OECD *Reviews of Regulatory Reform*

# REGULATORY REFORM
# IN MEXICO

ORGANISATION FOR ECONOMIC CO-OPERATION AND DEVELOPMENT

# ORGANISATION FOR ECONOMIC CO-OPERATION AND DEVELOPMENT

Pursuant to Article 1 of the Convention signed in Paris on 14th December 1960, and which came into force on 30th September 1961, the Organisation for Economic Co-operation and Development (OECD) shall promote policies designed:

- to achieve the highest sustainable economic growth and employment and a rising standard of living in Member countries, while maintaining financial stability, and thus to contribute to the development of the world economy;

- to contribute to sound economic expansion in Member as well as non-member countries in the process of economic development; and

- to contribute to the expansion of world trade on a multilateral, non-discriminatory basis in accordance with international obligations.

The original Member countries of the OECD are Austria, Belgium, Canada, Denmark, France, Germany, Greece, Iceland, Ireland, Italy, Luxembourg, the Netherlands, Norway, Portugal, Spain, Sweden, Switzerland, Turkey, the United Kingdom and the United States. The following countries became Members subsequently through accession at the dates indicated hereafter: Japan (28th April 1964), Finland (28th January 1969), Australia (7th June 1971), New Zealand (29th May 1973), Mexico (18th May 1994), the Czech Republic (21st December 1995), Hungary (7th May 1996), Poland (22nd November 1996) and Korea (12th December 1996). The Commission of the European Communities takes part in the work of the OECD (Article 13 of the OECD Convention).

Publié également en Français sous le titre :

LA RÉFORME DE LA RÉGLEMENTATION AU MEXIQUE

# FOREWORD

The OECD Review of Regulatory Reform in Mexico is among the first of a series of country reports carried out under the OECD's Regulatory Reform Programme, launched in 1998 in response to a mandate by OECD Ministers.

The Regulatory Reform Programme is aimed at helping governments improve regulatory quality – that is, reforming regulations which raise unnecessary obstacles to competition, innovation and growth, while ensuring that regulations efficiently serve important social objectives.

The Programme is part of a broader effort at the OECD to support sustained economic development, job creation and good governance. It fits with other initiatives such as our annual country economic surveys; the Jobs Strategy; the OECD Principles of Corporate Governance; and the fight against corruption, hard-core cartels and harmful tax competition.

Drawing on the analysis and recommendations of good regulatory practices contained in the 1997 OECD *Report to Ministers on Regulatory Reform*, the Regulatory Reform Programme is a multi-disciplinary process of in-depth country reviews, based on self-assessment and on peer evaluation by several OECD committees.

The country Reviews are not comprehensive, but, rather, targeted at key reform areas. Each Review has the same structure, including three thematic chapters on the quality of regulatory institutions and government processes; competition policy and enforcement; and the enhancement of market openness through regulatory reform. Each Review also contains chapters on sectors such as telecommunications, and an assessment of the macroeconomic context for reform in the country under review.

The country Reviews benefited from a process of extensive consultations with a wide range of government officials (including elected officials) from the country reviewed, business and trade union representatives, consumer groups, and academic experts from many backgrounds.

These Reviews demonstrate clearly that in many areas, a well-structured and implemented programme of regulatory reform has brought lower prices and more choice for consumers, helped stimulate innovation, investment, and new industries, and thereby aided in boosting economic growth and overall job creation. Comprehensive regulatory reforms have produced results more quickly than piecemeal approaches; and such reforms over the longer-term helped countries to adjust more quickly and easily to changing circumstances and external shocks. At the same time, a balanced reform programme must take into account important social concerns. Adjustment costs in some sectors have been painful, although experience shows that these costs can be reduced if reform is accompanied by supportive policies, including active labour market policies, to cushion adjustment.

While reducing and reforming regulations is a key element of a broad programme of regulatory reform, country experience also shows that in a more competitive and efficient market, new regulations and institutions are sometimes necessary to assure that private anticompetitive behaviour does not delay or block the benefits of reform and that health, environmental and consumer protection is assured. In countries pursuing reform, which is often difficult and opposed by vested interests, sustained and consistent political leadership is an essential element of successful reform efforts, and transparent and informed public dialogue on the benefits and costs of reform is necessary for building and maintaining broad public support for reform.

OECD 1999

The policy options presented in the Reviews may pose challenges for each country concerned, but they do not ignore wide differences between national cultures, legal and institutional traditions and economic circumstances. The in-depth nature of the Reviews and the efforts made to consult with a wide range of stakeholders reflect the emphasis placed by the OECD on ensuring that the policy options presented are relevant and attainable within the specific context and policy priorities of each country reviewed.

The OECD Reviews of Regulatory Reform are published on the responsibility of the Secretary-General of the OECD, but their policy options and accompanying analysis reflect input and commentary provided during peer review by all 29 OECD Member countries and the European Commission and during consultations with other interested parties.

The Secretariat would like to express its gratitude for the support of the Government of Mexico for the OECD Regulatory Reform Programme and its consistent co-operation during the review process. It also would like to thank the many OECD committee and country delegates, representatives from the OECD's Trade Union Advisory Committee (TUAC) and Business and Industry Advisory Committee (BIAC), and other experts whose comments and suggestions were essential to this report.

# ACKNOWLEDGEMENTS

This series of Reviews of Regulatory Reform in OECD countries was prepared under the direction of Deputy Secretary-General **Joanna R. Shelton**. The Review of Mexico reflects contributions from many sources, including the Government of Mexico, Committees of the OECD, representatives of Member governments, and members of the Business and Industry Advisory Committee (BIAC) and the Trade Union Advisory Committee (TUAC), as well as other groups. This report was peer reviewed in March 1999 in the OECD's Ad Hoc Multidisciplinary Group on Regulatory Reform.

In the OECD Secretariat, the following people contributed substantially to the review of Mexico: **Head of Programme:** Scott H. Jacobs; **Lead Drafters:** Michael Wise and Scott H. Jacobs; **Document preparation:** Jennifer Stein; **Economics Department:** Chapter 1 was principally prepared by Richard Kohl, and benefited from work by Giuseppe Nicoletti on regulatory indicators; **Public Management Service:** Cesar Cordova-Novion; **Trade Directorate:** Denis Audet; **Directorate for Financial, Fiscal and Enterprise Affairs:** Darryl Biggar, Patricia Heriard-Dubreuil, Patrick Hughes, Bernard J. Phillips, Sally Van Siclen, Michael Wise; **Directorate for Science, Technology, and Industry:** Patrick Xavier, Dimitri Ypsilanti; **General Secretariat:** Pierre Poret.

# TABLE OF CONTENTS

*Part* I

## Tables

## Annex Figures

## Boxes

*Part* II

*Part* I

# OECD REVIEW
# OF REGULATORY REFORM
# IN MEXICO

# EXECUTIVE SUMMARY

Over the past 15 years, Mexico has expanded regulatory reform as a central element in a broad transformation from an inward-looking economy to an open and market-based economy. The rapid pace, broad scope, and depth of regulatory reforms exceed those of most other OECD countries, and even compare to those of the emerging market economies in Eastern Europe who recently joined the OECD. This is in part evidence of how far Mexico had to go. Two decades ago, the Mexican economy was heavily regulated and protected. Industries and services in many areas were shielded from foreign and national competition. The federal government operated thousands of enterprises in sectors ranging from hotels to transport and mining. Export played a limited role as most industries concentrated on internal markets.

In the 1980s, a collapse in oil prices and default on a massive external debt, followed by five years of economic stagnation, triggered a major shift in this economic model. Mexico was one of the first Latin American countries to adopt market-based principles as a cornerstone of economic development. Under the new model, macroeconomic stabilisation policies were supported by trade liberalisation and privatisation. Most state-owned enterprises have now been sold, and opportunities opened for national and foreign investment in infrastructure. By 1998, virtually all price controls had been eliminated. A government-wide deregulation programme, adopted by President Zedillo in 1995, is whittling away the myriad forms by which the government intervened into economic activity and is promoting better regulatory techniques throughout the public administration (including at state and municipal levels). These efforts are supported by other efforts to modernise the Mexican state. A modern competition law adopted in 1993 created an over-arching framework for market-based principles, backed up by an effective watchdog. Domestic reforms were boosted and underpinned by international commitments as Mexico joined the GATT, APEC and the OECD, and signed NAFTA and other free trade agreements with Latin American countries.

Regulatory reform has already produced major benefits for Mexico by:

- Reducing prices and increasing quality and choices for Mexican consumers and businesses.
- Improving productive efficiency by reducing costs for such critical inputs as communications and transport services, and hence promoting competitiveness. This is contributing to the growth of Mexico's export sector.
- Promoting innovation in new products and technologies, and the adoption of modern, low-cost methods through new entry and investment. In transport, telecommunications, and other sectors, privatisation and elimination of red tape encouraged firms to invest in new technologies.
- Increasing the adaptability of the Mexican economy so that it can rebound more quickly and at lower cost from major economic crises.
- Establishing institutions and methods that permit Mexico to achieve its regulatory policy goals such as safety, health, and environmental protection more cost-effectively.

The social and distributional impacts of structural change are particularly important in Mexico. The emergence of a multi-party system and vibrant federalism has created many new actors with diverse interests who, depending on the distribution of benefits and costs, have challenged both traditional economic structures and regulatory practices, and the current programme of regulatory reforms. The sustainability of regulatory reform depends on the scope and depth of public and stakeholder support, the success of building constituencies for reform across a broader range of public and private interests, the willingness of political parties in the Congress to support reform, and communication to the public of the practical results of reform.

Chapter 1. *Sectoral structural reforms in Mexico have been broad and deep.* In most tradable goods and services sectors, complete deregulation of entry, exit and pricing has been achieved. The private sector's share of economic activity in Mexico is now among the highest in the OECD. Competition has increased in deregulated sectors, although there is a threat of reversal in important transport sectors (including at the sub-federal level). Output has increased in almost all deregulated sectors. But unstable macroeconomic performance has delayed achieving the full benefits of structural and regulatory reforms, and the reform agenda is not yet completed. In some cases, creation of efficient regulatory frameworks for privatised monopolies was delayed, and insufficient emphasis was placed on increasing competition. Instead, limiting competition in those sectors was believed necessary to finance needed investment. Complementary reforms are still necessary in factor markets, including water supply and energy (electricity reforms were recently proposed to the Congress), and in the legal framework for business, including the completion of current efforts to reform bankruptcy law.

Chapter 2. *The shift to market-oriented regulatory policies and instruments required major reforms of the public sector to reduce unnecessary intervention in the economy and effectively carry out important public policies.* The Mexican government is upgrading regulatory quality government-wide, based on institutional reforms, regulatory review, transparency, and consultation. The current deregulation programme (ADAE), launched in 1995, has been a sound basis for reducing regulatory costs while meeting public policy objectives. A ministerial-level Economic Deregulation Council provides political oversight, while the Economic Deregulation Unit in the Ministry of Commerce and Industry carries out day to day operations. The programme covers most business regulations, though some gaps should be closed. The ADAE and co-operation agreements between the federal and state governments are encouraging reform at subnational levels. Much has been done to improve transparency, in particular through the Economic Deregulation Council, but consultation is still uneven in scope and effectiveness. In 1997, regulatory impact assessment was made mandatory and its use has expanded, though analytical quality is often low. Many business formalities have been substantially reduced and simplified, but the pace of reform has slowed as projects have become more difficult. Attention now needs to shift to implementation of the regulatory reform agenda over the medium-term.

Chapter 3. *A key policy change was adoption of a new competition law and creation of a new Federal Competition Commission that rank among the best in the* OECD. The 1993 competition law and policy are sound, and establish an essential guiding framework for economy-wide regulatory reform. The clear rule against horizontal agreements is an efficient tool to abolish price controls. In key sectors, the competition authority identifies conditions of substantial market power and authorises regulators to control prices to protect consumers. The competition authority is also usually responsible for reviewing bids for public assets and concessions to guard against the accumulation of market power. Competition policy applies virtually universally in the private sector. Competition policy also applies to state-owned enterprises (but the law excludes strategic sectors such as energy), and preventing anti-competitive acts by local government bodies is a priority. The new competition agency is independent and increasingly vigorous, although its actions are often delayed by legal challenges. To ensure consistent application, the competition agency may need more power to check anti-competitive decisions by other regulators. The effectiveness of the competition agency will face major tests in the near future as issues of key importance in air transport and the asymmetric regulation of dominant firms will demand its attention.

Chapter 4. *Market openness policies launched regulatory reform and still anchor it.* Accession to the GATT and the OECD, and negotiation of NAFTA and other free trade agreements had a profound influence on Mexican regulatory policies and processes, and dramatically increased investment and trade. Between 1990 and 1997, imports and exports quadrupled, as did the annual rate of direct foreign investment in fixed assets. Market openness was instrumental in minimising the worst effects of the 1995 financial crisis and helped Mexico recover more quickly. It also made the economy more resilient in the face of the

1998 emerging markets crisis. Currently, the Mexican record on market openness is good, but some areas need attention. Transparency is improving, since Mexico leads in use of Internet-based methods, and has made substantial reforms in standards, procurement, and customs processing. Few problems of discrimination are reported, but some rules in services need attention. Mexico is a good performer in the adoption of international practises in official and voluntary standards. Mexico is now also moving toward greater recognition of equivalence of other countries' regulation, but the effort should be expanded beyond NAFTA. Some sectoral concerns about market openness remain (though for computers and automobiles, restrictions should be eliminated according to the NAFTA schedule).

Chapter 5. *The telecommunications sector illustrates aspects of Mexico's progress in reform, and remaining challenges.* In the past ten years, the regulatory regime in the Mexican telecommunications sector has undergone significant reform, which has transformed the sector from a poorly-performing state-owned monopoly to a sector increasingly reliant on competition to deliver benefits to consumers. These reforms have led to growth in competition in long-distance telecommunications services and have laid a foundation for competition in local services. Establishment of a new sectoral regulator was a big step in improving the transparency and quality of regulation. As a result, Mexican consumers have enjoyed improvements in quality and choice, and reductions of up to 50% in real long distance prices. These gains were aided by considerable foreign investment. Yet, in part due to the macroeconomic disruption caused by the 1995 crisis, progress has been slow in key areas, and further reform could generate large gains for Mexican consumers. OECD comparisons based on a standard basket of services show that access prices and prices to Mexican consumers remain very high in Mexico relative to other OECD countries, while the number of telephones per capita is by far the lowest of OECD countries. However, competition in local telephony is expected to begin in 1999 and new entrants have committed to investing in more than 9 million new telephone lines, which would double Mexico's teledensity. The independence of the sectoral regulator from the ministry could be strengthened, and the transparency and accountability of its decisions on regulations and conditions for concessions enhanced. Competition problems remain and, if not resolved, could reduce overall performance in the sector. In December 1997 and again in March 1998, the competition authority declared Telmex "dominant" in several telephone service markets, opening the door to possible new pro-competitive regulations. By mid-1999, these regulations were not yet finalised, though the regulator was in the process of deciding on additional asymmetric regulations to address the problems.

Chapter 6. *Conclusions and Policy Options.* Mexico's experience vividly demonstrates how liberalising trade, enhancing market competition, and reforming administrative processes are mutually supportive. Based on international experience with good regulatory practices, several reforms (further detailed in Chapter 6) are likely to be beneficial to improving regulation in Mexico. Mexico has made substantial progress in opening competition and reducing business burdens; now, it needs to rebalance toward a broader vision of social welfare and build a wider constituency for reform. A multi-year period of consolidation, sustained implementation, and refinement of the legal and policy reforms already on the table are also needed to help ensure that citizens and businesses see concrete benefits.

– *The potentially substantial benefits to the public of the current programme should be secured by pursuing a multiyear period of policy stability and by taking a series of steps to strengthen institutions and implementation capacities within the public administration.* Despite high-level political backing, the spread and scope of reforms, and the development of regulatory innovations and international best practices, the benefits of reform have not yet been widely realised. As in all countries, policy reforms of this magnitude require a period of sustained, consistent implementation. A high priority should be given to fine-tuning the policy, the institutions, and the tools of reform. Such steps include transferring the body that promotes reform to the centre of government (such as the Office of the President) or making it autonomous, while giving it more authority to co-ordinate related structural policies; broadening the scope of reform; enhancing the role of the competition agency in reviewing regulations and making it a formal member of the Economic Deregulation Council; improving and extending the programme of regulatory impact analysis to all areas of the government; and broadening powers of private actions to remedy anti-competitive conduct.

- *Gaps in the current policy framework for the use of regulation should be corrected to expand the use of competition and market-oriented principles.* Most of Mexico's reforms have been based on a pragmatic course built on opportunities that have arisen during the evolution to competition and on the need to resolve bottlenecks that have appeared. Though good progress has been made, important gaps and inconsistencies have inevitably arisen in the overall framework for regulation.

- *Regulatory weaknesses in some sectors, particularly in managing dominant firms after privatisation, continue to undermine sectoral performance and should be corrected to encourage effective competition.* Taking into account the experiences of other countries, the government should assess and correct regulatory frameworks in those sectors that have been reformed and where results have disappointed, and in those areas where regulatory requirements should be adapted to technological change. The role of the competition agency should be strengthened in overseeing sectoral frameworks. A comprehensive and independent review of the new regulatory agencies and a general revision of their mission statements would be a good first step to improving their efficiency, independence and accountability by strengthening their systems of governance, policy coherence, working methods, and relations with the competition authority.

- *More co-ordination and review are needed to improve the efficiency and coherence of regulations at state and local levels, and at the federal and state interface.* Regulatory reforms will have their fullest effect in Mexico only if state and municipal governments move in the same direction. Mexico has much to teach other federal countries in this regard, but efforts to prevent reversal of federal regulatory reforms by the states are essential.

- *Regulatory transparency should be enhanced throughout the public administration to boost investment, market entry, and innovation.* Transparency has improved significantly, but Mexico still falls short of OECD best practices, particularly in the use of public consultation. Adoption of notice and comment procedures at the federal level is a bold and important step forward, but there should be a comprehensive, standardised requirement for open public consultation.

- *To improve policy performance and coherence, existing regulations and conditions on concessions should be reviewed systematically to ensure that they are consistent with market-oriented policies and principles for quality regulation. Necessary reforms should be adopted as rapidly as possible to provide the maximum stimulus to economic growth.* There has been a great deal of review and reform activity in Mexico, and continued attention is needed to review and up-date existing laws and other regulations in crucial policy areas such as bankruptcy (where a draft reform law is being prepared), firms' governance (where a voluntary code is under development) and labour laws, as well as areas such as energy (where electricity reforms were recently proposed to the Congress), water management, and education. Recent activities in a number of these areas demonstrate a continuing commitment to reform, but these will succeed only if the reforms are supported by the Congress.

- *Consistent with current market-opening initiatives by the Mexican government, consumers will benefit from lower prices and more choice, and enterprises will gain from tougher competition and faster innovation as markets are more fully opened to international trade and investment.*

- *In the telecommunications sector, further regulatory reform and market opening would boost consumer benefits. Such reforms include enhancement of the independence and role of the sectoral regulator, as well as the openness of its decision procedures; implementation of asymmetric regulation on the dominant carrier, Telmex; and improvement of the foundation for interconnection charges.*

*Chapter 1*

# REGULATORY REFORM IN MEXICO

## INTRODUCTION

Over the past 15 years, Mexico has employed regulatory reform as a central element within a broader transformation from an inward-looking economy to an open and market-based economy. Regulatory reform has steadily proceeded, at first due to and later despite the external shocks and macroeconomic upheavals that accompanied this transformation. Indeed, reform may have helped reduce the severity of economic shocks by increasing the flexibility of the economy. The ground covered at the federal level and by several state governments is impressive. The pace, scope, and depth of regulatory reforms exceed those of almost all other OECD countries, excepting only the countries in transition in central and eastern Europe.[1]

This is in part evidence of how far Mexico had to go. Fifteen years ago, the Mexican economy was practically closed. Regulation in some sectors of the economy was extensive, pervasive and heavy-handed, while needed regulation was desperately lacking in other sectors. Industries and services in many areas were shielded from foreign and national competition. The government operated thousands of enterprises in sectors ranging from hotels to most energy services. Export played a limited role as most industries concentrated on the internal market.

*Mexico was one of the first Latin American countries to adopt market-based principles as a cornerstone of economic development...*

In the 1980s, external factors – a collapse in oil prices and default on a massive external debt – triggered a major shift in this economic model. Mexico was one of the first Latin American countries to adopt market-based principles as a cornerstone of economic development. Macroeconomic stabilisation policies were supported by a first wave of structural and regulatory reforms such as trade liberalisation and privatisation. The first wave of reforms uncovered further rigidities, and a second economic crisis convinced the government to embark on deeper reforms.

*... and since the early 1990s has undergone an extraordinary economic transition.*

As a result, from the early 1990s to the present, Mexico has undergone an extraordinary economic transition. Most state-owned enterprises were sold, and new opportunities were opened for national and foreign investment in infrastructure (*e.g.*, airports, railroads, natural gas, satellites). Price controls were progressively eliminated from 1992 to 1999. The government launched a deregulation programme aimed at the myriad forms of intervention into economic activity by federal and state administrations. A modern competition law created an over-arching framework for market-based principles, backed up by an effective competition watchdog. Reforms to the civil and commercial codes, the creation of a generic drugs market and a new regulatory framework for petrol station franchises are among the reforms intended to boost consumer welfare. Domestic reforms were underpinned by international commitments as Mexico joined the GATT, APEC and the OECD, and signed NAFTA and free trade agreements with other Latin American countries.

*Regulatory reform has evolved into a far-reaching strategy to modernise the economy and public governance of Mexico.*

Structural change was accelerated by renovation in the political and public governance landscape. The emergence of a multi-party system and vibrant federalism has created new actors with diverse interests who, depending on the distribution of benefits and costs, have challenged traditional economic structures and regulatory practices, as well as the current programme of regulatory reforms. Changes are occurring, too, in regulatory practices at all levels of government. Transparency and accountability are improving through administrative reforms. Expert and independent regulatory agencies have been created. New capacities for carrying out regulatory reform are in place across the government. A broad review programme to screen out poor regulations and a co-operative programme to help states and municipalities improve their regulatory capacities are good practices that compare well to those in other OECD countries and could contribute substantially to economic and social progress in Mexico.

*Unstable macroeconomic performance in Mexico has slowed the benefits of structural and regulatory reforms, but important benefits are now appearing, including enhanced economic flexibility that reduces Mexico's vulnerability to future shocks...*

The peso crisis of 1994, caused by external imbalances, delayed the benefits of these reforms and frustrated for a time the attempt to put Mexico on a stable growth path fuelled by market-led development. In fact, unstable macroeconomic performance in Mexico over the last 20 years has slowed the benefits of structural and regulatory reforms, since these reforms have maximum positive impact when the macroeconomic environment is stable and geared to growth. In addition, many reforms are too recent to show results. But in some areas, benefits are appearing and are driving further reforms. Market openness and deregulation helped create a vibrant exporting sector which, in turn, requires more competitive non-tradable network services, a transparent business environment, and efficient upstream and downstream sectors. Consumers have enjoyed better prices, higher quality, and greater choice, though have not yet seen the full benefits. The recovery following the 1994/95 peso crisis shows a new flexibility in the economy that is probably due to the move to market-led growth. The fast resumption of growth in the aftermath of the 1994 crisis, for example, contrasts with the economy's performance following the 1982 and 1987 crises.

*Yet the reform agenda is not yet completed. Gaps and mistakes are inevitable in such a broad and rapid transition, but mending them should not be postponed.*

Yet the reform agenda is not completed. Gaps in the reform programme should be closed and corrections made. The rapidity of the transition in Mexico and the need to take advantage of political opportunities has meant that reform was sometimes piecemeal and incomplete. For example, decisions on privatisation were not always followed up with establishment of regulatory safeguards to protect competition and consumer welfare. New reforms are warranted, particularly in infrastructure sectors like energy and water, the financial sector, and the legal and judicial frameworks. The benefits of reform for the Mexican population will continue to grow as these outstanding measures are implemented.

*A multi-year period of policy stability, implementation, and enforcement could lead to rapid and broad-based benefits for Mexican consumers.*

Even where reforms have been adopted, sustained attention is needed to implementation and enforcement. Despite large investments made in good regulatory policies and laws, concrete benefits have not yet been fully realised by citizens and businesses, and could be lost without a multi-year period of policy stability and enforcement to allow the reforms to take hold. For example, the transition to a transparent, accountable, and results-oriented administration that efficiently achieves public policy goals has had a good start, but has far to go. Some ministries have not made the cultural leap to a less interventionist role, and there continue to be serious weaknesses in policy implementation and enforcement by federal, state, and local bureaucracies. State and municipal governments are just beginning to adopt market-oriented policies and attention is needed to preserve and expand the benefits of reform as state responsibilities increase. Policy stability, combined with implementation and enforcement of the market-oriented reforms, could lead to rapid and broad-based benefits for consumers, due to positive synergies among these various reforms and the fact that many reforms require a minimum gestation period to bear fruit.

---

### Box 1.1. What is regulation and regulatory reform?

There is no generally accepted definition of regulation applicable to the very different regulatory systems in OECD countries. In the OECD work, **regulation** refers to the diverse set of instruments by which governments set requirements on enterprises and citizens. Regulations include laws, formal and informal orders and subordinate rules issued by all levels of government, and rules issued by non-governmental or self-regulatory bodies to whom governments have delegated regulatory powers. Regulations fall into three categories:

**Economic regulations** intervene directly in market decisions such as pricing, competition, market entry, or exit. Reform aims to increase economic efficiency by reducing barriers to competition and innovation, often through deregulation and use of efficiency-promoting regulation, and by improving regulatory frameworks for market functioning and prudential oversight.

**Social regulations** protect public interests such as health, safety, the environment, and social cohesion. The economic effects of social regulations may be secondary concerns or even unexpected, but can be substantial. Reform aims to verify that regulation is needed, and to design regulatory and other instruments, such as market incentives and goal-based approaches, that are more flexible, simpler, and more effective at lower cost.

**Administrative regulations** are paperwork and administrative formalities – so-called "red tape" – through which governments collect information and intervene in individual economic decisions. They can have substantial impacts on private sector performance. Reform aims at eliminating those no longer needed, streamlining and simplifying those that are needed, and improving the transparency of application.

**Regulatory reform** is used in the OECD work to refer to changes that improve regulatory quality, that is, enhance the performance, cost-effectiveness, or legal quality of regulations and related government formalities. Reform can mean revision of a single regulation, the scrapping and rebuilding of an entire regulatory regime and its institutions, or improvement of processes for making regulations and managing reform. Deregulation is a subset of regulatory reform and refers to complete or partial elimination of regulation in a sector to improve economic performance.

The challenge today is to consolidate the economic and institutional transformation so that Mexico can fully reap the benefits of an economy that is more efficient, competitive, and flexible. Strong support from the President and the Congress may be needed to avoid slowing down or even reversing the market-oriented reforms of the past several years, which would have potentially serious and long-lasting effects on market confidence and investment. Particularly since the benefits of reform are sometimes perceived to be narrowly targeted at organised business interests, it will be important for the government to broaden the constituency for reforms to more fully incorporate consumers and the Congress.

## THE MACROECONOMIC CONTEXT FOR SECTORAL REGULATORY REFORM

**The Mexican debt crisis in 1982 was a result of deep-seated structural problems in the economy, excessive borrowing, and negative external shocks.**

*After two decades of rapid growth, underlying structural flaws led to the emergence of macroeconomic problems in the 1970s.*

Beginning in the mid-1950s, the Mexican economy entered a time of "stabilising development", based on an import-substitution model of growth, led by domestic demand. Private industry was protected from foreign competition by high tariff and non-tariff barriers. The state was entrusted with a key role in the economy. Foreign investment was generally discouraged, and prohibited in most infrastructure sectors. Direct state ownership was constitutionally required in public infrastructure and was extended to many other sectors seen as strategic. The state heavily regulated private sector activity by controlling prices and limiting competition. Price controls and subsidies were used to keep prices of food and other basic consumer products low, often creating unfavourable terms of trade for agriculture. These factors, combined with high trade barriers, produced widespread industrial inefficiency, business rent-seeking and private and public monopolies, and reduced quality standards and competitiveness.

*A balance of payments crisis occurred in 1976, forcing devaluation.*

Nevertheless, Mexican aggregate economic indicators showed good performance for two decades under this strategy, as Mexico experienced rapid economic growth, financial stability, and relatively robust external accounts. The limits to this strategy emerged in the early 1970s when the economy slowed. Lower growth rates led to increases in government spending to address social inequalities, resulting in growing fiscal deficits.[2] Increased spending led to higher inflation, an overvalued exchange rate, and growing external deficits. Fiscal policies were not sustainable, and the government was forced to devalue the peso in 1976.

*The discovery of oil allowed Mexico to avoid significant structural adjustment.*

Despite a short-lived stabilisation effort in 1977, the discovery of oil allowed the government to avoid a resolution of the underlying problems that led to crisis. The "petrolisation" of the economy allowed Mexico to resume international borrowing, particularly for energy investments. Moreover, with support from foreign borrowing, the government increasingly expanded into direct production of goods and services. As a result the state sector accounted for an increasing share of the economy,[3] though it was characterised by poor planning and management, over-employment, and widespread inefficiency. By 1982, state-owned enterprises required subsidies and transfers equivalent to 12.7% of GDP (Aspe, 1993).

*These policies were ultimately unsustainable, provoking a debt crisis.*

Growing public sector investments, transfers and subsidies stimulated rapid growth in domestic demand which led to a reacceleration of inflation and exchange rate overvaluation.[4] External deficits steadily widened from 1975 to 1981. These policies were sustainable as long as oil prices were high, world real interest rates were low or negative, and growth in Mexico's primary export market, the United States, remained strong. When these conditions reversed in 1980-82, substantial capital flight ensued and Mexico faced increasing difficulty in refinancing its debt payments. The government responded with the temporary suspension of foreign debt service and the nationalisation of the commercial banks in September 1982, which marked the beginning of the international debt crisis of the 1980s.

### The 1980s debt crisis was followed by five years of economic stagnation.

*Contractionary macroeconomic policy and trade liberalisation were pursued to try to meet foreign debt payments and stabilise the economy.*

Economic policy after 1982 was driven by the need to earn the foreign exchange required to meet heavy debt service obligations and to stabilise the economy. The government pursued standard macroeconomic stabilisation policies of tighter fiscal and monetary policy to cut domestic demand and devalued the currency to restore balance-of-payments stability. The stabilisation measures were complemented by a first wave of structural reforms in the form of trade liberalisation measures as Mexico moved to reverse three decades of inward looking and interventionist policies. Initial privatisation of firms belonging to the traded goods sectors involve selling, merging, and closing more than 500 state-owned firms.

*These policies were not successful in stabilising inflation or restarting growth.*

These policies were only partially successful. Debt service was met, but largely by compressing domestic demand to generate trade surpluses (see Figure 1) as Mexico received little new lending.[5] Contractionary policies were reinforced by more negative external shocks as oil prices collapsed and Mexico City was hit with a severe earthquake in 1985. Real capita consumption and GDP fell at average annual rates of 2% from 1982 to 1988 (see Figure 2). Real wages also fell sharply (the average real manufacturing wage dropped by 35% from 1982 to 1988), while real interest rates increased sharply.

Moreover, inflation continued to be high. In the context of substantial internal rigidities, exchange rate devaluation initiated an inflationary spiral which was aggravated by wage and official price adjustments. Further depreciation was unsuccessful and the stock market crash in October 1987 resulted again in significant capital outflows. A broader-based effort was required to achieve a sustainable recovery.

**The authorities negotiated an incomes policy and began a process of comprehensive structural reform to create the basis for non-inflationary growth.**

*A new stabilisation strategy was needed to address widespread structural rigidities that eroded the benefits of trade liberalisation.*

The elements for a new economic strategy were based on lessons from the 1983-87 experience, namely, that devaluation and trade liberalisation were necessary but insufficient to generate sustained improvement in trade performance. Because of the complex and pervasive domestic systems of indexed wage setting, price controls, and subsidies and transfers, devaluation soon led to wage and price increases and increased government spending. This fed inflation and nullified the effects of the nominal devaluation on the real exchange rate, competitiveness and trade performance.

Trade liberalisation had indeed had positive effects. The successful *maquiladora* programme (under which companies engaged primarily in production for exports are granted free trade status, that is, exemption from paying tariffs and VAT on imported inputs) which was launched in the mid-1980s proved that Mexico could rapidly become a significant international exporter. But the elimination of protection and the opening up of the economy to external competition also revealed widespread structural rigidities that inhibited improvements in competitiveness, especially the reallocation of resources into traded goods sectors and the restructuring of sectors facing import competition. These problems were compounded by the policy of high interest rates and the nationalised and inefficient financial system, which diverted investment capital to inefficient loss-making firms and raised the cost of capital to private firms.

*The prerequisite for a new strategy was an incomes policy which allowed the government to break the link between devaluation and inflation...*

A prerequisite to any new strategy was to preserve the competitiveness benefits of devaluation by stabilising inflation; it was necessary to break the link between devaluation, inflation and higher public sector deficits. The administration brought all the participants in the economy together in a mechanism of consultation, resulting in the first of a series of agreements – the *Pactos*. The *Pactos*, first implemented in 1987, sought to break inflationary inertia caused by growing price-indexation and to distribute the costs of stabilisation. In the following years, the agreements were extended and covered the price of key government services and consumer goods, and cuts in subsidies in order to support increased supply flexibility and maintain downward pressure on prices.

*... and create a dynamic private sector.*

More importantly, through this mechanism, the government was able to negotiate support for exit from direct involvement in production through privatisation and other structural reform measures designed to create a dynamic private sector.

*Room for structural reforms to take effect was provided by external debt relief under the Brady plan.*

Despite these measures, external accounts deteriorated again in 1988. Following trade liberalisation in 1988, imports of consumers goods rose by 150.3%, a sign of long repressed demand. As noted in the 1991-92 OECD Economic Survey, it became clear that the debt service burden was incompatible with sustained growth: "[Mexico] could not make the heavy investments required to return to a sustainable and inflation-free growth path while at the same time transferring resources abroad to service external debt. ... [t]he resumption of growth with the consolidation of price stability was not viable if Mexico…needed to maintain large trade surpluses". In 1989 the Mexican government successfully negotiated a reduction in debt and debt service under the Brady Plan. More importantly, debt relief in combination with the comprehensive economic pro-gramme – tight macroeconomic policies, the *Pactos*, privatisation and deregulation – restored confidence in Mexico on the part of foreign and domestic investors, allowing for renewed capital inflows, a reversal of capital flight, and lower domestic real interest rates.

*Dramatic privatisation was key and was accompanied by price liberalisation and elimination of other structural rigidities.*

The government privatisations, which continue today, included rapid privatisation in 1990-91 of the previously nationalised major banks. In less than 12 years, the number of state enterprises was reduced from 1 155 to less than 213 (in 1993) and the state sector's share of GDP fell from nearly 50% to around 15% (Rogozonsky, 1994, p. 47). Barriers to efficient production were attacked. The govern-ment eliminated most price controls and cut subsidies for key goods and sectors. In particular, agricultural price supports and input subsidies were cut and, eventually, the land tenure system was reformed. The government started to privatise "regulated monopolies" in infrastructure services such as highways, telephony, and harbours. These measures were supported by steps to acceler-ate trade liberalisation, increasing external pressures on domestic prices,[6] and by measures to bolster new investment, such as lower interest rates, comprehensive (but incomplete) reform of the finan-cial system, and liberalisation of rules on foreign investment.

*A deregulation policy was launched to accelerate the structural changes.*

In concert with the privatisation of infrastructure services, the government launched an economic deregulation policy to accom-pany the other structural reforms. Its first priority was to eliminate bottlenecks to the flow and reallocation of goods, services, and cap-ital, and to make non-tradable services competitive. Between 1989 and 1995, the regulatory frameworks of harbours, transportation (road, rail, sea, air), electricity, tourism, water management, health and sanitary administration, telecommunication, petrochemicals, natural gas, packaging, textiles and salt industry, agriculture and fisheries industry, general commerce, and land ownership were reformed, together with a major overhaul of competition, consumer, patent, notaries, immigration and foreign investments laws.

### The result was strong economic performance, for a time.

To a great extent, the strategy worked. Inflation fell continu-ously, large fiscal deficits were eliminated and the stock of govern-ment debt dropped to one of the lowest levels in the OECD.[7] GDP growth recovered[8] (see Figure 2) and growth in export volumes sub-sequently exceeded the growth in Mexico's export markets. The mix of Mexican exports shifted away from oil to manufacturing.[9] Renewed confidence on the part of investors led to a rapid rise in capital inflows: foreign direct investment averaged 1.5% of GDP from 1988-94 and was substantially augmented by large inflows of portfo-lio investment in the domestic financial markets and renewed bank lending (see Figure 3). Domestic lending also recovered following the deregulation of the financial sector and privatisation of the banking system, and more and more this was directed to the private sector as government finances improved.

*External performance remained Mexico's Achilles heel.*

However, the Achilles heel remained the external accounts. Despite debt reduction efforts, the still large outstanding debt threatened the confidence of foreign and domestic investors in the peso.[10] Despite progress on inflation, Mexico's inflation rate remained above that of its major trading partners which, together with a predetermined exchange rate regime (crawling peg with a system of fluctuating bands), resulted in an underlying trend of real exchange rate appreciation. This trend was exacerbated by rapid growth in consumption and investment, which were made possible by large capital inflows and an expansion of credit following financial sector reforms.[11] The result was growing trade and current account deficits as exports began to slow and imports accelerated: the current account deficit rose from an average of 2.7% of GDP in 1989-90 to 7.0% in 1994 (see Figure 1).

## Devaluation was delayed until the end of 1994, with devastating consequences.

Despite regular adjustments to the exchange rate through a system of widening bands, the real exchange rate appreciated by about 30% from 1989 to end-1993 (see Figure 4). In the face of internal political shocks and high interest rates in the United States, the peso came under increasing pressure and in 1994 capital outflows occurred. The authorities faced several policy options: increase interest rates, accelerate exchange rate depreciation, introduce a large one-off devaluation, or float the peso. Very high interest rates were difficult in the face of an already troubled banking sector, while a devaluation could undermine confidence in the currency, with the risk of overshooting. The monetary authorities chose to sterilise in response to capital flight, given that pressures were thought to be largely temporary, and responded with a modest increase in interest rates. The increase proved to be insufficient to restore confidence[12] and the government was finally forced to devalue in late 1994 and eventually float the peso: the peso fell versus the dollar by 76% between December 1994 and May 1995.

*The recession of 1995 was the worst in a decade, returning per capita income levels to those of 1987.*

The immediate consequences were devastating. The stock market crashed by 40% – and GDP fell by 6.2%, while real wages, consumption, and investment fell even more. Almost 800 000 jobs were lost in 1995.

## The economy recovered quickly, partly due to structural reforms that speeded up the supply response to the recession.

*The rebound was more rapid than in the past. Renewed investors' confidence was based in part on the sustained commitment to pursue regulatory reform and market openness.*

The economy recovered remarkably quickly from the 1995 recession. GDP growth averaged 5.6% from 1996-98 and 2.1 million jobs were created from late 1995 through late 1997, an impressive performance. Most importantly, private investor confidence returned in 1996 with increasing inflows into Mexican financial markets, though these slowed somewhat during 1998 in the light of global concerns about emerging markets. An important factor for

Box 1.2. **Financial reform and the Mexican banking crisis**

Financial reform began in Mexico in the 1970s when the government modernised the institutional structure of the financial system. Numerous specialised institutions were merged into full-service commercial banks. Deposit rates were indexed to inflation, but the system was characterised by widespread controls on deposit rates, lending rates and the administrative allocation of 70-80% of credit through a complex system of credit targets and reserve and liquidity requirements. Problems began to emerge in the late 1970s as commercial banks borrowed heavily in dollars and lent these funds domestically in pesos, creating substantial foreign exchange risk. In 1982 the devaluation of the peso and the deep recession caused a substantial deterioration in commercial banks balance sheets. Several faced potential bankruptcy. In response, given the government's implicit policy of preventing bank failures and guaranteeing deposits, the Lopez Portillo Administration changed the constitution and nationalised the banks in 1982, consolidating them into 18 institutions.

Reform continued in the 1980s but was partial and incomplete leading to growing distortions and inefficiency, similar to the experience of other OECD countries. Lending rates were partially liberalised, creating distortions between regulated and unregulated lending markets. These distortions helped in banks' recapitalisation by generating substantial profits but simultaneously led to the increasing disintermediation of the banking system by less regulated securities markets, resulting in a decline in banks' share of financial assets and capitalisation.

In response to these problems the Salinas Administration undertook a programme of liberalisation and reform of the banking system. In 1989-90 the government deregulated deposit and lending rates, ended the system of credit allocation, removed restrictions on the types of business in which different financial institutions could engage, and amended the constitution to permit private ownership of banks. Simultaneously the authorities strengthened the system of prudential regulations by installing a system of loan classification, provisioning and capital adequacy guidelines compatible with those issued by the BIS. The government chose not to create a deposit insurance scheme, but permitted a pre-existing scheme (FOBAPROA) to remain in place which provided assistance to banks in difficulty. The reform process culminated in 1991-92 with the privatisation of most commercial banks. In some cases, however, screening of Mexican groups acquiring the banks from the government appears to have been lax.

The reforms to prudential regulation proved to be inadequate, particularly in the reporting of non-performing assets, large loan exposures and loans between different parts of the same financial group or to major stockholders. A rapid increase in lending followed deregulation and privatisation especially to finance construction. This was soon accompanied by an increase in problem and questionable loans, a result of banks' inexperience in lending, excessive optimism in the wake of NAFTA, large foreign capital inflows and rising stock prices, and close ties between bank owners and important economic interests, particularly construction companies.

The devaluation in 1994, combined with poor levels of capitalisation of some of the recently privatised banks and an expansion of credit provided by development banks that borrowed overseas, provoked another crisis in the banking sector. As in 1982 the combination of a substantial devaluation of the peso, a collapse in domestic demand and high real interest rates soared meant that many borrowers could no longer afford to repay, especially loans denominated in US dollars. Past due loans rose to a peak of 12% in mid-1995.

In response to the crisis the authorities introduced a package of special measures to rescue the financial system and reform the prudential regulatory system. Thirteen banks were actually taken over by FOBAPROA, three because of problems caused by fraud of the control groups that originally acquired the banks. The government created a recapitalisation and loan restructuring programme off-budget which permitted banks to swap problem loans for a ten year period in exchange for a new "asset", essentially the earnings on long-term government bonds; by the end of 1996 FOBAPROA had "purchased" 30.5% of outstanding loans. At the same time, a series of measures was introduced which provided government assistance to different types of creditors, such as mortgage holders and agricultural borrowers.

The bank rescue was largely successful, but at substantial cost. On the one hand, most problem banks have been either closed or recapitalised and reprivatised. On the other hand, past-due loans remain a significant problem whose cost has steadily risen. The loan restructuring programme was inherently flawed. In principle the government had built in specific incentives in for banks to collect on these loans.[1] In practice these incentives proved to be inadequate, especially in the context of a poorly functioning legal, judicial and bankruptcy system (see the main text). At the same time the series of debtor relief measures created a moral hazard problem, undermining their incentives to repay in expectation of further relief.

---

Box 1.2.   **Financial reform and the Mexican banking crisis** (*cont.*)

Whether corruption has been adequately prosecuted or the government should cover the entire costs of writing down the problem loans held by FOBAPROA was the subject of intense political debate in 1998. The poor incentives for loan collection and repayment had caused the value of the loans to steadily deteriorate: the cost of the banking reform, which was estimated at 5% of GDP in 1995 and 11.9% of GDP in 1997, rose to 14.4% of 1998 GDP. In December 1998 a partial political compromise was reached and Congress approved a package of measures which partly resolved the problem. The package replaced the liabilities of FOBAPROA with government-guaranteed traded securities. At the same time, a debt relief programme was introduced. FOBAPROA itself will be replaced, effective June 1999, with a decentralised public entity – the Institute for Bank Deposit Insurance – which will sell off assets, and provide deposit insurance.[2] Whether these measures will allow the value of problem loans to shrink, and ultimately be sufficient to durably strengthen the banking system, remains to be seen. In this latter regard the removal of the remaining restrictions on FDI in the sector is likely to be of major benefit.

---

1. The incentives included: 1) the ability to repurchase loans from FOBAPROA at the same price they were purchased, effectively a call option; 2) loss-sharing of any additional deterioration in loan quality, with the banks' absorbing 20-30% of the losses; 3) the lack of liquidity of the new asset, which was not tradable; and 4) interest on the new asset was below banks funding costs, creating a small carrying cost. Essentially the banks' would benefit from any increase in the value of the underlying loans, but their costs of doing nothing were small, especially since the government had already bailed them out twice in the past fifteen years. See Box 3 in the 1998 OECD *Economic Survey of Mexico* for further details.
2. During the transition period, FOBAPROA will continue to manage operations related to capitalisation and loan portfolio purchases, conduct audits, and if fraudulent loans are detected they will be returned to the banks.

---

renewed investors' confidence was the sustained commitment by the government to pursue regulatory reform and market openness.

*Structural reforms appear to have improved competitiveness and the supply response, lowering adjustment costs.*

Much of the basis for the more rapid turnaround appears to be structural reforms. The 1998 OECD *Economic Survey* noted:

> This greater responsiveness of the Mexican economy reflects the increased openness of the economy as well as enhanced flexibility engendered by the structural reforms implemented in recent years. (p. 13)

Many Mexican firms were able to reorient production from the depressed domestic market to exports – a possibility created by trade agreements such as NAFTA – reflecting comparable levels of quality, as well as flexibility in marketing and production.[13]

*Macroeconomic policies are now targeted toward avoiding the imbalances that have recurred in the past...*

Macroeconomic policy appears now to have finally created a stable framework for medium-term growth. The exchange rate, shift from a crawling peg to a free float, removes any tendency towards overvaluation such as occurred in the past. Central bank independence was established in 1994 and the Bank of Mexico has set a path of gradual disinflation to achieve long-term price stability. Consumer price inflation has declined steadily but gradually, and the fiscal stance, among the best in the OECD even prior to 1994, continues in that vein.

*... though several macroeconomic and structural problems remain.*

Despite these achievements, the current macroeconomic picture is mixed:

- Economic growth has been barely sufficient to absorb a rapidly growing labour force, while at the same time growth has been labour intensive – labour productivity has been zero or negative for most of the last decade.

• Export performance has been strong. The number of exporting firms grew by more than 50% from 1993 to 1997 and the exporting sector accounted for most of the jobs created since 1995, many of which pay higher wages than those found in other manufacturing firms. Exports continue to rely heavily on imported inputs, especially in the *maquiladora* sector. While domestic value-added is low, limiting backward linkages, it has been increasing. The *maquiladora* industry has consistently been extremely dynamic in terms of wages, employment and production.

• The decline of international oil prices in 1998 has revealed on the one hand that Mexican trade is much less dependent on the oil sector than in the 1980s, but on the other hand the continuing dependence of the government budget on oil revenues.[14] To maintain fiscal balance, in 1998 the government cut spending several times through the year.

• Growth of credit to the private sector was sluggish over the last few years and might become a constraint on economic growth. In part this constraint reflects the fragility of poorly capitalised banks, an appropriate tightening of bank lending requirements, and ongoing weaknesses in the quality of borrowers, since much of the private sector remains over-indebted. But delays in bank restructuring have been important and need to be resolved (see Box 1.2).

## SECTORAL IMPACTS OF REGULATION AND REGULATORY REFORM

As noted, structural reform in Mexico began in the 1980s in the wake of the debt crisis. Trade liberalisation was accompanied by privatisation, and as these tasks were completed, the government shifted its emphasis to focus on improving market competitiveness through broad-based regulatory reform. The 1994/95 crisis underlined these issues and thrust regulatory reform to the forefront of the recovery strategy. Despite lower labour costs, much of the business community outside the *maquiladora* industry was having difficulties and was urging the government to improve framework conditions for growth. Critics emphasised the need to upgrade the quality of crucial legal and regulatory services, like standard setting and patent protection, and to reduce pervasive and burdensome red tape.

**Improving trade performance was needed to launch a sustainable recovery.**

*Since 1985, Mexico has undertaken fast and far-reaching trade liberalisation...*

Improving external trade performance was essential to meet foreign debt obligations and restore investor confidence to allow for a resumption of domestic growth. The first step was trade liberalisation, in the context of exchange rate devaluation through the use of a fragile crawling peg. The goal was to reorient Mexico from an

25

import-substitution model to an open dynamic economy. Trade liberalisation was expected to expand the relative size of the tradable goods sector and to reallocate resources internally in line with world relative prices to reflect Mexico's comparative advantages.

Since 1985, Mexico has undertaken fast and far-reaching trade liberalisation (see Chapter 4 for details). Mexico eliminated most compulsory import licenses, abolished official import prices, reduced the maximum tariff by 80% (and cut the average tariff in half), joined the GATT, and entered into the North American Free Trade Agreement (NAFTA) and other trade agreements with Chile, Costa Rica, Bolivia, Colombia and Venezuela, and Nicaragua. The relaxation of historically rigid controls on foreign investment (a new Foreign Investment Law was enacted in 1993 and amended in 1997) played an important role in bringing capital and transferring research and development.

*... that quickly revealed pervasive structural rigidities and barriers to competitiveness and reallocation of resources toward traded goods.*

Trade liberalisation quickly revealed the extent to which structural rigidities were present in the economy. The quality of infrastructural services produced by state-owned firms was low and unreliable.[15] State-owned firms dominated many sectors and were inefficient, generating losses that required substantial subsidies and transfers to avoid bankruptcy and protect jobs. Many private sector firms were also inefficient due to regulatory barriers to competition. Price controls, import licenses, and subsidies produced "richer businessmen with poor businesses". These barriers led to a vicious circle of poor economic performance and rising subsidies. Increasing inefficiency and negative profits required higher prices and subsidies to maintain output, leading to further deterioration in efficiency. The disincentives in the system produced numerous bottlenecks, low levels of infrastructure investment, poor service quality and often shortages (for example, in telephone services).

### Privatisation was rapid and far reaching, resulting in one of the highest private-sector shares of economic activity of any OECD country.

*In turn, privatisation and price liberalisation were necessary to create a dynamic private sector and stimulate badly needed infrastructure investment.*

Privatisation was key not only to improving static efficiency through stronger market disciplines, but also to dynamic performance. A major constraint on productivity and efficiency was the poor quality of infrastructure, which had been starved by a lack of public funds under the austerity programmes of the 1980s.[16] Privatisation of infrastructure was expected to generate high levels of investment and produce substantial increases in the availability of services as well as their efficiency and quality. Most importantly, privatisation, like trade liberalisation, sent a strong signal to investors, domestic and foreign, about the commitment of the new administration to structural reform.[17] Privatisation complemented trade liberalisation directly by reducing the temptation for protectionist intervention.

Privatisation was also expected to aid in stabilising inflation, as improving efficiency and competition would lead to lower prices once the initial jump in price levels was absorbed. Privatisation would also affect inflation indirectly by helping achieve fiscal consolidation through increased revenues, by shifting investment spending onto the private sector, and by permitting cuts in transfers and subsidies to loss-making firms.[18]

Privatisation was carried out quickly and was accompanied by the merger or liquidation of many unprofitable enterprises. Between 1980 and 1994, private sector participation in gross domestic investment increased from 60.1% to 80.6%. Starting in 1992, sale of state assets was reinforced by opening up, through the auctioning of long-term exclusive concessions, sectors previously reserved to the state, such as rail transport, natural gas storage, transportation and distribution, and airports (all in the Zedillo Administration). Today, less than 100 firms remain in public hands, though these include some very large ones, such as Pemex and two vertically integrated regional electricity monopolies. The crisis in the banking sector has indirectly returned some previously privatised firms e.g. banking, toll highways, and airlines, to state ownership, although the government is not involved in day-to-day operations.

Price liberalisation and cuts in transfers and subsidies complemented the privatisation process. These were essential to create an environment in which the new private firms would face correct signals regarding resource allocation and investment.

### Privatisation was an unqualified success in most sectors, but speed and revenue maximisation were not always balanced with creating competition and appropriate regulatory frameworks.

In most sectors privatisation has been an unqualified success. Early privatisation efforts of smaller firms in competitive markets have produced important gains and generated substantial benefits in terms of improved productivity, lower costs and greater services, as discussed below.

*Reform of privatised monopolies in the initial years of reform was delayed, and little emphasis was placed on increasing competition.*

The second wave of privatising larger and public service enterprises stumbled into problems. This was particularly true for infrastructure industries, including toll highways and banking (see Box 1.2). As early as 1992, regulatory shortcomings were appearing in the airlines, in highways, and in the banking industry. Profits from the initial phase of liberalisation were concentrated in a few conglomerates, suggesting a lack of competition in many non-tradable sectors. It soon became clear that the need for appropriate regulatory regimes and institutions to protect competition and consumer interests in the new markets was insufficiently emphasised in the first years of structural reform. More competition was needed in the internal market – hence the passing of a competition law at the end of 1992 and the ensuing *Reglamento* in 1998, and the creation of new regulatory bodies in some sectors.

*Limiting competition was believed by some authorities to be necessary to finance needed investment through monopoly profits or to compete for international capital.*

Limits to competition were in some cases an explicit strategy to serve public policy objectives. Either the authorities chose to perpetuate monopoly or oligopoly conditions, or delayed in creating an adequate regulatory framework appropriate to new conditions, or both. The purported rationale for this was primarily to promote investment in infrastructure. Some authorities believed that full competition would not provide adequate infrastructure investment, particularly in network industries, nor extend service to poor rural communities, that is, provide for universal service.[19] Competition was thus constrained in some form so as to raise rates of return to presumably insure adequate expansion of the network.

Telecommunications regulation shows some aspects of this kind of policy (see Chapter 5 for details). Telmex was allowed to function as a complete monopoly in long distance services subject to regulation by the ministry from 1990 through 1996. Telecommunications rates were used to pay for investment, and maintain cross-subsidies to residential users as they were gradually reduced.

### Privatisation also suffered from failures to install adequate corporate governance and inappropriate sequencing.

*As privatisation proceeded, some problems appeared. For example, some of the new owners had inadequate management skills.*

Insufficient competition has not been the only drawback to privatisation. In the case of some banks, airlines and toll highways, the new owners of privatised firms, or holders of concessions, had inadequate management and financial skills. The most striking case has been the highway system, where concessions were granted combining highway construction and administration. Construction companies who had no experience in managing a toll road won most bids at prices which badly overestimated potential returns, resulting in overleveraged financing, excessively high prices, low utilisation rates and ultimately government intervention to rescue 23 financially troubled operations.[20]

*Other privatisations suffered from inappropriate sequencing and failure to simultaneously reform sectors in the production chain.*

Sequencing and co-ordination of reform proved to be a problem in many sectors, including banking, sugar, port services, transportation, petrochemicals, and vegetable oil. A common problem was that many of these sectors were links in a long production chain, or that privatised assets were inappropriately bundled. In vegetable oils, processing was privatised in the face of high effective tariffs on oil[21] and completely fragmented domestic oil seed production. The deregulation of petrochemicals failed to generate the hoped for large investments. 49% equity investment limits, together with the issue of pricing inputs by the state-owned company, diminished the interest of the private sector.

### In most non-infrastructure sectors, complete deregulation of entry and pricing has been achieved.

*Entry and exit requirements in a number of sectors have been eliminated or eased.*

Aside from the question of large infrastructure sectors, the Mexican authorities moved rapidly and effectively to liberalise entry and pricing in a number of sectors (see Table I.1). Perhaps the most successful cases were passenger buses and trucks, where federal restrictions on routes, material carried, and pricing were completely removed (see Annex 2). Other sectors where liberalisation occurred included port services and goods markets like horticulture products, seeds, matches, textiles and salt, among others. Entry was freed *de jure* in air transport as well; fares in air transport were fully deregulated in 1990. Routing licenses have also been substantially deregulated, but carriers continue to need licenses on a route by route basis.

Table 1.1. **Regulatory reform in Mexico**

| Industry | Previous situation/evidence for deregulation | Recent and outstanding reforms | Price regulation | Regulation of entry and exit | Other regulations which may affect competition |
|---|---|---|---|---|---|
| Air transport | Aeroméxico and Mexicana were state-owned in the late 1980s, then privatised in 1988 and 1989, respectively. In 1995, CINTRA (the holding company for both airlines) was permitted to maintain control of the airlines under the Federal Competition Commission's condition that Aeroméxico and Mexicana be operated independently. The government indirectly increased its control of CINTRA from 15 to 52% as a result of the take-over of bad bank loans, but does not participate in day-to-day operations. Up to 1989, rates had to be approved by the regulator. | Mexicana and Aeroméxico were privatised in 1988 and 1989, respectively. Fares and routes (in the latter case, not completely) were liberalised in February 1990. A new civil aviation law was enacted in 1995, and corresponding bylaws in 1998. | None, but prices must be registered with the Transport and Communication Ministry (SCT). SCT monitors some routes where the competition authority (CFC) has assessed market power. | Entry of new carriers and new entry and exit on individual routes is subject to SCT approval. Little industry exit or entry was observed in 1995-1998. In practice, some apparently insolvent firms have not exited the market. Such exit behaviour may constitute significant barriers to entry (potential entrants are dissuaded by the fact that some operating companies do not cover all of their costs). | Any transfer of corporate control of CINTRA must be approved by the Federal Competition Commission. Opening of airport operations to private capital initiated in 1998 reduce the likelihood that slot scarcity persists in airports, except possibly while a new airport is built for Mexico City. |
| Road transport (trucking) | Regulations allocated freight and dictated routing; freight handling was monopolised. Routes were granted by concession. Controls on entry created corrupt practices and inefficiency: empty backhauls, higher prices and poorer service. | Deregulation began in 1989 and culminated in amendments to the Federal Roads Law in 1992 Since 1997, the Federal government has signed 3 agreements with State governments to avoid back tracking on reforms at the sub-federal level. | None. | Permits are given to all firms that comply with the requirements spelled out in law. No exit barriers exist. | State and municipal authorities can regulate non-federal highways, imposing new regulations. Some parts of the regulatory regime recently reverted to reforms due to permits from concessions recently approved by the Mexico City government (including restrictions on foreign investment that seem to be incompatible with international obligations). |
| Rail freight | A state-owned monopoly provided low quality services at tariffs above international levels. Service was particularly poor in terms of delivery times. Deterioration in capital stock. Some maintenance facilities were privatised in the late 1980s, which paved the way for trunk line privatisations. | 1997-1998: privatisation of the national company. 4 companies created: 3 trunk line operators, and one in the Valley of Mexico in which the three trunk line operators have a 25% stake. The remaining 25% is held by the government. New framework establishes interconnection rates based on reasonable profits above costs. | 1993: liberalisation of freight charges in the customs zones, loading and unloading of freight Maximum prices established by SCT. | The SCT auctions exclusive, up to 50 year concessions to four main regional route-based companies. Vertical integration of the different functions or services (infrastructure construction and maintenance, traffic control and operation) is preserved, although functions may be unbundled where necessary. | Too soon to assess. Railroad concessions must grant rights of way to other operators. |

Table 1.1. **Regulatory reform in Mexico** (cont.)

| Industry | Previous situation/evidence for deregulation | Recent and outstanding reforms | Price regulation | Regulation of entry and exit | Other regulations which may affect competition |
|---|---|---|---|---|---|
| Ports | State-owned system. Private harbours were allowed only if owned by a single firm. | Deregulation of 1991 opened harbour services to private investors. | None. | The 1991 deregulation opened harbour services to private investors. In 1995, concessions were auctioned for port terminals and some integrated tourist port administrations to operate, plan and construct basic infrastructure. | |
| Highways | Underinvestment. Mexico had only 48 000 km of paved federal roads compared to 800 000 for Canada. But there were also 60 000 km of paved state roads. In 1989, there were only 1 230 km of national toll highways. | 52 concessions were awarded since 1989 for approximately 5 350 kilometres of road. | Tolls were allowed to increase semi-annually in accord with a CPI-X formula. | Concessions granted for up to 30 years to private investors if a free alternative exists to each proposed highway. Concessions periods were initially of 8 to 30 years, but some of the shorter periods were extended after renegotiation in 1995. | The government guaranteed usage levels of toll roads (as did many other countries until the early 1990s), which led to expensive bailouts. |
| Telecommunications | High prices and low density, suggesting underinvestment. Telmex was a state-owned vertically integrated monopoly, privatised in 1990 with a concession running until 2026, though long distance would open in 1996. Telmex was subject to price cap regulation and to any future legislative reforms. | A new Federal Telecommunications Law enacted in 1995 allowed for the spectrum sale through auctions. State-owned satellites and geostationary locations were privatised in 1998. In 1996, a new sectoral regulatory agency, Comisión Federal de Telecomunicaciones (Cofetel) was created. | Telmex prices are regulated through price caps. Other prices of service are set free. Terms of interconnection based on negotiation between long-distance operators and the operator of the public telephony network (Telmex). In case of standstill, SCT must establish the rates. | SCT delivers concessions for each service. Cofetel organises simultaneous ascending auctions of the radio frequency spectrum. Telmex monopoly of long distance services opened to competition in 1997. Competition in local service was opened up in 1990, but started in 1999. | In 1997, CFC determined that Telmex had substantial market power on five relevant markets. De jure local telephone services have been open since 1990; factual entry may take place in 1999. The Federal Telecommunications Law allows for asymmetric regulation (Article 63) of the dominant carrier. |
| Electric power | Underinvestment by the state-owned monopoly. | Reforms to the Electricity Law in 1992 allowed private participation in electricity generation through self-supply and co-generation (though no sale to end users is permitted). In 1995, an independent regulatory agency (CRE) was created. | The Ministry of Finance approves electricity prices. CRE approves methodologies for tariff calculation of all transmission related services. | CRE auctions concessions and issues permits. All persons that comply with legal requirements for self-supply permits and co-generation. No exit regulations for private generators. | In February 1999, the government submitted a constitutional amendment proposal to Congress. The reform would open the sector to private investment and introduce competition in the different segments of the industry. (Creation of an independent system and market operator and separate generation, transmission, and distribution companies.) |

Table 1.1. **Regulatory reform in Mexico** (*cont.*)

| Industry | Previous situation/evidence for deregulation | Recent and outstanding reforms | Price regulation | Regulation of entry and exit | Other regulations which may affect competition |
|---|---|---|---|---|---|
| Natural gas | Underinvestment by the State-owned vertically integrated monopoly. | Due to reforms in 1995, the private sector can now construct, operate, and own systems of natural gas transportation, storage, and distribution, and participate in marketing of natural gas. Several companies are already in operation in major urban centres. Regulations make unbundling of pricing compulsory (transportation, distribution and commodity costs must be itemised in the bill to the final user), even in the case of Pemex's first hand sales (commodity and transportation costs). | CRE regulates Pemex's (state monopoly) first hand sales price *via* netback. CRE also regulates transportation, storage and distribution tariffs by CPI-X formula. | CRE auctions concessions with a 5 to 12 year exclusivity period on a predetermined geographic zone. Permit holders must guarantee continuity of service. Transporters and distributors must provide open access. Physical bypass permitted in distribution zones. | Absence of many gas producers and brokers. Government controlled production. In the North of Mexico natural gas is easily imported. |
| Professional services (notaries) | Extremely high rates for notary services, in particular in low population density states. Slow and low quality of services in some states. In some states the local executive has extensive discretion in the granting of notary licenses. | The 1993 reforms permitted *corredores públicos* (public officials) to execute important mercantile acts that were exclusively done by notaries, in particular for the establishment of new enterprises. | Minimum prices set by local governments or notary associations. | Licence for "*corredores publicos*" issued by Trade and Industry Ministry (SECOFI) based on a professional exam. Notaries are regulated through state provisions. | 1997 CFC action against a collusive boycott in notarisation services against "*corredores públicos*". *Corredores* cannot be involved in real estate transactions, which are exclusively handled by local notaries. |

*Source:* OECD.

Since the mid-1990s, the government has begun to extend reforms to new sectors and the public administration itself. Customs procedures have been rationalised and measures to reduce corruption successfully introduced. Patent law and technical standards, including labelling, have been thoroughly improved. In health care, numerous reforms have been introduced including a simpler and quicker system for new drug registration, permission to use generic drugs, and private accreditation or certification of medical laboratories and other health services. Other far-reaching reforms include those in the mining and fisheries sectors, where entry controls were drastically reduced. There has been a major overhaul of the health and pension systems (see the 1998 OECD Economic Survey). A series of regulatory improvements has also concentrated on non-economic regulations, like in the environmental and sanitary sectors,[22] as well as reductions in red tape associated with formalities (see Chapter 2).

## The effects of reform have been positive in sectors where full competition has been introduced.

*Competition increased in deregulated sectors and economic performance improved rapidly.*

No general assessment of the benefits and costs of the multi-year programme of structural reform has been performed, though the competition authority has assessed effects on competition in its annual reports. Table I.2 summarises the available information on effects of reform in Mexico. A 1997 study, assessing the benefits of privatisation in Mexico, indicated that the economic performance of privatised firms improved rapidly – even in sectors with low levels of competition.[23] Reforms to mining law and regulations multiplied by 200 the sector's gross internal production of 1980 (BID, 1998, Table A2). In terms of market access, in most of the sectors where entry has been completely open there have been substantial new competitors, particularly in trucking, inter-city buses and urban transportation. The Ministry of Communications and Transport estimates there are over half a million truckers in Mexico. Unfortunately, these results may prove temporary, as open entry in trucking is threatened by attempts by some state governments to reintroduce entry barriers to favour firms from their area. Co-operation agreements between states were initiated by the federal authorities to prevent reintroduction of barriers, but only so far only three states have signed up.

In airlines, initial entry was substantial. New entrants' market share rose from 8 to 25% between 1989 and 1993 and at one time there were as many as 6 trunk carriers operating. However, for national traffic the process may have stalled or been reversed, and competition appears to have decreased since 1994-95. The reason for this appears to be the *de facto* merger, of the two major carriers, Mexicana and Aeroméxico and subsequently the government's re-acquisition of an ownership share through its bad loans recovery programme, an unintended consequence of the banking debacle (see Chapter 3 for details). Moreover, an implicit limited exit policy has been a deterrent to market entry in this sector. Nonetheless between 3 to 4 companies are serving most major routes.

Table 1.2. **Potential impacts of regulatory reform in Mexico**

| Industry | Industry structure and competition | Industry profits | Impact on output, price and relative prices | Impacts on service quality, reliability and universal service | Impact on sectoral wage and employment | Efficiency: productivity and costs | Future reforms needed |
|---|---|---|---|---|---|---|---|
| Air transport | Substantial new entry following deregulation in the late 1980s, increasing competition. By 1993, the share of Mexicana and Aeroméxico in the domestic market was over 71%, down from 91% in 1989. Increased competition created losses in Mexicana, taken over by Aeroméxico in 1993. Competition has declined with tighter enforcement of financial criteria for entry and safety regulations. | In the first three years after privatisation, Mexicana suffered heavy losses and Aeroméxico turned a small profit. After deregulation in 1992, both lost money. Aeroméxico and Mexicana were highly profitable in 1996 and 1997 by international standards. Profits in 1998 declined by 45% with respect to 1997, despite lower petrol prices and growth in the Mexican economy. | Prices (as measured by real yields, i.e., inflation-adjusted revenue per passenger-kilometre) decreased following privatisation and then increased after deregulation, more than reversing initial gains. Since the enactment of the civil aviation law (1995) and bylaws (1998), rates have been driven by market forces even though these forces were subdued by limited industry exit and entry. Prices have remained higher than in the United States. | | Cuts in Aeroméxico labour force from 11 505 in 1987 to a low of 4 218 in 1989 immediately prior to privatisation. Mexicana reduced its work force from 13 906 to 9 801 in 1992. Job creation by new entrants. From 1994 to 1995, employment in commercial aviation decreased 3%, from 21 419 to 20 756 employees. During 1996-1998, employment increased 21%. | Productivity estimates (revenue passenger kilometres per employee, air craft kilometres per flight crew member, passenger load factor) have increased. Revenues increased 15%, while operational and administrative costs decreased by 4% and 5%, respectively during 1994-1995. In 1998, revenues increased only 0.6% in nominal terms, operational costs increased 10.7% and administrative costs increased 18.5% with respect to 1997. | The competition authority should resolve whether CINTRA can (or cannot) be privatised as is. It will be important to ensure transparent slot allocation systems at temporarily congested airports, while additional capacity is built. The competition authority should screen bidders in slot auctions. |
| Road transport (trucking) (for more details see Annex 2) | Between 1989 and 1996, the number of registered units increased 92%. Many informal trucking companies were integrated. The industry is segmented into two categories: large, sophisticated firms and small, struggling ones. | Profits have been hard hit by the economic crisis of 1994-1995. | Between 1987 and 1994 trucking rates nation-wide declined 23%. Between 1995 and 1998, trucking rates declined 37% in real terms. | More competition in trucking promotes innovation and services. | A 5.2% increase in employment between 1989 and 1995. | Since 1989, traffic volumes increased 8.6% per year, measured in ton/km. | Harmonisation of state and municipal regulations with federal ones. Improved compliance with technical standards. |

Table 1.2. **Potential impacts of regulatory reform in Mexico** (cont.)

| Industry | Industry structure and competition | Industry profits | Impact on output, price and relative prices | Impacts on service quality, reliability and universal service | Impact on sectoral wage and employment | Efficiency: productivity and costs | Future reforms needed |
|---|---|---|---|---|---|---|---|
| Rail freight | The four main routes (one of these routes is for interconnection and manoeuvres in the Valley of Mexico) owned by each firm are designed so as to promote a "source competition" that may protect shippers in the absence of end-to-end railroad competition. Competition from trucking services. | N/A. | During 1994, rail freight rates decreased 6.6% in real terms, and 0.5% during 1995-1998. In 1998, after the opening to the private sector, the rates of the two main concessionaires increased, on average, 1.3% in real terms. | US – Mexico rail services terminals, crossing, and rail equipment have improved since 1991. Service has become much more reliable (timeliness of delivery in particular). High level of service improvement in the Mexico-Veracruz line in which there is direct competition. | The privatisation honoured all obligations between the government and the union (severance pay, rehiring of some employees, pension fund of the union). | Too early to assess, but thefts have decreased substantially. | |
| Ports | A competitive environment has emerged between the private operators of port terminals (API) and their service providers. | N/A. | Handling prices per ton for agriculture fell 42% in real terms since 1995. For minerals, prices were 35-50% lower, depending on the port. Costs of container service in Veracruz fell by 30%, and volume increased 47%. | N/A. | N/A. | Veracruz increased 40 to 75 number of containers per hour/vessel in operation; in Progreso, the unloading capacity of agricultural products went from 2 500 to 8 000 tons per day. In Acapulco, unloading of automobiles doubled, from 125 to 250 vehicles per hour. According to the SCT, the commercial cargo increased 16% per year and the handling of containers has increased by 26%. | Better integration of individual service providers with overall port authority. |

Table 1.2. **Potential impacts of regulatory reform in Mexico** (cont.)

| Industry | Industry structure and competition | Industry profits | Impact on output, price and relative prices | Impacts on service quality, reliability and universal service | Impact on sectoral wage and employment | Efficiency: productivity and costs | Future reforms needed |
|---|---|---|---|---|---|---|---|
| Toll highways | Most concessionaire affiliates of one construction company defaulted on loans. Local commercial banks were saddled with non-performing toll road loans estimated at US$4.5-5.5 billion. A trust fund for construction and operation of roads has been created, and creditors have priority in repayment. In 1997, 23 road projects were bailed-out by the federal government because of usage (traffic volume) guarantees. | Gross miscalculation of investment costs and operating income led to an unsustainable set of operating conditions and large losses. In the case of unfinished road projects, new investments were required. Extensive cross-subsidies exist in the bailed-out road projects. | Prices are still too high and not competitive. Users were left with some of the most expensive road tolls in the world. | Road system in Mexico is still inadequate for long-haul trucking, particularly to the US. Government estimated that another 6 500 kilometres of road are needed by 2000. There are few super-highways, although major arterial routes have been built between Mexico City and Guadalajara, Monterrey and Laredo. One infrastructure concern is the border crossing at Laredo, Texas, the gateway that handles over two thirds of Mexican-US traffic. A second concern is road conditions in the border states. | Employment was stimulated by highway construction, permanent increase on tolls and maintenance. According to unofficial estimates, over 225 000 temporary jobs were created for the construction and maintenance of road projects. | N.A. | Any future concessions should incorporate new schemes designed in the 1990s, and should not include government guarantees. |
| Telecommunication (for further details see chapter 5 and corresponding background report) | In long distance, new entrants quickly took about 30% of market share. Since 1997, several companies have obtained concessions for local service. Claims that Telmex is cross-subsidising long distance rates with higher local service prices. | For 1991, Telmex's net profit after taxes was US$1.7 billion, compared with a projection of US$1 billion, while in 1992 and 1993 it was in the range of US$2.5 billion. Despite being the 12th largest telephone company in the world Telmex's stock market capitalisation place it second in the world, next only to BT. | Long-distance and international services prices have fallen since 1997 (22% from January 1997 to October 1998), offset by large increases in local service price. However, for some subscribers the total price for telephone services may not have fallen given that the subsidies for local services have shrunk dramatically. | Investments improved technical performance of the sector. System digitalisation had increased from 29 to 83% by 1994. Growth in the number of telephone lines was modest but significant. Since 1994, the rate of investment has fallen off significantly, and performance on quality indicators has stagnated. | From 1985 to 1997, employment in telecommunication services increased 50%. | The number of lines per employee rose from 95.2 in 1989 to 151.5 in 1993, representing a cumulative increase of 46% in the three years following privatisation. In 1997, the number of lines per employee rose to 163.4. | |

*Source:* OECD.

*Competition in infrastructural sectors remains limited.*

In general, it is too soon to assess the effects of privatisation and reform on competition in the regulated monopoly sectors. Although in some sectors, like ports, the price decreases and better services give the impression of more efficiency and competition, in other sectors there are lingering problems. For instance, in telecommunications, Telmex earned substantial monopoly profits through the first half of the 1990s. Since long distance was opened up to competition new entrants have gained 30% of the market, but Telmex responded with aggressive price cuts so that new entrants now are sustaining operating losses. Telmex has recently been found by the competition commission (CFC) to have substantial market power in five markets (see Chapter 3). In rail the authorities are confident that intermodal competition from trucking will provide adequate competition.

**Output has increased in almost all deregulated sectors, but price movements have depended on the level of competition.**

*Prices fell in some reformed sectors and increased in others that had been subsidised...*

Prices in fully deregulated sectors like port services, trucking and inter-city transport fell substantially. Port services prices have dropped by over 40% in some cases. Between 1987 and 1994, trucking rates nation-wide declined 23% (see Table 1.2 and Annex 2). Prices in some sectors were artificially suppressed prior to privatisation, so that some increases occurred. This is true in railroads, local telephony and airlines. In airlines the fact that prices have gone from below to above US levels seems in part due to the reintroduction to informal barriers to exit discussed above apparently designed to maintain as much air service as possible.[24] In accordance with the rates rebalancing plan, telephones' residential prices rose steadily between 1994 from very low subsidised levels, and fixed installation charges rose even more (50% and 70%, respectively). The collapse of the market in 1995-96, when millions of subscribers cancelled their lines, forced Telmex, with the authorities approval, to slow down the rebalancing, further reducing the attractiveness for new entries. Domestic and international long distance rates have fallen since the sector was opened up to competition. Nonetheless, the aggressive price cutting by the incumbent is probably funded by cross-subsidies from local service, where it is still functioning as a monopoly.[25] In almost all sectors, the quality of service has improved enormously. Telephone installation waiting time has declined from 6 months to one day.

*... and efficiency increased substantially in most sectors.*

In most sectors efficiency has increased substantially. In port services loading and unloading rates have doubled or tripled, in telecommunications productivity increased by 8% annually in 1996-97 following a nearly 50% increase in lines per employee during the first few years following privatisation. Some enterprises in the primary non-energy export sector, such as agriculture and mining, have increased their international presence. Reforms in government services like customs, and more recently, tax administration, increased processing speed and greatly reduced corruption and the underinvoicing of imports. Efficiency in trucking improved modestly but has yet to benefit from any economies of scope or scale as no large carriers have emerged.[26] The ever-increasing numbers of small and medium-sized enterprises (SME) exporting, directly or indirectly through *maquiladoras*, indicate the existence of a new vibrant entrepreneurial private sector, a result achieved with little access to banking credit.[27]

### Effects on wages and employment are mixed.

*Insufficient evidence is available to assess any impact on sectoral wages.*

Wage effects of regulatory reform are difficult to assess because of the overall decline in real incomes caused by macroeconomic instability. Precise data is difficult to come by but there clearly was a huge drop in real wages in the 1980s. The recovery in wages which accompanied the resumption of growth in the 1990s was wiped out by the 1994-95 exchange rate crisis so that real wages levels remain below levels found in the early 1970s. Within that trend, the wages of high-skilled qualified workers have increased relatively because of economic liberalisation and market opening while low-skilled wages have suffered even more, in large part because of excess labour supply that is somewhat cleared through emigration.

*Employment losses were largely avoided by requirements in privatisation and concession terms...*

Potential losses of employment were confined, on the one hand, to transitional restructuring efforts, and on the other to infrastructural sectors characterised by overstaffing. Trade liberalisation and privatisation of inefficient firms had temporary negative employment impacts in some sectors, such as textiles, toys, and other manufacturing. But by mid-1998, nearly three million net formal sector jobs were created, almost half of which were in exporting companies. In many infrastructural sectors, such as railroads and, initially, air transport, employment cuts were avoided by explicit employment requirements contained in the concession titles Privatisation packages included contribution to union pension funds and severance packages which were important to avoid blocking by labour unions of the privatisations. Telmex was explicitly prohibited from releasing workers, as were the railroads; the subsequent expansion of output in telecommunications has permitted potentially redundant workers to be efficiently employed, and the authorities are hoping the same results can be achieved in rail transport. The one sector where employment losses occurred was air transport, though losses by the two dominant carriers were partly offset by increased employment on the part of new entrants.

*... while other newly liberalised sectors have began to show employment growth.*

At the same time, liberalisation has also stimulated job creation. Private sector entry in natural gas, for example, following reform has led to the creation of jobs, both directly and indirectly, as a result of network expansion.

### THE MACROECONOMIC EFFECTS OF REGULATORY REFORM

*Microeconomic benefits have largely been hidden by poor overall macroeconomic performance.*

Microeconomic reform is likely to have generated some macroeconomic benefits, but these are difficult to see. In terms of growth benefits were swamped by Mexico's macroeconomic instability. Instability was not attributable to reforms, with the notable and

*Supply flexibility has increased and the economy is less susceptible to inflation.*

important exception of problems in the banking sector, but rather resulted from Mexico's high debt service burden, the choice of a vulnerable exchange rate regime (crawling peg with fluctuating bands) external shocks, and domestic political shocks.

Trade and price liberalisation contributed substantially to the stabilisation of inflation, and growth performance has improved thanks to an improved supply response. The most compelling evidence of the effects of structural reforms on aggregate supply is Mexico's performance following the 1994-95 crisis.[28] Growth resumed almost immediately with strong and ultimately sustained export dynamism and inflation has steadily diminished, in marked contrast to the economy's performance following the 1982 and 1987 crises. In 1998, Mexican growth registered 4.8% despite the presence of unfavourable conditions in emerging markets and the fall of oil prices. This exceptional performance is due to fiscal discipline and the private sector's increased resilience, attributable mainly to regulatory reform and increased market openness.

**Future reforms in key sectors such as energy and waste will bring large benefits.**

Privatisation and deregulation need to proceed expeditiously and this is the intention of the government. In the immediate future, the government will continue to privatise or grant concessions in radio spectrum, paper mills, airports, natural gas, and ports, and self-supply and co-generation in electricity (in addition to the pursuit of additional reforms to increase private participation in electricity, including generation).

*Reforms are urgently needed in the provision of drinking water and electricity sector.*

An urgent sector for regulatory reform is water, given the need to allocate it efficiently in a context of growing scarcity. The 1992 National Water Law is of high quality (it allows for the trading of water rights and greater use of economic instruments), but lower level regulations – both federal and state – and the administration of water can be improved substantially by reducing discretion, setting rate guidelines and clearly establishing concession requirements. Recent attempts to involve private sector participation have often been unsuccessful due to an inadequate regulatory framework and a lack of sub-federal transparency. In some cases the municipalities have arbitrarily suspended concessions for political reasons.

The electricity sector is in need of a restructuring effort. In February 1999, the government addressed this need by submitting to Congress proposed amendments to the Constitution aimed at further opening it to private investment, accompanied by a new Electricity Law introducing competition in different segments of the industry. The reforms would involve the creation of independent system and market operators, and separate generation, transmission and distribution companies.

*Trade and investment liberalisation needs to be completed.*

Elimination of the few remaining restrictions on FDI and trade in goods and services would generate substantial benefits to Mexico. In the future, the removal of restrictions on car imports and used computers, which will ultimately expire under NAFTA anyway, should be accelerated.

**Complementary reforms are necessary in factor markets and the overall legal and regulatory climate.**

*Important complementary reforms are still lacking and if undertaken could amplify the benefits from reform.*

Important complementary reforms are still lacking and if undertaken could amplify the benefits from reform. A key area is the financial sector. A major reform was undertaken in 1997 when the pension system was completely overhauled. However important problems remain. Banks' bad debt problems have meant that the credit crunch is prolonged so that small and medium-size enterprises and consumers lack financing. Mexico recently eliminated restrictions on foreign investment in financial services and in the following months the rapid and complete implementation of the recent legal resolution of the bad debt problem (see Box 1.2) will be critical for growth. Additional financial reforms will be necessary to increase the pool of potential entrepreneurs and ensure against the re-emergence of problem debts.[29] One factor which contributed to the banking crisis was the lack of adequate credit information. No credit bureaux existed in the early 1990s and they are still under-utilised because of the possibility of information sharing amongst competitors.

*Legal and bankruptcy reforms are critical to improving the overall business climate...*

Legal and bankruptcy reforms are critical to improving the overall business climate. Important limitations and some problems still occur when enforcing contracts based on the merits of the law. Important areas for improvements concern the transparency and accountability of judicial decisions.[30] Most importantly, the current bankruptcy law does not provide for satisfactory allocation of claims, which has contributed to the slow progress in resolving the banking crisis, and commercial law in general is inadequate to the needs of modern business.[31]

*... and the reform process benefits from the support of a vigorous competition policy.*

As discussed in Chapter 3, the reform process needs to be complemented by vigorous competition policy. Continuing competition problems in air transport and telecommunications are a major source of concern; this is generally true of infrastructural network sectors where concessions have been granted. In other sectors, such as cement, and glass, high concentration and evidence of market power may require stronger responses from the competition authorities.

Finally, the regulatory environment in which SMEs operate still requires additional attention, as indicated in Chapter 2. The large informal sector is a daunting challenge to regulatory compliance. In addition, informal SMEs unfairly compete with formal ones, creating further negative incentives to comply. This situation also tends to sustain and fuel corruption amongst enforcers at the street level. A connected issue is that some mandatory technical standards are based on excessively rigid performance criteria and that formalities required from local governments for business opening and operation are sometimes excessively complex and duplicative. If this last link is not reformed, the final gains will be diluted or frustrated at the firms' level.

### Regulatory reform has improved competitiveness and overall efficiency.

*Reforms have enhanced confidence by international investors in the Mexican economy.*

The overall reform process, and the fact that momentum has been maintained through a major balance-of-payments crisis, recession and the associated income loss, has helped enhance the confidence of investors and world markets in the Mexican economy and its ability to meet its commitments. Particularly significant has been Mexico's participation in international organisations such as the GATT, APEC and OECD and trade and investment agreements with Chile, the United States, Canada, Costa Rica, Bolivia, Colombia, Venezuela and Nicaragua, in addition to WTO. The rights and obligations under these agreements have in many ways enshrined and guaranteed Mexico's commitments to regulatory reform.

Trade and price liberalisation, and deregulation are mostly successful, creating a framework in which firms can operate with appropriate signals for the efficient production and allocation of goods and services. This translated into an improved competitive environment and stimulated a massive reorientation of the economy towards exports and import competing sectors of production. Although the reorientation had its transitory costs the overall balance shows that price and trade liberalisation have had impressive results: they contributed to the stabilisation of inflation and improved external performance which in turn helped Mexico attract substantial capital inflows and maintain its external debt payments. Price liberalisation – from 1992 to 1999, all price controls have been eliminated – in particular is an impressive example which can be followed by other OECD Member countries which still retain controls.

*Rapid privatisation helped create an economy that is more efficient and dynamic.*

Privatisation has been in many ways a success. Privatisation achieved its major goal, the creation of a dynamic private sector with the incentive to produce efficiently. The speed with which it was achieved was remarkable and can serve as a benchmark for other countries. Privatisation contributed substantially to the reduction in fiscal deficits, increased investments in many sectors where it was needed, particularly infrastructural sectors, and attracted foreign direct investment which helped relieve pressure on the balance-of-payments.

Privatisation also had some problems. Privatisation may in some cases have placed too much emphasis in the first instance on maximising the sales prices, creating national champions and purportedly guaranteeing investment in infrastructure through exclusive concessions. Not enough emphasis was placed on creating long-term competition in privatised sectors, ensuring capable ownership of newly privatised firms and appropriate sequencing. Particularly striking was the failure in the early years of privatisation to establish new regulatory frameworks and corporate governance in advance of privatisation, a flaw which was particularly costly in the banking sector. As in other OECD countries these two factors fed into one another. Mid-stream reforms to the privatisation process have largely addressed these problems. What is urgent is that the banking sector restart functioning, that remedial actions be taken in monopolistic network sectors to induce as much competition as possible to minimise the long-term costs to the economy in terms of losses of dynamic efficiency. In this regard opening up the financial sector to FDI is an important step.

Mexican businesses and citizens have already benefited substantially from structural reforms at the micro level. Prices for most goods fell thanks to price liberalisation and the quantity and quality of services and products now available have improved. Prices fell even more in sectors where regulatory reform has been total, like trucking and port services, driven by substantial improvements in efficiency. Service in deregulated sectors improved across the board. New products and services have been introduced and are tailored to consumer needs. Costs in terms of employment losses are difficult to assess given the volatile macroeconomic environment, but are likely to be extremely small because Mexican privatisations explicitly introduced labour considerations in the privatisation processes.

*Reform improved Mexico's macroeconomic performance by increasing supply flexibility, allowing the country to rebound quickly and strongly from the crisis of 1994/95.*

Reform improved Mexico's macroeconomic performance by increasing supply flexibility, allowing the country to rebound quickly and strongly from the crisis of 1994/95. In the context of a more stable macroeconomic climate in place since 1995, reforms should substantially contribute to Mexico's overall economic growth. However, for these gains to be realised and sustained, regulatory reform needs to continue. Macro performance in 1998 was already quite strong despite a number of adverse external shocks.

Experience from other countries, and Mexico's own, indicates that the gains from reform can be magnified when reform is comprehensive and pursued on a number of fronts simultaneously. Similarly, other countries' reforms indicate that benefits develop over many years. New Zealand needed more than a decade in a steady macroeconomic environment to harvest the results of its reforms. For Mexico, this requires the full implementation and continuous enforcement of past reforms, greater emphasis on eliciting competition in non-contestable network industries such as telephones and airlines, the correction of past mistakes and the launching of complementary reforms in key framework areas like the bankruptcy and financial systems, and extending sectoral reform to new areas like the provision of water (sub-federal) and the energy sectors. In energy, the far reaching electricity reforms proposed by the executive depends on Congressional approval.

*Chapter 2*

# GOVERNMENT CAPACITY TO ASSURE HIGH QUALITY REGULATION

As structural reforms have introduced competition into formally regulated sectors, while fiscal constraints increasingly limit the scope of direct budgetary intervention, better economic performance for Mexico's citizens and businesses depends increasingly upon the efficiency and quality of the large numbers of regulations needed to carry out public policies and protect market competition. The shift to market-oriented regulatory policies and instruments has required major reform of the public sector to eliminate unnecessary economic intervention, while sustaining policy effectiveness in dynamic markets. Today, the key challenges for improving regulatory quality are implementing the reforms of the past several years throughout the federal, state, and local governments, making regulatory processes more transparent, fact-based, and responsive to ensure that needed regulations efficiently address the problems at hand, and building a wider constituency for reform by improving the public dialogue on the benefits and costs of reform among citizens and consumers, and in the Congress.

**Mexico's legal framework has undergone enormous reform affecting 90% of existing federal laws.**

*Economic reforms required changes in almost all of the nation's laws, a huge task...*

Implementing new policies of privatisation, market openness, and competition had a huge impact on Mexico's regulatory framework. From 1982 to 1997, over 90% of the national legislative framework was extensively modified, to support market mechanisms and links to the global economy, to reduce the state's role in market structure and function, and to reform the relationships among the constitutional branches of government, with states and municipalities, and with businesses and citizens.

*... but the quality and timing of the reform programme were uneven in some areas.*

This impressive task of revision and development of the country's basic regulatory frameworks contained some gaps, problems and inconsistencies that reduced actual benefits. Reforms in one area sometimes lagged needed parallel changes. For instance, in telephony, a long-term national concession was granted to a private operator six years before the new telecommunications law. This delay and the resulting inconsistencies led to problems in the development of the domestic market, as discussed in Chapter 5.

*Executive initiative drove early reforms, but now the base must be broadened.*

From the beginning, strong commitment at the highest level of the Executive branch was essential to sustaining such a broad reform programme. After 1997, a divided and increasingly activist Congress (in which no party has a majority) and increased participation from diverse interests in the larger society added new and powerful players to debates about regulation. The new market structures and political environment that emerged in 1997 combined to accelerate the change away from the traditional setting of the regulatory agenda by the Executive toward agenda-setting characterised by transparency, consultation, accountability, and open negotiation with interested parties. That is, the role of stakeholders has become more central to the direction and speed of change.

*Regulatory reform policy started with a narrow, deregulation approach.*

Regulatory reform policy started in the late 1980s as a targeted approach to accompany structural changes. The first explicit policy concentrated on improving economic performance and stimulating entrepreneurial energies. Since then, reform policy has expanded in three broad stages. The first stage was centred on classical deregulation. In 1989 the President created a special unit, the Economic Deregulation Unit (UDE), at the Ministry of Trade and Industry (SECOFI), to concentrate on deregulating or re-regulating specific economic sectors, and to facilitate the flow of goods, services and capital stimulated by trade liberalisation.

*The legal framework was adapted to participation by private and foreign firms.*

The deregulation effort focused on adapting the broader regulatory framework to an open economy, to provide a level playing field among existing firms and new firms regardless of the origin of capital, and to accompany the privatisation programme. Thus private and foreign participation was allowed in critical service sectors such as public infrastructure (highways, municipal public services) and electricity generation to attract international investment. Other important programmes pursued in this context were the deregulation of financial services and the reform of land ownership.

*Reformers then produced new basic laws, about standards, consumer protections, and competition.*

By the early 1990s, this economic deregulation programme was broadened to include efforts to review obsolete and inadequate regulations and build the necessary microeconomic conditions to increase efficiency and lower costs in all markets. This second stage of reforms has been driven by the need to support the structural reforms induced by external competition and investment attraction (railroads, airports, satellites, spectrum allocation, and natural gas distribution). The reforms aimed at providing legal certainty and eliminating contradictions, thus reducing transition costs and facilitating decision-making. The UDE originated three crucial laws, on standards and measures, on consumer protection, and on competition policy.

*Now, the process addresses the wider issue of regulatory management.*

The third stage, launched in 1995 by the incoming Administration of President Zedillo, aimed to establish a government-wide regulatory management system based on review, transparency, and consultation. But the economic circumstances of that year transformed the regulatory policy into a crucial element of the new industrial policy and an instrument to help businesses cope with the crisis.

---

Box 2.1.  **Managing regulatory quality in Mexico**

*Ensuring regulatory transparency*:

- A standardised procedure to create technical standards was established by law in 1992. Since then, standard-setting has involved a "notice and comment" process, detailed consultation, and cost-benefit analysis.
- Although there are no government-wide public consultation procedures, a Federal Administrative Procedure Law that came into effect in 1994 enhanced regulatory transparency and accountability.
- An official registry of all business formalities is published on-line in the Internet (http://www.cde.gob.mx/). The registry is updated though inclusion of all formalities that are justified and reviewed by the oversight unit.

*Promoting regulatory reform and quality within the administration*

- Since 1989, reform policies have been established directly by the President on the basis of presidential decree. The current programme – *Acuerdo para la Desregulación Empresarial* (ADAE) – established a regulatory management system based on central oversight by a co-ordination unit – *Unidad de Desregulación Económica* (UDE) – under the responsibility of the Trade and Industry Ministry.
- The ADAE established a high level Economic Deregulation Council where business and non-governmental representatives, with the main economic ministries, oversee progress.
- The UDE co-ordinates and monitors the regulatory reform programmes of the 31 federal states.

*Adopting explicit standards for regulatory quality*

- The current policy requires that draft laws and subordinate regulations justify that government action is needed, that potential benefits justify costs, that impacts on SMEs are minimised, that regulatory objectives cannot be achieved through better instruments, and that implementation is backed by sufficient budgetary and administrative resources.  The reviews of business formalities use the same criteria.

*Reviewing and updating regulations*

- In the past 15 years, 90% of existing federal laws have been reviewed, eliminated or modified to support a market economy and improve transparency and consumer protection.

*Assessing regulatory impacts*

- In 1996, the Administrative Procedure Law was amended to require regulatory impact analysis (*manfiestación de impacto regulatorio*) for all new draft laws and subordinate regulations with possible impacts on businesses.  The ministries carry out the analysis, and the UDE and the Economic Deregulation Council assure quality.

*Reducing administrative burdens*

- As part of the ADAE, a complete review of existing formalities was launched by the administration. By July 1999, 10 out of 12 ministries subject to the process had pledged to eliminate around 50% of mandatory formalities and simplify and improve 97% of remaining formalities. The inventory, set up in 1996 and accessible through Internet, is being transformed into an official registry to provide legal security to business – only registered formalities can be enforced – and serve as an electronic one-stop shop.

---

*The economic crisis speeded reform, to enable firms to respond and to address concerns about corruption.*

This new phase of regulatory reform needed to respond to important demands raised during the first months of the new administration. The business community demanded a more competitive framework, to take advantage quickly of new export possibilities following the devaluation in late 1994. And business urged the government to reduce the regulatory burden during the critical months that followed the economic crisis. The new policy emphasis also responded to public and business concerns about corruption and lack of transparency and accountability in the civil service. Furthermore, regulatory reform was considered a relatively low-cost policy with respect to the fiscal budget, as businesses can be significantly helped without the need for any explicit subsidies.

## Mexico has a coherent policy of regulatory management and reform, to review and improve existing formalities and new proposals.

*The ADAE programme is a sound basis for regulatory management.*

After consultation between the government and the business community, at the end of 1995 the new policy was embodied in a Presidential Decree, the *Acuerdo para la Desregulación de la Actividad Empresarial* (ADAE). The ADAE rejuvenated the UDE programme, reinforcing its administration capacities. It included most of the principles of good regulation established in the 1995 OECD *Council Recommendation on Improving the Quality of Government Regulation*. The policy was strongly reinforced in December 1996, when the UDE was empowered to manage a broad programme of regulatory impact analysis. The Mexican government has now established a sound basis for a regulatory management system.

*It covers most business regulations, but gaps could be troublesome.*

The policy framework covers most economic and business-related regulation. Some important policy areas, like public procurement and the financial sector, are excluded or partially exempted, though, and non-business regulations are not part of it. These are important gaps, which may create distortions and reduce public support for the policy.

*Reviewing existing business formalities was the first goal, responding to concerns of small and medium-sized enterprises (SMEs).*

One of ADAE's first goals was to establish a mechanism to review the stock of existing federal business formalities. Problems with these formalities are a particular concern of small and medium-sized enterprises, which could not take immediate advantage of the new export possibilities. Paperwork and red tape impose regressive, disproportionate burdens on smaller entities, compared to larger organisations that can afford the resources or spread the costs more widely. In order to avoid excessive or badly designed formalities, business often moves to the informal sector, leading to a habit of non-compliance that is hard to eliminate and that undermines respect for the rule of law generally. In addition, a large, unregulated informal sector creates unfair competition for "regulated" firms and impairs achieving the benefits that regulation and formalities are intended to produce.

*Next was a process to review and improve proposals for new laws and regulations.*

The second major element of ADAE was aimed at improving new administrative and legislative proposals. A new oversight system was established to review and improve the flow of proposals; this was later strengthened by the RIA programme. Contacts in every ministry must send to the UDE all proposals for new regulations. These require UDE's official approval. Proposals for more than 400 laws and subordinate regulations have gone through this review mechanism since 1996. The process helps eliminate or correct costly and flawed proposals, and also assures that new rules do not undermine reforms that were previously approved. The process has also encouraged important regulatory innovations, such as efficient auc-

46

tioning schemes in network or natural resources industries, the use of third party certification systems instead of *ex ante* controls, and the shift toward using permits based on technical criteria, to overcome the sometimes cumbersome and discretionary elements of the concession-granting process.

*Improvements continue in laws of general application.*

Third, the reform process continues to improve legislation and regulations with economy-wide application. For example, the UDE has improved important framework laws, like the law on technical standards, and drafted others, such as legislation streamlining civil and mercantile judicial procedures and creating mechanisms to improve credit allocation to individuals.

*ADAE encourages reform at local levels, through information and collaboration rather than central direction.*

Finally, UDE supports regulatory reform programmes at state and local levels. This is a crucial problem for a federal country. Each of the 31 federal states, the Mexico City federal district, and 2 377 municipalities has important regulatory powers, over issues such as land use, urban utility services, and business licenses and permits. Lack of progress in reform at local levels could reduce the benefits, to firms and the public, of federal-level reforms. Reforms at the state and local level have been patchy. This unevenness is explained in part by another, political aspect of reform: decentralisation. Until very recently, state and local governments took directions from the centre, despite the federal structure. Now, states and municipalities are increasingly autonomous. To accommodate the powerful demand for decentralisation, the federal government promotes local level regulatory reform mainly through exchange of information and best practice mechanisms.

*An important direct involvement was the overhaul of Mexico City's regulatory structure.*

One prime example of UDE's direct involvement with local governments, though, was the 1995-1997 programme to improve Mexico City's regulatory framework. A far-reaching co-operative project involving UDE, the 1994-1997 Mexico City administration, and the General Comptroller (SECODAM) permitted the elimination of nearly 40% of formalities and the reform of more than 14 major laws and regulations. New regulatory frameworks were established for the environment, public transport, and business inspection. A new permitting system was developed to allow most new firms to commence business in less than 7 days. Some of these reforms were not implemented, some were reversed after the change of local administration, and impacts on businesses have not yet been assessed. But the organisation and comprehensiveness of the effort could be a useful example for other local jurisdictions.

**To give regulatory reform a solid institutional basis, two new kinds of government bodies were needed: government-wide watchdogs and sector-specific regulators working on market principles.**

*Agencies with broad, "horizontal" oversight and control improve transparency and accountability.*

Reforms have created or strengthened horizontally-oriented bodies dedicated to supervision and quality control. This step contrasts with the administrative tradition of hierarchical and departmentalised services and organisations. The new or strengthened entities include the UDE itself and the SECODAM (the General

Comptroller). In addition, there is now a more powerful presidential legal counsellor, which oversees how regulations conform to legal requirements. A competition-policy authority, set up in 1993, has wide jurisdiction and a broad-ranging advocacy power. The ADAE created a new Economic Deregulation Council, which includes businesses, trade unions, rural organisations, and academics, as well as the most important economic ministries and the central bank. The Council plays a critical role by providing a forum for discussing and resolving important problems.

*Specialists in the reform process now have considerable expertise.*

These bodies have made a considerable investment in specialised expertise needed in supporting regulatory reform. They have developed routine processes that provide independent oversight to ministerial actions, to help make them more transparent and establish accountability and participation at high political levels. The developing co-ordination on legal, economic, and public management issues is very positive in exploiting the synergies between these related concerns and in producing a balanced and realistic programme.

*New regulatory agencies, with "vertical" mandates, aim to improve regulatory efficiency in key economic sectors.*

A second institutional development has been the establishment of sectoral regulatory agencies for network industries. Creation of these paralleled the general overhaul of the sectoral legal framework. The models are the agencies for energy (1994) and telecommunications (1996). Three characteristics common to these new bodies are technical specialisation, concentration on regulation and enforcement rather than policy or normative matters, which are left to the ministries, and some degree of autonomy, particularly concerning budgetary and human resources policies. New agencies are on the drawing board.

*Yet the new agencies raise concerns about consistent application of competition policy and continuing attention is needed to reduce the risk of capture by industry interests.*

Because their mandate is focused and they should be independent from political and private interests, these sectoral agencies should be able to do a better job of regulatory management. Yet these institutions are still in the process of establishing their credibility and sustainability. Two potential weaknesses are evident. First, there is a risk of inconsistency with competition policy. Some of these agencies share with the competition policy authority some responsibility in the application of policies to protect competition and consumer welfare in their industry. In the medium term, at least, parties interested in suppressing competition may take advantage of these overlapping responsibilities in ways that could erode consistent application of competition policy. Second, differences in the agencies' institutional designs and authorities may not be justified. Moreover, reproduction of basically similar agencies for each regulated sector could represent costly duplication and waste. In a labour market where network regulators are in short supply, each agency might end up too weak to stand up to strong, well-organised interests.

## Have new policies and institutions actually improved the capacity to produce better regulations?

Political support and technical innovation have been invested in improving how regulations are reviewed and improved. But have they improved the actual quality of regulations? In some respects the answer is yes. In others, the jury is still out.

*Transparency is much improved...*

One of the main improvements concerns transparency. Transparency of the regulatory system is essential to establishing a stable and accessible environment that promotes competition, trade, and investment, and helps ensure against undue influence by special interests. Systematically and quickly, the Mexican government has injected transparency into the regulatory process. The Technical Standards Law was a first step. Its notice and comment requirement was a radical deviation from the traditional method of elaboration of rules behind closed doors. A second step was the 1994 Administrative Procedure Law, which clarifies requirements for publication in the official diary and sets basic guidelines for public consultation. Further reforms to the Law in 1996 require regulatory impact statements for legislative and administrative proposals by the executive that can be made public at UDE's discretion. The ADAE also created the Federal Registry of Business Formalities, so the public would have a full set of all enforceable federal formalities. Overall, transparency is much better now than it was several years ago; however, except for the standards law, many of the provisions promoting transparency are voluntary or limited to sector-specific laws.

*... but consultation is still mostly voluntary, because there is no general "notice and comment" requirement.*

Many elements of the reform process have aimed at promoting consultation and participation before regulations are enacted. The technical standards law, which calls for consultations, was followed by the ADAE and the establishment of the Economic Deregulation Council, which has opened doors and improved co-operation. Since 1997, the Council has reviewed regulatory impact analyses for proposed regulations, including legislative proposals prepared by the executive. Still, formal requirements for public notice and comment are the exception, not the rule.

*Agencies use the Internet widely.*

Mexico's regulators have taken advantage of the Internet as a communication tool. Any business or individual can now check directly about formalities, technical standards, and the legal framework. Mexico's free-phone information centres and other on-line services are among the best developed in OECD countries.

*Transparency limits corruption and encourages businesses to leave the informal sector.*

Improved transparency helps confine discretionary powers and thus limit the potential for corruption and unethical behaviour. That, in turn, should also help shrink the large informal sector and bring those business activities into the regulated mainstream. Some important steps in this direction include reforms to the systems for inspection and licensing in customs, health and sanitation. A development that should be followed up is the use of third-party private certificators taking the responsibility to ensure that businesses comply with standards and rules.

*A major and needed reform to the judicial system is still to bear its fruits.*

Legitimacy and fairness are also critical. Acknowledging public criticism of the courts and concerns about the lack of fast and fair justice to citizens, President Zedillo launched a major reform of the judicial branch as one of his first acts of government in 1994. The reforms have strengthened and modernised the court system, under a stronger Superior Tribunal of Justice. Procedural reforms to the civil and commercial codes in 1996 speeded up commercial cases and reduced the number of trials significantly. But it is too soon to assess the overall results of judicial system reform.

## Use of regulatory impact analysis has grown.

*In 1997 Mexico adopted a well conceived regulatory impact analysis programme.*

The OECD Report on Regulatory Reform recommended that governments integrate regulatory impact analysis (RIA) into the development, review, and reform of regulations. In late 1996, Mexico amended two framework laws, the Administrative Procedures and Technical Standards laws, to implement this essential tool. With these changes, Mexico has joined the two-thirds of OECD countries using RIA to improve the quality of regulation. Mexico is one of a growing number of countries where the requirement is established by law, which gives it greater visibility and permanence. By fine-tuning the guidelines, working out problems with regulators and incorporating many best practices from other OECD countries, the UDE has tailored the RIA tool to the particular legal and traditional practices of the Mexican bureaucracy.

*The RIA programme has succeeded because it is supported by top leadership and well-focused; further improvements could be made, though.*

RIA is difficult to implement by independent departments not used to external scrutiny, and often staffed by public servants not skilled in analysis. Yet acceptance has been higher than expected, except in some areas of the federal government. In part, this success reflects political commitment at the highest level of the administration. Compliance with RIA needs to be monitored closely, and a third party evaluation of the system and its impacts on the quality of regulations should be planned. Already, some general issues are worth noting. One significant strength is the requirement for political accountability – an RIA must be signed by a deputy minister (or general director, for lower-level actions). Other strengths are the focus on costly regulations to maximise the impact of limited RIA resources, and the inclusion of a number of possible impacts and quality aspects to be assessed. But the RIA system could be improved through better training of regulators to prepare them to answer the complex questionnaire, greater use of quantitative cost and benefits information, better schemes to improve compliance, and routine publication of the RIAs themselves for public scrutiny. The Economic Deregulation Council and SECOFI currently publish a list of current proposals under review on the Internet which notes whether an RIA has been prepared (the site can be found at www.cde.gob.mx). Copies of draft texts and RIAs may be requested by all interested parties. Transparency is very important for promoting compliance by agencies. However, neither SECOFI nor the Council have the legal obligation to publish these lists. This makes the public availability of the lists dependent on SECOFI and the Council's political will. An important improvement would be to make full text publication of the proposals and RIAs under review mandatory by law.

## Traditional command and control regulations are still the norm, but there are promising new regulatory techniques in use.

*Mexico trails in the use of alternatives, but a programme to authorise methods meeting a test of "equivalence" may be a catalyst for innovation.*

Many OECD countries are expanding the use of alternative approaches to replace control-and-command regulations that create inefficiencies or distortions in the economy. Mexico took a major step in eliminating price controls and in implementing an equivalence principle for technical standards in the standards, environment and health and safety laws and regulations, but in other respects, it has been slower to do this than some countries, such as the Netherlands or the United States. But Mexico has launched efforts to adopt innovative alternatives in the past few years. Of particular interest to other OECD countries is the use of the principle of equivalence for technical standards and other performance rules. The concept is that a business could get a regulator's authorisation to use a process if the business can prove that the process can achieve the regulatory objective at lower costs. If this scheme works well, while satisfying criteria of transparency and accountability, this would be a promising and powerful tool to expand the use of performance oriented regulations. Another major area of innovation has involved changing inspection systems (particularly in health, labour and technical standards) to sampling-based approaches in order to improve regulatory compliance and the overall performance of the regulations and their enforcement.

*Care must be taken to ensure proper design of concessions.*

Where an activity is defined as a public service, there are legal constraints on the form of regulation. The Constitution provides that such services may be provided by the private sector, under a concession. The concession creates different legal rights and duties, compared to a licence or a permit. A concession, unlike a permit or license, also entails federal jurisdiction on labour, fiscal and other regulatory matters. Thus, when federal road transportation shifted to a permit system in 1989, regulatory powers devolved to the states and municipalities. Design of concessions also has economic consequences. If a concession period is too short, incentives to invest are reduced, and temptation to abuse is increased. The concession title also has accounting and fiscal effects, resulting from the fact that the firm does not own the assets. And concession titles can also raise administrative problems, as loosely defined concessions may permit excessive discretion and legal uncertainty.

*Some concession systems have been reformed, to make them more like permits.*

In the last few years, Mexico has tried to limit and improve some concessions. In some cases, the status of public service has been reformed to permit the creation of licences and permits, or other instruments were designed to regulate private property rights. In other cases, where the public service concept was maintained, the concession system has been revamped with longer terms, nearly automatic renewability, precise performance requirements, or dispute resolution mechanisms. These new forms of concession more closely emulate permitting or licensing systems. Indeed, in some cases they are even more transparent and efficient. The improvements have dramatically reduced regulators' discretion. The mining concession and the related auction procedures are a good examples.

*But innovation in social and environmental regulation is still limited.*

A major gap is the lack of progress to date in using economic regulatory instruments for social and environmental policies. Only two programmes are in place to use economic instruments to manage environmental externalities, for example. But the legislative foundation is in place, and the UDE continues to encourage ministries to find alternatives.

51

## Formalities have been reduced, but the pace has slowed.

*Systematic review of business formalities has made progress, but the pace has slowed as the projects have become more difficult.*

The review and reform of formalities, including information requirements, licenses, and permits, have proceeded systematically. Ten out of the twelve ministries subject to the process have now been reviewed. The process can be complex, and may require action at several levels, including the Congress. The programme has not exclusively targeted the formalities of greatest concern, but instead has moved methodically through reviews. As a result of the complexities and the methods used, only two-thirds of the existing stock of formalities had been reviewed after more than two years. The formal ministerial reform commitments, in the areas of finance and telecommunications, will be presented in 1999 to the Economic Deregulation Council. Because legal implementation can sometimes be complex and require congressional approval – an inherently lengthy process – the review process is ahead of the pace of the corresponding legal changes and implementation in the administration.

*How much burden has been lifted is unknown.*

The process has certainly improved transparency and simplified requirements. But there has been no overall assessment of the reduction in burden. Moreover, the review of formalities, and indeed the reform process generally, has generally been oriented toward businesses, though certain reforms are directly designed to benefit citizens and consumers as well, such as reforms to the civil and commercial codes and those permitting the creation of a generic drugs market and the reduction of entry barriers for gas station franchises.

## Continuing conflicts between reform programmes and traditional methods present transition challenges.

*Commitment to reform over a period several years is needed.*

Attention needs to shift now to implementation of the regulatory reform agenda over the medium-term. As noted in Chapter 1, the substantial investments in good regulatory policies and laws have not fully paid off in concrete benefits for citizens and businesses. Policy implementation by federal, state, and local bureaucracies is still weak. This is particularly relevant when old management practices coexist with new regulations. The private sector and society as a whole has an important role to play in stimulating this cultural change. In March 1999, the Mexican Business Council (*Consejo Coordinador Empresarial*) took an important step in this direction by publishing state rankings on the quality of regulations and regulatory improvement programmes.

*The most important intermediate-term goals: better implementation and enforcement, more transparency, clearer harmonisation, greater visibility, and broader constituency.*

Prospects for continuing and widening reform depend on an even deeper transformation of the regulatory environment. In particular:

- The gap between intentions and effective implementation of reforms among the regulators. Problems with human resources and public management, compounded by difficulties with compliance and enforcement, impede translation of regulatory reforms into real benefits. Mechanisms to improve the quality of and compliance with RIA are of particular importance. Upgrading human resources and public management performance will be crucial to the success of the new institutions being set up.

- Transparency has improved, but Mexico still falls short of OECD good practices. Mexican citizens still have no general right to comment on regulatory proposals and actions affecting their lives.

- Regulatory reform should be harmonised more clearly with other structural reform policies, in particular with competition advocacy and administrative reform.

- The central focus of reform, which has been in a ministry, SECOFI, could be more effective from a more central and/or independent management position.

- Better design of sectoral governance schemes, and more explicit recognition and protection of consumer interests are essential elements for future reform efforts. Sustaining regulatory reform will require broadening its constituency, to include consumers and citizens as well as businesses, and, in parallel, to increase involvement of the Congress, which is expanding its role in policy development.

*Chapter 3*

# THE ROLE OF COMPETITION POLICY IN REGULATORY REFORM

As a central part of its effort to open itself to the world economy and empower market institutions, Mexico has adopted a modern competition policy. The competition law, incorporating up-to-date economic analysis to promote efficiency, is new. The tradition of state control and protection is much older. The economy is still getting accustomed to new competitive realities. Much has been done to establish a sound policy and institutional foundation; the challenge now is to follow through and ensure that it becomes solidly established.

### Competition policy capped the reform legislation...

*A new competition law and enforcement agency reinforced the liberalisation programme.*

In 1993, the basic legal framework for reform was completed with the Federal Law of Economic Competition (LFCE), and the Federal Competition Commission (CFC) was created to enforce it. Liberalising trade, though a critical step toward competition, could not be enough by itself. Removing official trade barriers could not assure competition if those were simply replaced by private barriers. And import liberalisation could not ensure competition in non-traded sectors. A new, domestic law was needed.

### ... representing a clear break from traditional methods that had failed.

*The new approach reverses a tradition of state control and ownership.*

Competition policy, in the sense of protecting free competition rather than controlling prices and investment, is a new phenomenon in Mexico. The Constitution has prohibited monopoly since 1917, but the constitutional prohibition was not implemented. Instead, by the 1970s, much of the Mexican economy was under price or entry control or in the hands of state-owned monopoly, in an environment of import protection and strong state intervention and supervision. The effective policy about competition was to suppress it, not protect or promote it, and the result was to replace private monopoly and monopolistic restraints by public monopoly and state controls. The reforms that began in the mid-1980s changed economic direction, to replace control with market competition.

### Competition policy cements reform and sets a standard...

*Efficiency is the competition law's policy criterion.*

Mexico's competition law adopts advanced ideas and practices. The law balances efficient and strong treatment of the most harmful competitive constraints with economically sensitive analysis of others, and it applies an integrated treatment of market power in all relevant situations. Elegance and clarity show that the law is a product of technical expertise, more than political creativity and compromise. Efficiency is its primary criterion, and there are no doctrines about fairness or limiting concentration. Competition policies in many OECD countries have tended to emphasise efficiency more, so in this respect, and in others, Mexico's law reflects a general trend in the evolution of competition policy.

*Competition policy and reform are linked, in the new sectoral regulations that assign critical roles to the competition authority.*

The competition law's conceptual framework can provide a touchstone for measuring the adequacy and success of other reforms. The absence of a competition law had probably encouraged the business and government behaviours and policies that made reform necessary. Now, legislation for sectoral privatisation and deregulation is taking advantage of its new competition policy institutions' analytic and legal capacities. In several sectoral laws, regulation of prices or other conduct is only authorised if there is market power in the industry. Whether there is market power is determined by the competition agency, under the principles of the general competition law.

### ... reversing price controls by banning price fixing...

*The law uses two approaches: per se prohibition of "absolute" practices, and market-power analysis for "relative" practices.*

The law does not provide for correcting monopoly as such; rather, it addresses particular practices by which monopoly might be attained or strengthened. Practices are classified as either absolute or relative. Absolute monopolistic practices are prohibited *per se*. Violators are subject to administrative sanctions under the LFCE, and the CFC may report associated criminal conduct to the public prosecutor. Relative practices require that the agents have substantial power in a defined relevant market and the practices have an anti-competitive effect. The sanctions for relative practices are limited to civil remedies under the LFCE, and parties may offer efficiency defences.

*The clear rule against horizontal agreements is an efficient tool to reinforce an important early reform, the abolition of price controls.*

The absolute monopolistic practices that are subject to *per se* prohibition include price fixing, output restriction, market division, and bid rigging. Use of *per se* prohibitions balances the policy criterion of strict economic efficiency with an administrative criterion of enforcement efficiency. Prohibiting these agreements enforces one of the important reforms, the elimination of publicly sanctioned, but privately arranged, price control. When most prices were fixed by law, the ostensibly regulated price level was often the result of an agreement among the members of the industry, organised into "chambers of commerce and industry". As in other countries with corporatist traditions, semi-official industry trade bodies have been a common source of competition policy concerns. Much of the CFC's enforcement work, especially at first, has been directed at rooting out the old habits that this system of business chambers and price controls had supported.

*Support from local government does not excuse anti-competitive collusion.*

The ban on horizontal agreements has applied to agreements sanctioned by local government. For example, a municipal government encouraged an agreement among local *tortilla* producers that allocated areas of the market in order to prevent entry of new competitors; the CFC penalised the firms and issued a recommendation to the state government.[32]

*For vertical agreements, market power is the main concern.*

All kinds of vertical agreements are treated as relative monopolistic practices. Unlike most other OECD countries, Mexico does not prohibit resale price maintenance *per se*. The treatment reflects the law's thoroughgoing economic basis. The main criterion is substantial market power, so vertical agreements are allowed if the producers or distributors involved face sufficient horizontal competition.

### ... and preventing market power by controlling mergers and restructurings.

*Merger review aims to protect competition, while taking account of efficiencies and financial difficulties.*

Mergers whose objective or effect is to reduce, distort or hinder competition are prohibited. The CFC considers factors such as whether the merging parties could fix prices unilaterally or limit competitors' access to the market and whether competitors would inhibit that power. In addition, the CFC considers whether the parties have shown that they will achieve efficiencies, and a party's financial weakness may count in the assessment of the concentration's objective. The CFC's reported decisions about the significance of financial weakness are conclusory, though; the factual basis underlying its reasoning should be made clearer.

*Few mergers are actually blocked.*

Merger activity has increased in Mexico recently, as it has around the world. Few mergers have been challenged. In 1997, the CFC objected to only two and imposed conditions on three others. Most mergers are occurring in industries that are restructuring or consolidating either because of trade liberalisation and deregulation or because of financial crisis. Commercial banking, for example, has undergone substantial restructuring. The CFC has not blocked any mergers in the banking sector.

*Reviewing bids for assets and licences, which is much like merger review, has been a key CFC responsibility.*

At least as important as the merger review process has been the closely related responsibility to review privatisation proposals and applications for concessions and licenses. These cases, which amounted to 32% of the CFC's workload in 1997, require an analysis similar to that applied to mergers. The CFC performs these functions pursuant to laws and regulations that typically require that potential participants not be blocked by the CFC. Of the 154 reviews concluded in 1997, the CFC objected to two and imposed conditions on another.

*Some difficult merger decisions involved privatised or deregulated industries.*

Several notable merger-related decisions have involved privatised and deregulated industries. CFC investigation and communication of concerns evidently halted a proposed reconfiguration in the telecommunications and television industries. In another case, though, Telmex was allowed to buy a major cable firm (subject to obligations to provide network access). In airlines, the two major domestic air carriers were permitted to combine into a holding company, to improve their financial situation. (Before the competition law was adopted, the transport ministry had permitted Aeroméxico to acquire control over Mexicana.) The holding company arrangement is clearly unattractive from a competition policy perspective.

Despite safeguards in the arrangement, including giving the CFC power to dissolve the combination if the parties engage in monopolistic behaviour and competition does not improve, there are doubts about the vigour of the airlines' continued competition. The CFC has been investigating whether fare levels show the exercise of market power in some city-pair markets, calling for remedial action. This situation is a major test of the effectiveness of Mexico's competition policy and institutions.

## But the law does not attack monopoly directly.

*The law addresses monopolising practices, using the same market power test that triggers sectoral regulation of monopolies.*

Monopoly is prohibited, both by the LFCE and by the Constitution, but there is no separate section of the competition law about monopolisation or abuse of dominance. Rather, single-firm practices that may be defined as abuse of dominance or monopolisation in other countries are treated as relative monopolistic practices. The same legal predicate, a finding of market power, is applied to find liability under the competition law and in other, sectoral regulatory programmes, thus providing a critical link between competition policy and regulatory policy.

*The concern is the use of market power to exclude competition, rather than its exercise through higher prices.*

The LFCE does not address abusive (high) pricing.[33] Violation is defined in terms of exclusionary practices at the expense of competitors, and not in terms of exploitative practices at the expense of consumers. The reasoning behind this approach is that the conduct is self-correcting, because exploiting market power by charging high prices will normally invite new competitors to enter. In addition, direct remedies are difficult to implement. Controlling high prices would require CFC to act like a utility regulator. Requiring divestiture could raise constitutional issues. Thus, the principal response is vigorous enforcement against exclusionary practices. If the dominant firm tries to maintain or enhance its dominance by engaging in a monopolistic practice–that is, by excluding competitors – the CFC will step in. Thus, the law does address predatory pricing, treating it as a potentially exclusionary device. Surprisingly, for a law that is in other respects economically sophisticated, the legal standard does not include a judgement about the likelihood of post-success recoupment of losses suffered to force a competitor out.

## Typical regulated network monopolies are subject to sectoral regulation.

*Network monopoly problems are handled with sectoral programmes, although in principle the LFCE might also reach access problems.*

A common concern in all OECD countries is the monopolised network industry. Restructuring such an industry is not within the scope of the Mexican competition law; instead, it is dealt with within sector-specific laws and privatisation programmes. Some early privatisations paid too little attention to the need for restructuring, with the result that the newly private industries were born as inadequately regulated monopolies. Problems of network access, where the concern is discrimination or cross-subsidisation that harms competition in complementary markets, might in principle be reachable under the LFCE. But the usual approach has been for the sectoral legislation or regulation to set out rules governing access, rather than to apply the LFCE's general principles and procedures.

*Regulating monopoly pricing depends on a CFC finding of dominance.*

Similarly, because monopolistic pricing is something the LFCE does not remedy, other agencies apply sector-specific regulations to control abusive pricing by dominant firms. A necessary precondition for this price regulation is the existence of dominance, that is, substantial market power. Laws about railroads, airlines, natural gas and telecommunications include this market power standard. The CFC is responsible for assessing and identifying market power in those sectors. If the CFC finds there is market power, that finding becomes the basis for price controls imposed by the sectoral regulator.

*The law has prevented exclusionary practices in deregulated or protected industries.*

The LFCE has been applied to other practices involving dominant firms in protected, privatised, or deregulated industries. In 1995, for example, the CFC took action against price discrimination by a subsidiary of Pemex. And the CFC challenged one of the major domestic airlines, Aeroméxico, for vertical division of markets and refusal to deal with travel agencies that sold other airlines' tickets.

### In principle, competition policy applies virtually universally...

*Competition policy applies very broadly; there are few exemptions.*

The LFCE applies to all areas of economic activity, including those areas subject to specific, sectoral economic regulations. There are few exceptions from the LFCE. Some of the activities excluded are like those excluded in most countries. Technically, authorisation by a federal or state official does not excuse private conduct that violates the LFCE. Practically, the CFC recommends that other authorities not encourage or issue rules or orders that put parties in that position.

*In principle, competition policy fully applies to regulated sectors.*

Regulated sectors are still subject to the competition law and the CFC's authority, even if there is a separate sectoral regulatory agency or ministry department. As a basic principle, other laws that affect competition policy, such as those governing former state enterprises, must be applied consistently with the competition law.

*Competition policy also applies to public enterprises.*

Public enterprises are not exempt as such. The state, its agencies, and its companies as economic agents are subject to the LFCE. Government entities that restrict competition through conduct beyond their authorised power may get an admonition, rather than an order or a fine, where they are not participating in the conduct as economic agents and the CFC thus does not have jurisdiction over them. For example, an action against a collusive boycott in notarisation services concluded with economic sanctions against the private parties involved and a recommendation to the public official whose action on behalf of a government entity eased the boycott effort.[34]

*Preventing anti-competitive acts by local government bodies is a high priority.*

An enforcement priority is state government action that restricts trade between the states. The LFCE[35] implements the Constitution's prohibition against these measures by empowering the CFC to declare their existence. Restrictions on interstate trade are nevertheless pervasive. Many of them pre-date the LFCE and the effective enforcement of the constitutional ban. The CFC lacks the power to punish a local government, yet CFC statements have in specific cases proven to be effective in eliminating trade barriers. Thus, the CFC's usual action about a government entity's restraint is a recommendation; if the local government does not take action itself to remove it, that is followed by a declaration that the restraint is legally void.

*Smaller firms are also fully subject to competition enforcement.*

Small and medium sized firms receive no special treatment under the LFCE. There is no *de minimis* rule, and hard-core horizontal agreements are prohibited *per se*, regardless of the size of the firm. But there is a degree of implicit protection in the rule-of-reason approach taken for all other conduct (although substantial market power depends on firm's size relative to its market, not its absolute size). Theory suggests that price fixing agreements between firms with small market shares would be uncommon, because those firms lack the market power that would make those agreements effective. But experience shows that small firms nonetheless collude enthusiastically, perhaps showing that in small markets they may indeed have at least short-term market power when they act together. In any event, the CFC has brought exemplary enforcement actions against small firms in those conditions. This rigorous enforcement runs some risk of alienating potential allies in small business. On the other hand, collusion among small businesses may also have a directly observable effect on another important constituency, consumers.

### ... but some major sectors remain state-protected monopolies.

*"Strategic" sectors are legally protected monopolies, but firms in those sectors may still be liable for anti-competitive conduct.*

The strategic sectors reserved to the state under the Constitution are excluded from the law's prohibition of monopoly. That exclusion is limited, though: entities, even state-owned ones, engaged in the strategic sectors may be liable for conduct that falls outside the scope of the permitted monopoly. Pemex has been subject to several actions for practices outside the sector where it enjoys constitutional protection. The strategic areas now include coinage and paper money, postal service, telegraph and radiotelegraphy, petroleum and other hydrocarbons, basic petrochemicals, radioactive minerals, nuclear energy, and electricity. Recently, satellite communications and railroads were taken off the list (by constitutional amendment), in order to open up those sectors to competition. And the electricity sector has been partially opened up to private participation. For instance, private parties may generate electricity for their own use or for sale to the state-owned electricity monopoly.

### In principle, competition policy articulates well with regulatory authority...

*The CFC is involved in competition policy decisions across the government.*

The CFC participates in several inter-ministerial groups that are concerned with issues that affect competition policy, such as privatisation, public spending and financing, local telephone services, norms and standards, and foreign trade, and has been invited to the Economic Deregulation Council since March 1999. The CFC may comment on the effects that existing laws, regulations, agreements and administrative acts may have on competition, on the effects of contemplated changes to federal programmes and policies, and, upon request by the Federal Executive, on the effects on competition of new laws and regulations proposed to Congress.

*Competition policy has a central role in decisions about privatisation and auctions for permits and concessions.*

Partly as a result of its competition advocacy, the CFC has important roles under laws and regulations dealing with transport, telecommunications, natural gas, and pension funds. The CFC typically has two functions in these sector-specific programmes. First, the CFC can determine which economic agents may participate in auctions for public enterprises, concessions, licenses and permits. Although it is not usually a voting member of the groups that manage privatisation and grant concessions, the CFC exercises significant power in the ensuing processes, by determining whether firms can participate.

*Sectoral economic regulation depends on CFC findings about market power.*

Second, the CFC may determine whether effective competition exists, or whether one of the agents has substantial market power, as a condition for a sectoral regulator to impose regulation such as price caps. In that connection, the CFC may also determine that competition has been restored, because of changes in market conditions, so the regulation should be terminated.

*A prime example of a "market power" finding is the CFC's March 1998 decision about Telmex.*

In telecommunications, the CFC's most important action has been its finding that the incumbent, Telmex, has market power. The sector regulator, Cofetel, can regulate the tariffs and services of dominant firms in order to facilitate entry and enhance competition. But that power depends on the CFC, for it is up to the CFC to determine whether a carrier is dominant. The CFC concluded in December 1997 that Telmex does indeed have substantial market power in five relevant markets: local telephony, interconnection services, national long distance, international long distance and the resale of long distance. This decision was reaffirmed in February 1998 and submitted to Cofetel. The next step is for Cofetel to design and implement appropriate regulations.

*Competition policy decisions have affected rules, auctions and privatisations in telecommunications.*

In other aspects of telecommunications, competition policy has been enlisted in the privatisation of the satellite system, in several spectrum auctions, and in designing rules about telephone services. All satellite assets were privatised in one package, as the CFC concluded that the eventual winning bidder would still face sufficient competition from other satellite systems or other technologies. Treatment of bidders in spectrum auctions has varied with particular market conditions and prospects for the bands being auctioned. The CFC has supported simultaneous ascending auctions, limits on holdings, and measures to discourage collusion and hoarding. In one microwave auction to build supply for point to point systems, structural restrictions were found sufficient to protect competition. By contrast, the CFC imposed few conditions (delayed entry) on Telmex's participation in an auction for frequencies used by wireless and PCS services, despite its ownership of large parts of the spectrum and its dominance in local service.

*In other network infrastructure industries – railroads, port services, air transport, and natural gas transmission – rules protect competition and the CFC reviews bidders and makes market power determinations.*

In the railroad privatisation, concessions and licenses were granted through a two-part competitive bidding process. The CFC issued opinions about bidders for five railways. Rules limit cross-ownership and obligate railroads to grant tracking and haulage rights in some settings to avoid market power abuses. Rules also set out procedures for setting rates when, in the CFC's opinion, conditions of competition do not exist. For harbour and port services, the rules for privatisation and issuing concessions prevent combining terminals that provide the same kind of service in the same relevant geographic market. Here too, the CFC is involved and must approve particular bidders. The airports and civil aviation laws include provisions related to competition, such as criteria for concessions and permits, and regulation of mergers and acquisitions. The CFC participated in the discussion and preparation of these laws with the transport ministry. If the CFC determines that there is market power in a relevant market, typically a city-pair or associated airport markets, then SCT may regulate the fares. In natural gas, the CFC must approve participation in auctioning exclusive distribution permits. The CFC also contributed to the 1995 regulations that laid the groundwork for introducing private market competition. The process is complicated by the fact that the incumbent in much of the country is Pemex, which retains a constitutional monopoly on natural gas production and also still owns much of the pipeline network. Price and rate regulations may be removed when, in the CFC's opinion, conditions of competition exist.

### ... but in practice, regulators may resist or promote other agendas.

*Competition policy may be understood differently by the CFC and by sectoral agencies.*

The CFC's relations with other regulators have sometimes been difficult. Not only is the CFC's jurisdiction under the LFCE very broad, but also several sector-specific laws give the CFC authority over important issues in other ministries' or agencies' jurisdiction. The LFCE and sector-specific laws regarding cross subsidisation and price discrimination may lead to different results. Some competition-related sectoral rules are more stringent than the generally applied competition law, for example. In some sectors, notably telecommunications, there have been disagreements about the design of competition-related regulations and remedies. In air transport, the ministry applies a test of likely profitability in permit and route decisions, ostensibly to protect safety, which may prevent potentially efficient new entry.

*Other regulators may also promote goals that are not consistent with competition policy.*

Other ministries may advance development-related goals that may not be consistent with promoting competition conceived as efficiency. In air transport, public policy has included the goal of creating or protecting a large, nationally based firm. In the division of responsibility between the competition authority and the regulator, it is the regulator that most often has the final say in designing and applying the rule to control market power, and thus it is the regulator's conception of policy balance that governs as a practical matter. That conception is not always consistent with efficiency-based competition.

## The new enforcement agency is independent and increasingly vigorous...

*The CFC has roots in the institutions that monitor and promote regulatory reform.*

The CFC is a separate entity attached to SECOFI. The CFC has sole responsibility to apply the LFCE. Competition policy issues related to regulation are also considered by the Economic Deregulation Unit in SECOFI, described in Chapter 2. The UDE participated in drafting the LFCE, and continues to participate in review of regulations and regulatory proposals, including those of the CFC.

*The CFC's structure protects its decisional independence.*

Decisional independence is protected by the terms of the Commissioners' tenure. Appointed for ten year terms, and removable only for grave cause, the Commissioners are insulated from the usual practice of virtually complete personnel turnover after presidential elections every six years. In contrast to some sectoral agencies, the basis for the CFC's independence is in the law, not a lower-level normative act, and the Commissioners are appointed by the President, not by ministers. They are still exposed to political pressure and other persuasion, but their tenure protects them somewhat from consequences of decisions that conflict with other ministries' designs.

*Responding to concerns about transparency, the CFC now publicises its decisions better.*

Some have criticised the CFC for lack of transparency in its decision criteria. So far, the principal means of explaining its decisions has been its annual report, which includes summaries of the most illustrative cases. The CFC has now begun publishing its decisions and reasoning in a periodical gazette; in addition, summaries will also be published in the government's official journal. The complete texts of the law, regulations, annual reports, and summaries of recent decisions are available at the CFC's Internet website.

*The LFCE is the only source of general competition law, and the CFC is the only body that applies it.*

Application of competition policy is focused on the CFC and the LFCE. There is no other source of substantive law about competition policy issues, either at the state or federal level. No other officials have responsibility to enforce it, and private enforcement is limited to a claim for damages after the CFC has found a violation. This avenue has not yet been used. The CFC's discretion is not unlimited; when the CFC receives a complaint that meets the conditions for standing, it must deal with the case and reach some decision.

*Resources devoted to applying competition policy are being increased now.*

Commitment to effective enforcement, as measured by resources employed, has been stable. In terms of personnel, CFC staffing has held steady for several years, but the budget fell about 30% (in real terms) between 1994 and 1997, reflecting budget and economic troubles that have hit Mexico since the 1995 financial crisis. For 1998, the budget increased significantly. A high priority, in terms of staff time, has been given to regulatory and related issues.

## ... but its actions are often delayed by legal challenges.

*If CFC decisions have seemed to take long, it is often because of court challenges.*

Clear deadlines and time targets control CFC proceedings. Nevertheless, some observers have criticised the CFC for deciding slowly. Often the reason has been delays due to court appeals, or punctilious observation of necessary procedures to reduce the risk of losing such appeals.

*The constitutionally-guaranteed amparo action can delay administrative enforcement, repeatedly.*

Appeals to the courts can take two forms. A party who claims that a legally protected interest has been infringed by CFC action may resort to the *amparo* action before a Federal District Court, to challenge the legality or constitutionality of the CFC's decisions.[36] Parties have often availed themselves of this constitutionally granted process right, and the result has been to delay CFC proceedings. Not only do parties challenge final CFC decisions, but they also take the CFC to court to dispute preliminary and intermediate actions. This leads to repeated delays, for once the *amparo* is initiated, the judge can enjoin the administrative proceeding pending the judicial decision. Until a comprehensive regulation appeared in March 1998 explaining how the law was being interpreted and applied, many *amparo* suits complained (generally unsuccessfully) that the LFCE was unconstitutionally vague. In addition, fines can be appealed to an administrative court, the Federal Tax Appeal Tribunal. The CFC believes its success rate in both *amparo* suits and administrative appeals has generally been good, at least on important substantive issues.

**The law and policy are modern and sophisticated; now, it is important to ensure that they are widely understood and supported.**

*Competition policy is well conceived and well integrated with regulatory policy.*

The analytic quality of the competition law is a significant strength. The CFC has spent a commendable proportion of its effort on advocacy and dealing with competition policy problems outside of traditional law enforcement. The same standards are applied by the same expert body whether the issue is merger or other competition law enforcement, or licensing, privatisation or natural monopoly regulation. This consistency integrates competition policy into regulatory policy.

*But competition policy has been a subject for experts; it needs a broader base of public understanding and support.*

Expert craftsmanship is a clear strength. But that strength implies a weakness as well. The competition law, like the rest of the reform programme, is the product of experts in the government. Although legislators are increasingly interested in the CFC's work, and the CFC receives an increasing number of complaints, the constituency for competition policy is not well identified. Moreover, there has little visible effort to develop a public constituency, through media relations, systematic relationship with consumer protection institutions (which are admittedly rudimentary), or otherwise. The lack of a clear public message and broader support could make competition policy less effective, just as Mexico's reforms are entering the stage in which general, horizontal principles like competition law, rather than sectoral regulatory decisions or trade policies, will be more important tools for ensuring that the promised benefits of reform are achieved.

*To ensure consistent application, the CFC may need more power over remedies imposed by other regulators.*

Making the commitment to thorough competitive reform more effective may call for re-examining the division of regulatory responsibilities. Giving the CFC the important task of identifying market power is analytically sound. Having another body, such as Cofetel for telecommunications, decide what will be done about that problem shows that another entity may have the effective power to decide that competition policy issue. To make sure competition policy is applied consistently, the CFC may need stronger tools to recommend and oversee implementation of remedies. For competition policy and enforcement to cement reform, other agencies must learn to accept its results, rather than resist them on behalf of industry clients.

# Chapter 4

# ENHANCING MARKET OPENNESS THROUGH REGULATORY REFORM

By reducing its regulatory barriers to trade and investment, a country can increase the benefit from its comparative advantage and innovation and increase the benefits to its consumers from regulatory reform. An open world trading system depends on regulatory styles and content that promote global competition and economic integration, that avoid trade disputes, and that improve trust and mutual confidence across borders. As traditional barriers to trade have been progressively dismantled, "behind the border" measures have become more relevant to effective market access, and national regulations are exposed to unprecedented international scrutiny by trade and investment partners. Regulatory quality is no longer (if ever it was) a purely "domestic" affair.

### Market openness launched reform and still anchors it.

*Reform has transformed an inward-oriented economy based on import substitution toward a market-based and open economy integrated into the world economy.*

Mexico underwent a significant transition in the last decade and a half from an inward-oriented economy based on import-substitution policies toward a market-based and open economy integrated into the world economy. Reforms that opened the economy to trade and investment have created new and equitable market opportunities, accelerated the modernisation of Mexico's productive capacity and stimulated the growth of its economy. A variety of concrete actions worked together to produce these benefits. Although the simple average tariff remained at about 13% between 1993 and 1997, the weighted average fell from 7.8% to 2.7%.[37] Mexico eliminated most compulsory import licenses, abolished official import prices, adhered to the GATT, and made commitments through its membership in the North American Free Trade Agreement (NAFTA) and in free trade agreements (FTAs) with six Latin American countries. Other reforms rationalised standards and procedures, and removed rent-generating restrictions and bureaucratic red tape.

*Accession to the GATT and negotiation of NAFTA had profound influence on Mexican policies and processes.*

International co-operation to open markets was instrumental in shaping reform in Mexico. Mexico's accession to the GATT in 1986 consolidated key commitments regarding transparency, non-discrimination and trade liberalisation. The negotiation of NAFTA had a profound influence on how Mexico formulates policy. Under NAFTA, almost all trade in goods, including agricultural products, and services is subject to complete liberalisation over fixed time periods. A comprehensive set of domestic policies with trade-related dimensions was subject to specific disciplines, on a reciprocal basis. The subjects include the transparency of domestic regulations, technical standards and certification procedures, investment, government procurement, intellectual property rights, customs procedures, and dispute settlement.

*Opening markets dramatically increased investment and trade.*

Between 1990 and 1997, imports and exports quadrupled. So did the annual rate of direct foreign investment in fixed assets, which reached US$12.5 billion. The composition of trade has changed markedly. By 1997, manufactured products, rather than petroleum and agricultural products, were by far the most important exports.

*Mexico's commitments anchored policy during the 1995 financial crisis.*

The financial crisis of early 1995 confronted Mexico with difficult policy decisions. In many respects, its WTO and NAFTA commitments served as effective policy anchors to discourage backtracking on reform. As discussed in Chapter 1, far from reversing reforms, the Mexican government extended the deregulation programme in the aftermath of the crisis by accelerating privatisation and further liberalising the investment regime. Sectors previously reserved to the state, such as railways, satellite communications, and natural gas storage and distribution, were opened to foreign ownership.

*Market openness helped Mexico recover quickly.*

Mexico's commitment to openness helped it stage an impressive recovery from its crisis. GDP grew 7% in 1997, and at a rate above 5% during the first half of 1998. Foreign direct investment in fixed assets remained strong, and portfolio investment returned after the 1995 shock. The foreign trade sector play a key role in leading the recovery. Between 1994 and 1997, total exports nearly doubled, and the trade balance moved from deficit to surplus. In 1997, strong domestic demand increased total imports by 30.7%. And this is not just a NAFTA phenomenon: though trade within NAFTA accounted for over 80% of imports and exports in 1996, about two thirds of the incremental trade in 1997 was outside NAFTA, attesting to the success of Mexican FTAs with other countries.

*The world trading environment continues to present challenges to reform.*

Mexican competitiveness has been hard hit by the Asian crisis and its ripple effects. Despite substantial depreciation of the peso, Mexican products have lost competitiveness compared to those of more depreciated Asian currencies. Textiles, clothing and electronic equipment sectors have been particularly vulnerable. In addition, the steep drop in crude oil prices dampened the economy. Continuing reform based on market openness principles confronts a difficult world economic environment, which will test Mexico's resolve.

### Principles of "efficient regulation" sustain market openness.

*Six principles promote market openness: transparency, non-discrimination, non-restrictiveness, harmonisation, recognition, and competition.*

So that regulations do not reduce market openness unnecessarily, reform should ensure that the process incorporates principles of efficient regulation. Following these principles will help foreign suppliers compete in the national market free from conditions that are discriminatory, restrictive or excessively burdensome. The six principles described in the OECD *Report on Regulatory Reform* are:

- Transparency and openness of decision making.
- Non-discrimination.

- Avoidance of unnecessary trade restrictiveness.
- Use of internationally harmonised measures.
- Recognition of equivalence of other countries' regulatory measures.
- Application of competition principles.

*How has Mexico incorporated these principles into its regulatory system?*

These principles, identified by trade policy makers as key to market-oriented and trade and investment-friendly regulation, underpin the multilateral trading system. These principles are used by the OECD in determining how Mexico's current regulatory procedures and policies contribute to market openness.

*Regulatory reform and trade issues are linked institutionally.*

The institutions responsible for overseeing the comprehensive deregulation programme also have responsibilities for trade-related issues. SECOFI, which houses the UDE and performs other reform roles, also participates in the Commission on Foreign Trade, which provides opinions on all issues concerning trade policy and reviews all trade and trade-related laws and regulations. SECOFI thus plays a co-ordinating role in encouraging government-wide awareness of and respect for international obligations relating to domestic regulatory matters, and in doing so oversees the implementation of obligations of the WTO and other trade agreements.

### Transparency: Mexico leads in use of Internet-based methods...

*Access to information and to consultation opportunities is open to all.*

Mexico ranks favourably among OECD countries with respect to opportunities for public consultation and comment, publication of draft technical standards measures, and notification to international organisations. Where there are public consultations, nationals and non-nationals alike may participate, without distinction. In practice, non-nationals are submitting comments on draft regulations and their comments are taken into consideration.

*The range of Internet-available material is wide.*

The type and range of regulatory information that Mexico makes available through the Internet, a medium that is readily accessible to foreign participants, is notable. Virtually all federal business formalities were identified and published on an Internet site by December 1996. Since February 1998, a compendium of all current laws and other major regulatory measures is continually updated there. Foreign participants thus have an open access to a comprehensive set of Mexican laws, regulations and business formalities at their computer tips. Sectoral programmes can be downloaded from the Internet or obtained from the corresponding ministries. Upon prior registration, it is also possible to access the Internet version of the Mexican Official Diary. A list of all regulatory proposals under review by the UDE and the Economic Deregulation Council is published and updated weekly on the Internet (the site can be found at www.cde.gob.mx).

### ... and made substantial reforms concerning standards...

*Standards-related processes are generally open to participation by foreign firms.*

Transparency about standards and conformity assessment procedures reduces the risk that domestic groups might capture the process to make imported products less competitive. Technical standards in Mexico reflect a mixture of government and private sponsorship. Most – over 90% – approved standards are voluntary standards sponsored by the private sector. The decentralised process requires that standards be based on a consensus of the interested sectors after public consultations, and that they be based on international standards unless those are determined to be inefficient or inappropriate. There is no distinction under the law or process between nationals and non-nationals, and foreign participants can participate in any of the standard-setting groups.

*Mexico has responded to complaints with special "fast track" revisions.*

Despite this effort to open the process, trading partners have complained about lack of transparency, rigid implementation of labelling and marking requirements, and difficulty keeping up with changes in standard-related requirements. In response, Mexican authorities have applied a so-called "fast track procedure", established in 1996 as amendments to the Standards Law, to provide more flexibility in rapidly modifying standards that cause unforeseen problems. To counterbalance the absence of public consultation, these revised "fast-track" measures cannot impose new or stricter requirements.

### ... procurement...

*An Internet procurement system reduces costs and makes access easier for foreign firms.*

The costs of participating in the public procurement process, of retrieving information and meeting deadlines, could be substantial for small and medium-sized enterprises and firms based in foreign countries. In March 1996, Mexico responded to this need with an innovative process of organising government procurement through the Internet, called COMPRANET, implemented by SECODAM, to improve transparency and efficiency. Small and medium-sized firms, and foreign firms in remote locations, have the same access to procurement information as large domestic enterprises. Government agencies also gain from greater competition, because spreading the information wider attracts more bids. Mexican authorities want to develop COMPRANET so participating agencies can use electronic means for follow-up and control, too. Electronic signatures, cryptography and international standards in electronic data transmission may permit submitting bids through COMPRANET.

### ... and customs processing.

*Customs procedures have been reformed radically.*

Lack of transparency or uneven application of customs regulations and procedures, in any country, can be particularly frustrating to market participation by foreign firms. Wide discretion can encourage corruption. And inefficient procedures impose significant costs of delay. As a necessary complement to trade liberalisation, Mexico has made important changes in its customs procedures and administration (see Box 4.1).

*More transparent, efficient customs process produced substantial benefits.*

Mexico is a leader in the implementation of an integrated electronic-based customs system. Transparency and efficiency have improved dramatically. The maximum clearance time fell from up from 24 hours to a few minutes. Certified customs brokers increased from fewer than 400 in 1989 to nearly a thousand in 1997, while the number of Customs officials fell, yet the number of import and export operations increased substantially. The more transparent system made duty collection more efficient. Simplifying and automating procedures and investing in infrastructure have significantly reduced the risk of uneven application at different ports of entry. And reducing the discretionary power of Customs officials has improved integrity.

---

Box 4.1.  **Customs procedures in Mexico**

**Private administration:** import transactions must be processed through certified customs brokers, and customs duties are payable via commercial banks. Customs brokers are responsible for import declarations and duty assessment on behalf of their clients. These measures were intended to improve the duty collection system and reduce the incidence of fraud and corruption.

**Random inspection and checking:** the principle of 100% physical inspection has been dropped. Instead, Mexico uses a random system. About 10% of all shipments are subject to physical inspection. There is a second level of inspection, also random, performed by private firms, which is intended to detect malfeasance by customs officials and brokers. And post-audit verification of importers' files and transactions can also detect false declarations and frauds.

**Deadlines:** each stage of inspection must be done within a time limit, of two hours.

**Automation:** an Integral Automated Customs System allows for electronic exchange of information between the General Customs Administration, Customs offices, customs brokers, warehouses, and banking institutions that are authorised to collect duties. Entry documents can be validated or refused prior to the actual clearance. Since May 1997, the NAFTA countries have been experimenting with an Internet-based system for truck carriers, using encoded windshield stickers and laser readers to permit instant decisions about the need for inspection.

---

**But consultation is left to agency discretion and is uneven.**

*A weakness is that public consultation, although encouraged, is not required, as Chapter 2 describes.*

Chapter 2 describes consultation procedures in detail. The Federal Administrative Procedure Law does not require public consultation, though it does recognise the need for consultation. It sets a default timetable for consultations, to be applied when another law requires that proposals under it be published for public comment. Although not mandatory, the Economic Deregulation Council and the UDE promote public consultation and transparency, by making public the titles of the proposed regulations they are reviewing, and sending the complete text of the proposals and their corresponding regulatory impact analysis to all individuals who request them. Internet publication of regulatory impact assessments, if it is implemented and kept up to date, will help participants understand even better some of the potential implications of proposed regulations.

*Authorities should remain vigilant in enforcing transparency reforms.*

Some key features of the programme are still new. In some sectors, there are signs that regulatory bodies are not following transparency requirements. Authorities should remain vigilant in pursuing improved transparency all across the government structure.

71

## Non-discrimination: few problems are reported, but the issue is omitted from formal review criteria...

*Laws and regulations generally conform to non-discrimination principles.*

Two of the basic principles of non-discrimination in the multi-lateral trading system – most-favoured-nation and national treatment – aim for effective equality of competitive opportunities between like products and services, irrespective of country of origin. In Mexico, international treaties it has entered are supreme law and do not technically require the adoption of domestic legislation for internal application. Nonetheless, several domestic laws have been modified to make them fully compatible with international commitments and to facilitate their application. Agencies are obliged to comply with the principles in those international agreements. That requirement is not formalised, but SECOFI, as an oversight agency, ensures that non-discrimination commitments are effectively implemented. Within the WTO dispute settlement process, there were no complaints from trading partners alleging infringement of Mexico's non-discrimination obligations.

## ... and preferential agreements and some services items may call for attention.

*Mexico is a party to several preferential trade arrangements.*

Mexico is a party to six free trade agreements[38] and a network of bilateral investment agreements. Mexico is currently negotiating several others, including a comprehensive one with the European Union, and it also participates actively in multi-country initiatives, such as APEC and FTAA. Mexico is keen to exchange liberalisation commitments, that go beyond current WTO obligations, and it supports current talks for the launching of a new round of multilateral trade negotiations.

*Mexico shares information and the benefits of these arrangements widely.*

Mexico's trade and investment agreements are managed in a highly transparent manner. Mexico has extended on a non-discriminatory basis to all WTO Members the benefits of its free trade agreements in the areas such as investment, customs procedures and intellectual property. Overall, available evidence points to well-orchestrated and good faith efforts in Mexico to share information about its trade and investment agreements as widely as possible.

*But Mexico maintains some deviations from non-discrimination, about financial services.*

Mexico participated in and signed the WTO General Agreement in Trade in Services (GATS) and more recently the Financial Services Agreement. Mexico's commitments, like those of many countries, maintain some deviations from the non-discrimination principle, particularly concerning financial institutions and services. Under the GATS, Mexico undertook several sector-specific commitments. Mexico's services commitments remain broader in NAFTA than in the GATS.

## Unnecessary trade restrictiveness: this should be made a formal criterion in the review process.

*Several aspects of the regulatory review process can promote the avoidance of unnecessary trade restrictiveness.*

Policy makers should use instruments that do not restrict trade any more than necessary to fulfil a legitimate objective. This principle could lead to using standards based on performance, rather than design, as the basis of a technical regulation, or to considering taxes or tradable permits rather than mandates to achieve the same goal. Whether this principle is applied effectively depends on several factors. Are there specific requirements or means to encourage regulators to avoid unnecessary trade restrictiveness? What rationales are permitted for any exceptions to the principle? How is the impact of new regulations on international trade and investment assessed? Are trade policy bodies, and foreign traders and investors, consulted in the regulatory process? How are foreign parties assured access to dispute settlement?

*The principle is omitted from the formal review criteria, but it is implied by others and may thus still be considered.*

The principles of Mexico's deregulation programme do not formally include the avoidance of unnecessary trade restrictiveness. But related considerations are taken into consideration informally, and more so than in other OECD countries. The principle is no doubt implicit in considering two of the explicit criteria, whether alternatives may accomplish the same objectives at a lower cost and whether the proposed regulations minimise the negative impact on business. And nothing bars SECOFI from suggesting or promoting alternative regulations that are least trade restrictive. But because the principle of avoidance of unnecessary trade restrictiveness is not included in the guiding principles for regulatory impact assessments, there is no guarantee that it would be effectively taken into consideration.

*Formal application of the principle could clarify whether the benefits of some restraints are worth their costs.*

The severity of some remaining trade restrictions could call for more formal application of this principle, to be sure that reaching the objective is worth the cost incurred. Some import licence requirements, such as those for used motor vehicles and used computer equipment, result in *de facto* prohibitions. These restrictions will be eliminated for North American goods in accordance with the calendar established in the NAFTA (for used motor vehicles, the licence requirement will be totally eliminated in 2019). The continued use of this most highly trade restrictive instrument, which substantially increases consumer prices for these products in Mexico, suggests that the current set of guiding principles for regulatory reform is incomplete. The additional principle of "avoidance of unnecessary trade restrictiveness" should be included in the preparation of regulatory impact statements to discourage creation of such restriction in the future.

### International harmonisation: Official standards are moving toward compliance with international standards...

*Most official Mexican standards conform to international standards.*

Consideration of internationally-harmonised measures as the basis of domestic regulations can facilitate expanded trade. Mexico's law on measures and standards calls for technical standards to consider international standards, except when those are judged to be inefficient or inadequate to achieve the desired objectives. Since January 1998, agencies preparing regulatory impact analysis for proposed standards must justify on scientific bases the reasons for not using international standards or for deviating from them. Approximately 65% of the *normas oficiales Mexicanas* are partially or totally in accord with international standards.

73

## ... but the situation is less clear for voluntary standards.

*It is less clear whether private bodies are basing voluntary standards on international models.*

For voluntary standards, there is no requirement to prepare regulatory impact analyses, and the process is thus somewhat less transparent. It is not clear whether the privately-sponsored organisations that issue these voluntary standards make genuine efforts to base their standards on international ones. They should have *a priori* no objections to using available international standards that are cost efficient and less burdensome. And they are subject to legal requirements that should help them to stay abreast with relevant international developments and best practices applied abroad.

### Recognition of equivalence: Mexico is now moving in the right direction...

*Mexico has taken steps toward recognising the equivalence of other countries' regulations.*

Disparities in regulatory measures and duplicative systems of conformity assessment should not become barriers to trade. That result can be avoided by recognising the equivalence of trading partners' regulatory measures or the results of conformity assessment performed in other countries. Mexico is following both routes, in various ways. Recognising certifications by foreign laboratories is one example. Such recognition can be accorded unilaterally or through the mechanism of a Mutual Recognition Agreement (MRA) between trading partners.

*Conformity assessment certification procedures are SECOFI's responsibility.*

Conformity assessment procedures are performed by several government agencies in Mexico and by private bodies. Private bodies need accreditation by SECOFI and approval from the relevant government agencies. A private entity, EMA, has recently taken over SECOFI's accreditation function. SECOFI is responsible for concluding agreements with international or foreign institutions about mutual recognition of conformity assessment in Mexico, and for approving privately negotiation by Mexican accredited bodies of mutual recognition agreements with foreign institutions. There are no foreign-owned conformity assessment bodies currently operating in Mexico, but there are no restrictions preventing foreign bodies from obtaining accreditation and the criteria are the same for all applicants.

*Mexico must now accredit NAFTA parties' conformity assessment bodies; some mutual recognition agreements have been reached.*

Under NAFTA, Mexico had a four-year grace period to give its conformity assessment bodies time to upgrade their technical and competitive capacity. The grace period ended in January 1998, so Canadian and the United States conformity bodies can now seek accreditation for certifying relevant Mexican standards. Mexico has negotiated two agreements with the United States so far, for the mutual recognition of test results for tires and telecommunications equipment. Mexico is negotiating with Canada an agreement on telecommunications equipment. Since the end of the NAFTA grace period, Mexico has been moving in the right direction about recognition of equivalence of other countries' regulations and conformity assessment procedures.

### ... but the effort should be expanded beyond the NAFTA context.

*Mutual recognition arrangements should be extended beyond the NAFTA parties.*

The stage is now set to work towards reduction in duplicative certification procedures among NAFTA parties. But in addition, Mexico should move toward mutual recognition of conformity assessment over a wider geographic reach. Ongoing negotiations for free trade agreements and other multi-country discussions under APEC and the FTAA are opportunities for this. To be sure, there are practical limits to the time and resources that can be spent negotiating agreements. As SECOFI's accreditation functions have been privatised, though, some of its resources will be redirected to the important task of negotiating more broad-reaching MRAs.

## Competition principles: The competition agency has acted to keep markets open...

*The Competition Commission can prevent private conduct that impairs market access and thus reduces competition.*

*Foreign investment is not allowed in Pemex service stations.*

Ensuring market openness requires that parties have avenues for complaint and relief against regulatory or private actions that impair market access and effective competition by foreign firms. In Mexico, firms can take such complaints about private conduct to the Competition Commission (CFC). For example, a Mexican subsidiary of a multinational corporation complained that Mexican producers had entered into contracts with domestic retailers, granting a rebate if the retailers would not sell appliances produced outside the NAFTA area. The CFC ordered the firms to remove these clauses from their contracts and warned them that failure to comply would lead to fines. And the CFC took action to stop Pemex from distorting markets not within its authorised monopoly through its rules about petrol service station leases.

## ... but it cannot always persuade other regulators.

*But against regulatory action that has the same effect, the Competition Commission's powers are more limited.*

Where the concern is regulatory, rather than private, action that anti-competitively impairs market access, the available remedies are more limited. The CFC plays a role as an advocate with other governmental institutions, but its opinions are not legally binding, although they are often taken into account. Examples of successful advocacy are Railroad Service Law and Federal Telecommunications Law, which incorporate competition provisions that emphasise market access opportunities for both domestic and foreign service providers.

## Sectors where market openness concerns have concentrated include telecommunications services...

*The telecommunications sector has been privatised and liberalised, and some foreign-backed firms have entered.*

The Mexican market for telecommunications services is one of the largest and fastest growing in Latin America. The industry has been privatised and the legislative and regulatory structure has been overhauled since 1990. And in the GATS negotiations, Mexico made specific liberalisation commitments about basic telecommunications services. Some foreign competitors have moved quickly to capitalise on these new market conditions, structuring their investments to be consistent with Mexico's foreign ownership restrictions.[39] Faced with the dual challenge of expanding the network and fostering competition, Mexico has made progress towards liberalisation while still in early stages of infrastructure development. The stage is set for a trade- and investment-friendly regulatory regime.

*But foreign carriers report lack of transparency and other failures to follow principles of efficient regulation.*

But, as detailed in Chapter 5, the experiences of some new carriers seeking to compete in the Mexican market suggest that certain features of the regulatory framework may be undermining market openness. Some trading partners have expressed concerns about transparency in this sector, such as uncertainty about procedures to follow in pursuing complaints. Foreign ownership in most subsectors remains subject to restrictions. Throughout 1998, new carriers became increasingly vocal about alleged regulatory barriers to effective market access and presence. Concerns about market openness in this sector have been mitigated by some recent actions, to increase market access for foreign providers of satellite mobile services and to reduce interconnection rates. Still, as Chapter 5 suggests, greater efforts seem to be required to ensure more cost-based interconnection rates and the implementation of the six principles of efficient regulation in telecommunications.

### ... telecommunications equipment...

*Frictions about telecommunication equipment call for greater attention to mutual recognition, harmonisation, and avoidance of trade restrictiveness.*

Apparent differences in interpretation of the obligations arising under NAFTA-related provisions have led to growing concerns about Mexican market openness in this sector. Sector-specific NAFTA provisions have aimed to alleviate these concerns, and might have provided a model for wider multilateral application, but fundamental differences about implementation and standardization issues have arisen. Of greatest importance here is renewed attention to recognition of equivalence, particularly of conformity assessment procedures, and greater reliance on internationally-harmonised measures. A comprehensive re-evaluation of the fundamental objectives of the current regulations to ensuring that they do not unnecessarily restrict trade seems warranted.

### ... and automobiles and parts.

*Regulation of the automobile industry is highly trade-restrictive.*

Automotive production and trade are highly regulated. Imports of new motor vehicles by individuals are subject to very stringent conditions, and in practice, import licences are essentially granted to manufacturers on the basis of their import and export balances. These regulations are to be eliminated at the end of December 2003 as provided under NAFTA. For used vehicles, there is a *de facto* import prohibition, as import licences are simply not granted. Under NAFTA, licences will be gradually issued for some imports of used vehicles originating from the United States and Canada beginning in 2009, and the licence requirement will be eliminated in 2019, 25 years after NAFTA's entry into force.

*Mexico has established a competitive auto industry; the benefits of this have come at the cost of higher prices for Mexican consumers.*

These delays significantly distort trade in the automobile sector; however, the intent to open the market is a marked improvement relative to the previous programme based on import substitution. In production, foreign direct investment is now welcome. The local content and trade balancing requirements are gradually being relaxed. Restraints in this industry, combined with Mexico's overall trade liberalisation, were instrumental in Mexico becoming a large exporter. The benefits have come at the cost of higher prices for consumers. Manufacturers established in Mexico are export success stories, and the trade balancing requirements do not now exert any real restraint on import manufacturer imports.

**Mexico generally follows the principles of efficient regulation, even where they are not codified, and has benefited from doing so.**

Not all of the six efficient regulation principles examined in this review are expressly codified in Mexican administrative and regulatory oversight procedures. But they are given ample expression in practice. Highlights are the transparency and openness of decision-making and measures to ensure non-discrimination.

Market-opening regulation promises to promote the flow of goods, services, investment and technology between Mexico and trading partners. Expanded trade and investment generate important consumer benefits through greater choice and lower prices, raise the standards of performance of domestic firms through the impetus of greater competition, and boost GDP. The transformation of the Mexican economic policies was instrumental in making Mexico the largest recipient of foreign direct investment among emerging economies, after China, during the 1990s.

With about two thirds of exports accounted for by manufactured goods, Mexican export performance reflects the improved competitiveness of Mexican firms in international markets. This itself is partly a reflection of trade and investment liberalisation and domestic deregulation. The growing importance of trade appears in the growing number of exporting firms, which increased by nearly 70% between 1993 and 1997.

Trade and investment friendly regulation need not undermine the promotion and achievement of legitimate Mexican policy objectives. High-quality regulation can be trade-neutral or market-opening, coupling consumer gains from enhanced market openness with more efficient realisation of domestic objectives in key areas such as the environment, health and safety. But it is doubtful that this can be achieved in the absence of purposeful, government-wide adherence to the principles of efficient regulation.

77

*Chapter 5*

# REGULATORY REFORM IN THE TELECOMMUNICATIONS INDUSTRY

The telecommunications industry is extraordinarily dynamic, with rapid technological evolution shaking up industries and regulatory regimes that had long been based on older technologies and market theories. Twenty-three OECD countries now have unrestricted market access to all forms of telecommunications, including voice telephony, infrastructure investment and investment by foreign enterprises, compared to only a handful a few years ago. The industry's very definition is blurring and merging with other industries such as broadcasting and information services.

*Strong competition policies and efficiency-promoting regulatory regimes are crucial to the performance and future development of the industry.*

The role of regulatory reform in launching and shaping the rapid evolution of the industry has been described by some as pivotal, and by others as at best supportive. It is nonetheless clear that strong competition policies and efficiency-promoting regulatory regimes that work well in dynamic and global markets are crucial to the industry's performance and future development.

## Mexico has pursued sound policy objectives and has made progress toward regulatory reform.

*The first step toward reform, in 1990, was to privatise the monopoly incumbent and modernise its concession.*

The regulatory regime for Mexico's telecommunications sector has undergone significant reform. The two pillars of reform were privatisation and competitive entry. The monopoly incumbent, *Telefonos de Mexico* (Telmex) was returned to private control in 1990. Under the modified concession granted at that time, Telmex was the only carrier allowed into the domestic and international long distance markets until 1996. Other carriers could, in theory, enter local service markets. The continued monopoly in long distance was permitted so that Telmex could achieve network expansion targets and rebalance its rate structure. Telmex, which is under the effective control of a conglomerate, Grupo Carso, is now the largest company listed on the Mexican stock exchange.

*Expanding service is a fundamental policy goal.*

The promotion of universal service and network expansion was, and continues to be, an important policy objective. Many households have no telephone line. In 1997, telephone penetration was only about 9.8 lines per 100 persons (the regulator, Cofetel, calculates that penetration rates had reached 10.3 per 100 in 1998); by contrast, the average rate in OECD countries is around 50 per 100 persons.

*The second step was to invite new entry, in long distance and mobile services.*

Steps were taken to open markets to competitive entry, most notably into domestic and international long distance after 1996. New entrants in long distance include firms backed by MCI and

AT&T. Entry has led to price competition in long distance service, and has eroded Telmex's market shares. In long distance, new entrants quickly took about 30% of the market. Granting multiple concessions for cellular service and allocating frequencies through spectrum auctions have promoted competition in mobile service markets. The largest new entrant there is backed by Bell Atlantic. Telmex's subsidiary, Telcel, is the largest mobile carrier, with a share of about 60%. Telmex still controls virtually 100% of fixed-wire local service and interconnection.

## The Federal Telecommunications Law is a potentially solid policy foundation.

*The 1995 law brings the legislative foundation up to date, relying on market methods and promoting competition.*

The Federal Telecommunications Law (FTL), adopted in 1995, is a well-conceived statute that incorporates central elements of effective regulation. The FTL promotes market mechanisms for the allocation of scarce spectrum rights. It also sets out a framework for interconnection by rivals to the incumbent's public switched telephone network. The FTL codifies the goal of promoting network expansion and universal service. And it also codifies the goal of promoting competition among providers, to benefit users through better services, diversity, and quality.

*A key feature of the FTL is that it establishes the institutional arrangements for regulating the telecommunications sector.*

Importantly, the FTL also establishes the institutional basis for regulation of the telecommunications sector, by establishing a regulatory agency separate from the government and the major industry players. This regulator, Cofetel, has been delegated many of the powers exercised by the SCT under the FTL, including, importantly, the power to recommend conditions on new concessions and the power to resolve interconnection disputes.

---

Box 5.1. **Key features of the 1995 Federal Telecommunications Law**

A new **sectoral regulator**, Cofetel, is created. Cofetel is given powers to issue opinions on the issuing, modifying and revoking of concessions and permits, can establish policies and resolve certain disputes. In addition Cofetel can regulate **pricing** of carriers that the CFC determines to have significant market power.

The FTL establishes new service authorisation requirements. A **concession** is required for a provider using frequency or operating a fixed network. A **permit** is required for a carrier engaged in other commercial telecommunication operations. **Registration** is required for a provider of value added services.

The FTL requires the government to hold public tenders (**auctions**) for all public concessions concerning the use of spectrum frequency. A condition for a firm to participate in an auction is approval by the Federal Competition Commission (CFC).

**Interconnection** with the incumbent's network is mandated. In the event of failure to negotiate interconnection terms and conditions, operators can request Cofetel to set the terms and conditions of issues in dispute. Interconnection tariffs should cover incremental cost.

**Foreign investment** is permitted. For an operator of a fixed network, foreign ownership is limited to a 49% share. For cellular carriers, higher levels are permitted, subject to the approval of the National Commission on Foreign Investment.

### The role for competition is well designed...

*General competition policy is applied to sectoral decisions, about market power and entry.*

The general competition law applies to the telecommunications sector, and thus the CFC has the authority to take enforcement actions and provide competition policy advice as in other OECD countries. In addition, the FTL explicitly gives the CFC the responsibility to determine whether a firm has significant market power and thus authorise Cofetel to regulate its prices. CFC must also approve firm's participation in spectrum auctions. In principle, the structure of the interface between competition law and sector-specific regulation is well designed.

### ... and so is the spectrum allocation regime.

*Auctions are used to promote competitive entry.*

Mexico has effectively used market-based methods to allocate spectrum. Auction processes, in which the CFC has played an important role, have produced a competitive market structure in mobile communications. Subscriber growth rates have been strong, and the market share of the largest competitor (a subsidiary of Telmex) is at about the same level as elsewhere in the OECD; however, penetration rates remain low compared to other OECD countries. Still, the potential competitive strength of mobile services may be important, because wireless technology, particularly wireless-local-loop, may be a more likely substitute for wireline access in countries facing network penetration challenges.

### But there remains room for increasing the independence of the regulator...

*Full regulatory independence is necessary to build confidence in the market.*

The establishment of Cofetel as a regulatory agency distinct from the SCT was an important step towards developing an independent and transparent regulatory framework in Mexico. However, the independence of Cofetel, and the transparency and accountability of its decisions, do not go as far as is desirable. Regulatory independence from day to day political pressures is essential to build confidence of all market participants that government intervention in the telecommunications market will be transparent. There is a need for strengthening Cofetel's independence from regulated companies to further ensure transparent, fair, and reasonably predictable decisions.

*The transparency and accountability of Cofetel could be enhanced by making it more independent of the government.*

Arrangements differ in each country, but the essential features include complete independence from the regulated companies, a legal mandate that provides for separation of the regulators and the regulatory body from political control (*e.g.* by removing the power over appointments to the regulatory body from political control), a degree of organisational autonomy, well-defined obligations for transparency (*e.g.* publishing decisions) and for accountability (*e.g.* appealable decisions, public scrutiny of expenditures). The combination of transparencies – of objectives, powers, processes, decisions, and information – enables the public to evaluate how the regulator is fulfilling its role as a neutral arbiter of market competition and enforcer of regulation. In addition, the remaining powers held by the SCT (relating to the issuing and revoking of concessions) should be delegated to Cofetel.

81

## ... increasing the quality and transparency of the regulator's decision-making processes...

*The transparency and quality of Cofetel's decision-making processes could be enhanced through the adoption of a formal, transparent consultation process.*

Although Cofetel has widely consulted with the industry on an informal basis, Cofetel has not, to date, implemented a formal public process of consultation before taking important decisions. Before the second semester of 1998, Cofetel did not publish the reasoning behind its decisions, contributing to a general lack of transparency in the decision-making process, and enhancing the scope for legal challenge. The adoption of processes involving a public, transparent and accountable procedure of notifying for comment, publicly accepting or rejecting other positions based on reasonable standards and the regulatory framework, and issuing final resolutions based on such procedures, would result in a more credible, less contentious and more efficient regulatory process.

*The voice of the competition authority should be heard.*

A key component in any new consultation procedures would be granting the opportunity for other government agencies including, especially, the competition authority, to express its views publicly on the policies of Cofetel. Although all input is important, the competition authority has a special role due to its mandate of promoting competition and its experience in controlling the behaviour of dominant firms.

## ... and improving the coverage of the government's regulatory quality review processes.

*The application of wider government regulatory quality control processes could be improved.*

The Mexican government, like many other OECD governments, has established quality control processes for reviewing the exercise of its regulatory powers. Until 1997 the concession regime shielded the sector from these quality control processes. More recently, Cofetel and SCT are still in the early stages of compliance with this regulatory quality control policy.

### The concession system requires careful handling...

*Concession terms remain very important.*

As in other countries, the need to obtain a license or concession represents a potentially important source of barriers to entry. The FTL requires Cofetel to scrutinise the business plan and the legal, administrative, financial and technical capacity of new entrants. Cofetel can recommend that conditions be placed on concessions, including, most importantly, the concession to build network infrastructure. Much of Cofetel's power to regulate carriers, including Telmex, derives from the terms and conditions of concession titles.

*Concession conditions should be strictly limited.*

Although a relatively large number of concessions have been granted, and although Cofetel asserts that it has been weakening the requirements for obtaining a concession, nevertheless, the certainty and transparency of entry requirements could be enhanced by limiting the discretion of Cofetel to place conditions on concessions. Such a change would also encourage a movement towards a more formal system of rules-based regulation, rather than regulation based on conditions in concessions.

## ... as do requirements to register and publish prices.

*Requirements to publish prices may facilitate collusion.*

The FTL requires that Cofetel register and publicise the prices of all firms, including non-dominant firms. Such a system may facilitate collusion among competing firms. Sustained profitable collusion requires the detection of "cheating" on the agreed prices. If firms are required to publicly disclose all their prices, the detection of such cheating is much easier. Under the current system, firms cannot discount without it becoming public knowledge even before the discounts apply. Long-distance prices have fallen significantly in Mexico, but with a relatively small number of large players, collusion remains a long-term threat in this industry.

## Interconnection prices have come down rapidly...

*Interconnection charges have dropped rapidly.*

The charges for the interconnection of long-distance competitors to Telmex's local network have dropped from around 6 US cents per end per minute in 1997 to around 2.6 US cents per end per minute in 1999. This represents a rapid decline relative to other countries.

## ... but interconnection issues remain highly controversial.

*High interconnection charges in Mexico may reflect choices regarding the balance between local and long-distance prices.*

As in other countries, issues surrounding interconnection charges have been intensely controversial. International comparisons suggest that current levels of interconnection charges in Mexico, though they have declined rapidly, remain high by world standards. This may be due to the choice, in Mexico, of a different "balance" between the sources of revenue (monthly rental fees, local call usage fees and interconnection charges) that are necessary to cover the costs of the local telephone service. Interconnection charges may be higher to keep the cost of local telephone service down.

*The charges for interconnection of local networks make a distinction between types of networks.*

In the case of the interconnection of local networks, Mexico distinguishes between networks which have substantial coverage of the local area and those which do not. Networks which have substantial coverage of the local area (and which therefore serve more residential customers) receive a higher payment for terminating calls.

*The basis for setting interconnection charges could be made more transparent.*

OECD price comparisons suggest that overall telecommunications prices remain high in Mexico. The transparency of interconnection decision-making could be enhanced through steps such as *a*) carefully identifying the size of a deficit on local services that is covered through interconnection charges, *b*) identifying the component of interconnection charges which contributes to that deficit and *c*) the establishment of an explicit transparent fund mechanism for covering any deficit on local services.

## The system of price-controls set out in the Telmex concession was far-sighted...

*The focus on a basket of prices rather than individual prices is sound.*

The Telmex concession includes a system of price controls which fixes the level of a basket of prices. In principle, the focus on a basket of prices allows the regulated firm to use any private information that it holds to properly adjust individual prices to reflect underlying costs and demand elasticities, while helping to prevent the firm from exercising market power overall. The basic structure of this system of price controls is sound and was far-sighted at the time the Telmex concession was implemented.

*Rebalancing to eliminate distorted rate structures before introducing competition was an important step.*

The initial rationale for including local and long distance services in the same basket was to permit rate rebalancing. As in most OECD countries, rate structures in Mexico historically embodied implicit subsidies. Prices for business users and for long-distance services were above competitive levels, so rates for local or rural service could be kept low. The concession's flexible price cap design permitted Telmex to change the relationship, to reduce long distance rates and increase local rates, without significant loss of revenue. Rebalancing to correct rate distortions is often a necessary step toward competitive markets. It promotes economic efficiency by reducing incentives to bypass the most efficient long distance network or refrain from using efficient local service. It enhances allocative efficiency, since subscribers face prices that reflect true costs and adjust their consumption decisions accordingly. And the greater efficiency enhances competitiveness, since telecommunications is an input to business activity in many other sectors.

*But rebalancing was not completed on time due to the peso crisis of 1994.*

When the concession was entered in 1990, it envisioned that Telmex would complete rate rebalancing before competition was permitted in 1996. Entrants would then be responding to efficiency considerations rather than rate distortions. And the incumbent's price changes would then respond to relative economic costs, rather than predation. Telmex postponed rate restructuring, largely because of the peso crisis in 1994. As a result, when the market was opened to competition, Telmex could reduce long distance prices and, at the same time, increase local prices.

### ... but may need to be modified to prevent anti-competitive behaviour.

*The current price-cap may provide incentives for Telmex to price aggressively in long-distance markets.*

By including both competitive services (long-distance) and non-competitive services (local telephony), the Telmex price cap arrangement may enhance the incentives of Telmex to price below cost in its competitive markets, because it can recoup any loss in revenue by raising prices in the non-competitive markets. Although pricing below cost is not permitted, it can be difficult and time-consuming to detect. These incentives could be removed by eliminating competitive prices from the cap.

### The problem of the incumbent's substantial market power has been diagnosed...

*The CFC has determined that Telmex has market power in five markets.*

The CFC concluded in March 1998 that Telmex has substantial market power in five relevant markets: local telephony, interconnection services, national long distance, international long distance and the resale of long distance. Telmex virtually owns all of the local public networks and provides local and interconnection services. Although there has been entry in long distance services, the entrants' infrastructure is still modest and the entrants rely on

Telmex's capacity both for their access to final consumers and to provide long distance services in some routes. Telmex's vertical integration and its ability to set prices without other competitors being able to offset such power, as well as the existence of important entry barriers, were taken into account in determining its dominant position.

### ... but the regulatory response has been delayed.

*The market power finding authorises regulation under the FTL, but new regulation has not yet been implemented.*

The CFC's finding authorises additional regulation to control or remedy the exercise of market power. But the new regulation has not yet been implemented. The development of these additional regulations presents an opportunity to place the regulation of Telmex under a formal regulatory instrument, rather than relying on its concession title. In addition, these additional regulations present an opportunity to improve the system of price controls on Telmex, by focusing the price controls on those services for which competition is limited.

### The arrangements for the international exchange of traffic restrict competition.

*Mexico prevents competition in the termination of international traffic.*

The majority of Mexico's international traffic is with the US. Like many countries, Mexico does not allow its domestic companies to compete in the termination of calls from the US, but sets a single, common termination tariff, with incoming traffic shared amongst the firms in the same proportion as their outgoing traffic. Due to the imbalance in calls between Mexico and the US, this mechanism preserves a substantial revenue flow to Mexican telecommunications companies. The elimination of this system would lead to immediate price reductions on international calls and benefits to both Mexican and foreign consumers.

### Despite the problems, the regulatory regime has attracted sources of new competition...

*Competition is developing in those markets where it is currently limited.*

Competition has developed quickly in the long-distance market and competition is developing in the local market. Cellular service is offered by several firms, and the number of cellular subscribers doubled between 1996 and 1998, although penetration rates are still the lowest in the OECD. Satellite providers are possible source of competition. The communications satellite system was sold off by auction in 1997. Other non-wireline resources are being developed. A 1997 auction was aimed at building a capacity supply market for microwave point to point and point to multi-point systems. In the longer term, new entry into local markets could be a competitive force. Several firms have received concessions for both fixed and wireless local service.

### ... and recent decisions about local competition are promising.

*Cofetel has also adopted new rules to encourage local service competition.*

Cofetel's December 1998 decision about local competition rules introduces several useful measures. Applying the principle of "calling party pays" for mobile service is an important step. It means mobile service subscribers can control their phone bills, and thus eliminates an artificial incentive to turn off the phone or to choose wireline instead. Where this charging system has been implemented, mobile telephony has developed much faster. In addition, Cofetel is reducing the number of local calling areas, to simplify investment requirements and promote scale economies, and expanded the stock of numbers available.

### Indicators of performance present a mixed picture.

*After early progress, some performance improvements continued, while others slowed...*

In the late 1980s and early 1990s, investments were made in the Mexican telecommunications system, which are reflected in improved performance of the sector over this period. By 1994, system digitalisation had increased from 29% to 83%. Growth in the number of telephone lines was modest but significant. Since 1994, the rate of investment has fallen off significantly. There has been almost no growth in the number of new lines added to the system.

*... for example, prices have not declined much overall.*

Competitive entry into long-distance and international services has led to pronounced decreases in those prices. But the introduction of competition has not reduced prices overall, because large increases in the price for local service offset savings for long distance.

*Compared to other OECD countries, Mexico remains at the low end in penetration rates...*

In indicators of performance, Mexico remains at the low end of OECD cross-country comparisons. Price levels exceed those in other OECD countries by a large margin. The penetration rate is the lowest in the OECD, and is only half of the next lowest country, Poland (which has doubled its rate, from 10 to 20 per 100 persons, since 1990).

### Further progress on regulatory reform could lead to further and more significant benefits to users and consumers.

*Additional reforms will produce benefits across the entire economy.*

Privatisation and creation of a more modern legislative and administrative system were important steps. Technological progress in telecommunications has been dramatic. But further regulatory reform could produce significant benefits for the Mexican economy. Progress in promoting penetration in other countries shows that reliance on competition and market forces can be effective. Because telecommunication services are used in many other markets, the price reductions, quality improvements and increased network penetration that can be achieved would generate benefits throughout the economy.

# Chapter 6

# CONCLUSIONS AND POLICY OPTIONS FOR REGULATORY REFORM

*Reform sustains economic and political development...*

Regulatory reform has been a vital step in the process that began in the 1980s of opening Mexico's markets to competition. Reforms in regulation create the framework for enduring improvements in Mexico's economic and public life. Mexico's economic performance for the last two decades has been uneven, even disappointing. But regulatory reform has not been the reason; rather, the difficulties have pointed out the need for reform. And reforms accomplished already have helped Mexico rebound from crises more quickly and be less vulnerable to a volatile international environment. Reform has been necessary to avoid even greater problems and to establish a foundation for longer-term growth. The major benefits of reform have been:

*... by making business more competitive...*

- Improving productive efficiency, by reducing costs for such critical inputs as communications, land, and transport services, and hence promoting competitiveness. This is witnessed by the growth of Mexico's export sector.

*... by encouraging innovation...*

- Promoting new products and technologies, and the adoption of modern, low-cost methods through new entry and investment. In transport, telecommunications, and other sectors, privatisation and elimination of red tape have encouraged firms to invest in new technologies.

*... by reducing prices and increasing choices...*

- Permitting competition – and enforcing new laws to prevent collusion – has reduced prices and increased choices, for consumer products as well as business services.

*... by reducing fiscal imbalances...*

- Saving and redirecting resources, so that Mexico could weather its major economic crises more successfully.

*... and by promoting sound government methods.*

- Establishing institutions and methods that will permit Mexico to accomplish its regulatory goals more effectively.

The process of policy reform in Mexico has been instrumental in changing the economic direction toward integration with the world economy and in changing the governing culture toward one of greater openness and accountability. Mexico's experience vividly demonstrates how liberalising trade, empowering market competition, and reforming administrative processes are mutually supportive complements.

**Liberalising trade and privatising assets, followed inevitably
by stronger competition policy and regulatory reform,
have promoted development.**

The economic transition staged in Mexico in the last decade
and a half is extraordinary by any standards. The Mexican government, facing fiscal crises, recognised the need to move the basis of
its economy away from protection and privilege and undertook a
long-run plan to do so. The plan included international commitments to maximise the likelihood of policy perseverance.

Mexico's accession to the GATT in 1986, APEC in 1993, the
OECD in 1994, and the negotiation of NAFTA and other free trade
agreements have had profound impacts on domestic policy and
regulatory formulation processes. Entering these trade and investment agreements announced a fundamental change in policy. Moreover, Mexico's commitments under these agreements acted as
catalysts for domestic regulatory reforms and provided strong policy anchors which have contributed to minimise the adverse effects
of the crisis in 1995 and helped Mexico stage an impressive recovery. Continued multilateral liberalisation of trade and investment
should bolster future regulatory reform efforts (including the negotiation of a FTA with the European Union and continued negotiation
of bilateral investment protection agreements).

The significant privatisation programme, in conjunction with
the removal of many restrictions on foreign direct investment and
control, constituted another fundamental change in policy.

Removing price controls made clear that markets would be
allowed to function, and adopting a modern competition law
announced that market competition would be the norm for business
and investment.

Some reforms in administrative and regulatory processes are
among the most advanced in the OECD. The process for developing
technical standards is of interest in the development of best practices
in this important area. On-line searchable databases of regulatory formalities puts Mexico at the forefront in the use of this important tool.
Integration of federal, state and local government regulatory reforms is
also an area in which Mexico is in the front rank. Virtually all states have
now agreed to implement reform programmes based on consistent
principles, and there has been progress in encouraging commitments
from municipal governments to do likewise. Reform activity seems to
have been successfully "leveraged" by the federal reform strategy.
Transmission of reform to the sub-national levels of government should
help broaden its base and deepen its roots. The private sector has hastened this process by publishing (and making available on the Internet) its first annual rankings of quality of regulations and regulatory
reform programmes in the states.

**Mexico's experience shows the value of a comprehensive
approach, and the challenge of transforming regulatory cultures.**

*High-level support for
comprehensive reform empowered
the reform process.*

The Mexican experience offers lessons that should be considered by other Member countries. Regulatory reform has
received clear and sustained support at the highest level of the

federal government, a factor that has been of key importance in empowering the bodies within the administration charged with co-ordinating, monitoring and promoting reform. These administrative bodies have been given clear, well formulated roles and high quality staff and have been active in pursuing reform. Other key strengths include a well-formulated set of RIA requirements including, unusually, consideration of the feasibility of enforcing regulations.

*Mexico has made substantial progress; now, it needs to rebalance and build a wider constituency for reform.*

Mexico has moved further and more quickly than most OECD countries in bringing its old regulatory system up to international standards. The only countries that compare in terms of the magnitude of the policy response are eastern European countries involved in the transition to market democracies. The distance yet to travel is large, though, and progress will slow as the multi-party system develops. Because the regulatory reform programmes are relatively recent and have moved so quickly, gaps in concept, design, and administrative implementation and enforcement have developed and remain to be resolved. What is needed now is a rebalancing of the programme toward a broader vision of social welfare to help build a wider constituency, combined with a multi-year period of consolidation, sustained administrative implementation and enforcement, and refinement of the legal and policy reforms already on the table. This will permit legal and policy reforms to spread through the administration so that citizens and businesses see concrete benefits.

*The gap between sound reform plans and actual implementation of better regulatory capacities must be reduced.*

- As in all countries, policy reforms of this magnitude require a multi-year period of sustained, consistent administrative implementation and enforcement. Translating reform programmes into real benefits is hampered by problems of human resources and public management and by some weaknesses in compliance and enforcement. The problems are not limited to regulatory management. They affect the culture of government generally. A more transparent, results-oriented, and accountable approach is slowly emerging, but it is fragile, and the broader administrative environment does not support it.

*More consultation is critical.*

- Transparency has improved significantly, but Mexico still falls short of OECD good practices, particularly in the use of public consultation. Procedural requirements in some areas are helpful, but not enough; there should be a comprehensive, standardised requirement for open public consultation, making use of RIA requirements and procedures.

*Policies should be better harmonised.*

- Other structural reform policies, in particular competition advocacy and administrative reform, should be harmonised more clearly with regulatory reform.

*Reform should have higher institutional visibility.*

- Visibility and effectiveness of the regulatory reform effort need to be improved by moving the organisations responsible for the process to a higher and more central or independent management position with greater operational and budgetary autonomy.

89

*The focus must continue
to be on regulatory improvement
rather than deregulation.*

- After some setbacks in the aftermath of initial privatisation efforts due to the lack of appropriate regulatory frameworks, the Mexican government has shifted its attention to regulatory improvement and the re-regulation of certain sectors rather than deregulation. Sustaining this regulatory improvement effort requires reaching out to a broader constituency, to citizens and consumers as well as businesses, and to the Congress as well as the bureaucracy. The implications and benefits of reform to the general public, in sectoral governance and consumer protection, must be communicated more effectively and more widely.

Regulatory reform is part of an historic process of social, political and economic change. It is a key contributor to these broader changes, and those changes constrain and shape reform, too. The future prospects for regulatory reform are linked with the evolution of these wider changes.

## POLICY OPTIONS FOR REGULATORY REFORM

This report is not a comprehensive review of regulation in Mexico. Nonetheless, the areas reviewed show that the policy effectiveness in Mexico's regulatory regimes can be improved.

This section identifies actions that, based on international consensus on good regulatory practices and on concrete experiences in OECD countries, are likely to be beneficial to improving regulation in Mexico. The summary recommendations presented here are discussed in more detail in the background reports to Chapters 2 to 5, published separately. They are based on the recommendations and policy framework in *The* OECD *Report to Ministers on Regulatory Reform.*

*The current programme's benefits for the public are potentially substantial, but realising those benefits depends on effective administrative implementation and enforcement of reforms, which requires a multi-year period of policy stability and a series of steps to strengthen the institutions and capacities within the public administration.*

Despite the high-level political backing, the spread and scope of reforms, and the development of regulatory innovations and international best practices, the benefits of reform have not yet been widely realised. A crucial element for this to happen is their administrative implementation in the culture and practice of regulators as well as reducing the lag in legal implementation in specific ministries. The main challenge is execution by each of the involved agencies, not conceptualisation, of regulatory reform. A high priority should be given to fine-tuning the policy, the institutions, and the tools of reform. Until the reforms permeate into the regulators' "culture" and filter into the public administration, the new capacities will not be realised. It is undeniable that this will be an arduous effort that will require continuous political support. But it is necessary to fulfil urgent demands for tangible outcomes.

*Put CDE/UDE in the centre of government or make it autonomous and broaden the scope of the policy.*

- *Transfer the central reform body (CDE/UDE) to the centre of government, with cross-cutting management and co-ordination authorities, and strengthen its attention to consumer protection and citizen welfare.* The Ministry of Trade and Industry has carried regulatory reform very far indeed, reflecting its strong position in economic policy and commitment to competitive markets. The next step in the reform process is integration of regulatory quality concepts and processes into the core policy-making machinery of government. Experiences in some OECD countries suggest that placing a systematic regulatory management in the centre of government linked to the offices of the President, Prime Minister, or budget, or making it autonomous (akin to the CFC) enhances the authority and oversight needed to steer the process and obtain results. This is particularly likely in the Mexican setting, where administrative hierarchy has high value. Moving from a line ministry to the centre of government also has important implications for the content and scope of the programme. Broadening UDE's responsibilities, reducing exemptions, and pursuing a government-wide approach to regulatory quality should accompany the up-grading. In particular, a wider view of how good regulation and deregulation together can maximise social welfare would be necessary to maintain the legitimacy and effectiveness of the UDE at a higher management level. The transfer should also be an important occasion to improve co-ordination with other entities in charge of structural reform policies, as well as with those closely related to budget and public human resource policies. Furthermore, a new setting could be the occasion to widen the reform strategy and more actively involve Congress and other non-businesses parties. This will increase the credibility of a new unit, and broaden its appeal. For instance, the UK's Deregulation Unit moved in 1996 from the Trade and Industry Ministry to the Cabinet Office and changed in 1997 its name to the Better Regulation Unit.

*Enhance the CFC's role in the CDE process.*

- *Make the competition authority (CFC) part of the Ministerial Economic Deregulation Council (CDE), to ensure that competition policy issues are regularly considered at the highest levels in regulatory reform efforts.* The CFC has not been regularly involved in the CDE's review process. Although it is consulted on an *ad hoc* basis, the lack of formal and accountable responsibilities diminishes the role of competition principles in the reform process. In March of 1999, the CFC was extended a permanent invitation to the meetings of the CDE. Bringing the CFC into the CDE should lead to a more stable process for resolving disputes among competing policy interests and give the CFC a forum to explain and reason various opinions and resolutions. If promoting market-based approaches is an important goal, then that importance should be represented by high-level participation in this body. Continuing participation will also help ward off regulations that are more anti-competitive than necessary to accomplish their purposes, thus economising on enforcement efforts in the long run.

*Ensure uniformity of RIA preparation.*

- *Take measures to ensure uniformity in the preparation of regulatory impact analysis (RIAs) and in the implementation of regulatory requirements by all Federal and Regulatory Agencies.* The requirement to prepare a regulatory impact assessment for proposed regulations having a potential impact on business activities is still very recent. This regulatory requirement should be more widely and uniformly implemented by all Federal ministries and regulatory agencies. Additional resources for RIA review and technical assistance may be needed if Mexico is to take its legislative obligations seriously. Higher quality RIA would be achieved, in part, by requiring that all regulatory projects and RIAs be systematically published and widely available to the public.

*Improve RIA, encourage alternatives to traditional regulation, and improve drafting.*

- *Strengthen disciplines on regulatory quality by refining tools for regulatory impact analysis, use of alternatives, and law drafting, and training public servants in how to use them.* Since its creation, the UDE has been instrumental in designing and implementing new tools to improve regulatory quality. To be sure these tools are incorporated effectively and regularly in administrative practice, action would be useful in improving the skills of public sector employees in how to conduct the regulatory impact analysis. Alternative to traditional "command and control" regulations should also be actively encouraged and supported through training, guidelines and expert assistance. Moreover, the UDE should foster improvements in regulatory clarity and simplicity by adopting the principle of plain language drafting. For instance, quality controls on technical law drafting should be put into place in each ministry. Here again, controls could be supplemented by training and guidelines to improve drafting skills and standardise approaches.

*Improve the powers of private action to remedy anti-competitive conduct.*

- *Broaden the available enforcement resources by expanding the right of private action.* As a supplement to the CFC's resources, the right to take private action against restraints on competition should be expanded. Making all decisions under the competition law completely dependent on the CFC ensures consistency, but risks leaving problems unaddressed because of resource limitations. Expanding private actions will require addressing other institutional problems in the judiciary, though.

*The current policy framework for the use of regulation is founded on competition and market-oriented principles and is a sound basis to improve regulatory efficiency and effectiveness. But gaps in the framework should be corrected to ensure that reform brings benefits for consumers as well as for business development.*

Most of Mexico's reforms have been based on a pragmatic course built on opportunities that have arisen during the evolution to competition and on the need to resolve bottlenecks that have appeared. Good progress has been made, though gaps and inconsistencies have inevitably arisen in the overall framework for regulation. Mexico should thus dedicate new resources to build on its achievements to date.

*Expand good practices; eliminate exemptions and loopholes.*

- *Establish consistent government-wide standards for regulatory quality by closing gaps, eliminating exemptions and incorporating non-businesses regulations in the current policy framework.* Good regulatory practices already established for significant portions of Mexican regulatory activity should be expanded government-wide. Broad exemptions from important parts of the programme, combined with the non-mandatory nature of some policies, have resulted in a fragmented application of regulatory powers. These gaps limit the use of regulatory impact analysis, independent review, codification, and public consultation. The Administrative Procedures Law, which sets down the general guidelines for the government interaction with the public in all administrative procedures and the legal remedies to those aggrieved by administrative action, would be an important vehicle to improve and strengthen the regulatory process, from "cradle to grave". Any exemptions should be very narrowly drawn. Loopholes, such as those that have permitted regulations about telecommunications under concessions to avoid the supervision of the ADAE process, should be closed.

*Consider carefully the benefits and costs of monopoly protection for strategic sectors.*

- *Competition principles should be strengthened in the overall policy framework.* As reform proceeds and competition spreads across the economy, problems due to remaining pockets of market power will become even more obvious. Economic distortions will result from trying to sustain monopolies in economically competitive industries or not eliciting competition in non-contestable, non-tradable network industries. Mexico will have to consider carefully the benefits and costs of the remaining public and private monopolies.

*Add avoidance of unnecessary trade restrictiveness to the RIA checklist.*

- *Complement the current sets of guiding principles for the preparation of RIAs with the additional principle of "avoidance of unnecessary trade restrictiveness".* This would allow interested firms, particularly foreign firms or investors, to check proposed regulations and legislation systematically against a more comprehensive set of principles when regulatory impact statements are carried out.

*Work to broaden public support for competition-based reform and further strengthen attention to consumer protection.*

- *Broaden the base of support, through greater media exposure and co-ordination with consumer protection activities.* The UDE and the CFC should publicise their actions to a wider audience than the business press. To accomplish the goal of wider public understanding of the benefits of competition and better regulation and increased transparency, it will be necessary that reform actions result in consumer benefits that can be clearly and convincingly communicated. And the UDE and the CFC should develop a structure of co-ordination with consumer protection activities, which could also help build a broader base of understanding and support. It would be consistent with the economic foundation of Mexico's competition policy for the CFC to take on responsibilities for some "consumer protection" issues that are also often treated as matters of unfair competition doctrine, like deceptive advertising, which have direct effects both on consumers and on the health of market competition.

*Past reforms are producing significant gains for Mexico, but regulatory imperfections, particularly in managing dominant firms after privatisation, continue to undermine sectoral performance. Corrections are needed to encourage effective competition in these areas.*

During a period of thorough, broad and rapid reform, countries have great difficulty in maintaining and ensuring the coherence and quality of changes realised across policies and sectors. This has been the case for some important reforms undertaken in Mexico. Although significant gains have resulted from reforms and privatisation, benefits have not always lived up to the expectations held by their promoters, and have in some cases provoked new regulatory problems, inefficiencies and costs. They may erode public support for further reforms. It is thus important that Mexico urgently concentrate in correcting past shortcomings in sectors that have been reformed.

*Review carefully the structure and experience of the sectoral agencies.*

- *Launch a comprehensive, independent review of the new regulatory agencies and a general revision of their mission statements, as the first step toward improving their efficiency, independence and accountability by strengthening their systems of governance, policy coherence, transparency of their decisions, statutory goals (mission statements), working methods, and relations with the competition authority.* The rapid appearance of autonomous and semi-autonomous regulatory agencies is changing the legal and administrative environment. These agencies have been created case by case, without a consistent framework permitting comparability and co-ordination. Questions remain about the relationships between regulatory agencies and with the competition authority, and about the application to them of the procedures of the judiciary system. A central element of this review would be to evaluate the feasibility, in the Mexican context, of a multi-sectoral regulatory institution that could share resources, facilitate learning across industries, reduce the risk of industry or political capture, and deal with blurred industry boundaries. The economies of density in a country with limited human capital resources such as Mexico could be an important factor to consider. An independent expert group should review the architecture in order to propose a new, harmonised framework. Recent experiences in the UK, where a Green Paper was recently prepared, or the in-depth work done by the inter-ministerial commission of Chile could be model to consider. Australia's model of combining the regulatory oversight body with the competition authority could also be a reference.

*Focus competition policy on regulated and privatising sectors.*

- *Maintain competition policy attention to regulatory issues and regulated and privatising sectors, with analysis, publicity, and enforcement, as long as competition is still impaired by controls on entry and by other kinds of potential regulatory bias.* In competition policy, focus should be maintained on the sectors where regulation and privatisation are still important issues, despite the difficulty and the political and resource cost, until better outcomes are achieved in the major sectors affected. Analysis and advice should be accompanied by law enforcement in these sectors, too. The CFC can take advantage of the law's comprehensive reach, for few industries, even regulated ones, are technically exempt. This emphasis would have the additional, desirable effect of focusing attention on higher-impact matters concerning collusion and exclusion. If more enforcement is desirable for institutional reasons, it would be better to target the largest economic forces, the largest consumer and market harms, and the most important anti-competitive situations. These are likely to coincide with the subjects of privatisation, deregulation and needed regulation in non-contestable markets, that is, the same sectors that are now receiving the CFC's regulatory-policy attention.

*Give the CFC means to ensure that its market dominance findings result in effective remedies.*

- *Provide for effective power to ensure that regulations to remedy market power actually achieve that aim, by requiring CFC approval for those regulations or a right of intervention and appeal concerning regulatory decisions that implement its market power findings.* In form, the method for incorporating competition principles into the regulatory system appears sensible. The CFC applies its general expertise about assessing market competition to determine whether there is a market power problem that needs a solution, and if there is, then a regulatory body that is expert about the particular sector designs and implements that solution. The practice, however, demonstrates that the formal arrangement has weaknesses. In some sectors, capture and lack of adequate oversight appear to be significant problems. Regulators tend to protect "national champions" in communications and transport, and the Constitution protects them in energy and petroleum. Competition policy confronts development concerns in telecommunications. In energy, it must compromise with national history. And in many sectors, it is in conflict with concentrated financial interests. Regulators who share industry interests in preserving established institutions are unlikely to apply competition policy effectively. One option would be to give the CFC a strong oversight role to monitor solutions, for instance, and require CFC approval of the proposed network industry regulation before it could become effective. A less intrusive option would be for the CFC to accompany its market power findings with clear, performance-based standards and necessary controls that regulations must include. The CFC could be more effective if it had the clear power to intervene in actions that apply those regulations, to ensure that the other agency is following through correctly and effectively. As the experience in the telecommunications industry illustrates *au contraire*, a finding of dominance by the CFC should be accompanied by recurrent public reports on the effectiveness of competition which identify changes to the regulatory framework that would address competitive issues. The results of this report should be made public (or at least providing for intra-governmental oversight) and submitted to the regulator, so it can craft, and then implement, regulatory provisions that satisfy the general properties articulated by CFC. Where relevant, the CFC report should consider the potential benefits of measures such as the form of price cap regulation that will avoid anti-competitive cross-subsidisation.

*Enhance the independence of Cofetel.*

- *In the telecommunication sector, enhance the independence and role of Cofetel by appointing Commissioners for overlapping fixed terms, enhancing their tenure by making removal from office difficult, and delegating the power to issue, enforce and revoke concessions from SCT to Cofetel.* In the long-term, investment in the telecommunications industry requires the assurance that a regulatory framework will be developed, and disputes will be resolved, in an impartial, considered and efficient manner. It is desirable therefore to enhance the credibility and the independence of Cofetel by distancing the Commission even further from the SCT and from the political process in this way.

**More co-ordination and review are needed to improve the efficiency and coherence of regulations at state and local levels, and at the federal and state interface.**

The quality of Mexico's regulation is both hindered and boosted by the federal state structure. State level regulation may be frustrating reforms made at federal level. Progress in decentralising and deconcentrating regulatory powers to bring them closer to citizens and business may also create potential concerns about the future coherence and efficiency of the national regulatory system. A federal country must work harder to establish quality regulation and maintain it over time. Static losses from uncoordinated state actions can be large and durable. At the same time, the role of the states and municipalities as innovators and testing grounds for new ideas should be a national asset the can speed up change and regulatory responsiveness.

*Promote state-based reform.*

- *Co-ordinate with the state and local governments to help them to develop management capacities for quality regulation.* Initiatives in this area to date are pioneering. Still, the process is far from complete. The adoption of state based programmes of reform based on consistent principles should form the basis for more formal co-operation measures, including consideration of establishing fora for resolving issues arising from regulatory conflicts. An additional and complementary strategy should continue to be developed to help the states encourage municipalities to launch regulatory reform programmes; it is encouraging that 23 states have signed regulatory co-operation agreements with their municipalities of greatest economic importance. Continued leadership from the centre to encourage experimentation will be needed.

*Review and reform the subnational regulatory framework associated with the supply of private local infrastructure.*

- *Improve local governments' regulations governing the private sector provision of public goods and services, private concessions and government procurement.* The provision of efficient and adequate public services is crucial to attracting investment and improving competitiveness of firms at the local level. This is also a key element for territorial development. As fiscal discipline is maintained greater involvement of the private sector should be expected. This will happen only if an appropriate regulatory framework exists at the state and municipal level. The private sector has a very important role to play in the improvement of state and municipal regulations. Citizens must demand better regulation of local governments and participate in the design of schemes to improve it. Government should provide incentives to make such participation attractive or lower the costs associated with it. General solutions will be hard to impose due to the decentralisation and deconcentration efforts. Nevertheless, this should not reduce concerns for improvements. One possible model to be further investigated is the one used by a federal agency, the *Fondo para la Vivienda* (FOVI), to provide concrete incentives to implement reform proposals in the states.

*Encourage local governments to adhere to principles of efficient regulation.*

• *Heighten awareness of and encourage respect for the OECD efficient regulation principles in state and local regulatory activities affecting international trade and investment.* Because states and municipalities have important regulatory responsibilities, conflicting regulations could frustrate the free circulation of goods and services and deregulation reforms sponsored at the Federal level. With improved transparency in the preparation and adoption of Federal regulations and procedures, the absence or lack of transparency in the preparation and adoption of regulations and procedures at the state and municipal levels will also become more visible.

### Regulatory transparency should be enhanced throughout the public administration to boost investment, market entry, and innovation.

*Adoption of notice and comment procedures is a bold and important step forward. A number of other steps would also improve transparency.*

Transparency in regulatory decisions and application helps to cure many reasons for regulatory failures: capture and bias toward concentrated benefits, inadequate information in the public sector, policy rigidity, market uncertainty and inability to understand policy risks, and lack of accountability. Moreover, transparency helps create a virtuous circle – consumers trust competition more because special interests have less power to manipulate governments and markets. Also, the administration should be accountable for its use of regulatory discretion and for the policy performance of regulation. Mexico has made significant efforts to increase transparency in its regulatory procedures. Nevertheless, further enhancement is needed for it to become ingrained in the public administration's practices. As previously recommended, a great opportunity for change lies in expanding the scope and authority of the Administrative Procedures Law and linking it more explicitly to regulatory reform. Professional and cultural change in the administration will not come easily. The policy reforms suggested will require new training programmes, new skill mixes, and new funding in some cases.

*Make public consultations a requirement, not a suggestion.*

• *Further improve transparency by extending legal requirements for notice and comment procedure to all ministries and agencies during the develop-*

97

*ment and revision of regulation. Procedures for openness should be standardised for all advisory bodies.* Adoption of a general consultation requirement covering all substantive new laws and lower-level rules would promote both the technical values of policy effectiveness and the democratic values of openness and accountability of government. Notice and comment processes are based on clear rights to access and response, are systematic and non-discretionary, and are open to the general public as well as organised interest groups. Advisory groups may continue to be needed to establish dialogue with experts and interest groups, and standard procedures for their use are necessary to ensure that they do not undermine the transparency of the regulatory system.

*Make RIAs more widely available to the public for information.*

- *Make mandatory the publication through the Internet of the regulatory impact analysis (RIAs) prepared for proposed regulations.* While Mexico is well advanced in disseminating federal formalities and regulations through the Internet, greater public availability of RIAs for all proposed regulations would further assist the public, including foreign participants, in understanding potential implications of those regulations. It would also act as an additional check and balance feature to minimise potential risk of regulatory capture.

*Enhance the consultation arrangements in the telecommunications sector.*

- In the telecommunications sector, establish formal consultation and transparency procedures for Cofetel with the government, the industry and the public to enhance the level of participation and improve the quality of decision making. Improved decision-making and consultation processes and publication of the reasons for all decisions would reduce the risk of litigation and would improve the overall quality of Cofetel's decisions. Cofetel has indicated that it intends to implement this policy during 1999. It should make all deliberate haste to do so. In particular, the CFC should have full opportunity to express its views.

**To improve policy performance and coherence, regulations should be reviewed systematically to ensure that they are consistent with market-oriented policies and principles for quality regulation.**

The Mexican regulatory reform policy started with very focused reviews of sectoral laws and regulations. Progressively, the UDE invested resources in organising a regulatory management system based on central oversight of the flow of new regulations. This effort was complemented by a systematic review of existing formalities. Despite this combined effort, more attention and resources are needed to review and up-date the vast body of existing laws and other regulations, in such crucial horizontal policy areas as bankruptcy, corporate governance or labour laws, as well as some economic and social areas such as water management (which is shared with sub-federal governments). The 1999 reform proposals in the electricity sector appear to be a step toward a more dynamism and efficiency in this important sector. Meanwhile, technological changes in telecommunications and electricity and the need to promote competition in airlines and other transport modes will require constant updating and adjusting of their regulatory environments.

*Make the review of existing requirements more systematic and effective.*

- *Adopt a more systematic and comprehensive approach to the review of existing laws and regulations.* More attention should be paid to systematic review and upgrading of regulation, by means such as a rolling review based on a prioritisation of policy areas. Structuring of an effective review process will be key to its results, and may require strengthening the capacities and resources of the UDE and co-ordination with the competition authority. The Australian competition principles review, which includes both federal and state governments, provides an interesting model. Such reviews should be based on benefit-cost principles, that is, on maximising social welfare. In key sectors, the reinvention principle should guide the reviews. The effectiveness and speed of more comprehensive sectoral plans based on all policy measures needed for results, including regulations but also other forms of intervention such as subsidies, procurement policies, and tax policies, has been demonstrated in other countries. The "reinvention" of sectoral regimes, based in part on international benchmarks, allows reformers to consider policy linkages and related measures needed to make reform effective, to package related reforms into a coherent programme, and to reassure market entrants that reform is credible and predictable. Adopting reform steps in law, rather than leaving the timing of the steps to the ministries, will further strengthen the accountability, credibility, and sustainability of reform.

- *Review laws and regulations in order to improve the concession system. In the past, concessions have been a costly, complex, opaque and overly discretionary way to regulate the private sector in the Mexican network and natural resources industries.* In many sectors, a more precise delimitation of which activities should be considered public services would help to transform many concessions into permits and licences or even replace them with other regulatory alternatives. A second and parallel initiative could be to review the remaining concessions related to a smaller core of specific public services and improve them in order to reduce the unnecessary discretion involved in their management.

- *In the telecommunications sector, ensure that full use of mandatory quality controls established by the government for the review of its regulatory powers is made in the telecommunications sector.* The regulatory policies of Cofetel are among the more important regulatory controls in any sector. It is especially important that the powers of Cofetel be subject to the government's regulatory quality controls.

***Progress has been made, but consumers will benefit from lower prices and more choice, and enterprises will gain from tougher competition and faster innovation, if markets are more fully opened to international trade and investment.***

- *Intensify efforts to use existing international standards when they are efficient and to participate more actively in the development of internationally-*

*harmonised standards as the basis of domestic regulations.* Reliance on internationally-harmonised measures as the basis of domestic regulations can facilitate the expansion of domestic production capacity and support the export-orientation of Mexican firms.

- *Seek to ensure that bilateral or regional approaches to regulatory co-operation are designed and implemented in ways which will encourage broader multilateral application.* Mutual recognition of regulations or conformity assessment procedures and other approaches to intergovernmental regulatory co-operation offer promising avenues for the lowering of regulatory barriers to trade and investment. Efforts carried out under regional agreements should actively be pursued in a broader perspective of international organisations with multilateral applications.

**In the telecommunications sector, further regulatory reform and market-opening would boost consumer benefits.**

- *Delegate the power to issue, enforce and revoke concessions from SCT to Cofetel.* The value of establishing an independent, transparent regulatory entity is reduced when its powers are limited. The power to issue, enforce and revoke concessions is appropriately exercised by Cofetel.

- *Disclose the total amount of spectrum that could technically be used for a new service prior to auctioning new spectrum.* Spectrum auctions provide the government with a financial interest in the artificial creation of spectrum scarcity and consequent reduction in competition. In order to offset concerns that more spectrum may be available than is sold, Cofetel should disclose the total amount of spectrum that could be feasibly made available for a particular technology prior to auctioning new spectrum.

*Implement new regulations on Telmex as a dominant carrier.*

- *Implement and enforce asymmetric regulation for the dominant carrier in conformance with Article 63 of the FTL.* The Telmex concession played an important role in the transition to competition by establishing a fixed timeline for the rebalancing of Telmex's charges and establishing procedures and policies governing interconnection and other competition safeguards. However, this rebalancing is now complete (or almost complete) and the important competition safeguards are more fully set out in the FTL. As has been argued, the price-cap regime in the Telmex concession creates competition problems. Transparency and legal certainty would be enhanced by placing Telmex under the regulation that is appropriate for a dominant firm, applied under Article 63 of the FTL.

*Ensure that barriers to entry are kept as low as possible.*

- *Limit the discretion of Cofetel to grant concessions and to impose conditions on concessions. Issue concessions that do not restrict lines of business. Minimise coverage and commitments required of the concessionaires.* One of the most important requirements for healthy competition is low barriers to entry. At present Cofetel has the power to impose conditions on concessionaires. Although there is little evidence that the conditions imposed have significantly hindered new entry, this power may itself in the longer term become a potential threat to competition.

- *Reconsider the proportional return system for international traffic with the US and with other countries as competition develops.* The proportional return system with the US and other countries is a restraint on competition in the international long-distance market which increases prices paid by Mexican consumers.

- *Amend the FTL to eliminate, for carriers which are non-dominant, the requirement for Cofetel to register and publicise prices.* Competition on prices is one of the most fundamental forms of competition. This competition is threatened by a system in which competitors have advance knowledge of each other's price changes and can observe each other's discounts. This requirement should be eliminated for all except dominant carriers. This would require changes to the FTL.

**Improve the transparency of the interconnection regime.**

- *Undertake a number of policies to improve the foundations on which interconnection charges are set, namely: clearly identify the components of interconnection charges which are designed to compensate for the fixed and common costs of local service; allow the process of rebalancing to be completed by allowing Telmex to raise its prices for local service (especially business local service) to eliminate any remaining deficit; and pursue other approaches to the covering a deficit on local service (if one exists) through other mechanisms (such as the fund mechanism below).* The deficit on Telmex's local service is an important component in Cofetel's argument for above-cost interconnection charges. At a minimum the portion of access charges which is intended to contribute towards this deficit should be separately and clearly identified. Restraining Telmex's rebalancing increases the size of the deficit on Telmex's local service and thereby raises interconnection charges. Ideally, it is more appropriate for the deficit to be funded through a broad-based tax on general revenues or a tax on less elastic telecommunications services, which can be more easily achieved through the use of a formal fund. Finally, under current proposals, Cofetel is forced to make arbitrary, controversial decisions as to when networks qualify for the higher interconnection charges. This could be eliminated by basing charges on whether the originating line serves a residential or business customer.

- *Structure interconnection charges according to the underlying cost – especially, adopt a flat per call charge for interconnection for local calls and reduce real interconnection charges over time according to best practice to ensure that Telmex improves productivity.* Given that local calls are currently charged on a per minute basis in Mexico, charging interconnection for local calls on a per-minute basis introduces opportunities for distorting and anti-competitive behaviour. Reductions in the costs of providing interconnection services should be passed on to new entrants.

**Establish a competitively and technologically neutral funding mechanism for universal service.**

- *Promote network expansion, universal service and economic efficiency objectives by establishing an explicit, portable, competitively and technologically neutral funding mechanism.* There is some evidence that local service rates in Mexico are approaching consumers' willingness-to-pay. It may therefore be appropriate to subsidise consumers on to the network at the margin, using a mechanism that relies on market forces, is competitively and technologically neutral, and is administered in a transparent fashion.

*Implement number portability and access to rights of way as soon as possible.*

- *Develop and carry out plans to implement number portability and access to rights of way as soon as possible.* Plans to introduce number portability and rules to assure access to rights-of-way appear to be at an early stage. An absence of number portability acts as an artificial disincentive for customers to switch from the incumbent to a new entrant because such switching imposes transaction costs, such as the burden of informing others of their new number. Moving forward toward full implementation of a permanent form of number portability would be an important step to assuring that subscribers do not face artificial disincentives to switching between carriers in response to price competition. Similarly, progress on developing an effective regime to assure appropriate access to rights-of-way is also quite important in order to ensure that there are no artificial regulatory barriers to entry into local service markets. This especially applies to the activities of local authorities.

- *Restrict the price cap to only those services in which there is an absence of competition.* A revenue cap that covers both competitive and non-competitive services enhances the incentives on the incumbent to act anti-competitively in the competitive market. With the present degree of competition in the long-distance market, it is no longer necessary to regulate Telmex's rates. These rates should be removed from the price-cap by relaxing the price regulation set out in the concession or regulating Telmex's prices through some other mechanism, such as Article 63 of the FTL.

- *Dominant local carriers should be prevented from restricting competition by acquiring existing cable television infrastructure.* Cable television infrastructure is an important source of potential competition in local telephony. In most cases strict enforcement of competition law can prevent a local telephony provider from purchasing a cable television infrastructure (on the basis that it reduces potential competition). In addition, requiring Telmex to divest its existing holdings in cable television should be considered.

*Develop formal co-operation arrangements between Cofetel and CFC.*

- *Develop formal co-operation arrangements between Cofetel and CFC for the joint enforcement of competition law prohibitions in the telecommunications sector.* Given the substantial links between the functions of Cofetel and CFC, it is important for them to develop a consistent approach to preventing anti-competitive behaviour. This could be facilitated through explicit formal co-operation and interaction arrangements.

- *Increase the maximum sanctions set out in the FTL to a level at which the sanctions could have a material impact.* The current maximum monetary sanctions in the FTL are derisory. The threat to revoke a concession after three violations is a draconian measure that is unlikely to be taken in practice. The monetary sanctions should be enhanced to a level where they could be expected to make a real impact on even the largest concessionaires.

## MANAGING REGULATORY REFORM

Notwithstanding the extensive support from the business community, a fundamental issue to sustaining regulatory reform will be to broaden its constituency to consumers and citizens and, in parallel, to increase involvement of the Congress, which is expanding its role in policy development. The guiding principle for reform of sectoral governance, namely regulatory quality rather than deregulation, should be made more explicit and its implications clarified to a wider range of social interests.

It can also be expected that producing these public benefits will entail some private costs, as competition erodes the security of those who benefit from market power. Thus shareholders in these sectors are likely to resist change, in order to avoid those losses to themselves. Efforts to avoid costs to these parties will impose costs on the economy and the consumer, as the competitive benefits of lower prices and greater choice are deferred.

# NOTES

1. **Milestones in the management of regulatory reform:** creation of the Economic Deregulation Unit (1989); Federal Metrology and Standards Law (1992, 1997); Federal Competition Law (1992, 1998); Federal Administrative Procedures Law (1994, 1996); Presidential Decree for Business Deregulation (1995); and Regulatory Impact Analysis (1996-1997, 1999).
   **Specific external reforms include:** GATT (1986) and unilateral tariff reductions; APEC (1993); OCDE (1994); and free trade agreements with Chile (1992), the United States and Canada (1994), Bolivia (1995), Colombia and Venezuela (1995), and Nicaragua (1998).
   **Specific internal sectoral reforms include:** trucking and bus transportation (1989-1990); maritime transportation (1991-1993); land tenure reform (1992); co-generation and self-supply of electricity (1992-1993); roads (1994); ports (1994); telecommunications (1995); railroads (1995); natural gas (1995); satellites (1995-1996); civil aviation (1995, 1998); foreign investment (1996); civil and mercantile judicial procedures – federal, Mexico City and Nuevo León (1996); mining – auctions (1996); environment (1996); reforms to the commercial code (1996); guarantee trusts and Mortgage securitization – reforms at the federal level and in 16 states (1996-1998); pension funds (1997); airports (1997-1998); generic drugs (1997-1999); and the removal of all price controls -- including tortilla (1992-1999).

2. According to Gavin (1996), a failed 1972 attempt to reform the tax system left tax revenues stagnant.

3. By 1982, state-owned enterprises produced 14% of national output, employed 4.4% of the labour force, and accounted for 38% of fixed capital investment.

4. It reached almost 30%. Source: Banco de Mexico, 1990.

5. The balance on goods and services averaged +1.4% of GDP between 1983-87, while net new lending averaged 0.7% of GDP, and this came from international financial institutions as foreign banks steadily reduced their exposure.

6. Maximum tariffs were lowered from 45% to 20% and practically all import licences were eliminated, with important exceptions in key sectors like automobiles.

7. The 1995 OECD *Economic Survey* noted: "Mexico's fiscal position in 1994, in terms of both the primary surplus and the overall financial balance, was one of the most favourable among OECD countries, while its public-sector debt was among the lowest", p. 25.

8. Real GDP growth in 1989 averaged 3.2% but was not so high in per capita terms; Mexico's population grew at 2.7% over the same period.

9. Manufacturing, including the *maquiladora* sector, moved from 61% to 81% of total exports between 1987 and 1994. OECD (1996), Table 2.

10. Averaged over 1991-1993, the present value of Mexico's future debt service obligations (a measure of the stock of debt) amounted to 184% of exports of goods and services and 36% of GDP. On the World Bank Debt Tables, Mexico's debt stock relative to its level of exports places it in the moderately indebted category. World Bank (1998).

11. The 1995 OECD *Economic Survey* noted: "[Following financial sector privatisation and reform] the area of most rapid credit growth were in personal-sector lending, including mortgages and credit card loans... in 1994, there was a major acceleration in bank financing to businesses." In fact rapid credit expansion shared many of the characteristics of asset bubbles found in other OECD countries (*e.g.* US, Japan) in the mid-1980s, and with ultimately similar results (see Box 1.2).

12. In fact these interest rates were sufficiently unattractive to foreign investors given the perceived increase in risk that the government had to resort to issuing dollar-denominated debt – "tesobonos" – during 1994 to

meet its financing, needs. For a more detailed and nuanced account of the difficult choices facing the Mexican authorities at the time, see Chapter 1 in the 1995 OECD *Economic Survey*.

13. This was revealed in the strong performance of exports – dollar manufacturing export volumes grew by 29% in 1995, compared to 12% increase in export market growth, and the trade balance went from –2% to +4% of GDP (see Figures 1, 3).

14. Oil represented 80% of Mexico's exports in 1982; it only represented 6.5% in 1998.

15. In the case of rail freight, service was so unreliable that customers never knew where, when or whether their freight was going to arrive. Problems were similar for passenger services.

16. The status of infrastructure in several key sectors:

   • Highways: most of Mexico's highway infrastructure was completed prior to the 1980s. New road developments reached a virtual standstill after 1982. During this period, the federal government started to divert toll revenues to nonhighway uses. Towards the end of the decade, the backlog in road maintenance affected about 50% of the federal highway system.

   • Railways were characterised by increasingly poor and unreliable service and declined in importance. During the 1980s the volume of freight and passenger transport dropped by over 25%.

   • Energy production: from 1983 on Pemex postponed and cancelled investments in the petrochemical and natural gas sector.

   • In ports, the inadequate services provided and the lack of modern infrastructure resulted in a low level of activity compared with other countries.

   • In telephony, demand was increasing at an annual rate of 12%. The government was incapable of financing the needed infrastructure investment, and neither was Telmex. Revenue per line was 60% of levels found in the US and the UK. This led to a widening capacity gap. See Tandon (1996).

17. In 1982, state-owned enterprises received subsidies and transfers equal to 12.7% of GDP, produced 14% of national output, employed 4.4 per cent of the labour force, and accounted for 38% of fixed capital investment. For instance, according to Tandon (1996), for the period 1982-87, Aeroméxico (one of the state-owned airlines) received subsidies each year from the government equal to about 15% of its revenues. SIDERMEX, a steel conglomerate, accumulated losses in two decades of more than US$10 billion. Aspe (1993). It must be pointed out, however, that not all SOEs were poorly run or unprofitable. Telmex, for example, was among the better run state firms in Mexico.

18. Annual subsidies to the railroads alone were running at $300 million prior to privatisation.

19. This was in part based on the turn of the century experience of seeing foreign investment concentrate in the small, urban and rich market.

20. The government actions came in response to the failure of traffic volumes to meet guarantees contained in the original contracts.

21. Effective tariffs measure the tariff of a final good relative to its imports, so that high effective tariffs encourage imports of the raw material inputs and not the final good.

22. OECD (1997), *Environmental Performance Reviews for Mexico* stated that "the government has put forward in the past two years a steady number of reforms by instituting integrated permitting, increasing the economic efficiency of regulation; simplifying administrative procedures; strengthening enforcement procedures; extending mechanisms to improve compliance; furthering decentralisation and devolution; guaranteeing the right to know; and enhancing public participation", pp. 20-21. The Industry and Trade Ministry indicated that deregulation of sanitary licences in this area has benefited over 450 000 companies, without any resulting danger to public health.

23. "Privatisation [was] followed by a 24 percentage point increase in the ratio of operating income to sales... The gains in profitability were roughly decomposed as 10% of the increase is due to higher product prices; 33% of the increase represents a transfer form laid-off workers, and productivity gains account for the residual 57%. Transfers from society to the firm are partially offset by taxes which absorb slightly over half the gains in operating income". La Porta, Rafael, Florencio Lopez-de-Silanes, 1997, p. 1.

24. Data provided by CINTRA, the holding company for Mexicana and Aeroméxico, shows lower prices in Mexico. This data presents prices on individual routes of comparable length between the two countries rather than average prices, and the individual route pairs chosen are systematically those US routes subject to very low volumes and levels of competition. Data from private consultants reports confirms the statement in the text.

25. This seems to be occurring despite strict accounting separation. Pre-tax returns on assets for local calls in 1997 was 18% compared to a loss on long distance assets of around 12%, plus the local market is bigger.

26.  The average owner-operator is 17 years old, single person/single truck firms, and small firms are unable to expand due to lack of financing and entrepreneurial capacity.

27.  95% of the firms which started to export between 1993 and 1997 were firms exporting less than US$10 million.

28.  In addition, Mexico's international commitments (WTO, NAFTA, FTAs) were essential in bolstering Mexico's adherence to open markets. Mexico regained access to international financial markets in seven months in 1995; after the 1982 crisis, it took Mexico seven years.

29.  One of the winners of a railway concession is one of the construction companies involved in the highway debacle. Though this may reflect problems in transparency in the bidding process, the fact that the same companies reappear over and over in terms of ownership of privatised assets and concessions reveals both the concentration of financing and managerial expertise and the need for financial sector reforms to increase the pool of potential owners. Mexico's law forbids discriminatory rejection of companies applying for concessions. If a firm is in good standing, then its proposal must be considered in the same manner as all others.

30.  Reforms in civil and mercantile judicial proceedings in 1996 (including the Commercial Code) greatly reduced both the number and the duration of trials.

31.  The federal government is currently preparing a reform to the public registry of commerce. The public registries of property are under municipalities' jurisdictions. The federal government is working on a scheme to promote modernisation of the property registries so that they may be compatible and simultaneously searchable.

32.  Comision Federal de la Competencia (1998), *Annual Report [to OECD Competition Law and Policy Committee] on Competition Policy Developments in Mexico* (1997).

33.  OECD Competition Law and Policy Committee (1997), *Aide-Memoire of In-Depth Examination of Competition Policy in Mexico.*

34.  Comision Federal de la Competencia (1998), *Annual Report [to OECD Competition Law and Policy Committee] on Competition Policy Developments in Mexico* (1997).

35.  Article 14 of the Mexican Constitution.

36.  See Richard D. Baker (1971), *Judicial Review in Mexico: A Study of the Amparo Suit.*

37.  See the submission of the Mexican Government in the context of the 1997 WTO Trade Policy Review. Mexico indicated that it had unilaterally eliminated tariffs on an MFN basis on 1 200 products, thus increasing the number of duty-free products from 414 in 1993 to 1,658 in 1997. This tariff elimination primarily concerned inputs and machinery used in agricultural, chemical, electrical, electronic, textiles and publishing sectors.

38.  NAFTA and the five other Free Trade Agreements, respectively with: Colombia and Venezuela (G-3); Costa Rica; Bolivia; Nicaragua; and Chile. Mexico also grants unilateral preferences to a number of developing countries under the Generalised System of Preferences.

39.  One important example was the creation in 1994 of AVANTEL, a venture between MCI Communications Corporation and Grupo Financiero Banamex-Accival (Banacci) to offer long distance and other telecommunications services in Mexico. MCI owns 45% of the company.

*Annex* 1

# FIGURES

Figure 1. **Mexico exports, imports and trade balance**

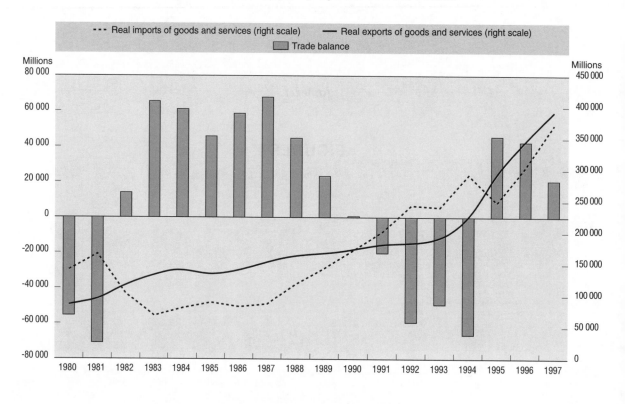

Figure 2. **Mexico income indicators**
Annual growth rates in percentage

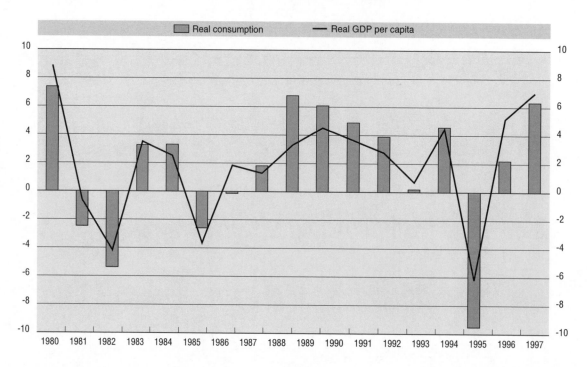

*Source:* OECD database.

### Figure 3. **Mexico external inflows and outflows**
As a percentage of GDP

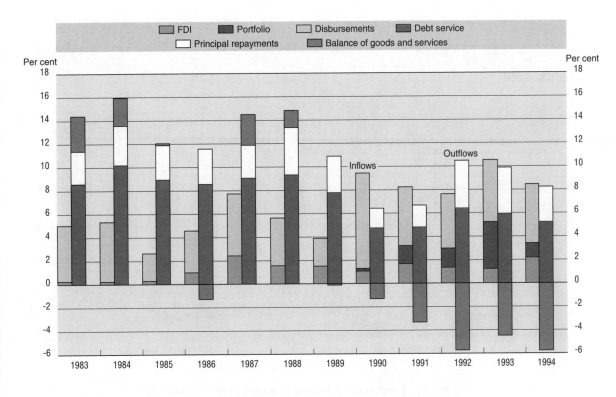

### Figure 4. **Real exchange rate and external balances**

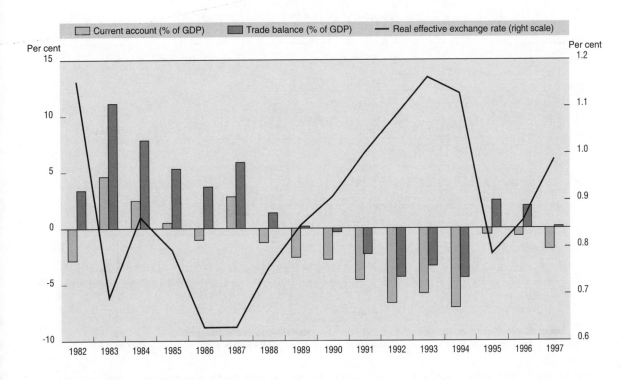

*Source:* OECD database.

*111*

Figure 5a. **Mexico growth performance in manufacturing**
***vs* OECD countries**

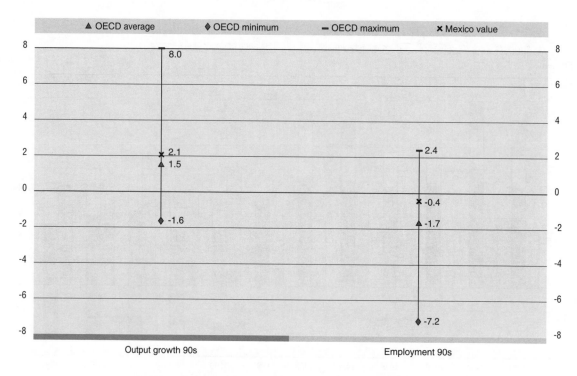

Figure 5b. **Mexico performance in levels in manufacturing**
***vs* OECD countries (OECD = 100)**

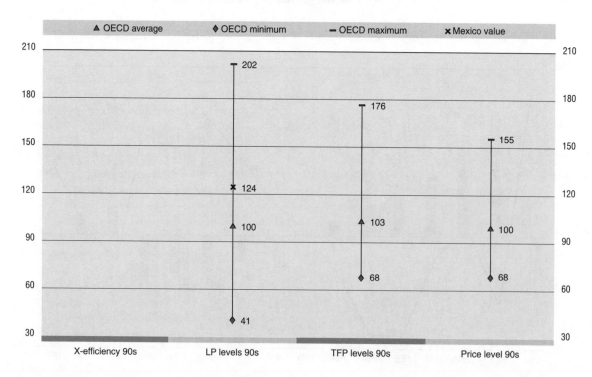

*Note:* For each figure the vertical line covers the range of all values from the maximum to the minimum of the relevant group of countries.
*Source:* OECD.

OECD 1999

Figure 6a. **Mexico growth performance in electric power**
***vs* OECD countries**

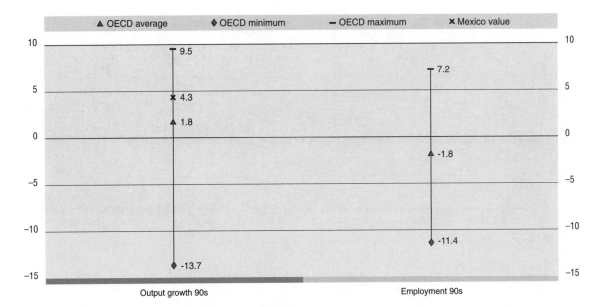

Figure 6b. **Mexico performance in levels in electric power**
***vs* OECD countries**

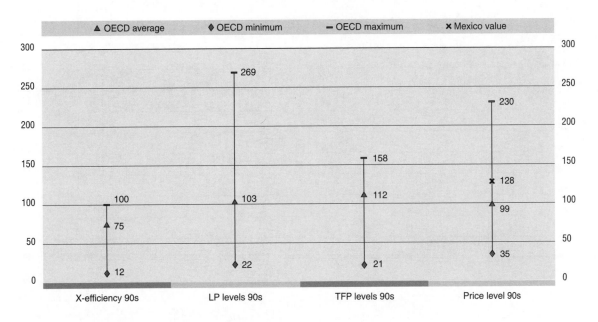

*Notes:*  For each figure the vertical line covers the range of all values from the maximum to the minimum of the relevant group of countries.
Output = net electricity production.
Employment = total employment.
Labour productivity (LP) = net electricity production/employment.
Total factor productivity (TFP) = output is net electricity production, inputs are employees and total installed capacity (the labour share is set 0.25 which is the OECD average for electricity, gas and water).
DEA = data envelope analysis with net electricity production as output and labour and installed capacity as inputs.
Price level = business electricity price, converted with GDP-PPP.
*Source:*  International Energy Agency.

Figure 7a.    **Mexico growth performance in telecommunications
*vs* OECD countries**

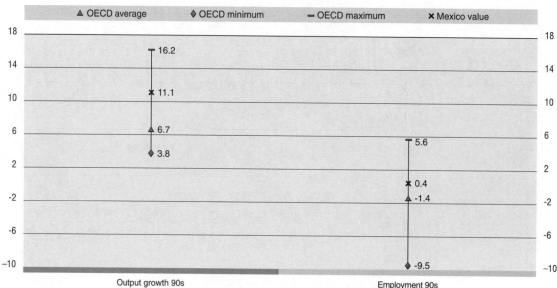

| ▲ OECD average | ◆ OECD minimum | — OECD maximum | ✕ Mexico value |

Output growth 90s

Employment 90s

Figure 7b.    **Mexico performance in levels in telecommunications
*vs* OECD countries**

| ▲ OECD average | ◆ OECD minimum | — OECD maximum | ✕ Mexico value |

X-efficiency 90s          LP levels 90s          TFP levels 90s          Price level 90s

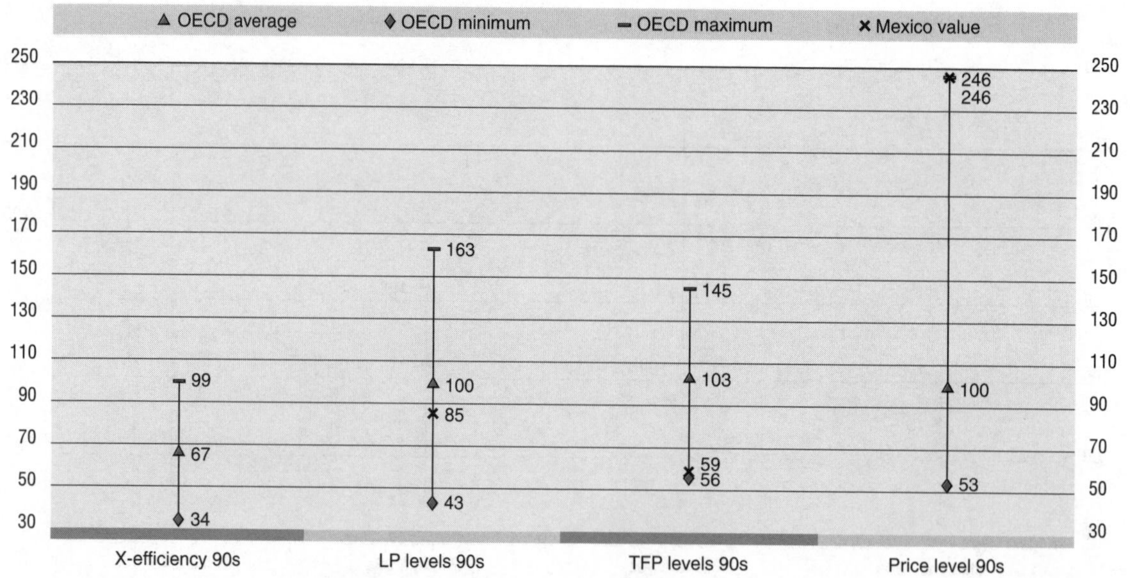

*Notes:*    For each figure the vertical line covers the range of all values from the maximum to the minimum of the relevant group of countries.
Output = mainlines + cellular subscribers.
Employment = total employment.
Labour productivity (LP) = mainlines + cellular subscribers/employment.
Total factor productivity (TFP) = capital is calculated using the perpetual inventory method and the investment PPP (the labour share is set to 0.54 which the OECD average for communications).
DEA = results of data envelope analysis with revenue (converted with sectoral PPP), mainlines + cellular subscribers and numbers of pay phone as output concepts and employment and capital (as in TFP) as inputs.
Price level = simple average of a basket of services (including business and residential prices of local, trunk and international fixed voice telephony, mobile telephony, leased lines and Internet).
*Source:*    OECD Telecommunications database 1997, *OECD Communications Outlook* 1997.

Figure 8*a*. **Mexico growth performance in air passenger transport**
*vs* **OECD countries**

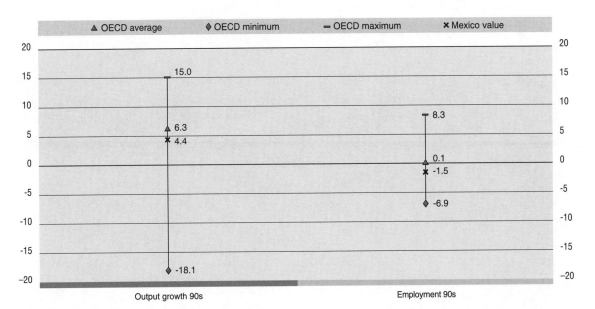

Figure 8*b*. **Mexico performance in levels in air passenger transport**
*vs* **OECD countries**

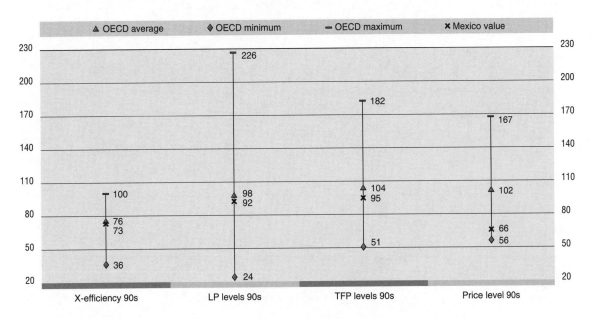

*Notes:* For each figure the vertical line covers the range of all values from the maximum to the minimum of the relevant group of countries.
Output = transported passenger-km (TPK).
Employment = total employment.
Labour productivity (LP) = TPK/employment.
Total factor productivity (TFP) = output is TPK and capital is total seating capacity (the labour share is set to 0.6, which is the OECD average for transport).
DEA = data envelope analysis using passengers transported and TPK as output and total personnel, numbers of planes, km flown and total seat capacity as inputs.
Price level = operating revenue per TPK.
*Sources:* Institut du transport aérien (ITA) and OECD.

Annex 2

# REGULATORY REFORM IN ROAD TRANSPORTATION

*This annex was written by Mark Dutz (World Bank), Aydin Hayri (Deloitte and Touche) and Pablo Ibarra (Woodrow Wilson School, Princeton University). It was prepared under funding from the World Bank research preparation grant "Competition and barriers to entrepreneurship" (RPO-682-57).*

One of Mexico's major reform programmes has been deregulating its road freight industry. Transportation service is a critical input to other businesses. Inefficiency in transportation services and monopoly in transportation markets add costs and cut output in other sectors of the economy. Today, more efficient transport and logistics systems have become a source of competitive advantage. Tolerating inefficiencies in freight transport can cripple a country's efforts to enhance its overall competitiveness.

Before the reform process began in 1989, freight transport on Mexico's federal highways was subject to rigid regulation. The number of firms was limited, and competition among them was minimal. Companies could not compete with better service or with lower prices, so service was poor and prices were high. After ten years of reform, entry and pricing are free, the industry is growing strongly, prices are declining, and service and innovation are improving. More needs to be done, particularly to bring the informal trucking sector up to modern standards, but the benefits of reform to date are already clear.

### Trucking, a vital service in Mexico, was regulated as a cartel.

Road freight services are the most important of all transport services in Mexico. In 1995, road freight accounted for 40% of gross value added of the transport and storage sectors. Competition between road and rail freight is limited, because officially-set tariff policies led to the two sectors concentrating on different kinds of freight. In addition, the rail system was hampered by the radial structure of the track network and operational problems in the state-run rail company.

A background issue affecting the efficiency of the trucking industry is the quality of the road system. Despite its heavy reliance on trucking, Mexico's highway system is sparse and inadequate. Of its nearly 50 000 km of paved federal roads, about 6 000 km are so-called concession highways, which are privately-owned toll roads. Most of these have been built since 1989. Although a welcome development, these new highways are grossly under-utilised, mostly because their tolls are very expensive.

Government regulation of the trucking industry in Mexico extends back to the late 1940s. The apparent rationale for regulation was concern that open competition might disrupt economic activity, because prices would be variable and service would be uncertain, especially in remote areas. In addition, it may have been feared that competition would encourage excessive cost cutting and lead to more accidents or pollution.

Federal policy strictly controlled entry. To provide general freight services to the public, truckers needed a federal trucking concession, issued by the Ministry of Communications and Transport (SCT). Incumbent firms received preferences in expanding fleets and in objecting to expansion by others. Operating permission was route-specific. Regulations required channelling all traffic through freight centres, a process that helped police the resulting cartels. Official trucking tariffs were set by SCT, presumably above the competitive level and high enough to balance, on average, both fixed and variable costs and yield "reasonable" profits. The rate was uniform for all seasons and for all regions of the country.

The state also accepted cartels and monopolies in other aspects of freight handling. Multimodal, created by SCT, had a monopoly on door-to-door delivery of international container traffic. And SCT granted other concessions for handling cargo movements at borders and railroad stations, limiting entry and encouraging cartels.

Economic issues were thus heavily regulated. But other aspects of trucking operation, such as vehicle dimensions and weight limits, technical vehicle safety, or pollution, were not. That is, the system depended on the presumed effect of eliminating competition to promote these goals.

The net result of the complex of regulations, whatever their motivation, was what is typically expected from cartels: poor service, high prices, and inflexibility. Route controls and other restrictions encouraged firms to offer services jointly, so shippers often had no choice of carrier. And they required costly empty backhauling and market segmentation that further prevented competition. Collusion between Multimodal and the freight centres led to a system of surcharges and unofficial payments which often far exceeded the stated tariffs. Poor service confined container traffic to port areas, undermining its potential efficiency.

Rigid regulations not only stimulated collusion among formal truckers, but also led to the development of a substantial informal trucking sector. These small-owned operators, the *transportistas piratas*, avoided all legal constraints, incurred lower administrative costs, and paid no taxes. Even under extensive regulation, there was thus a certain degree of competition, at the low-end of the market, from illegal operators offering bargain prices.

The regulatory regime ended up limiting the supply of higher-quality logistics services. Shippers that required better and faster service could obtain it at negotiated, higher-than-official prices. But the system of cargo-sharing made it difficult even for a larger trucking company to provide such service consistently. The freight centre system and intervention by the national trucking industry chamber, CANACAR, usually prevented shippers and carriers from developing long-term relationships in which reputation and quality of service matter. So there was little investment in quality improvements.

### Trucking was an early object of the reform programme.

Trucking was one of the first objects of the government's move toward deregulation in the late 1980s. The government's vision was a competitive trucking industry with free exit and entry and market-based pricing, without intrusive government regulation. Unblocking this major supply bottleneck and correcting the market imperfections were deemed essential to achieve more rapid and sustainable growth. The United States had deregulated interstate trucking a few years before, and the economic benefits were evidently substantial. Since regulation was even more heavy-handed in Mexico, the Mexican authorities had every reason to expect even bigger welfare gains. A 1987 SCT report estimated the welfare costs of trucking regulation at 0.5% of GNP.

The reformers had to deal with the possibility that opposition from CANACAR could have immobilised the country. To avoid interest-group pressures, the draft proposal was prepared by a small group outside the transport ministry, indeed without open consultations with SCT or other parties. To gain support from the CANACAR, the proposals emphasised modernisation, rather than deregulation, and did not identify strengthening competition as an explicit objective. The government negotiated an agreement with CANACAR in 1989, under which CANACAR agreed to cooperate with deregulation and modernisation, and the government offered loans at preferential rates to truckers who wanted to renovate their fleets.

A regulation issued the following day, July 7, 1989 eliminated most entry restrictions. Thus the government effectively abandoned the public service concept of requiring concession. These regulations also allowed discounting, by treating the "official" tariffs as maximum rates. Six months later, another decree eliminated the maximum rate controls, too, so rates to be freely negotiated between truckers and customers. The principal reason the delay between the two decrees was SCT's concern that if all deregulation actions were taken at once, the forces of competition might have been too weak to prevent sharp price rises.

Deregulation was thus implemented by presidential regulation, rather than legislation. The new law was not published until late 1993, and the new regulation, not until late 1994. This delay generated uncertainty, as many carriers were not clearly informed of the new rules or expected them to be reversed. The motivation for this phased approach was strategic. The reformers anticipated that legislative reform would take substantial time and meet stiff resistance in the Congress. In the meantime, between the 1989 regulation and the 1993 legislation, the imminence of NAFTA accelerated the effective implementation of the reforms.

### The new law indeed represents a fundamental departure from the old system.

Entry is free, requiring only a permit, not a concession. An entrant need only prove identity and vehicle ownership, and establish insurance and pollution compliance to get a federal trucking permit. The federal state no longer has any discretion regarding authorisation. The law abolished the limits on the number of entrants and the incumbent trucking companies' power over the entry process. Private own-account operators can transport third-party cargo, and thus all restrictions on backhaul are eliminated. Containers can be transported without Multimodal's services. In January 1990, customs restrictions on using international containers for domestic cargo were lifted, and new regulations ended exclusive rights for cargo handling services customs facilities, and border crossings.

Routes are no longer controlled. Trucks can transport interstate cargo throughout Mexico, and direct shipments between former corridors are permitted without additional costs. Freight centres no longer control cargoes. Truckers do not have to belong to freight centres to obtain cargo and shippers are free to use the trucker of their choice.

These changes greatly reduced SCT's responsibilities. Its road transport functions now include road maintenance, transport policy, and highway safety. It took some time to reduce the number of SCT personnel, though. Reportedly, as the benefits of the new policy have become evident, and as SCT staff previously involved in regulatory matters have departed, SCT has become strongly committed to the new policy.

### In response to the new freedoms, the industry grew, but it remains segmented.

The number of registered trucks increased dramatically. Between 1989 and 1996, the number of registered units increased 92%, with the most striking increase between 1989 and 1992, precisely concurrent with the regulatory reform. And in spite of a 7% decline between 1993 and 1994, the number of units in 1996 had again surpassed 1993 levels. Three reasons for the increase are entry of new firms, expansion of existing firms, and legal registration of formerly non-registered *transportistas piratas*. With entry barriers lower, many informal carriers decided to register and avoid the risks and costs of operating illegally. Still, most of the increase was new entrants, suggesting that the amount of competition among truckers may have increased substantially. Lower tariffs and improved service induced some producers to give up their own in-house truck fleets, and instead contract for services from public providers.

The segmentation of the industry between technologically more advanced, concentrated large firms and low-technology, small fringe firms has continued. The number of large firms (with over 100 trucks) is increasing, from about 150 in 1988 to nearly 190 in 1996. They accounted for 65% of national haulage and 87% of transborder transport in 1994. These firms provide services based on long-term contracts and cover main routes. Foreign ownership restrictions have fostered formal agreements and alliance between United States carriers and larger Mexican trucking companies. By contrast, the large number of owner-operators and small firms cover short hauls, urban markets and cargo consolidation.

## Competition enforcement supported reform.

The long history of government intervention and control left a strong imprint on post-reform market conduct. When regulation by government was removed, previously-favoured market participants tried to replace government control by inter-firm agreements. Sustaining reform required strong competition policy enforcement.

In 1994, the Mexican competition authority, CFC, took action against CANACAR for price fixing. CANACAR had prepared and distributed a reference price guide for truckers to use in negotiating with shippers. The document's specific aim was to set minimum prices. CFC exacted a fine from CANACAR and ordered CANACAR not to do it again and to withdraw the price guide from circulation.

CANACAR then consulted the CFC about a cost accounting programme for its members. The CFC concluded that better information obtained by using this costing methodology could improve efficiency. But the CFC also took into consideration CANACAR's price fixing record. So CFC warned CANACAR that examples on how to use the methodology would have to be strictly illustrative, and ordered that materials must state that using the methodologies and estimates to fix prices would violate the law.

And in 1997 the CFC challenged market division agreements in the transport and distribution of diesel fuel. One was for distribution of products sold by *Pemex-Refinacion* (which tacitly accepted the arrangement).

## The economic benefits of reform have been great.

As expected, introducing competition lowered prices and increased output. Prices for services of equivalent quality have fallen by at least 30%. Between 1987 and 1994, trucking rates nation-wide declined 23% in real terms. Traffic volume increased over 50% between 1989 and 1995. And distances travelled increased substantially more than volumes carried, showing that one effect was longer trips to new and further locations.

Better quality services are now available, too. NAFTA, as well as other structural reforms and other international commitments, has allowed large retailers and manufacturers to adopt faster and more complicated logistics systems, forcing truckers to improve their services. Some larger firms are doing so through alliances with United States firms, which are transferring know-how, computer software, and equipment. These services cost more. Most large companies have taken advantage of computer systems to improve administrative controls and to upgrade their communications systems with customers. All large companies significantly modernised their freight tracking systems to ensure timely delivery, with a majority investing in modern satellite or cellular-based communications systems to institute some kind of tracking system. By contrast, small trucking firms have adopted fewer, more modest innovations, and many have done little since 1989.

Trucking firms have become more responsive to their clients, who have profited from lower costs and higher quality service. Delivery times and transit losses have decreased substantially. Lower inventory levels have led to reported cost savings. Better logistics means firms can offer new products and serve new markets. A more competitive, efficient trucking market allows firms to outsource transport requirements, in effect converting a fixed cost into a variable cost. This will enhance new entry and rivalry in other markets that use trucking services.

The general benefits are already being realised. SECOFI has estimated that, overall, distribution costs for commodities in Mexico declined about 25% in real terms between 1987 and 1994.

## What remains to be done.

One remaining issue is the division of regulatory responsibility between the federal and local governments. States and municipalities have some powers over the use of their roads, that are not in the federal road system. Substantial differences between federal and state-level liberalisation could increase costs. The federal government encouraged state governments to undertake similar deregulation within their own jurisdictions.

SCT devised a plan for harmonising federal trucking regulations with state regulations through a series of bilateral agreements between the federal government and the states. These agreements were expected to be finalised by March 31, 1991. But although states, such as Chiapas, have deregulated intrastate trucking, the harmonisation agreements have not been finalised yet. Progress with bilateral agreements has been much slower than planned. And the CFC may not have effective power to eliminate anti-competitive intra-state tariffs, schedules and reserved routes that are set by local governments.

Lack of harmonisation could lead to backtracking, not just concerning competition, but also environmental and safety objectives. The problem of lack of harmonisation does not appear to be widespread, at least not yet. The most significant issues have arising in only two local jurisdictions; however, one of those is the Federal District, where the local jurisdiction has reverted to issuing concessions, rather than permits.

An important issue will be the achievement of environmental goals in the transport sector. This will be motivated in part by outside pressures and obligations. The challenge is to implement high quality regulations that minimise costs and improve compliance in Mexico's still-evolving industry settings.

Two regulatory quality problems are reportedly of particular concern to the industry. One concerns rules about weights and dimensions, which are thought by some to be either nonexistent or at best unclear, and inconsistently applied. The second is the level of the per-truck license payment, which has been set to achieve full-cost recovery of highway maintenance expenditures. This may represent an improvement in regulatory quality, though, over the previous situation, in which trucks paid less than a sixth of the costs they imposed on the highway network.

**Obstacles remain in the way of further successful reform.**

Segmentation, between the large, technologically sophisticated firms and the low-technology fringe mirrors a division in the broader Mexican economy. Those sectors that are not operating internationally remain much less developed, relying on informal establishments for distribution and retail sales. These sectors cannot afford, and may not need, improved services. The large fringe of owner-operators provides haphazard but inexpensive service, which may be a lifeline for small, informal businesses, But the fringe imposes a cost on the rest of the economy. Technically inadequate trucks are a threat to road safety, and until they can consolidate and increase their efficiency, larger carriers will face less competition.

Small and informal truckers have encountered some difficulty in complying with technical standards and maximum load restrictions. Better enforcement of technical standards, not only in trucking but also in other areas, will no doubt force out some informal businesses, but the ensuing consolidation could create new opportunities of greater benefit to the economy.

Because of resistance in the United States, the transportation related provisions of NAFTA have not been implemented. To be sure, Mexico already feels pressure from increased intensity of competition. A full opening with the United States could lead to further significant gains from additional competition. United States-Mexico integration has lagged behind the needs of the market, with negative consequences for Mexico's international competitiveness.

**Mexico's trucking deregulation experience offers some lessons for others.**

Successful reform requires careful planning, execution and high-level political support. Strategy must carefully take into account key interested stakeholders, both supporters and opponents. Some officials in the SCT had close relations with the industry, or feared losing their positions. To avoid confrontation or even early sabotage, the reform project was undertaken elsewhere, at SECOFI and UDE, and were supported by the Finance Ministry. It may be that reforms must be designed and implemented by third parties, rather than the traditional regulator. Then, reform was presented to the industry in terms of "modernisation" along with the promise of soft loans in exchange for the chamber's non-opposition. Deregulation was sequenced, to prevent a possible consumer backlash if prices rose too quickly. And the project had unconditional support from the highest political levels, namely the President himself.

The oversight institution will need attention and resources to help it adapt to post-reform conditions. Regulatory reform causes profound changes in the sectoral institution that formerly had responsibility. Resources must be applied to assist with such tasks as defining the organisation's new role, re-organising its structure and facilitating re-deployment of its staff.

Pro-market rules to offset remaining market failures should be introduced concurrently with removal of distortionary anti-competition rules. Ideally, any new regulations to be introduced as appropriate complements to a more market-oriented framework (such as programmes of highway safety, control of vehicle weights and dimensions, and inspections of vehicle emissions) should be implemented at the same time as the deregulation actions. Clear attention to these values will make for a smoother transition from the government-controlled regime to the post-reform market-determined one.

Competition policy plays a critical role. In general, the national competition agency should help lay the groundwork for reform. (That did not happen in the process of reforming road transport in Mexico, simply because the competition agency had not been established yet). The competition agency may be uniquely placed to make a compelling case about the costs of the pre-reform regime and the expected benefits of reform, working through media relations and with representatives of consumer and producer interests. In addition to this pre-reform advocacy and education role, the competition agency must play a careful post-reform enforcement role, to ensure that cosy cartel-like behaviour stimulated by tight entry restrictions does not persist. Mexico's experience here is a clear illustration: the CFC has had to take three actions, so far, to ensure that the industry does not return to its history of non-competition.

# BIBLIOGRAPHY

Acuerdo para la Desregulación de la Actividad Empresarial (ADAE) (1995),
Diario Oficial de la Federación, 23 November.

Aspe, Pedro (1993),
Economic Transformation the Mexican Way, MIT Press, Cambridge MA.

Baker, Richard D. (1971),
*Judicial Review in Mexico: A Study of the Amparo Suit.*

Banco Interamericano de Desarrollo (BID) (1998),
El Sector Privado en Mexico: Obstaculos a la Inversion, Serie de Estudios Economicos y Sectoriales, April,
Washington, D.C.

Banco Nacional de Comercio Exterior (Bancomext) (1998*a*),
*Trade Policy in Mexico*, Mexico.

Banco Nacional de Comercio Exterior (1998*b*),
*Sectorial Information*, Bancomext Business Center, Mexico.

Berrt, S. Vittorio Grilli and Florencio Lopez-de-Silanes (1992),
"The Automobile Industry and the Mexico-US Free Trade Agreement", NBER Working Paper Series No. 4152,
Cambridge MA.

Blanco Mendoza, Herminio (1994),
*Las Negociaciones Comerciales de Mexico con el Mundo*, Fondo de Cultura Económica, Mexico.

Borrell, Brent (1991),
"The Mexican Sugar Industry: Problems and Prospects, Policy, Research, and External Affairs", Working Papers,
International Trade, International Economics Department WPS 596, February.

Broder, Ivy E. and John F. Morall III (1997),
"Collecting and Using Data for Regulatory Decision-making" in *Regulatory Impact Analysis – Best Pratices in* OECD
*Countries*, OECD, Paris.

Chavez, M. (1990),
"Desregulacion y Consumo Popular" in *Momento Economico*, Mexico.

Comisión Nacional de Agua (1998),
Situacion del Subsector Agua Potable, Alcantarillado y Saneamiento a diciembre de 1996, Gerencia de Agua
Potable y Saneamiento en Zonas Rurales, CNA, Mexico.

Comisión Presidencial de Modernización de la Institucionalidad Reguladora del Estado (1998),
*Modernización de la Institucionalidad Reguladora del Estado*, Informe Final y Anexos, Santiago de Chile, Chile, August.

Consejo Coordinador Empresarial (CCE) (1997),
*Guias para el Cuestionario sobre la Experiencia Empresarial con los Tramites Estatelaes y Municipales en Gestion de Gran Impacto
Economico*, Mexico.

Craig, M. and M. Epelbaum (1994),
"The Premium for Skills: Evidence from Mexico", mimeo, Columbia University.

Department of Trade and Industry (1998),
"A Fair Deal for Consumers. Modernising the Framework for Utility Regulation", United Kingdom.

Elizondo, Carlos (1993),
"The Concept of Property of the 1917 Mexican Constitution", Working Paper 10, Division de Estudios Politicos,
Centro de Investigación y Docencia Economica, Mexico.

Feliciano, Z. (1994),
"Workers and Trade Liberalization: The Impact of Trade Reforms in Mexico and Wages and Employment", mimeo, Harvard University.

Fix Fierro, Hector (1998),
"Poder Judicial" in Gonzáles, Ma. del Refugio y Sergio López Ayllón, eds. *Transiciones y Diseños Institucionales*, UNAM, Mexico.

Fix Zamudio, Hector (1965),
"Sintesis del derecho de amparo" in Instituto de Derecho Comparado, *Panorma del Derecho Mexicano*, UNAM, Mexico.

Gavin, Michael (1996),
*The Mexican Oil Boom*: 1977-1985, Office of the Chief Economist, Inter-American Development Bank, Working Paper-314, January.

GEA Economico,
Al 15 de abril de 1998, Mexico.

GEA laboral
No. 58 al 31 de octubre de 1995 Sindicalismo El sindicato azucarero: nuevo liderazgo, mismos retos, Mexico.

GEA Sectorial
No. 1, abril de 1997, Calzado, y autopartes, Mexico.

GEA Sectorial
No. 2 julio de 1997, prendas de vestir, Mexico.

GEA Sectorial
No. 4 febrero de 1998, Ensamble de automoviles y camiones, Mexico.

Gil-Diaz, Francisco (1998),
"The Origin of Mexico's 1994 Financial Crisis", *The Cato Journal*, Vol. 17, No. 3.

Guasch, J. Luis and Pablo T. Spiller (1997),
*Managing the Regulatory Process: Design, Concepts, Issues and the Latin America and Caribbean Story*, World Bank, New Direction for Development series.

Hanson, G. (1995a),
"Regional Adjustment to Trade Liberalization", NBER Working Paper No. 4713, Cambridge MA.

Hanson, G. and P. Krugman (1993),
"Mexico-U.S. Free Trade and the Location of Production" in Peter Garber ed., *The Mexico-US Free Trade Agreement*, MIT Press, Cambridge MA.

Hanson, Gordon (1998),
*North American Economic Integration and Industry Location*, NBER Working Paper Series No. 6587, Cambridge MA.

Johnson, Simon, Daniel Kaufmann, Pablo Zoido-Lobaton (1998),
"Regulatory Discretion and the Unofficial Economy", *Government in Transition*, Vol. 88, No. 2.

Kalter, E. (1992),
*Mexico: The Strategy to Achieve Sustained Economic Growth*, Fond Monétaire International, Études hors série No. 99, Washington, D.C.

Kim, C. and Y. G. Kessel (1996),
*La Regulación del Mercado de Gas Natural en México*, Instituto Tecnológico Autónomo de México, mimeo.

Krugman, P. and R. Livas (1996),
"Trade Policy and the Third World Metropolis", *Journal of Development Economics*, 49: 137-150.

La Porta, Rafael, and Florencio Lopez-de-Silanes (1997),
*The Benefits of Privatization: Evidence from Mexico, Public Policy for the Private Sector*, The World Bank Group, Note No. 117, June, Washington, D.C.

Levy, Santiago and Rafael del Villar (1996),
"Contribution of Competition Policy to Economic Development : The Case of Mexico", in *Competition Policy 1994 Workshop with the Dynamic Non-Member Economies*, OCDE/GD(96)59, Paris.

Levy, Santiago (1993),
"Trade Liberalization and Economic Deregulation in Mexico" in *Public Administration in Mexico Today*, Fondo de Cultura Economica y Secretaria de la Contraloria General de la Federacion, Mexico.

López Ayllón, Sergio (1995),
"Notes on Mexican Legal Culture" in *Social and Legal Studies*, Sage, Vol. 4.

López Ayllón, Sergio (1997),
*Las transformaciones del sistema jurídica y los significados sociales del derecho – La encrucijada entre tradición y modernidad*, UNAM, Mexico.

Lustig, N. (1992),
*Mexico, the Remaking of an Economy*, The Brookings Institution, Washington D.C.

Martinez, Gabriel and Guillermo Farber, *Desregulación Económica* (1989-1993),
(1994), Serie "Una Visión de la Modernización de México", Fondo de Cultura Económica, Mexico.

Morales Doria, Juan (1998),
"The Role of Regulatory Reform/Deregulation – The Private Sector as Main Participant in the Deregulation Process". Presentation at the APEC Symposium on Regulatory Reform, August.

"Notes: Liberlismo contra Democracia: Recent Judicial Reform in Mexico" (1995),
*Harvard Law Review*, Vol. 108.

Noyola, Pedro and Enrique Espinosa (May 1997),
"Policy Competition and Foreign Direct Investment: The Case of Mexico", SAI *Laws & Economics Paper*, Mexico.

Núñez, W. Peres (1990),
"From Globalization to Regionalization: The Mexican case", Technical Paper No. 24, OECD, Paris.

OECD (1997),
*Issues and Developments in Public Management: Survey*, Paris.

OECD (1997),
*Regulatory Impact Analysis. Best Practices in OECD Countries*, Paris.

OECD (1998),
*Environmental Performance Reviews: Mexico*, Paris.

OECD (1997),
*The OECD Report on Regulatory Reform: Synthesis*, Paris.

OECD (1992),
*OECD Economic Surveys 1991/1992: Mexico*, Paris.

OECD (1996),
*Trade Liberalisation Policies in Mexico*, Paris.

OECD (1998a),
*OECD Economic Surveys 1997-1998: Mexico*, Paris.

OECD, (1998b),
"Railways: Structure, Regulation and Competition", Competition Policy Roundtables No. 15, Mexico Policy, Paris.

OECD (1998),
Note by Mexico. Mini-Roundtable on Relationship between Regulators and Competition Authorities, (DAFFE/CLP/WD(98)20), Paris.

OECD/PUMA (1998),
Mexico's Responses to the Review Questionnaire on Competition Policy, Paris.

Office of the President (1995),
*Plan Nacional de Desarrollo, 1995-2000*, Mexico.

Office of the President (1997),
*Tercer Informe de Gobierno*, Mexico.

Ozorio de Almeida, Anna Luiza, Leandro F Alves, Scott E.M. Graham (1995),
*Poverty, Deregulation and Employment in the Informal Sector of Mexico*, Education and Social Policy Department, World Bank, mars.

Procuraduria Federal del Medio Ambiente (1998),
Press Communication, April, Mexico.

Ramamurti, R. (1996),
"Telephone Privatization in a Large Country: Mexico", in R. Ramamurti ed., *Privatizing Monopolies*, The Johns Hopkins University Press Ltd., London.

123

Ramirez, Miguel Angel (1996),
   *Tiempo Contado de la Industria Azucarera*, Comercio Exterior, June, Mexico.

Randolph, R. Sean (1994),
   "Economic Reform and Private Sector Development in Russia and Mexico", *Cato Journal*, Vol. 14.

Revenga, Ana (1995),
   *Employment and Wage Effects of Trade Liberalization: The Case of Mexican Manufacturing*, La banque mondiale, Latin America and the Caribbean Country Department I Country Operations Division 1, Policy Research Working Paper 1524, October, Washington, D.C.

Rogozonsky, Jacques (1994),
   *La privatizacion de empresas paraestatalse*, Fondo de Cultura Economica, col. Una vision de la modernizacion de Mexico, Mexico.

Ruster, Jeff (1997),
   A *Retrospective on the Mexican Toll Road Program* (1989-94), The World Bank GroupViewpoint, Public Policy for the Private Sector, Note No. 125, September, Washington, D.C.

Sachs, J. Aaron Tornell and Andres Velasco (1995),
   "The Real Story", *The International Economy*, March/April.

Secretaría de Comercio y Fomento Industrial (1998),
   *Programa de Desregulación Económica*, July, Mexico.

Secretaría de Contraloría y Desarrollo Administrativo (1998),
   *Programa "Usuario Simulado"*, Carpeta Ejecutiva. Coordinacion General de Estudios Especiales, June, Mexico.

Secretaria Tecnica de la Comisión Intersecretarial de Gasto-Financiamiento (1998),
   *Reporte de los Procesos de Desincorporacion de las entidades paraestatales correspondientes al mes de diciembre de 1997*, 13 de enero.

Sempe, Carlos (1997),
   *Tecnica Legislativa y Desregulacion*, Editorial Porrúa, Mexico.

Tandon, Pankaj (1996),
   "Divestiture and Deregulation: The Case of Mexico's Airlines", in R. Ramamurti ed. *Privatizing Monopolies*, The Johns Hopkins University Press Ltd., London.

Taylor, Michael (1997),
   "Why No Rule of Law, in Mexico? Explaining the Weakness of Mexico's Judicial Branch", *New Mexico Law Review*, Vol. 27, winter.

Tokman, Victor (1992),
   *Beyond Regulation – The Informal Economy in Latin America*, Lynne Rienner Publishers, Boulder, London.

Tovar Landa, Ramiro (1997),
   "Policy Reform in Networks Infrastructure – The Case of Mexico", *Telecommunications Policy*, Vol. 21, No. 8.

Tribunal Superior de Justicia del Distrito Federal (1997),
   *Justicios presentados en materia mercantil y civil, juzgados de Primera instancia del D.F. 1989-1997*, Mexico.

United States Department of Agriculture (USDA) (1996),
   NAFTA: *Year Two and Beyond*, Rapport du NAFTA Economic Monitoring Task Force, Economic Research Service, April.

Vazquez Cano, Luis Ignacio (1993),
   "Administrative Simplification in Public Administration" in Vasquez Nava, Maria Elena ed., *Public Administration in Mexico Today*, Fondo de Cultura Economica y Secretaria de la Contraloria General de la Federacion, Mexico.

World Bank (1997),
   *The Private Sector in Infrastructure: Strategy, Regulation and Risk*, Washington, D.C.

World Bank (1998),
   *Mexico Country Review*, World Bank Web Page, Washington, D.C.

World Bank (1990),
   *Mexico: Industrial Policy and Regulation*, Report No. 8165-ME, Country Operations Division I, Department II Latin American and the Caribbean, August 15, Washington, D.C.

*Part* II
# BACKGROUND REPORTS

# BACKGROUND REPORT
# ON GOVERNMENT CAPACITY TO ASSURE
# HIGH QUALITY REGULATION*

* This report was principally prepared by **Scott H. Jacobs**, Head of Programme on Regulatory Reform, and **Cesar Cordova-Novion**, Administrator for Regulatory Management and Reform in the Public Management Service. It has benefited from extensive comments provided by colleagues throughout the OECD Secretariat, by the Government of Mexico, by Member countries as part of the peer review process, and by the Trade Union Advisory Committee and the Business Industry Advisory Committee. This report was peer reviewed in June 1998 in the OECD's Working Party on Regulatory Management and Reform of the Public Management Committee.

# TABLE OF CONTENTS

## Tables

## Figure

## Executive Summary

## Background Report on Government Capacity to Assure High Quality Regulation

Is the national administration able to produce social and economic regulations that are based on core principles of good regulation? Regulatory reform requires clear policies and the administrative machinery to carry them out, backed up by concrete political support. Good regulatory practices must be built into the administration itself if the public sector is to use regulation to carry out public policies efficiently and effectively. Such practices include administrative capacities to judge when and how to regulate in a highly complex world, transparency, flexibility, policy co-ordination, understanding of markets, and responsiveness to changing conditions.

Since the early 1980s, the pace, scope, and depth of Mexico's structural reforms have exceeded those of most other OECD countries. Policies of privatisation, market openness, public sector modernisation, competition enhancement, and regulatory reform have substantially reduced the direct role of the state in the economy, strengthened competitive market forces, and in some sectors, boosted the efficiency of regulation needed to protect public policies and promote competition. This process of deep structural change, still underway, has been accelerated by a transformation of the political landscape toward a multi-party system, the rapid development of federalism in governance structures, and integration of the North American economy through NAFTA. As part of these changes, regulatory decision-making moved from opaque and highly centralised processes, in which policy decisions at the centre were undermined by weak policy implementation at lower levels, toward more decentralised, flexible, transparent and accountable approaches. These changes have moved Mexico closer to good international regulatory practices. By end-1998, Mexico had established a solid policy, legislative and managerial basis at the national level for addressing the serious regulatory problems that remain.

In 1989, Mexico launched its first explicit regulatory reform policy to improve economic performance and to stimulate entrepreneurial energies. The reform programme expanded in three stages: 1) sectoral deregulation was followed by 2) improvements to sectoral regulatory frameworks, which were complemented by 3) efforts to establish a government-wide regulatory quality control system based on critical review, transparency, and consultation. Government capacities for carrying out regulatory reform have been built over the past six years, including enactment of laws (such as an administrative procedure law and a law on standard-setting) to improve regulatory transparency and other aspects of regulatory quality.

Since 1995, the current administration has reinforced these capacities through implementation of a broad review programme for new regulations and existing formalities, launching of a co-operative programme to help states and municipalities improve their regulatory frameworks, and establishment of new government-wide regulatory reform tools, such as regulatory impact analysis, a Federal Registry of Formalities, and an equivalence test to speed the adoption of performance oriented regulatory alternatives. Several of these initiatives are good practices that should be considered by other OECD countries. These regulatory initiatives were supported and implemented through new institutions, such as a ministerial-level Economic Deregulation Council, a team in the Ministry of Trade and Industry, and specialised regulatory agencies for telecommunication, energy and competition policy. The judicial branch is being strengthened and modernised, though there is room for further progress in fortifying the role of judicial review of the use of administrative discretion.

Attention needs to shift now to implementation of the regulatory reform agenda over the medium-term. Despite large investments made in good regulatory policies and laws, the full benefits have not yet been realised by citizens and businesses on the ground, and could be lost without a multi-year period of policy stability and determined implementation to allow the reforms to take hold. During the present transition phase when old and new still coexist, the contradictions between a market-oriented policy regime, a rigid administrative environment, and a complex and inflexible legal framework must be worked through. For example, the transition to a transparent, accountable, and results-oriented public administration has far to go. Some ministries have not made the cultural leap to a less interventionist role, and there continue to be weaknesses in policy implementation by federal, state, and local bureaucracies. In the new political context, the constituency for reform must be broadened to the general public and Congress to consolidate and build on past achievements.

The OECD's policy options for Mexico are to:

- *Establish consistent government-wide standards for regulatory quality by closing gaps, eliminating exemptions in the current policy framework, and expanding the review programme beyond "business" regulations to all significant regulations.*

### Executive Summary

### Background Report on Government Capacity to Assure High Quality Regulation (*cont.*)

- *Further improve transparency by extending legal requirements for notice and comment procedures, already required for technical standards, to all ministries and agencies during the development and revision of regulation. Procedures for openness should be standardised for all advisory bodies.*

- *Improve the efficiency, independence and accountability of the new regulatory agencies by strengthening their systems of governance, policy coherence, working methods, and relations with the competition authority. A first step should be the launching of a comprehensive and independent review of the performance of the new regulatory agencies, followed by appropriate revisions to their missions, authorities, and work methods in laws and other regulations.*

- *Promote quality regulation by transferring the CDE/UDE to a location at the centre of government with cross-cutting management and co-ordination authorities, such as the President's office, and by strengthening its attention to consumer protection and citizen welfare.*

- *Strengthen disciplines on regulatory quality in the ministries and agencies by refining tools for regulatory impact analysis, lawdrafting, and use of alternatives to regulation, and training public servants in how to use these tools for regulatory quality.*

  i) *require that RIAs be systematically published during the notice and comment process for each regulation;*

  ii) *train public sector employees in how to conduct regulatory impact analysis;*

  iii) *promote the adoption of alternatives to traditional regulation by developing guidance and training;*

  iv) *improve regulatory clarity and simplicity through better lawdrafting.*

- *Speed up effective reform by adopting a systematic and comprehensive approach to the review of existing laws and regulations.*

- *Review laws and regulations to improve concession processes.*

- *Further encourage regulatory reform by co-ordinating with the states and helping them to develop management capacities for quality regulation.*

## 1. THE INSTITUTIONAL FRAMEWORK FOR REGULATORY REFORM IN MEXICO

### 1.1. The administrative and legal environment in Mexico

Recent years have seen a transformation of the Mexican state that has involved profound changes to the style and content of regulation. Sweeping modernisation launched in the 1980s and 1990s was aimed at changing government's relations with society toward more transparent and decentralised forms. Recent events such as the congressional elections of 1997 indicate the existence of a pluralistic and open political system, which will reinforce the trend to a more transparent, responsive and accountable public administration in which clientelist relations are diminished. These changes are still underway, but important progress has been made in a brief period, ranking Mexico among the OECD's best performers in terms of the speed with which regulatory reform is advancing toward international standards of good practice. An understanding of the present situation and future trends is possible only by reviewing the basic features of the former system.

A *centralist tradition*. For most of this century, Mexico's system of governance could be characterised as bureaucratic, hierarchical, and centralised.[1] This was exemplified in the *de facto* one-party system, in which the *Partido Revolucionario Institucional* (PRI) dominated national and state politics for nearly 70 years, since the founding of the modern Mexican state. This centralised pattern could be seen in both the "vertical division of power" (between federal, state and local governments) and in the "horizontal division of power" (between the legislative, executive and judicial branches).

In the "vertical" dimension, Mexico is divided into 31 states and a federal district for Mexico City. Each of these has an elected governor, an assembly, and a state judicial system and is further divided into municipalities. Each of the 2 377 municipalities is governed by a municipal president and a small rule-making council. This is not obviously a centralised state. For example, the Constitution formally gives important regulatory powers to sub-national levels of government (see Section 2.3 below). In practice, however, political and policy power, supported by national controls over fiscal and budget decisions, has accumulated at the centre, and the federal government has also made most regulatory decisions.

Concerning the "horizontal" division of power, the federal government was itself centralised. The president at the top – also the *de facto* head of the PRI – exerted a near monopoly of power *vis-à-vis* the legislative branch and exerted strong influence through administrative, legal and constitutional reforms of the judicial branch.[2] The two elected chambers of Congress, the Senate, and the Chamber of Deputies, together with the Supreme Court, deferred in practice to decisions taken by the president and ministers. Legal proposals were prepared by a small staff in a single ministry. After being signed by the president, they were sent to the Congress who rapidly approved and enacted them, often in less than a week. In contrast, the constitutional grant of power to Congress and the states to initiate and enact laws was, until recently, never used.[3] The Constitution itself was a policy and regulatory tool, and was frequently revised to support policy decisions, some concerning the economic role of the state.

A strongly hierarchical approach to public administration exerted a powerful and long lasting influence on public service culture. All members of the Cabinet and the chief executives of regulatory agencies are directly appointed by the president. Each minister or chief executive then builds a team that is personally loyal. With few exceptions, there is no career civil service in the administration. The public administration is staffed by a mixture of unionised and non-unionised bureaucrats with different incentives for performance and service quality improvement. The unionised group is guaranteed job security, but its promotion opportunities are limited. In contrast, the second group of non-unionised "technocrats" is largely in control of public institutions but, though they have a higher level of income, they face uncertainty, do not have a clear professional development path and lack compensation if they lose their jobs. Most policy-making powers are centralised in the minister and his/her personal team, who are usually in place for only a few years, in the face of high turn-over.

Effective control by a small and temporary group of high officials over most of the government's decision-making mechanisms has important impacts on the design and implementation of regulatory reform. On the positive side, in the period leading up to the current co-habitation between the government and Congress, policy coherence is more easily assured, and legal reform can happen very quickly and forcefully when there is agreement in this group to move forward. On the negative side, such centralisation can also reduce government efficiency, transparency, and accountability. Understanding and control of the implementing capacities of the administration by this group is weak, and longer-term institution-building is neglected in favour of short-term policy announcements. Simple regulatory decisions, such as approvals, are checked at higher levels, creating severe delays in regulatory processes. Periodic transfers of top officials from one position to another diminish long term commitment and policy stability, as well as institutional memory when implementing policies. There is little follow-up or accountability in terms of results achieved. In some cases, implementation never takes place. Furthermore, the hierarchical culture based on loyalty to superiors is so strong that *de facto* independence of regulatory agencies from the sectoral ministries is hard to establish (see Section 3.4). In sum, the "top down" approach to policies, can make implementation of programmes and reforms confused in form or substance, delayed, or even non-existent.

A *complex regulatory framework*. Paralleling the rigid, centralised administrative system is a complex, legalistic, and rigid regulatory system. Under Mexico's civil law system, regulations are hierarchically organised, each one explicitly based on a superior rule until it refers to a specific article of the Constitution. In 1998, this pyramid-like structure was composed of 258 laws, 2 111 international treaties, 374 presidential regulations ("*reglamentos*"), 766 presidential decrees or agreements, and 585 mandatory standards known as Normas Oficiales Mexicanas (NOMs). The Constitution caps this federal framework. The legal structures of state and municipal governments are similarly organised, with individual state constitutions forming the point of the pyramids of state laws and regulations. An added complexity arises where states' regulations involve a sharing of regulatory responsibilities with the federation and the municipalities, for instance in environmental protection and water management (see Section 2.4).

After enactment by the Congress, laws are made effective by promulgation (*i.e.* signed and ordered into effect) by the president and publication in the Federal Official Gazette (*Diario Official de la Federación*). By constitutional mandate the president, as head of the executive, has broad powers to execute, interpret and enforce laws through a variety of regulatory instruments, the most important being the *reglamentos*. Previous to the current regulatory management policy, regulators could establish lower level subordinate regulations and requirements, such as formalities or NOMs, with traditionally few constraints on their discretion in exercising those powers.

Important features of the legal framework contribute to a rigid administration that is often more concerned with procedural duties than delivering good policy results. As in all civil law countries, the legal system of Mexico is based on the concept of certainty. In practice, this implies an effort to develop written legal codes with as much detail as possible. Unlike in a common law system, implementing laws and regulations are, under the Mexican constitution, meant to be an "exhaustively complete code of rules, procedures, rights, and duties for [the authorities as well as for the citizens] [...] Rules may not be implied, but rather must be expressly spelled out".[4] Articles 27, 28 and 73 of the Constitution not only define the general objectives and scope of government intervention but specify the activities and sectors subject to state monopoly. In a similar manner, laws, rather than lower-level regulations, tend to enumerate all the procedures with which a business must comply.

Reliance on detailed laws did not, however, avoid delegation of broad discretionary powers to regulators because the laws tended to concentrate on a mass of procedural details ("rights and obligations") rather than on setting down substantive criteria for decisions (policy results). Hence, for example, regulators must examine information whose provision is mandated by law, but have more freedom on how to weigh the information in their decisions. Too, the accumulation of procedures increased the arbitrary nature of administration, because it was impossible to know or comply with all requirements, leaving administrators to decide which rules to enforce, and how. Similar to experiences in the United States, the pursuit of certainty in regulations produced so much complexity and detail that they reduced the performance of the whole.[5] Paradoxically, then, the Mexican legal system seems to be characterised by both too much detail and too much discretion.

Lastly, Mexico's legal environment consists of a complex web of linkages and cross-references which includes laws, subordinate regulations and other delegated instruments. In the extreme (but not completely unusual) case, business requirements can be derived from two different laws and several sets of subordinate regulations which cross federal and state jurisdictions.

Some of these features make reform, revision and replacement of existing regulations a major and laborious process of co-ordination and re-drafting, if the consistency of the system is to be preserved, and policy objectives of reform are to be achieved.

Until very recently, the administrative setting and the legal framework were able to coexist in relative harmony, though policy effectiveness suffered. Weaknesses in the judicial branch encouraged a low level of compliance and enforcement, consistent with the capacities of the administration. A huge gap existed between, on the one hand, the real legal environment where since the colonial period "the law was to be obeyed, but not fulfilled" and, on the other hand, the constant search for a perfect, but impractical legal system.[6] Previous to the current composition of Congress, the predominance of the Executive branch permitted constant legal reform, overriding the structural rigidity of the system. For instance, though a change in the Constitution must be achieved via a procedure requiring approval by a two-third majority of the Senate and approval by each state's assembly, from 1917 to 1996, 346 amendments were made to its 136 articles. Subsequently, these modifications slowly trickled down to the lowest levels of regulation.[7]

The strongly executive-driven nature of governance allowed a small reforming elite to accomplish an impressive "silent revolution" of the Mexican legal system over the past 15 years to support the ambitious economic modernisation programme. It is during this period that most of the government capacities and initiatives discussed in this Chapter were launched. Between December 1982 and December 1994, 107 new laws were enacted and 57 were reformed out of a total of more than 200 laws in force at that time. In effect, 80% of the legal framework was extensively modified. The pace of change accelerated in the last 6 years of this period, when 61 new laws entered into force (see Box 2 for the major economic regulatory activities). The aggregate effect of these legislative reforms was to support the establishment of market mechanisms and links to a globalised economy (*i.e.* market openness) through reducing the state's role in market structure (*i.e.* privatisation), in its functions (*i.e.* deregulation), in its relationship with the other constitutional branches of government (*i.e.* political, electoral and judiciary reforms), with the states and municipalities (*i.e.* decentralisation) and with citizens in general (*i.e.* transparency and administrative procedures).[8]

Paralleling this astonishing legislative transformation are changes to the traditional governance system forced by internal factors. In the past few years, the centralised system has rapidly lost ground. A multi-party system has emerged, and in 1997, the PRI lost control of the lower house of Congress for the first time. Today, federal, state and municipal governments operate in a more pluralistic setting with greater balance between the effective powers of the arms of the state. An active federal Congress and local assemblies are learning to exert their autonomous regulatory powers. Civil society is demanding a more transparent and accountable State. As new voices enter the debate and a new balance is found between executive and legislative powers the public debate about regulatory reform is becoming more vigorous, supporting the trend toward good regulatory practices. Support by the new Congress for continued movement toward market-oriented policies will be essential to sustain reform and reap the benefits of past reforms.

During the present transition phase where old and new uneasily coexist, the contradictions between a market-oriented policy regime, a progressively less rigid administrative environment, and a complex and inflexible legal framework raise important questions about the future of regulatory reform.

---

Box 1.   **Good practices for improving the capacities of national administrations to assure high-quality regulation**

The OECD Report on Regulatory Reform, which was welcomed by Ministers in May 1997, includes a co-ordinated set of strategies for improving regulatory quality, many of which were based on the 1995 Recommendation of the OECD Council on Improving the Quality of Government Regulation. These form the basis of the analysis undertaken in this report, and are reproduced below.

**A.  BUILDING A REGULATORY MANAGEMENT SYSTEM**
  1.  Adopt regulatory reform policy at the highest political levels.
  2.  Establish explicit standards for regulatory quality and principles of regulatory decision-making.
  3.  Build regulatory management capacities.

**B.  IMPROVING THE QUALITY OF NEW REGULATIONS**
  1.  Regulatory Impact Analysis.
  2.  Systematic public consultation procedures with affected interests.
  3.  Using alternatives to regulation.
  4.  Improving regulatory co-ordination.

**C.  UPGRADING THE QUALITY OF EXISTING REGULATIONS**
  (In addition to the strategies listed above)
  1.  Reviewing and updating existing regulations.
  2.  Reducing red tape and government formalities.

## 1.2. Recent reform initiatives to improve public administration capacities

Rapid industrialisation of Mexico in the 1950's and 1960's, in what is known as the period of stabilised development, was fostered in a domestic economy highly protected by tariff and non-tariff barriers. In this environment, the economy grew at an average rate of 6.5% from the 1950s until the early 1980s. Governments relied on an economic growth model that featured subsidies and protectionist measures to encourage development of a private sector oriented to producing substitutes for imports. Restrictions on direct foreign investment were accompanied by steady expansion in tariff protection and quantitative restrictions. Fiscal incentives and subsidised credit programmes were enjoyed by sectors deemed to be a priority. Regulations were pervasive in the economy, favouring a selected group of industries and controlling business entry and operations. While achieving some of their objectives, the regulations had negative consequences, such as diminishing competitive pressures, reducing flexibility and discouraging efficient changes among producers. Accumulating rigidities and inefficiencies culminated in the debt crisis of 1982 and painful adjustment that has taken many years to work through.[9]

The process of economic structural change that began in 1983 continues today. This process has been built on two pillars. First, public finances had to be put on a sound footing to strengthen the government's ability to influence macroeconomic variables. To achieve this goal, the government's size and its role in the economy had to be redefined. Secondly, the government sought to expand the space for market-driven decisions in order to promote a more efficient economy. To this end, the government has gradually withdrawn from its role as a producer in various markets and has allowed market forces more latitude in determining the allocation of resources.

Two general strategies – privatisation and free trade – served as the framework and starting point for regulatory reform in Mexico. A huge privatisation process transferred commercial activities from the public to the private sector and the free trade program dramatically increased competition. The embracing of market policies called for a new regulatory framework that would clearly define the rules of the game and give certainty to investors. These policies were supported by two other strategies of reform: the emergence of a structured competition policy and the modernisation of the public administration.

*Privatisation of State-owned enterprises.* Through liquidations, mergers, transfers, and sales, the number of government-owned companies fell from 1 155 in 1982 to fewer than 200 in 1996. This process significantly reduced the proportion of employment and production accounted for by the public sector. At the same time, privatisation was an important short-term financing source for the government.

*Opening markets.* After initial and modest liberalisation efforts, Mexico launched a rapid and far-reaching liberalisation of the manufacturing sectors as part of the stabilisation and adjustment programme after the debt crisis of 1982. The aims were to expand the tradable sector and open the economy to international competition to encourage efficiency in exporting and import-substitution activities. Trade liberalisation accelerated in 1986 with accession to GATT, resulting in the correction of relative prices and reduction of price distortions. Further steps included bi-lateral and multilateral trade negotiations, the most important of which was the North American Free Trade Agreement (NAFTA) which went into effect on 1 January 1994.

GATT did not have a major direct impact on the regulatory framework, except for those regulations directly related to trade, such as standards. Regulations concerning non-tradable sectors remained more or less untouched. This was not the case with NAFTA. This wide-ranging trade treaty had important impacts on the regulatory framework (compelling reforms to investment law, patent protection law, etc.) and significant implications for the competitiveness of previously unreformed sectors and policy areas including services, investment and even the rule of law. It was also important in establishing a number of disciplines in the Mexican regulatory system that were deemed necessary to market openness and a level playing field (*e.g.* consultation mechanisms, transparency, conflict resolution mechanisms).[10]

*Deregulation and regulatory improvements.* From the end of the 1980's, these structural reforms were complemented by a major overhaul of laws and regulations to improve the functioning of markets. A deregulation policy was not explicit in the structural reforms in 1982, when the government concentrated

---

## Box 2. List of major sectoral regulatory reforms since 1990

*Trucking and bus transportation* (1989-1990). The entire sector was deregulated at the federal level, allowing for a simple and transparent license and permit system, the end of geographic restrictions, the elimination of limitations on the loading and unloading freight, and the eradication of all price restrictions.

*Electricity* (1992-1993). The new electricity law and corresponding implementing rules made co-generation and self-supply by independent producers possible.

*Maritime transportation* (1991-1993). Changes in the law allowed for the private sector to obtain port services concessions.

*Land tenure reform* (1992). A far reaching modification of ownership rights of poor farmers (*ejidatarios*) to allow all forms of rural business ventures. Domestic and foreign corporate entities may now own and operate land for agriculture, livestock and forestry production within certain legal limits.

*Natural Gas* (1995). The law was amended and by-laws (*reglamentos*) issued in order to allow private transportation, storage and distribution of natural gas. Transportation permits are given on a first-come first-serve basis. The initial permit in each geographic zone is allocated through an auction in which the bidder offering the lowest end-user fee is declared the winner. The winning bid also sets the average revenue from which the revenue cap regulation is begun.

*Telecommunications* (1995). A new Federal Telecommunications Law was enacted in 1995, allowing for asymmetric regulation of the dominant telephone carrier and for the sale of the radio spectrum through a competitive bidding process. New entrants in long distance telephone services began operations in 1997.

*Civil aviation and airports* (1995-1998). A new Civil Aviation Law was enacted in 1995, and its corresponding *reglamento* in 1998. Prices and routes are no longer subject to government control, except for monitoring of routes where some carriers exhibit significant market power. The opening of airport operations to private capital began in 1998.

*Railroads* (1995-1999). As a result of 1995 Constitutional reforms, the national railroad company was divided into four separate companies and sold through a competitive bidding process.

*Foreign Investment* (1996). The ban on foreign entities owning land was removed. Calculation of foreign investment in a restricted enterprise no longer takes into account minority foreign participation in the entities that would own the enterprise (if the entities are controlled by Mexican nationals). Limits on foreign investment in financial group holding companies was raised to 49% (up to 100% for US and Canadian Nationals). With prior government approval, entities with majority foreign investment may now participate in the bidding for the privatisation of airports and railroads.

*Civil and mercantile judicial procedures in the Federal District and in the State of Nuevo Leon* (1996-1997). Court procedures in the capital were significantly streamlined, reducing the typical case's duration from two to three years to six to 18 months. From 1995 to 1997, the number of trials in Mexico City decreased by 41%. Because it is now much more difficult to delay trial proceedings unscrupulously, many more commercial disputes are being resolved outside the courts.

*Guarantee trusts and mortgage securitisation* (1996). Restrictions on the use of guarantee trusts in lending transactions were eliminated, thereby increasing access to capital for small and medium size businesses. Unnecessary mortgage registration and information requirements in Mexico City were removed, reducing the costs of selling mortgage portfolios between financial institutions and enabling the bundling and securitisation of mortgages. The states of Nuevo León, Aguascalientes, Campeche, Chiapas, Coahuila, Colima, Durango, México, Nayarit, Oaxaca, Puebla, Quintana Roo, Sonora, San Luis Potosí, Tabasco, Veracruz and Zacatecas have also passed similar reforms.

*Mining* (1996). The process for the granting of mining concessions was simplified through implementation of an auction system.

*Environment* (1996). The entire Environment Law was substantially changed, rationalising the use of environmental impact statements, allowing for the introduction of tradable permits, and clearly delimiting federal, state and local jurisdictions.

*Health* (1997). Implementing rules for the General Health Law were modified in order to improve the way in which sanitary licenses are administered and to allow for the creation of a generic drugs market in Mexico.

*Labour* (1997). Although the Labour Law has not been reformed, the implementing regulations related to worker training and safety, and to labour inspection procedures were substantially simplified.

*Pension funds* (1997). A major reform of the social security system allowed the creation of individual retirement accounts administered by competing fund-management companies.

on privatisation efforts related to fiscal consolidation. However, since the beginning of the administration of President Salinas in 1989 an explicit national policy on regulatory reform has been in place and has steadily expanded in scope and ambition. An important element of this strategy was the creation in 1989 of an economic deregulation unit called the *Unidad de Desregulacion Economica* (UDE) in the Ministry of Trade and Industry, *Secretaria de Comercio y Fomento Industrial* (SECOFI).

The Mexican regulatory reform effort can be divided into three periods.[11] At its beginning, the UDE concentrated on deregulating or re-regulating specific economic sectors to facilitate the flow of goods, services and capital stimulated by the trade liberalisation measures. The UDE also worked with other ministries to establish new regulatory frameworks for privatised infrastructure sectors such as telecommunications and harbours. Secondly, the deregulation effort focused on adapting a broader range of regulations to an open economy to provide a level playing field between existing and new firms regardless of their origin inside or outside Mexico. Thus private, including foreign, participation was allowed in strategic service sectors such as public infrastructure (for instance in highways, municipal public services and co-generation and self supply of electricity) to attract international investment Other important programmes pursued in this context were the deregulation of financial services and the reform of land ownership.

By the early 1990s, this economic deregulation programme had broadened to include an effort to review obsolete and inadequate regulations and build the necessary micro economic conditions to increase efficiency and lower costs in all markets. This second stage of reforms was driven by the advancing pace of structural reforms induced by external competition and investment attraction. The reforms aimed at providing legal certainty and eliminating contradictions, thus reducing transition costs and facilitating decision-making. The UDE originated three crucial laws: the Federal Metrology and Standards Law (*Ley Federal de Metrologia y Normalizacion*), the Consumer Protection Law (*Ley de Proteccion al Consumidor*), and the Competition Law (*Ley Federal de Competencia*) (see Box 3).

The administration of President Zedillo in December 1994 commenced a new phase of reform. Three considerations were paramount during preparation of the new policy. First, regulatory reform was central to the recovery strategy after the peso devaluation of late 1994. Second, although the previous programme was regarded as successful, its selective approach based on targeting .priority sectors to

---

Box 3.    **Milestones in managing regulatory reform in Mexico**

**1989 (February):**    Creation of the UDE through an executive order: the *Acuerdo por el que la* SECOFI *Procedera a Revisar el Marco Regulatorio de la Actividad Economica Nacional.*

**1992 (July):**    Federal Metrology and Standards Law enacted. It establishes for the first time a regulatory process with a detailed consultation procedure and a cost-benefit analysis requirement for new technical standards.

**1992 (December):** Federal Competition Law enacted. It establishes modern antitrust regulations and creates an independent Federal Competition Commission.

**1994 (December):** *Ley Federal de Procedimiento Administrativo.* Clarifies important aspects of the regulatory process, in particular concerning appeal rights.

**1995 (November):** *Acuerdo para la Desregulacion de la Actividad Empresarial* (ADAE) Creation of the Economic Deregulation Council. The UDE gains more review powers and a review process for existing formalities and new regulations is established.

**1996 (December):** Reforms to the Federal Administrative Procedure Law, regulatory impact analysis (RIA) mandated for all new regulations.

**1997 (April):**    Reforms to the Federal Metrology and Standards Law. The cost-benefit analysis is replaced by a RIA. A five yearly sunsetting mechanism and a fast-track procedure to eliminate obsolete technical standards (NOMs) are established, and a performance oriented system for new standards is encouraged.

*137*

maximise efficiency gains was considered too slow and partial. The business community considered that the administration had placed too much importance on minimising political costs, and had avoided reforms that would have confronted some powerful interests. Business representatives also wanted to include reforms aimed at what they saw as the high costs of social and environmental, as well as sub-national, regulations, all of which had previously been beyond the scope of reform policy. Last, from the viewpoint of a government struggling with a budgetary crisis, regulatory reform was the form of "industrial policy" which was least fiscally demanding.

In late 1995, a comprehensive policy, called the *Acuerdo para la Desregulacion de la Actividad Empresarial* (ADAE), was enacted in a new executive order, and was confirmed a few months later in the National Development Plan. It gave the UDE greater review powers, created an Economic Deregulation Council (CDE) and, most important, established a scrutiny process for new regulatory proposals and existing formalities (see Section 2.1 below).

*Competition policy.* Competition policy is central to the restructuring of the Mexican economy that was closely tied to the deregulation efforts. While previous initiatives had been taken in this area, it was in 1993, with the entry into force of the Federal Economic Competition Law that an explicit policy was launched to modernise competition policy. The UDE authored the new law, and co-authored its *"reglamento"*, and the first president of the competition authority was its former chief (see Chapter 3 for details).

*Modernisation of Public Management.* In parallel with previous reforms, the Mexican federal government launched a broad policy of administrative modernisation based on two axes: administrative simplifica-tion, and a systematic effort to eliminate unethical and corrupt practices in the bureaucracy. These pro-grammes have been managed by the Ministry of the Comptroller General (*Secretaria de Contraloria y Desarrollo Administrativo* or SECODAM). Recently, the modernisation programme has focused on four areas: citizens service and participation, decentralisation and delegation of public administration pow-ers, measurement and evaluation of public management performance, and reform of human resources policy in the public sector.[12]

## 2. DRIVERS OF REGULATORY REFORM: NATIONAL POLICIES AND INSTITUTIONS

### 2.1. Regulatory reform policies and core principles

The 1997 OECD *Report on Regulatory Reform* recommends that countries adopt at the political level broad programmes of regulatory reform that establish clear objectives and frameworks for implementa-tion.[13] The 1995 OECD *Council Recommendation on Improving the Quality of Government Regulation* contain a set of best practice principles against which reform policies can be measured.[14]

Since 1989, Mexico has had an explicit national policy, set out in an executive order (*Acuerdo Presi-dencial*), on reforming regulation. In November 1995, President Zedillo ratified and expanded it through the executive order named Agreement to Deregulate Business Activities (the ADAE).[15] It is designed to increase the competitiveness of Mexico's businesses and promote job creation by reducing and stream-lining requirements for the establishment and operation of firms, specially SMEs, by limiting bureau-cratic discretion, and by reducing uncertainty in commercial transactions due to obsolete laws and the high cost of using the courts to enforce contractual obligations. It also aims to enhance the transparency of the regulatory process by making draft regulations available to the private sector through a ministe-rial-level Economic Deregulation Council (CDE) and, since October 1998, publishing weekly the list of draft regulations under review on the CDE's Internet website.

The ADAE spells out both regulatory reform criteria and a permanent process for reviewing regula-tions in detail. Thus, reform is transformed from a "one off" initiative into a systematic and permanent review process. It significantly increases the UDE's powers to implement the policy, and sets out several important elements:

– Review and reform of all existing federal business formalities (stock).[16]

– Review and reform of all new administrative or legislative proposals (flow).

– Proposal of economy-wide legislative reforms to improve Mexico's regulatory framework.

– Support to regulatory reform programmes at state and local levels.

The ADAE reviews have, as an explicit policy goal, "deregulating all requirements and response time needed to start up and operate a business in Mexico imposed by federal authorities".[17] This goal makes clear that, consistent with its roots in the economic modernisation programme, the ADAE is primarily producer oriented, concentrating on deregulating government requirements on businesses but excluding other regulatory policies affecting consumers or citizens. Oddly, given the broader nature of reforms in Mexico, the ADAE does not mention improving the efficiency of markets, increasing competition, or improving trade openness. Moreover, no consumer protection organisation or association, which are undeveloped in Mexico, is a statutory member of the CDE.

Consistent with OECD recommendations that governments establish principles of good regulation to guide reform, the ADAE has explicit standards for regulatory quality. The following five criteria are used as a check list in the review process:

– There must be a clear justification for government involvement. Regulations must be vehicles for the processing of government services or must respond to concrete economic or social problems such as health or environmental hazards, or inadequate consumer information.

– Regulations must be maintained or issued only on evidence that their potential benefits exceed their potential costs.

– There should be no regulatory alternatives that can accomplish the same objectives at lower cost.

– Regulations must minimise the negative impact they have on business, especially small and medium size businesses.

– Regulations must be backed by sufficient budgetary and administrative resources to ensure their effective administration and enforcement.

The content of these quality standards is comprehensive and well-conceived, and compares favourably to regulatory quality standards in place across the OECD area, and in the OECD Recommendation of 1995 (the OECD Recommendation was, in fact, an input to the policy). The inclusion of a check on implementation capacities is a useful response to systematic implementation weaknesses in the regulatory system. Although it is named the "deregulation" programme, the ADAE also established for the first time a regulatory management system which in practice creates an on going "better regulation" exercise. The implicit focus (in the benefit/cost test) on using good regulation to improve social welfare rather than only seeking ways to reduce business costs mitigates to some degree the unduly narrow business-oriented goals of the ADAE. The visible focus on business costs probably reflects the need to maintain strong support for the programme among the ministry's business constituency, though the programme itself is pursuing broader regulatory quality goals. Further emphasis on an overall policy for better regulatory quality controls in the future, including but going beyond minimisation of business costs, should boost the social gains from the programme and help broaden the appeal of the programme to a wider constituency. One important and continuing gap, however, is the absence of any principle on public consultation or transparency beyond the creation of the high-level CDE.

The ADAE review powers were supplemented in 1996 and 1997 by modifications to the Federal Law of Administrative Procedures and the Federal Law of Metrology and Standardisation that introduced a Regulatory Impact Analysis implemented by the UDE (see Section 3.3).

Together, the ADAE and these legal changes established a broad framework of principles for regulatory quality, covering most existing and proposed federal regulations regardless of legal form. However, the policy framework has important gaps in its scope. In addition to regulations without business impacts, the UDE does not review:

– Regulations related to contributions (taxes and payments made to the federal government), the financial sector, federal government property, public servant obligations, electoral regulation, agrarian and labour justice, and those established by the Justice (*Procuraduría* General) and

Defence Ministries (but the UDE automatically reviews any business formalities contained on these regulations).

- Regulations related to the IMSS (Mexican Social Security Institute), the INFONAVIT (national housing funding agency), concessions, government procurement and public works (but the UDE can review any business formalities contained in these regulations *if* it and the CDE explicitly request them).

### 2.2. Mechanisms to promote regulatory reform within the public administration

Reform mechanisms, including the allocation of explicit responsibilities and authorities for managing and tracking reform inside the administration, are needed to keep reform on schedule. As in all OECD countries, Mexico emphasises the responsibility of individual Ministries for reform within their areas of responsibility. But it is often difficult for ministries to reform themselves, given countervailing pressures. Further, maintaining consistency and systematic approaches across the public administration is necessary if reform is to be broad-based. Mexico has established a series of centralised oversight mechanisms for implementation of the reform programmes considered in Section 2.1 above.

Two main bodies promote regulatory reform in Mexico: at the political level, the ministerial council for Economic Deregulation (CDE), and at the expert administrative level, the Economic Deregulation Unit (UDE) in the Ministry of Trade and Industry. The CDE is at the centre of the promotion programme. The CDE is chaired by the Minister for Trade and Industry who reports directly to the president. In practice the CDE acts as Mexico's supreme regulatory policy forum. Other standing members of the CDE are the Comptroller General as vice-chair, the Ministers of Finance and Labour, the Governor of the Bank of Mexico, five representatives of the business sector, four representatives of the academic sector, three from the labour unions and two representatives of rural workers.

The ADAE establishes accountability for performance of regulating ministries by instructing them to name a deputy minister responsible for the implementation of their regulatory reform programmes and inviting them to report periodically to CDE. This has provided the CDE, and the UDE acting as its technical secretariat, with enhanced leverage in their negotiations with agencies. It has also improved incentives for ministries to place regulatory reform higher on their list of priorities.

The full CDE meets approximately six times a year and its executive commission approximately every six weeks. During these meetings, proposed reforms and reports on the implementation of previously approved reforms are discussed. Most of the recommendations taken by the CDE are prepared by its executive commission. This high-level group is co-chaired by the chief of the UDE and the Head of the Deregulation Programme of the Mexican Business Council (*Consejo Coordinador Empresarial* – CCE), and is attended by representatives at vice ministerial level of the members of the CDE. Depending on the topics, other vice ministers, state officials, academics or concerned parties are invited. A detailed performance indicators table summarising the state of reform and supported by a comprehensive list of approved and implemented proposals is presented in each meeting. The executive commission establishes *ad hoc* advisory working groups in order to prepare reform proposals. Co-ordinated by a UDE desk officer, these working groups concentrate on a particular body of regulation within a ministry. Their main function is to provide technical advice to the executive commission in the form of detailed proposals.

As the technical secretariat of the CDE, the UDE manages the programme. It also reports directly to the Minister of Trade and Industry as counsellor on regulatory matters. The UDE is staffed by 16 to 20 officials, mostly economists and lawyers, and is supported by consultants and advisors. Its main task is to formulate and analyse reform proposals and prepare the programme's activities to be presented to the CDE. The UDE is organised around specific "desks" dealing with particular ministries. Each desk officer is responsible for organising reviews, preparing reform proposals for CDE opinion, and following up the implementation of commitments by the ministries. Since January 1998 desk officers have also been in charge of reviewing regulatory impact analyses prepared by the ministries.

The Office of the President's Legal Counsel (*Consejería Jurídica del Executivo Federal* – CJEF) has been an important driver in regulatory reform. CJEF reviews all law proposals to be sent to Congress and all the implementing regulations that require the signature of the president (*i.e. Reglamentos, Decretos y Acuerdos Presidenciales*). The main formal functions of the CJEF are to verify the constitutional adequacy of proposed regulation and act as legal advisor to the president. It also has a role in improving the quality of new regulations and enjoys a *de facto* power to stop any regulations it considers as being of unsatisfactory quality. It has been instrumental in reducing duplication and overlap among regulations and enhancing the quality of law drafting. Given its crucial position at the end of the drafting process for major regulation, CJEF has improved the credibility of the regulatory reform policies by asking ministers to present regulatory impact statements (or a waiver issued by UDE) with each proposal. However, in the case of lower-level regulations not requiring the president's signature, the CJEF has no role.

Regulatory reform is reinforced by other bodies working on related structural reform policies. Since the early enactment of the policy, the ADAE has run in parallel to efforts to improve the Mexican public management services, in particular through a process of administrative modernisation and anti-corruption measures. Significantly, the Comptroller General was appointed vice president of the CDE. In practice, officials from the office of the Comptroller General participate in the review processes, concentrating on enforcement issues (*e.g.* inspections aspects) and on reducing excessive administrative discretion that may be a source of corruption. The office of the Comptroller General has also been responsible for monitoring the speedy and effective implementation of agreements reached with individual ministries. This auditing function has now been integrated with the Public Sector Modernisation Programme. The office of the Comptroller General has powers to sanction officials that do not comply with CDE decisions. According to the UDE, this threat has had important effects in the rapidity of establishing the review process and its "acceptance" by a large part of the ministries and agencies.[18]

*Assessment*: this complex of bodies strategically located at various points in the regulatory system compares well to mechanisms in other OECD countries to promote and sustain regulatory reform. As noted, under the leadership of the Ministry of Trade and Industry it has produced very rapid legislative and regulatory policy change. There has been considerable investment in specialised expertise in regulatory reform, in developing routine processes through which ministerial actions are more transparent and are independently overseen, and in establishing accountability and participation at high political levels. The developing co-ordination of legal, economic, and civil service auditing issues is very positive – and ahead of most countries – in exploiting the synergies between these related concerns and in producing a balanced and realistic programme.

Yet there are limits to the continued effectiveness of the current mechanism, justifying an examination of other strategies to carry the programme forward. The first is that the current structure places enormous strains on the Ministry of Trade and Industry as the primary body promoting reform in other ministries. The Ministry is a natural leader, due to the origin of regulatory reform in market openness and structural adjustment concerns. Yet the Ministry has no traditional management authority over other ministries, and hence its authority rests almost entirely on strong presidential support, backed up by its extensive contacts in the business community and its persuasive analysis. This can be an effective combination for a time, but is not a solid institutional basis for sustaining reform over the longer-term. Other OECD countries are locating regulatory reform mechanisms closer to the centre of government in order to exploit government-wide policy and management authorities and to improve co-ordination and consistency in reform efforts. Mexico, with its strong presidential system, offers a natural alternative to the Ministry of Trade and Industry for the next phase of reform.

A related problem is that the competition authority (CFC) and CJEF interventions and participation to the CDE are based on informal agreements. Thus, these arrangements can effectively be modified or abandoned at any time. This demonstrates a general informality in co-ordination arrangements. Notwithstanding the close working relations among officials in charge of structural policies, the ADAE does not refer to competition or trade openness. No official relationship or co-ordination mechanism is spelled out. Each policy is essentially developed and implemented by a separate ministry or agency. Disagreements among them are resolved at the Cabinet level. This may be a residue of the centralist tendencies formerly prevailing in the Mexican government. For instance, although, the competition authority has been invited to participate in the CDE since the beginning of 1999, its explicit advocacy

141

powers on existing and future regulations, have not been co-ordinated with other structural reform mechanisms and institutions. In a similar way, although the Comptroller General (SECODAM) is the vice-president of the CDE and is legally responsible for ensuring the implementation and compliance of reform commitments to the CDE, co-ordination between public management reform and performances management of the public sector, and regulatory reform could be made more explicit. Consideration should be given to improving formal co-ordination procedures between these bodies.

A conspicuous absence is consumer protection policy. In part due to the fact that very few consumer groups exist in Mexico with the organisational skills and resources to participate, no formal or active mechanisms have been established to involve consumer NGOs, or even the consumer protection agency. In addition, except for formal academic, labour, agrarian institutions and associations, no official device or transparent mechanism for involving any other non-governmental bodies in the CDE, other than through explicit invitations. This imbalance has probably reduced the appeal of the programme outside the business community, and limits the pace and scope of further reform.

### 2.3. Co-ordination between levels of government

The 1997 OECD *Report* advises governments to encourage reform at all levels of government. This difficult task is increasingly important since regulatory responsibilities are shared among many levels of government: supranational, national, and subnational. High quality regulation at one level can be undermined or reversed by poor regulatory policies and practices at other levels, while, conversely, co-ordination can vastly expand the benefits of reform. Mexico regulatory reform policy clearly acknowledges this issue. The same day President Zedillo signed the ADAE in 1995, all state governors co-signed individual co-ordination agreements containing commitments to implement conceptually similar regulatory reform programmes. The only other federal country to carry out the same ambitious level of regulatory reform co-ordination among the states is Australia.

These non binding agreements have, in practice, formed the basis of a considerable programme of reform activity at sub-national levels in Mexico. This programme is important, as the extensive regulatory powers of the states and, in particular, the municipalities have considerable potential to frustrate changes at the federal level (see Table 1). Moreover, in the new federalist and co-operative environment the federal government has very few instruments with which to stimulate reforms at state and municipal levels, although the Federal Competition Law enables the competition authority to contest state laws and regulations that restrict free trade across the country. This capacity has in practice been used many occasion in the last few years by the CFC to take action against state barriers imposed by several governments on interstate trade in flowers, eggs and fresh meat, among others.[19]

Most of the regulatory problems deriving from relations with sub-national governments can be grouped into two broad categories.[20] First, many state and municipal rules overlap with federal regulations in specific sectors and activities, creating overlap, duplication and inconsistency. Many sub-national regulations also provide excessive discretion to regulators. Administrators issuing licences will often evaluate compliance against a mix of formal requirements and subjective criteria. The amount of time and resources and the unpredictability of the results that often accompany administrative and judicial appeals against an official's decision exacerbates the difficulties for SMEs. Moreover, a large number of permits and licences are justified as a substitute for local taxation. For instance, annual licences for bars and restaurants in some towns represent an important source of income for municipalities.

A second and important problem concerns regulations related to the provision of goods and services to the public by states and municipalities. Fiscal constraints of the past two decades have meant that a number of these services are provided by the private sector. However, many sub-national governments have had great difficulties in establishing and enforcing transparent and efficient regulatory frameworks to govern the provision of public goods and services, private concessions and government procurement. According to a recent study of the regulatory framework of a leading reforming state, *Aguascalientes*, important inefficiencies exist in at least three areas. First, complex and opaque cross-subsidies distort the pricing structures for public lighting, water and other public services. Second, important inadequacies exist in the terms of the concessions that have been signed by municipalities with private firms to attract investment in water treatment plants, urban water systems and solid waste management, among other services. Finally, problems have been found concerning local procurement regulations where, in spite of the effort at the federal level, local laws still include discriminatory measures against foreign and even interstate suppliers not established in the state, and have weak dispute settlement provisions.[21] A co-ordinated effort – perhaps based on benchmarking criteria – in these topics should be launched to resolve these barriers to national economic growth and regional development.

These problems are exacerbated by short-term political considerations and the constitutional requirement that mayors cannot serve two three year terms in a row. A consequence of this situation has been that many technically and financially complex contracts are negotiated too rapidly, and contain medium term problems that require renegotiation by a new administration. This "political risk factor" is, of course, added to the costs of the installations and services.[22]

In part based on the co-operation agreements of 1995, the UDE, with the help of the CDE, has organised an activity to "provide support to regulatory reform programmes and state and local level". Two initiatives fall under this activity: first, efforts to convince states to establish the regulatory management tools developed at the federal level and, second, co-operative efforts to reform specific local regulations.

Table 2 shows that most states have instituted regulatory reform programmes and that 24 have signed agreements with their most economically prominent municipalities. Analysing results by state, it appears that the most important factor in determining local initiatives is more related to the political commitment of the administration in place rather than to the stage of economic development, geographic location or the political party in office

Another concrete initiative of UDE has been to provide technical support for the reform of local regulations. The most important example of this was the launching of an ambitious deregulation programme in the Federal District of Mexico City between 1995 and 1997.[23] In the old centralised system,

Table 1.  **Division of main regulatory powers**

| Policy area/public service | Federal level | State level | Municipal level |
|---|---|---|---|
| National defence | x | | |
| Foreign relations | x | | |
| International trade | x | | |
| Monetary policy | x | | |
| Air transport | x | | |
| Railway transport | x | | |
| Post Office | x | | |
| Domestic trade | x | x | |
| Redistribution | x | x | |
| Culture | x | x | |
| Industry and agriculture | x | x | |
| Environment | x | x | x |
| Public transport | x | x | x |
| Education | x | x | x |
| Health care | x | x | x |
| Water | x | x | x |
| Urban planning | | x | x |
| Housing | x | x | x |
| Staple markets | | | x |
| Slaughterhouses | | | x |
| Waste disposal | | | x |

Note:  In the case of environment, this does not necessarily imply an overlapping regulatory jurisdiction, as the Federal Environmental Law (reformed in 1996 with the UDE support) clarifies the different levels of government who are in charge of regulating specific media (water, soil, air, toxic waste, etc.).

Source:  Adapted from OECD (1998) *Decentralisation and Local Infrastructure in Mexico. A New Public Policy for Development*, p. 76.

*143*

the Chief of the Federal District was appointed directly by the president. In 1994, a constitutional reform gave to the Federal District a similar political, legal and administrative status than those of the 31 states. However, the change did not take effect until end 1997. During this transition period, the CDE/UDE and the appointed Chief of the Federal District launched an extensive programme to review all existing formalities and reform most of the local laws and regulations. In addition to improve the regulatory environment of the most important economic city of the country, the project also aimed to reduce the size of the informal sector (see Section 3.1.6) and serve as a model for other state and local governments. The results of these reforms are substantial in terms of the regulatory framework: nearly 40% of formalities were eliminated, and 14 major regulations (local laws and *reglamentos*) were reviewed and modified. New regulatory frameworks were established in crucial policy areas like the environment, public transport, businesses inspection and a new permitting system was created which allows most new firms to commence business in less than seven days. The actual impact on businesses are yet to be assessed.

Although infrequently, some federal agencies have used direct incentives to foster reforms at the local level. For instance, *Fondo para la Vivienda* (FOVI), a federal state-owned trust which provides housing credits, facilitated access to larger credit lines to those states that undertook reforms of their civil and judicial proceedings laws in order to increase certainty of repayments and allow the securitisation of mortgages. To date these reforms have been passed by 16 states.

The UDE has also tried to tackle the co-ordination and compatibility problems between federal regulations and state and municipal regulations. Clarifications have been made in important laws like the environment law or the health law in the past few years. But these efforts may not be sufficient. Some local governments, using their constitutional rights, have started to establish regulations controlling their markets. For example, in 1989-1990 the federal government successfully deregulated road transport for both passengers and freight. However, as the reformed regulations apply only to federal highways, interest groups were able to lobby successfully for more restrictive licensing and safety regulations to apply to state and municipal roads. This has permitted the appearance in at least one state and in Mexico City of new and restrictive regulations which undercut the federal deregulatory initiatives as lorries and trucks may be obliged to load and unload when they change from a federal to a state road. As a pre-emptive measure, the federal government has sought individual agreements with each state permitting compatibility between state and federal transportation regulations. By mid-1999, three states had signed such agreements.

Changes in regulatory frameworks often do not indicate clearly the extent to which the actual regulatory environment for businesses and citizens has changed. There have been two recent attempts to measure directly and benchmark the regulatory environment in different Mexican .states in recent

Table 2. **States' efforts to improve the quality of the regulations**

| Capacities and initiatives | Number of states implementing |
| --- | --- |
| Co-ordination agreement between the Federation and the State | 31 |
| Co-ordination agreement between State and municipalities | 25 |
| Enactment of a State Policy framework (*Acuerdo Estatal*) | 31 |
| Establishment of a State Deregulation Council | 31 |
| Establishment of a State Deregulation Unit | 25 |
| Enactment of a state RIA | 1 |
| Programme of Regulatory Auditing | 3 |
| Programme to accelerated businesses start ups | 3 |
| Programme to improve inspection and enforcement systems | 2 |
| Programme to review new regulations | 9 |
| Programme to review existing formalities | 31 and Federal District |
| Establishment of one-stop shops | 31 and Federal District |
| Setting up of an Inventory of formalities | 25 |

*Source:* Consejo Coordinador Empresarial, Direct communication with OECD, October 1998.

times. In 1996, the *Instituto Tecnológico de Estudios Superiores de Monterrey*, a private university, published a comparative analysis of the investment friendliness of the states. The study included criteria such as the regulatory environment and the capacity of the judiciary to ensure an adequate rule of law. It stirred much attention and controversy but helped accelerate reforms. Candidates for state governorships are using its results in their election campaigns. A second benchmarking exercise published in March 1999 by the Mexican Business Council (CCE) compared the actual performance of regulatory environments across the 31 states, based on surveys of officials and businesses. For example the study benchmarks states in relation to the quality of their regulatory reform programmes, their efficiency in processing licenses and permits for zoning, construction, environment, water, etc. and the time needed to comply with them and will also look at the performance of local courts in dispute resolution (see http://www.cce.org.mx/).[24]

## 3. ADMINISTRATIVE CAPACITIES FOR MAKING NEW REGULATION OF HIGH QUALITY

### 3.1. Administrative transparency and predictability

Transparency of the regulatory system is essential to establishing a stable and accessible regulatory environment that promotes competition, trade, and investment, and helps ensure against undue influence by special interests. Just as important is the role of transparency in enforcing the legitimacy and fairness of regulatory processes. Transparency is a multi-faceted concept that is not easy to change in practice. It involves a wide range of issues, including standardised processes for making and changing regulations; consultation with interested parties; plain language in drafting; publication, codification, and other ways of making rules easy to find and understandable; and implementation and appeals processes that are predictable and consistent. The Mexican regulatory system has made progress in these areas, but important problems, in particular to reduce excessive discretionary powers and improve accountability, still exist.

### 3.1.1. *Transparency of procedures: administrative procedure laws*

The Mexican Constitution sets out general procedures to be followed in promulgating higher level regulations: *i.e.* laws and presidential rulings (*reglamentos*). The main element of this procedure is the requirement that proposed laws be signed by the president before being sent to Congress, in the case of laws, or published by the Federal Official Gazette in the case of *reglamentos*. This ensures a minimum degree of central oversight, co-ordination and accountability in respect of these higher level regulations. For lower level regulations, the Federal Public Administration Organisation Law (*Ley Orgánica de la Administración Pública Federal*), together with individual laws, gives broad powers to ministries and agencies to establish, to implement and to enforce regulations. Prior to the recent creation of the ADAE and the introduction of regulatory impact analysis for business regulations (see Section 2.1), these lower-level regulations were prepared without standard oversight or transparency procedures.

In the past few years, the degree of control exercised on administrative discretion has increased. Three important complementary initiatives to establish a formalised system for making new regulations are notable. The first is the introduction of a new and precise system for developing technical standards and process regulations, known in Mexico as *Normas Oficiales Mexicanas* (NOMs). The Federal Metrology and Standards Law of 1992 was designed to clearly establish the role and status of these instruments, thus reducing uncertainty and improving accountability. It sets out very detailed administrative procedures for drafting and publication of this type of mandatory regulation, which usually aims to control health, safety and environmental risks and provide consumer protection for products, services and processes sold or provided in Mexico. To harmonise and control the development of product and process standards, only nine ministries (out of 17) can issue NOMs. All NOMs must be drafted within one of the 22 national consultative committees (*comites consultivos nacionales de normalizacion*). Each committee is specialised in a regulatory area such as pesticides and risk related chemicals, health and safety at work, etc. The committees are chaired by the lead regulatory agency and are composed of government and private sector experts. Preparation of a NOM follows four steps: first, a ministry prepares a pre-project and presents it to a consultative committee. Since

*145*

January 1998 the pre-project must be accompanied by a RIA and must also be presented to the UDE. Second, having obtained UDE and committee approval the ministry publishes the NOM proposal in the Federal Official Gazette and seeks comments. After a consultation period of 60 days, the ministry publishes, in the same gazette, an official response to any comment. Finally, not less than 15 days after this last publication, the ministry can publish the NOM in its final form. Two important additional procedures are a sunsetting every five years of all NOMs and provision for affected parties to comply with a NOM through an alternative deemed equivalent (these features are discussed further below)

A second improvement to the process of creating new regulation was the enactment in July 1994 of the Federal Administrative Procedure Law. This law established a set of principles and criteria for the interaction between authorities and citizens. Some of its main improvements related to regulatory procedures include:

– Clarification of the requirements for publication of all regulations in the Federal Official Gazette.

– Public access to information possessed by regulators.

– A clearer administrative appeal mechanism.

– Time limits for authorities to respond to a public request for information or authorisations.

– Minimum criteria to be followed by public officials during an inspection.

In December 1996, an amendment of the law established the regulatory impact analysis (RIA) process. As described below, this had a major impact on the process of writing new regulations (see Section 3.4). .

---

Box 4.  **Transparency of regulatory systems in selected OECD countries**

Based on self-assessment, this broad synthetic indicator is a relative measure of the openness of the regulation-making and regulatory review system. It ranks more highly national regulatory systems that provide for unrestricted public access to consultation processes, access to regulation through electronic and other publication requirements, access to RIAs, and participation in reviews of existing regulation. It also ranks more highly those programmes with forward planning of regulatory activities, a consultation system open to any member of the public, the publication of a consolidated registry of all subordinate regulations, the obligation of publicly release RIA documents for consultations. Mexico has a poor score on these criteria.

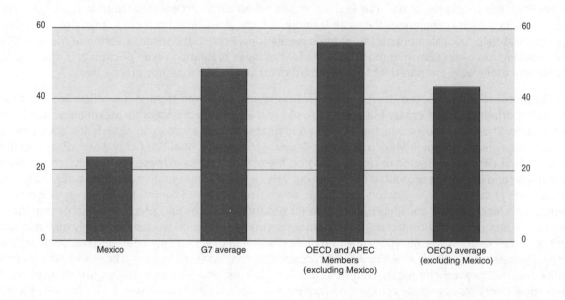

Finally, the ADAE in November 1995 established a review process for all new regulatory proposals likely to have an impact on business activity. The mechanism has permitted review of more than 250 regulations (see Table 3). It was supplemented, for regulations that require the president's signature, by a second external review to be completed by the CJEF prior to the proposal being sent to Congress for approval or published in the Federal Official Gazette. The ADAE review programme has focused consistently on defining clearly the amount of discretion necessary in each step of a regulatory procedure: from granting a permit to completing an inspection.

According to the UDE, the level of compliance with this new process has generally been high. During the initial implementation in 1995, the compliance stresses normally associated with establishing new requirements of this kind were overcome by the need for rapid regulatory responses in a number

Table 3. **Regulatory proposals received by the UDE, 1996-1998**

|  | Laws | Presidential regulations (*reglamentos*) | Decrees | Ministerial orders | Technical standards (NOMs) | Other | Total |
|---|---|---|---|---|---|---|---|
| 1996 | 13 | 20 | 8 | 8 | 0 | 16 | 65 |
| 1997* | 7 | 37 | 8 | 23 | 15 | 7 | 97 |
| 1998 | 3 | 13 | 16 | 17 | 102 | 44 | 195 |
| 1999 (January-June) | 2 | 6 | 5 | 7 | 42 | 17 | 79 |

* Since September 1997, the ADAE individual reviews have been strengthen with the inclusion of the mandatory RIAs submitted to the UDE.
*Source:* UDE, direct communication, June 1999.

Box 5. **Critical approach in selected OECD countries**

Based on self-assessment, this broad synthetic indicator is a relative measure of the critical approach to government intervention and its nature. It ranks more highly national regulatory systems that provide the opportunity to affected parties to give views on the necessity of intervention, the use of precise threshold tests to justify action to be considered, and the inclusion in the RIA of benefit/cost principle and risk assessment requirements. Mexico ranks slightly below the G7 and OECD average on this score.

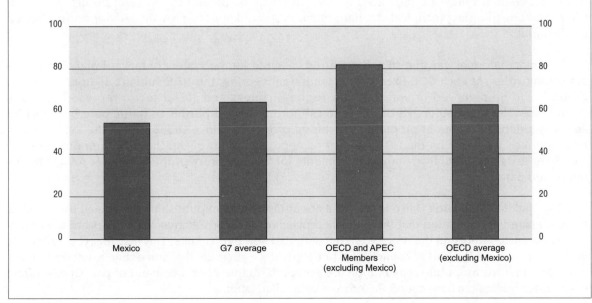

of areas to deal with the economic crisis following the 1994 peso devaluation. As in other countries, minor rules or politically sensitive regulations may still be implemented without review by the CDE/UDE. However, the strong support of the Comptroller General and political support at the highest level show potential to establish a new regulatory culture in Mexico.

The dual element of central oversight by the UDE and openness of the CDE have the potential to bring about substantial change. Evidence suggests that quality of new regulations has greatly improved. Reducing excessive regulatory discretion has been implemented as part of UDE systematic reviews of regulations. A key change has been the systematic elimination of the formerly widely used legal drafting technique of adding "among others" to any list of mandatory requirements or criteria.

However, some improvements would boost programme benefits. The scope of the UDE review of new regulations is too narrow. As indicated previously, the ADAE and the Administrative Procedures Law exempt important regulatory areas like public procurement and financial sector (unless they contain a business formality). A similar problem exists in regard to the preparation of technical rules and standards by ministries exempted from the Federal Metrology and Standards Law, for instance in the financial or telecommunication sectors. Another design issue is that a review mechanism based on a sequential analysis is not well adapted to dealing with important co-ordination and duplication issues arising either in relation to regulations enacted previously by the same ministry or those enacted by another ministry.

### 3.1.2. *Transparency in implementation of regulation: forward planning of regulatory actions*

A number of OECD countries have established mechanisms for publishing details of the regulation they plan to prepare in future. The objective of this forward planning is to foster the participation of interest parties as early as possible in the regulatory process and, to some extent, to reduce transition costs through giving more extended notice of forthcoming regulation.

Two recent Mexican initiatives are worth noting on this respect. The 1992 Federal Metrology and Standards Law mandates that the National Standards Office (*Direccion General de Normas*) publish annually in the Federal Official Gazette a list of all technical standards to be considered during the coming year by each of the 22 consultative committees. The list includes, for each committee, the name, address and telephone number of its president, who is responsible for disseminating information and organising the activities of the committee. The time frame for the consideration of each proposed standard must be indicated to give all participants and the general public an idea of when the corresponding technical standard might be issued, and to provide early opportunities for public input.

In a more informal way, the UDE has started to implement a system of forward planning of regulatory activities. At each CDE Executive commission meeting, the UDE submits an updated list of proposals to be reviewed or under review to the business and social sector representatives in attendance. The main objective of this is to call for interested parties to participate in the *ad hoc* advisory groups in charge of preparing the reform proposals. Since October 1998 the list has been made publicly available on the CDE Internet homepage; upon request, the UDE then provides the complete texts and regulatory impact statements for all regulatory proposals under review to any interested parties.

The National Standards Office is sceptical about the results of publishing the annual list of NOMs to be prepared. It has argued that the published plans of most consultative committees are too imprecise to stimulate interest in the process among potential new participants. This may reflect a deliberate lack of openness on the part of committees, but experience suggests that some time is needed before new opportunities for public consultation are accepted. Active encouragement of participation from government bodies can help speed the process of familiarisation.

### 3.1.3. *Transparency as dialogue with affected groups: use of public consultation*

Mexico does not have a comprehensive law or government policy requiring the use of consultation in making, modifying or repealing legislation and regulation. However, laws and government policies requiring consultation exist in some areas and a wide variety of forms of consultation are used to some extent (including notice and comment, circulation for comment, information consultation, advisory groups and public hearings).

Formal procedures to ensure public consultation have been limited. The Federal Administrative Procedure Law does not establish a specific, mandatory mechanism for citizen participation in the rule-making activities of the federal government. The Law does contain minimal recognition of public consultation procedures. While leaving the issue of when consultation is to be undertaken to be determined in sector specific laws, it requires that, if a law establishes a "notice and comment" mechanism, the period of time allowed should not be less than 60 days. Other than that minor limitation, the consultation process is largely at the discretion of the ministry or agency preparing the regulation, unless constrained by provisions of a specific law. In practice, informal consultations occur most of the time and at all stages of the process – both before and after the formulation of policy proposals and later when the detailed draft regulation is ready. Generally a ministry submits the draft to selected representatives of interested parties to receive comments and suggestions. Negotiation meetings are sometimes organised for major reforms.[25]

Important initiatives have recently been taken. The public consultation procedure stipulated by the Federal Metrology and Standards Law, described in Section 3.1.3, is the most detailed in Mexican law. A 60 day period for receiving comments follows publication of the project in the Federal Official Gazette. After that period, the National Standards Office must publish its response at least 15 days before issuing the final version in the Federal Official Gazette.

The participation of businesses, and in some respect, of other interested parties at the CDE also improved the openness of the process of making new regulation. The dozen or more *ad hoc* consultation groups organised under its umbrella to review existing formalities and new regulations have had an important impact on improving consultation. These groups have been successful in improving the quality of draft regulations and the business community has welcomed them as an important advance.

Some specific laws have established particular consultation processes:

– The Law on Foreign Trade demands that any proposed regulation which may have impacts on international trade should be submitted for comments to the Commission of External Trade (*Comision de Comercio Exterior* – COCEX).

– The general environmental protection law states that the Environment Ministry must convene *consultative commissions* to receive comments from government agencies, academic institutions, and social and business organisations on the design and evaluation of environmental policy. On creating new regulation, the Environment Ministry must state the reasons for accepting or rejecting opinions presented by the commissions. The Ministry must also consult with the public during the evaluation of applications for environmental permits, which includes making environmental impact statements (EIAs) public and assuring that the public right to make observations and propose changes to EIAs has been respected.

– Another type of consultation procedure applies in the case of regulation of the natural gas sector. The major implementing rules stipulate that any directives proposed by the Energy Regulatory Commission must be published for public comment at least ninety days before the final publication.

*Assessment of public consultation.* Together, these separate steps represent solid but incremental changes toward opening up the decision-making process for regulations. In that sense, Mexican initiatives are consistent with the international trend towards more transparent and accessible regulatory processes. However, important gaps continue in Mexican consultation processes. This gap is due to the absence of a generally applicable consultation requirement for higher-level laws. An extension of the "notice and comment" system applied to NOMs to these laws (with necessary adjustments) would be an important step forward. Many OECD countries have found that notice and comment mechanisms of this kind are a minimum guarantee of regulatory transparency.

Second, as noted above in relation to publication of prospective NOMs, international experience indicates "notice and comment" should be supplemented by active mechanisms to encourage participation of a wide range of interests, particularly when a participative tradition to regulatory decision-making has yet to take root. Mexico has been quite successful in increasing participation by targeting certain groups. However, it will be important to scrutinise the diversity of participation on regulatory issues, in order to avoid capture of the process and the regulators by narrowly based interest groups.

---

### Box 6. Use of public consultation in selected OECD countries

In this synthetic indicator of the scope and systematic use of public consultation, Mexico is under the OECD average score. This indicator looks at several broad aspects of the use of consultation and ranks more highly those that are routine, non-discretionary, accessible to all interested parties, and used earlier in decision processes. Despite the increasing use of public consultation in Mexico, its consultation programme is used in some cases, is less open to all interested parties, and gives regulators more discretion about when and how to consult, potentially reducing transparency and raising the risk of capture by special interests.

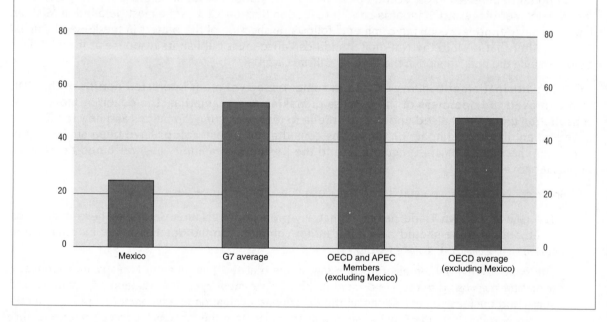

---

### 3.1.4. *Transparency in implementation of regulation: law drafting*

Legal clarity is essential to good regulation. If rules and regulations are poorly written or unnecessarily complex in structure, problems will arise during implementation and enforcement. Unclear or unspecified legal terminology can lead to major compliance problems. As in several aspects of the transparency of its legal system, Mexican experience in this respect shows a mixed pattern.

Law drafting responsibilities accrue in the first instance to a specialist unit in each ministry or agency in charge of preparing proposed regulations. Prior to the establishment of the ADAE regulatory review programme there was little external review of the regulation produced by the individual agency. The only exception was the requirement for higher level regulations to be signed by the president. In practice, this involved scrutiny by the president's legal office. This system had limited success in ensuring regulatory quality. Imprecision and the use of obscure legal terms were relatively common. Laws were written to be deciphered by lawyers or other specialists, rather than to be intelligible to laymen.

Lawdrafting has not been regarded as part of the regulatory reform programme in Mexico. However, the CDE/UDE and the CJEF have progressively added quality assurance filters. For instance, as part of the CDE review, UDE's internal lawyers and external legal service providers have established minimum criteria for legal quality of regulations. Perhaps the key issue addressed during these legal analyses is verification of the legal standing of the regulation. In the past, many ministries and agencies have tended to extend, unilaterally, their statutory powers by making unanticipated uses of broad powers delegated to them to make lower level rules. By applying a simple check of the authorising law, the UDE has eliminated many such abuses of discretion.

A second key change has occurred at the end of the economic and technical review, where a more detailed and in depth study is now undertaken. At this stage the focus is on the structure and clarity of the text to ensure understandability and compatibility with existing regulation. This check is repeated by the CJEF, the body ultimately responsible for the legal quality of legislative proposals and major implementing rules. However, these new processes do not proceed from clear and formal principles and guidelines and, to this extent, can be difficult for individual agencies to anticipate. No policy on "plain language" has been established to improve simplicity and clarity of regulations. Moreover, as in other key parts of Mexico's reform initiative, no training programmes have been developed.

### 3.1.5. *Transparency in implementation of regulation: communication, compliance and enforcement*

*Communicating regulations*

Complex and unclear regulation, and difficulties at the judicial level with interpretation and enforcement, have meant that Mexican regulation has long been the source of considerable uncertainty and confusion to citizens. Aware of the negative impact of this situation on achievement of regulatory objectives, federal and state governments have launched programmes to improve the communication and enforcement of regulation. In the early 1990's, the Comptroller General launched a government-wide programme to establish definitively the status and content of all formalities. After laborious effort, a first inventory of formalities and services was established in 1994. Its impact was, however, reduced by problems as to its completeness and by difficulties of access to its information (it was published in two or three dozen binders). Moreover, the information soon became obsolete after the restructuring of the ministries in 1994. This effort was most important as a learning process which contributed to the imple-mentation of a subsequent programme, undertaken by UDE as one of its first tasks, to complete and update an inventory of formalities. In 1996, a new inventory was prepared and published on the Internet, including more than 2 400 business formalities applied by federal authorities, and became the dataset of existing formalities to be reviewed (see Section 4). In 1998, this Internet inventory of formalities was completed by the addition of the official list of standards (NOMs) and a compendium of all current laws and other major legal regulatory instruments. The same year, a free telephone service to access infor-mation in these inventories was established. Similar approaches are now being pursued in states and municipalities. Leapfrogging the printing press, creative initiatives based on the Internet have enhanced communication and information about the regulatory framework. Recently, private entities have also begun to produce lists of regulations on the Internet, with search capacities and other value-adding devices.

Efforts have also been made to improve the public's awareness of its rights and of the obligations of inspectors (see below). In 1993 the Comptroller General launched a open access phone-based ser-vice (SACTEL) to enable complaints to be made against public servants and to provide information on federal and administrative procedures and formalities. A second, more ambitious, project concerns the reform of the Mexico City business inspections system (see Section 2.3). In a joint initiative of the previ-ous government of the Federal District and the CDE/UDE a phone service was created to permit busi-nesses to check the validity of inspections by telephone (LOCATEL). Only inspections confirmed by phone could be carried out. This system was developed as a fight against excessive discretion from enforcers and the existence of "pirate inspectors" trying to extort payments from small businesses.

---

#### Box 7.   On-line search of business formalities

In June 1998, the UDE launched an ambitious communications project: an electronic one-stop shop based on the inventory of formalities supported by Internet search capacities. Based on the six digit ISIC definition of activities, a user-friendly on-line search tool available on the CDE web page (www.cde.gob.mx) permits any person to retrieve a list of formalities needed to start up or operate his business. With the transformation of the inventory into the official federal registry, these lists will provide near 100% accuracy and legal security (see Section 4 on the establishment of the federal registry).

The procedure includes three steps:

1.   The applicant defines the economic activity from the ISIC catalogue. If the person does not know the six digit number, a key word search engine or a progressive narrowing down from division, group, class and activity helps him to fix it.

2.   The search is further narrowed when the system asks two additional attributes: *a*) the type of administrative procedures corresponding to the business development: *e.g.* constitution of the business, start up the activity, operation, export or import or closure of the business, and *b*) boundaries to the search by specifying the type of formality, either voluntary or mandatory.

3.   A list of formalities is then presented, specifying the agency or Ministry in charge of administer it.

By clicking into the formality code, the system links directly to the official Inventory. At this point a standard format describes the selected formality. The following details are included: the place to present it, the agency in charge of responding, all the information requirements (together with attachments), the time the agencies have to respond (along with the existence of an automatic approval after that date), the fees and charges needed to apply it and additional comments.

---

*Enforcing regulations*

The enforcement of regulations is problematic in Mexico. Traditionally, a law or a subordinate regulation was a vehicle to set down a policy as well as to establish rights and duties.[26] In general, enforcement policy was delegated to lower levels. This created stresses on low level administrative units without adequate resources. A related problem was the excessive discretion allowed to regulators to implement enforcement strategies. Finally, the situation was aggravated by serious inefficiencies in the judicial system. These three issues, though connected, are analysed separately.

A major concern driving regulatory reform since the beginning has been that enforcement deficiencies create corruption opportunities for businesses and civil servants, with a disproportionate impact on SMEs. Mexico is rare among OECD countries in specifically including in the regulatory review policy a test of whether regulations are backed with sufficient budgetary and administrative resources to ensure their effective administration and enforcement. Based on these considerations the federal government has in recent years tried to re-invent the inspection and enforcement aspects of its regulatory systems.

Two approaches have been used. First, the UDE has promoted the use of third party certification of compliance with technical standards. Through this system, regulators can concentrate on controlling only the third party entities, significantly reducing the budget costs of inspections. In general, the participation of the private and social sector (*e.g.* universities) has resulted in efficiencies which have reduced time and paperwork for businesses. This technique is used, for example, to check car pollution emissions in some cities including Mexico City, in sanitary licenses, environment audits, authorisation for forestry programmes, granting mining concessions, etc.

A second approach is re-engineering of inspection systems, replacing *ex ante* controls with *ex post* notification and random checking. Two examples of this approach are the customs administration of the Ministry of Finance and the licences and permits area of the Ministry of Health.

The customs administration was the first to introduce random inspections of arriving passengers and importers. Its objectives were, in part, to fight against smuggling and corruption and in part to speed processing times at the borders. Passengers or importers in the custom premises push a button, leading a red or green light to appear randomly. Those who receive a red light are inspected (see Box 5 in the background report on Enhancing Market Openness through Regulatory Reform.

A similar approach was applied successfully in the Ministry of Health, where the system of sanitary licenses has been completely overhauled. Before the reform, sanitary licenses were among the most restrictive and costly regulations. Most businesses had to be inspected prior to receiving a sanitary licence.[27] In practice, this created a large backlog of inspections that delayed business openings and provided incentives for non-compliance with the law. Reforms to this system eliminated low risk activities from sanitary controls and allowed businesses in some activities to simply notify the Health Ministry of operations. These businesses are randomly inspected to ensure compliance. The reduced number of "high risk" activities must still undergo *ex ante* inspection. Sanitary controls are required solely in cases where there is a clear danger to the final consumer. The authorisation of some sanitary licenses is further hastened when the solicitor presents a registered third party certification. This greatly reduced controls: 92 of 297 previously regulated activities were exempted from sanitary controls. The number of activities requiring a sanitary license was reduced by 81%, and are now limited to chemical, pharmaceutical and medical products and services. The result is that over 450 000 firms are benefiting from more flexible sanitary controls.

The Comptroller General, in parallel efforts, has also undertaken innovative programmes to improve ethics and fight corruption in the public sector. Its main tools have been auditing, investigation of corruption and misallocation of resources, establishment of precise standards for public auctions, public contracts and other monetary transactions involving public servants, and introduction of an array of reporting requirements and controlling mechanisms. They have also established a large programme of "sleuth users" as a random checking mechanism. This involves the Comptroller General employees applying for a range of licences and evaluating the authorities' responses.[28]

The informal sector is a daunting challenge to improving regulatory compliance. By definition, informality is the condition of non-compliance with a given set of standards and regulations, like prohibitions, inspection requirements, zoning laws, labour legislation, and tax regimes.[29]

As in many emerging economies, the Mexican informal sector is quite large. According to the World Bank, 41% of the work force in major cities is employed on this sector. In the 1980s and 1990s its size increased.[30] Domestic services and retail trade, and to a lesser extent construction, have been the typical activities where informality has developed. A very large majority is formed of micro-firms between one and five employees that rely on family ties for labour. They often operate without accounts and premises, producing low quality/low costs products and services. Transactions typically take place on the street in family stores or in kiosks.[31]

Many factors have fuelled the growth of the informal sector: demographic pressures, migration linked to rural exodus to urban cities, education, and, of course, the series of economic crisis that hit Mexico in the past two decades. Rationalisation linked to increased international competition and other structural reforms have also contributed in the short term.[32] Exposed to rapid and strong internal and external competition, some large, medium-sized or "formal" firms have temporarily used the informal sector as a way to downsize sub-contracting semi-finished goods or distribution with informal firms.[33] In many ways, the informal sector has functioned like a spontaneous safety net, in which poor families seek refuge from the effects of protracted growth, inflation and low wages, waiting for conditions to improve.

Growth of the informal sector is also due to problems in the regulatory framework. The design, administration, and cumulative effects of regulations create strong incentives for total or partial evasion.

Regulations, even if justified, can have negative impacts on small firms. The well known regressive effect of regulations relative to firm size means that compliance costs are disproportionately higher for small firms. The nature of regulations used in Mexico further increases compliance costs. Many of the regulations relevant to the informal sector are administrative, mostly carried out through *ex ante* formalities such as registries, licences, fees, contracts with public authorities, zoning authorisations, and other regulations affecting start-up. The costs of this market entry paperwork in terms of time and money can be difficult for the hurried entrepreneur. For instance, in Mexico the cost of legal entry were estimated in the early 1990s at 83 to 240 days, and represented an expenditure of $210 to $368.[34] "Variable regulatory costs" present another problem. The flexible, changeable and mobile nature of many informal operations make it difficult for micro-firms to comply adequately with regulations based on the number of employees or revenues (such as regulations implementing tax, labour and social security legislation). As a result, informal firms develop a regulatory strategy where they reduce (or eliminate) compliance costs enforced by the government, while paying more flexible "evasion costs" such as bribes to official inspectors, or protection fees to vigilantes, gangsters and other non-official authorities who impose their own regulation in whole neighbourhoods, stretches of sidewalks, lines of business, etc.[35]

A second disincentive to comply concerns legal security problems and the related social and cultural environment. Compared to a distant and sluggish government and its deficient welfare system, a micro firm receives prompt services, support and protection in the non-official social and economic environment where it operates. This reduces further the private and social benefits of "official" regulations.

Additionally, some regulations pose direct problems to micro-firms. For instance, interest groups can capture regulatory authorities to set up entry barriers to smaller competitors. This was the case until 1992 in the federal road freight transport sector. Harder to detect, particular regulations or policies have also important side effects with a strong impact against micro-firms. For instance, a perverse effect of governmental anti-inflationary policies used until recently, such as price controls of basic goods like bread, tortillas and essential groceries was that they severely limited the earnings of informal commercial kiosks (and therefore had a regressive dimension).[36]

Progressively these effects feed on themselves creating a vicious circle. The informal sector has little incentive to pay taxes or social security contributions as they are excluded from many government expenditures, entitlements and subsidised services set up since the 1950s, like vacation, household subsidies, housing credit, export support, etc. But at the same time it "unfairly" competes with the "formal" SMEs, obliging the latter to switch to "evasion strategies". This reduces further the tax base, which reduces the government's budget for improving a more adapted enforcement mechanism or for establishing programmes to help this sector. At the end of the day, the existence of such a high level of non-compliance has a corrosive effect on the rule of law, creating a pervasive culture of non compliance.

However, it is important to note that being informal does not mean that a micro-firm is privileged in its cost structure compared to a formal firm. A team from the World Bank calculated that in Mexico "regulatory costs" (including compliance and evasion costs) correspond to approximately 24% of total costs of informal firms. For repair and other services, these costs fluctuate between 50 and 63% of total cost.[37] With such "regulatory costs", these micro-firms are trapped in informality since their capacity to grow is bleak.

Since the mid-1980s, Mexican officials have taken measures to reduce the informal sector to achieve a more balanced and equitable economic society, to fight corruption, and to encourage entrepreneurial energies. During the Salinas administration, the Ministries of Labour, Commerce and Industry, Finance, Social Development, development banks, like *Nacional Financiera*, NGOs and local entities launched an array of measures targeted at these firms. Key components of such strategies were the provision of finance, technical assistance, promotion of inter firm organisation and administrative simplification. For instance, tax reforms in the late 1980s were intended to help small firms by lowering tax rates and reducing paperwork. In 1987, Congress enacted a law that created the concept of *"Ventanillas Unicas de Gestion"*, literally the "only window for management". Since then, dozens of one-stop-shops have been set up to provide information, and in some cases administer, over 70 formalities ranging from sanitary licences and notification to tax registration and social security registration.

However, despite partial successes, these initiatives did not reduce the growth of the informal sector or improve their chances to become "formal" businesses. In part, this is due to poor economic performance, but also most of the programmes were unco-ordinated and dependent on expensive "facilitators" making them extremely costly to sustain.

Since 1995, the government has tried a complementary approach to "re-legalise" the informal sector. Its main component was to reduce regulatory compliance costs, either their official components, their "evasion costs", or both. An important government response was the deregulation programme launched in Mexico City in 1996 (see Section 2.3). To reduce official compliance costs, a new licensing system was set up in which 73% of activities (which created 78% of the added value in Mexico City) were deemed "low risk" and could comply with land use, fire prevention, construction and pollution control requirements through a single format. An automatic authorisation was established after seven days if regulators had not commented. In parallel, these efforts were completed by deregulation of federal formalities in important sectors such as sanitation, environment, taxes, and social security (see Section 4).

To reduce "regulatory evasion costs", three strategies were used. First, the government declared a general pardon for businesses out of compliance. This amnesty permitted more than 10 000 micro-firms to "formalise" tax or other regulatory situations without paying arrears or fines. Second, in order to combat discretionary abuses by inspectors and private "vigilantes" as well as to grant legal security to businesses, Federal District authorities and the Mexican Business Council (CCE) launched in 1997 a certification programme where after a simple audit a business premise was recognised as "in compliance" with local regulations and a corresponding official document delivered. Third, UDE together with the Comptroller General and Federal District authorities developed a verification system where inspectors and business were chosen at random and where different transparency rules were created to reduce abuses and harassment during enforcement.

It is too early to assess the results of these measures. As indicated above, the roots of informality go beyond the regulatory framework, and complete deregulation would not solve the excess supply of unskilled labour or the scarcity of capital and education supporting the informal sector. However, Mexico's initiatives are worth noting, as they recognise the explicit link between regulatory reform, non-compliance and the need to help micro-firms to grow.

### Reform of the judicial branch

Enforcement and compliance are, of course, highly dependent on the rule of law prevailing in the country. As indicated in Section 1, the centralist and authoritarian administrative environment, in place until recently, resulted in a judicial branch that was politicised, weak and inadequate. In addition to their lack of real autonomy, courts and judicial bodies were constantly underfunded. This made the pace of justice extremely slow. Years were needed before a dispute could be settled. Lack of resources also created vast opportunities for corruption and abuses among civil servants employed in the judicial branch. Dearth of training and career development programmes bled the tribunals.[38]

As a result, access to justice was often achieved through different means. First and foremost, the writ of Amparo permitted any citizen to appeal to the Supreme Court and to the other courts affiliated to the federal judicial system. The Amparo is a mechanism through which citizens can challenge any infringement by the government of individual rights granted by the constitution.[39] This specific habeas corpus enabled many citizens and businesses to successfully oppose and even repeal flawed rules or improper actions by the administration. As such, the Amparo also serves as an ex ante control to verify the quality of regulations as regulators writing regulations are deterred by possible challenge in court by any person or business.[40]

A second mechanism used by the Mexican government to improve access to justice was the progressive creation of an array of partially independent quasi-judicial bodies within the administration. From the early 1930s the government established administrative tribunals and entities in the field of labour disputes (Junta Federal de Conciliacion y Arbitraje) agrarian affairs (Tribunal Agrario), electoral controversies (Tribunal de lo Contencioso Electoral Federal), fiscal matters (Tribunal Fiscal de la Federacion), and other administrative dispute settlement (*Tribunal del Contencioso Administrativo*). It should be noted that in 1992 and 1996, respectively, the agrarian and electoral tribunals were incorporated in the judicial branch and a totally independent *Instituto Federal Electoral* has now been created.

There is no doubt that the *Amparo* mechanism and the quasi-judicial tribunals solved many problems and speeded settlements. However, for most private citizens and firms they did not provide an adequate solution. Resources and time were still needed to win or to avoid reprisals. As public participation increased, the demand for a fairer and more efficient system prevailed.

This became a major policy of the Zedillo administration. In the days after coming into power in December 1994, the president submitted a legal package of major constitutional and legal changes, which has since been enacted as the Judicial Reform. They were part of a policy explained a few months later in the 1995-2000 National Development Plan:

*Today, our legal and institutional framework is not totally adequate to the expectations and conditions of our time. Important backwardness, vices and needs on public security, prosecution and delivery of justice, combat on corruption and impunity, legal certainty and acknowledgement of fundamental rights, particularly of most vulnerable of social groups subsist. Consequently, many members of our national community have legitimate doubts and concerns about the enforcement and reality of the State of Rule, and for equality in front of the Law and public institutions.*[41]

The president's reforms endeavoured to expand the constitutional power of the federal judiciary overhauling the composition of the Supreme Court to make it more accountable for its jurisprudence and less vulnerable to pressure from executive and legislative branches.[42] The main characteristics of the reforms are the following:

– Restructuring and renewing the Supreme Court to strengthen the federal judiciary (number of Supreme Court Ministers reduced from 26 to 11; term limits increased from six years (which use to coincided with the presidential term) to 15 years; nominations, which will be staggered and scheduled to avoid overlapping with transition in the executive branch, made subject to public congressional hearings and approval by two thirds of the Senate; and the freeing of the Supreme Court from administrative duties relating to the federal judiciary).

– Creating the Federal Judicial Council (*Consejo de la Judicatura Federal*), now in charge of managing and modernising the federal judiciary system, including the selection, promotion, policing and general improvement of the quality of federal judges and magistrates (the Council is comprised of the President of the Supreme Court, three members elected by judges and magistrates, two designated by the Senate and one by the president of the Republic).

– Enabling federal and state legislators and the Attorney General to contest the constitutionality of laws before the Supreme Court, whose decision becomes broadly applicable to all citizens (in contrast, when a person wins an *Amparo* trial, the law in question only ceases to apply to that person in particular).

– Granting municipalities access to the Supreme Court for the settlement of disputes with other municipalities, states, or the federation (only the states and the federation had such access before), and clarifying the basic principles for the judicial procedures that apply to jurisdictional disputes of all types.

The efforts of the CJEF and the UDE also contributed to streamlining court procedures. In May 1996, reforms were implemented to facilitate the resolution of business disputes and to provide businesses with greater access to loans by eliminating the requirement that guarantee trusts (*fideicomisos de pago*) be administered by third parties. According the *Tribunal Superior de Justicia del Distrito Federal*, the reforms reduced the number of trials in Mexico City by 41% between 1995 and 1997.[43] Similar reforms were passed in the northern state of Nuevo León in 1997, resulting in a 52% reduction in the number of trials between 1996 and 1998. Because it is now more difficult to unscrupulously delay trial proceedings, many more commercial disputes are now being resolved without going to court.

These changes helped to strengthen judicial oversight of administrative discretion. Yet Mexico is still in a transition phase, where new mechanisms co-exist, sometimes uncomfortably, with older ones.

Improvements and legal reforms are still needed. The most challenging task will be to gain the confidence of citizens through concrete results. This will only be achieved through a continuous effort to deepen and strengthen the professionalism, technical skills and specialist knowledge of the courts and their officers. Reforms of this kind involve the building of new cultures and institutions and are inherently long-term in nature.

### 3.2. Choice of policy instruments: regulation and alternatives

A core administrative capacity for good regulation is the ability to choose the most efficient and effective policy tool, whether regulatory or non-regulatory. The range of policy tools and their uses is expanding as experimentation occurs, learning is diffused, and understanding of markets increases. At the same time, administrators often face risks in using relatively untried tools. Bureaucracies are highly conservative and there are typically strong disincentives for public servants to be innovative. A clear leading role – supportive of innovation and policy learning – must be taken by reform authorities if alternatives to traditional regulation are to make serious headway in the policy system.

The use of alternatives to traditional regulation is fairly new in Mexico's regulatory processes. Until the middle of the 1990's most regulations were based on the "command and control" principle. Mexican regulators and enforcers often focused on compliance with rules and procedures rather than results. More recently, some reforms have been launched. In 1994, the Environment and Energy Ministries attempted to introduce a market for SOx pollution permits in the main industrial zones. However, concerns raised by publicly owned enterprises in the oil and electricity sectors and poor design of the scheme compromised this effort. In 1995, ADAE established an explicit review criterion which required agencies to ensure that "[…] no regulatory alternatives exist that can accomplish the same objectives at lower cost". This test was subsequently reinforced by a special Section in the RIA reporting system. Based on these tools, and through negotiations with regulators, the government has been designing regulations providing more information to consumers, using random ex post compliance verification schemes, seeking implementation of voluntary rather than compulsory standards (self-regulation or co-regulation), providing flexibility in regulatory compliance, regulating ends rather than means, eliminating underlying economic distortions, and using insurance schemes. It is too early to judge their final impact but some examples can illustrate the scope of current efforts.

As in many OECD countries, most innovations have concentrated in the area of environmental protection. Mexico receives mixed marks here. The positive steps include:

- The Ministry of Environment was the first ministry to enact, in its reformed law of 1996, the use of the "equivalent principle" to prepare technical standards (NOMs). The objective is to allow any business to propose more efficient compliance mechanisms that achieve equal or superior performance to that achieved via NOM. Approval of a business' proposed alternative requires that it be presented in detailed form to the National Office of Standards, who, after advice from an appropriate committee, issues a certificate of conformity or rejects the proposal. Automatic approval is granted if the application receives no response after a set time. Approvals are announced in the Federal Official Gazette. This last feature is intended to grant the same benefits to other parties by alerting them to the existence of an approved alternative compliance mechanism. To date, this process has been used for NOMs in three policy areas: fisheries control, health and safety, and environment. In the latter area, a group of businesses proposed an alternative to a NOM controlling the size of the mandatory buffer zone surrounding explosive vessels and installations with risk. The accepted alternative consisted of a smaller buffer zone protected by special installations and devices.
- Environmental enforcement has used as an alternative to traditional enforcement approaches a programme of eco-audits. These audits are in-depth and interdisciplinary reviews of a company's production process to identify pollution and risk conditions. The audits cover discharges into all media (including water) and determine the degree of compliance with regulations and international engineering practices. Following the audit, the company signs an agreement with the authority on the steps to clean up its operations, committing itself to specific timelines. By agree-

ing, the firm avoids criminal sanctions and can often reduce its insurance premiums. By August 1997 the Environment Ministry had approved 2 110 audits (775 in border states with the US) and 698 had been completed (198 in border states).[44]

On the other hand, the record of Mexico is poor with respect to the use of economic instruments, particularly in the area of managing externalities (for instance, linked to environment, water and fisheries management). Only two schemes are reported: water effluent charges and transferable hunting rights. But as mentioned in the previous section, the UDE also made a major effort in finding alternatives to permitting and enforcement systems and has promoted economic instruments like transferable permits, concession auctioning, etc in areas such as federal transport and bidding schemes for mines and spectrum franchises. In particular, a significant number of *ex ante* permits and licences have been replaced with general rules (often performance based) and *ex post* checking.

Efforts to adopt innovative alternatives have been too recent to allow for a definitive evaluation of their impact. A major gap in efforts to date is the lack of progress in establishing economic regulatory instruments for social and environmental regulations. Some significant initiatives have been taken, even if overall Mexico is trailing other OECD countries in this field. Of particular interest to other OECD countries is the innovative use of the equivalence principle in relation to NOMs, an approach that is currently being considered in Australia. If it performs well while satisfying transparency and accountability standards, this would be a promising and powerful tool to expand the use of performance oriented regulations. The Mexican implementation seems to be the first broad use in practice of this mechanism, and should be monitored.

### 3.3. Understanding regulatory effects: the use of Regulatory Impact Analysis (RIA)

The 1995 Recommendation of the Council of the OECD on *Improving the Quality of Government Regulation* emphasised the role of RIA in systematically ensuring that the most efficient and effective policy options are chosen. The 1997 OECD Report on Regulatory Reform recommended that governments integrate regulatory impact analysis into the development, review, and reform of regulations. A list of RIA best practices is discussed in detail in *Regulatory Impact Analysis: Best Practices in OECD Countries*[45] and provide a framework for the following description and assessment of RIA practice in Mexico.

With the 1996 amendments to the Federal Administrative Procedure Law, Mexico joined the two thirds of OECD countries using RIA as a tool to improve the quality of regulation, and the small group of countries where such a requirement is established by law. The law states that all draft regulations with a potential impact on business activity must be submitted to UDE for review, along with a regulatory impact statement (RIA). As in other countries, development of RIA in Mexico has not been entirely smooth. The benefit-cost analysis (BCA) requirement for preparation of NOMs that was established in 1992 encountered major implementation problems. Consultative committees in charge of preparing the BCA had great difficulties in producing scientific or objective data. BCA was often little more than a list of qualitative benefits and political considerations set against a description of minor transition costs. In effect, BCA became an extra layer in the paperwork process, rather than a guide to decision-making.

Between the establishment of the ADAE (January 1996) and the effective establishment of RIA requirements (January 1998), the UDE and regulators gained valuable experience, based sometimes on frictions and problems between agencies. At the beginning, the regulatory review occurred at the very end of the drafting process. Regulatory agencies were not accustomed to having their proposals reviewed by a third party, and did not allocate sufficient time to incorporate comments. The review process was characterised by regulators as a bottleneck that impeded important regulations, and even regulatory reforms. The review process was undermined by confrontation and lengthy and sometimes sterile negotiations. Analysis of these problems and a six month pilot phase has resulted in a fairly successful launch of the new RIA programme. To correct earlier problems, the programme is designed to enhance communication between the UDE and ministries/regulatory agencies and to provide incentives for incorporating quality regulation criteria earlier in the drafting process to avoid "unpleasant surprises" for the ministries at a later stage.

UDE's current RIA requirements were developed from a study of international best practices. The objectives are to provide CDE/UDE with more detailed information on the benefits and costs of regulations and to help regulatory agencies to consider ADAE criteria early in the regulatory process. The ultimate goal is to foster a cultural change among regulators.

A major element of this initiative was the preparation of a detailed manual, accessible and acceptable to ministries. A draft manual was sent to the ministries in June 1997. After incorporation of comments a final version was distributed throughout the federal government in September 1997. The manual specifies instructions for completing the six sections of RIA:

1. *Purpose of the regulation.* Agencies must list the behaviour to be regulated and the reasons for government intervention. Providing explanation and evidence of the problems that the proposed regulation purports to solve is essential. There are, however, no standard criteria or threshold tests used to evaluate these justifications. Risk assessment is sometimes used for environmental regulations, but not very widely. The quality and scope of data available are rather meagre, so priority setting is seldom done according to pre-established technical criteria. While individual ministries often set regulatory priorities, there has been no serious attempt to do this on a government-wide basis. This Section of the RIA must also include an explanation of the legal basis for the regulation. A description of all related regulations (including any international obligations) is included, as well as the reasons they have proven unsatisfactory in dealing with the problem.

2. *Alternatives considered and proposed solution.* Regulators are asked to identify all possible regulatory and non-regulatory responses (including the option of doing nothing) to the problems at hand. The alternatives must be described and the reasons for rejecting them clearly stated. International standards must be considered and preferentially applied based on a case-by-case analysis.

3. *Implementation and enforcement.* Implementation and enforcement schemes must be described in detail (sanctions, verification mechanisms, etc.). It is particularly important for the regulatory agency to explain where it expects to obtain the resources needed to apply the proposed regulation effectively.

4. *Public consultation.* Ministries are required to list all parties consulted (including names and telephone numbers) and their opinions. The description of the results of public consultation has often been found to be the most useful part of RIA. Because the data employed in the analyses are rarely of high quality, the opinions of affected parties (appropriately discounted for biases and self-interest) are frequently seen as the most accurate way to evaluate the potential effects of regulations. Nonetheless, an unsurprising tendency for regulatory authorities to minimise any conflicts or differences of opinion and present the chosen regulation as the consensus option has been observed.

5. *Anticipated benefits and costs.* RIAs must include a structured description of the potential costs and benefits of the proposed regulation. The level of quantification and detail of the costs and benefits Section is expected to be proportional to the importance of the project. Only regulations of major impact need to quantify benefits and costs extensively. Different types of costs and benefits must be identified and discussed (effects on capital costs, operation costs, salary costs, consulting/legal costs, conformity assessment costs, health environment or other social costs, administrative costs, etc.), and distributive implications made explicit. The UDE has developed a list of criteria to help regulators self-assess the relative impact of their proposals and thus prepare an appropriate RIA (see Table 4). According to UDE, the biggest problem for the costs and benefits Section of the RIA is that the quality of data is generally poor and thus a quantitative analysis of proposals is virtually impossible. Regulatory authorities are not asked to produce net benefit estimates, for fear of creating additional incentives to distort already inadequate data. The UDE has stated that one of its top priorities for further development of RIA is to improve the availability and use of high quality data.

6. *Identification of business formalities.* All formalities created, modified or maintained by the proposed regulation must be listed and described. This is important because it enables the UDE to track changes in formalities and update the federal inventory of formalities on the Internet (see Section 4). Agencies must give specific information regarding the formalities including the legal basis, rules of application, criteria for decisions, the regulatory authority's maximum

Table 4.  **Threshold criteria in preparing a RIA**

| Level of impact | Characteristics of costs | Level of quantification required |
|---|---|---|
| Low | Total annual costs do not exceed 5 million pesos (1997). Negligible impact on employment and business productivity. | No quantification required. Qualitative description of costs and benefits. |
| Medium | Annual costs between 5 and 500 million pesos (1997). Non-negligible impact on employment and productivity. Affects some economic sectors but effects are neither substantial nor generalised. | Quantification of costs and benefits suited to quantification. Qualitative description of the rest. |
| High | Annual costs greater than 500 million pesos (1997). Generalised impact on multiple sectors of the economy, employment and business productivity. Substantial impact on a particular sector, industry or region. | Complete quantification of all costs and benefits. |

---

Box 8.  **RIA grading mechanism**

To track the quality of RIAs by type of regulation and by regulatory agency, the UDE has devised a simple internal RIA grading mechanism. The grade given to each RIA reflects its overall quality, measured as a function of the care with which each distinct sub-component of the RIA was prepared.

There are 14 distinct sub-components by which RIA are measured, and for each of these a grade ranging from –2 (very bad) to +2 (very good) is assigned. These sub-components are:

1. Definition and evidence of the existence of the problem to be resolved.
2. Legal basis for the proposed regulation.
3. Description of existing regulations relating to the same issue.
4. Quality of regulatory alternatives presented.
5. Description of the proposed regulation.
6. Table relating problems identified to regulatory (or non-regulatory) solutions proposed.
7. Description of implementation and enforcement schemes.
8. Quality of implementation and enforcement schemes.
9. Quality of public consultation undertaken.
10. Description of different opinions presented during public consultation.
11. Quality of the description of potential costs and benefits.
12. Quality of the quantification of potential costs and benefits.
13. Degree to which distributional consequences are explicitly stated.
14. Degree to which formalities are identified and described.

The grading of each of the 14 sub-components gives an overall grade of –28 to +28, which is then transformed to a scale from 0 to 10. Agencies have received average grades ranging from 4.4 to 7.3, with an overall average of 6.3. The average quality of RIAs for regulatory agencies/ministries is almost a (positively-sloped) linear function of the number of RIAs sent to the UDE. With this system, the UDE has targeted technical assistance to 30% of RIAs, increasing their score to 1.5 point more than the general average score of 6.0 for all RIAs reviewed.

permissible response times, and all associated data requirements. Listing thesecharacteristics often helps ministries take a more careful look at their business formalities and make them as simple as possible. Thus, this element of the RIA *pro forma* creates a link between RIA requirements and the review of formalities underway as part of the broader regulatory programme. This innovative aspect of Mexican RIA content may be a promising practice given the widespread attention in OECD countries to administrative and paperwork burdens and means of reducing them.

Between the start of the programme in September 1997 and June 1999, the UDE reviewed 286 RIAs. The UDE provided technical assistance to regulators in 93 cases to assist them in improving the quality of the RIA. According to the UDE, in the first year of implementation the quality of RIAs and analytical sophistication have slowly improved as regulators develop skills. UDE has developed and applied an innovative scoring system for individual RIAs (see Box 8) that allows tracking of RIA quality on a systematic basis over time. The trend in the scores is upward. The scoring system is also used to identify systematic problems.

A more fundamental aspect of RIA compliance has also been tracked and shows a gradual improvement. In the first few months, at least a quarter of the regulatory proposals received by the UDE were not accompanied by a RIA. Subsequently, CJEF has required that any proposals submitted to it without an accompanying RIA be returned to the proposing ministry and resubmitted. As indicated previously, a letter sent by the Comptroller General to all deputy ministers in charge of implementing regulatory reform programmes, reminding them to comply with the RIA programme, was very useful in getting the RIA programme off the ground. According to the UDE, without it, compliance would undoubtedly have been poorer. As of May 1999, the UDE also sends fortnightly reports to Comptroller General on the degree of compliance with RIA requirements. These reports allow the Comptroller General to issue warnings to non-compliant ministries, even in the case of lower-level regulations.

### Assessment against best practices

As the RIA requirement is recent, no evaluation of the system or its impact on the quality of regulations has been made. Yet framework issues and methodological aspects are worth noting.

*Maximise political commitment to* RIA. The use of RIA to support reform should continue to be endorsed at the highest levels of government. The Mexican system rates highly on this criterion. RIA has become a central element of the regulatory reform programme. One important means used in Mexico to achieve this is the requirement that RIAs for proposed laws, presidential regulations (*reglamentos*) and decrees be signed by high-level officials such as the deputy minister, and for other subordinate regulations by general directors before being sent to the UDE. An additional element to assure political support and the credibility of the instrument has been the voluntary use by CJEF of RIAs when analysing regulations requiring the president's signature.

*Allocate responsibilities for* RIA *programme elements carefully.* To ensure ownership by regulators while at the same time establishing quality control and consistency, responsibilities should be shared between regulators and a central quality control unit. The Mexican approach has mixed results on this standard. On one hand, except for regulations not covered by the Administrative Procedure Law and the Standards Law, draft regulations must have a RIA reviewed by the UDE. However, the UDE cannot oppose the implementation of poor regulations. UDE's statutory powers permit it delay the implementation of regulatory proposals, oppose the establishment of business formalities, and make public its opinion. For instance, cases of non-compliance with the RIA requirements in the telecommunication sector and of some areas of the Finance Ministry have been reported.

To help regulators fulfil their new responsibilities the UDE established a technical assistance facility. UDE desk officers are encouraged to approach the regulators and help them to understand and implement the new tool. As analytical requirements become more complex these capacities are expected to need enhancement. There is also concern that technical assistance and final review are provided by the same desk officers. Conflicts of interest or even capture may occur as UDE administrators are involved consistently with the same agency.

*Train the regulators*. Regulators must have the skills to do high quality RIA. As previously indicated the RIA programme was intended to nurture a cultural change among regulators. Mexico has not developed a systematic training programme on RIA. Early in the RIA implementation process, the UDE organised one day general training sessions for regulatory agencies. Subsequently, the UDE has relied on improved guidelines and technical assistance arrangements. With funding from a development bank, BANOBRAS, a pilot seminar on implementing a RIA programme was organised to train public officials in the states. Room for improvement clearly exists. The initial implementation phase of RIA is when the benefits of systematic training will be highest, both in imparting technical skills not widely available and in hastening broader cultural changes within Ministries.

*Use a consistent but flexible analytical method*. The experience with initial BCA requirements for NOMs was negative. It was difficult to reach an adequate level of analytical sophistication when starting from a very low initial base, and lack of an external review reduced incentives for serious work. As a result, the current RIA guidelines have concentrated on changing rational thought processes within regulatory agencies rather than obtaining precise values. Broad quantification of costs, but not benefits, is required. No accounting methodology is proposed. Alternatives not considered need only be described, rather than analysed. However, two additional features of the Mexican RIA programme should be noted. The first is the requirement for a detailed table, cross referencing the problem to be solved with the solution proposed, including the contribution of each part of the regulation. Any requirements left out of this table need to be specifically justified. Secondly, analysis of proposed formalities must be more extensive,

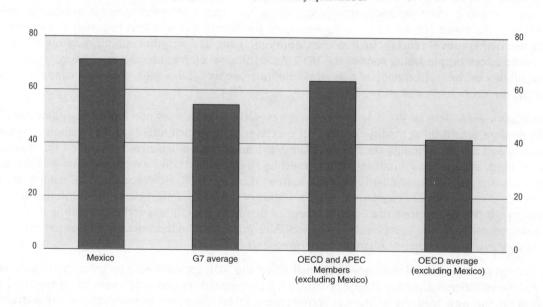

Box 9. **Use of regulatory impact analysis in selected OECD countries**

This synthetic indicator of different elements of regulatory impact analysis (based on self-assessments) ranks more highly those RIA programmes where benefits and costs are quantified, and where a benefit-cost test is used in decision-making. Mexico ranks above the G7, APEC and OECD average on this score. Its score was reduced by the fact that there is no requirement to publicly release RIA documents, and that benefits and costs are not consistently quantified.

including an identification of the existing formality (where applicable) or, in case of a new formality, a justification of why approval is needed rather than notification.

*Develop and implement data collection strategies.* An essential part of the RIA guidelines consists of a thorough discussion of the consultation process during preparation of the proposal. This is to encourage regulators to solicit views from affected parties of the likely impacts of proposals. From the UDE view, the list of consulted parties provides information about the quality of the data collection strategy as well as potential bias. However, the RIA guidance material developed by the UDE has not incorporated elements to help agencies to develop data collection strategies, such as surveys, structured public consultation, econometric tools, etc.[46]

*Target RIA efforts.* RIA resources should be targeted to those regulations where impacts are most significant, and where the prospects are best for altering outcomes. In all cases, the amount of time and effort spent on regulatory analysis should be commensurate with the improvement in the regulation that the analysis is expected to provide.[47] The Mexican approach can be characterised as "partially targeted", in that, while the RIA requirement applies to all draft regulations, three broad levels of analytical rigour and effort are distinguished by guidelines, depending on the importance of the regulation (see Table 3 above). The intention is to target the use of resources without losing the possibility of building a complete regulatory inventory.

*Integrate RIA with the policy-making process, beginning as early as possible.* The UDE believes that the current RIA approach is less confrontational and more co-operative than the previous system. In particular they underline their emphasis on the provision of technical assistance early in the drafting period.

*Involve the public extensively.* RIAs have become important working tools for the reviews by the UDE and the CDE working groups. Even if the UDE cannot prevent the passage of a proposed regulation with a RIA that is deemed unsatisfactory, the law permits it to make public its concerns. To promote public participation, the UDE has begun to publish on its Internet web page a listing of all proposals that indicates if they complied with RIA requirements. This possibility is also very important for promoting compliance by agencies that may otherwise try to bypass regulatory oversight. However, neither SECOFI nor the Council has the legal obligation to publish the RIA. Public availability of RIAs and the Internet listing of proposals dependent on SECOFI and the Council's political will. A clear requirement for open public consultation based on RIA, incorporating key procedural safeguards, remains a significant gap in the Mexican system. The concerns expressed by reform officials about data quality in RIA highlight the potential gains from addressing this shortcoming.

*Apply RIA to existing as well as new regulations.* RIA disciplines are equally useful in the review of existing regulation as in the *ex ante* assessment of new regulatory proposals. Indeed, the *ex post* nature of regulatory review means that data problems will be fewer and the quality of the resulting analysis potentially higher. Currently, Mexico has not used RIAs to analyse existing regulations, or even formalities. This is a major area into which RIA use could be extended.

### 3.4. Building regulatory agencies

Implementing systems for regulatory scrutiny and review is necessary but not sufficient for a successful programme of regulatory management and reform. Also of primary importance is the development of well-designed regulatory institutions and a change of culture among regulators. Three issues should be considered in this respect. First, how can accountable and independent institutions which resist capture by interest groups, either public or private, be established. Second, how can the accountability of regulators be improved. Thirdly, how can regulators be trained and equipped with the requisite skills and attitudes for the making of high quality regulation.

In parallel to the general overhaul of the legal framework, the pace of institution building has accelerated and a new type of regulatory institution has appeared in Mexico.[48] These new entities have three common characteristics: a high degree of technical specialisation, a concentration on regulatory or enforcement aspects, leaving policy or normative matters to the ministries, and a greater degree of autonomy, particularly concerning budgetary and human resources policies.

However, the new institutions are quite different from one another. For instance, in relation to their legal autonomy *vis-à-vis* the executive branch, these entities can be divided in broad terms into four categories (the dates noted are those of the most recent reforms):

- *Independent from the Executive branch*: The Central Bank (*Banco de Mexico*) (since 1994); the Electoral Institution (*Instituto Federal Electoral* – IFE) (since 1996).

- *Independent inside the Executive branch*: National Commission for Human Rights (CNDH) (since 1992), the Federal Competition Commission (CFC) (since 1994).

- *Policy setting partially autonomous and technically independent*, Regulatory Energy Commission (CRE) (since 1995).

- *Technically autonomous from the sectoral ministry*: Federal Telecommunication Agency (COFETEL) established in 1996,[49] the banking and security industry commission[50] (*Comision Nacional Bancaria y de Valores*), the Unit of Unfair International Trading (*Unidad de Practicas Desleales de Comercio Internacional*), the National Institute of Ecology, or the National Water Commission (CONAGUA), Revenue administration (*Servicio de Administracion Tributaria*) in 1997, etc.

Additionally, midway between the judicial and executive branches, some new prosecutorial agencies have been created for specific policy areas such as consumer protection in 1994 (*Procuraduria Federal del Consumidor*), the environment in 1993 (*Procuraduria Federal del Medio Ambiente*) and family and minors issues (*Procuraduria del Menor y la Familia*).

This increasingly complex institutional setting offers great potential in improving regulatory efficiency. The specialised and more autonomous regulators have created important "checks and balances" to match the powers of ministries and interest groups and increase the speed and quality of regulatory decisions. Their operation are also more transparent and accountable. Most of the new regulators have their own budgets and human resource policies. Economic regulatory agencies, like CFC, CRE, and COFETEL, have moved to the use of fixed term appointments for their most senior executives, with removal possible only on limited grounds. Academics and businessmen have begun to be nominated to the boards of these organisations.

Some issues remain unresolved. First, appointments to most of the institutions are still made by ministers, rarely by the president and even more rarely (notably in the case of the central bank and electoral institute), are confirmed by the Senate. Thus, for many appointees, independence is constrained by career considerations. A conflict with the minister in charge of the sector may be costly for the individual regulator and for the institution. Second, though some of the new regulatory agencies have a more autonomous, and thus more "attractive" staff policy, they are still severely limited by the quality of personnel. The rapid rate of creation has put a high premium on technical specialists in an already tight professional labour market. The superior attractiveness of jobs with the independent agencies has, at the same time, further weakened the ministries' ability to recruit and retain high quality regulatory staff, while a lack of training of the regulators (see below) ensures that the problem persists. A consequence is that economic regulators are technically vulnerable to special interests supported by private consultants. Third, their legal status has not always guaranteed *de facto* autonomy from the ministries. The agencies are dependent in many ways on the relevant sectoral Ministry. In a highly hierarchical administrative culture, most chief regulators must convince "their" minister to implement their decisions. Additionally, in some cases the procedures of the independent agencies are deficient in terms of accountability and transparency. For instance, the existence of a large amount of discretionality in the definition of powers of COFETEL and CRE may create incentives to act as active proponents of an industrial policy protecting national champions.[51]

Lastly, the creation of this web of regulatory institutions has been a product of partial modifications and has lacked a coherent and explicit design. In some aspects it resembles the US and UK models of sectoral regulatory commissions. In others, it resembles the French model of ministerial control through the grant of concessions. Important economic sectors lack an independent regulator, for instance the audio-visual and rail and freight transport sectors. Regulatory powers among the established regulators vary in scope and scale. For example COFETEL is less independent from the Ministry of Transport and Communication than the CRE from the Ministry of Energy, but the latter deals mainly in a sector where powerful state-owned players are still dominant. The Water Commission has not only important regulatory powers but also executive duties, employing more than 24 000 employees around the country. Further, vital co-ordination and harmonisation mechanisms are lacking, even when much of the theoretical foundations are similar. For example, essential issues like controlling prices or managing access arrangements for "essential (or network) facilities" or interconnection prices differ between agencies. This may lead rapidly to institutional erosion as rent-seeking firms attempt to arbitrage among the regulators in an attempt to find the most attractive protected niche activities.[52] Crucially, legal and institutional consistency is lacking between the competition authority and the sectoral regulators, in particular in regard to the extent and form of the oversight role of the competition authority. Presently the CFC links with sectoral regulators through its participation to inter-ministerial committees at sub minister level, through the authorisation of participants to the privatisation process, and through binding opinions for existing regulations and non-binding opinion for new regulations. These are important elements but additional co-ordination mechanisms and improvement of CFC oversight role may be needed in the future[53] (see also background report on the Role of Competition Policy in Regulatory Reform).

Another contributor to the quality of the civil service in the regulatory bodies is the training of regulators. Some important regulatory failures can be blamed upon lack of expertise among the personnel concerned. For instance, administrative failures by the highways regulator (*Caminos y Puentes Federales*, part of the Ministry of Communication and Transport) in managing the concessions to private operators, induced higher than expected construction costs and further exacerbated their financial situations after their privatisation.[54] Equally, some responsibility for the financial sector crisis of 1994 has been attributed to major failures in regulatory supervision.[55]

In the rapidly changing environment of Mexico of the late 1990's, human capital shortages cannot be solved in the short term. Nor can reforms wait on the availability of optimum implementation capacities. However training regulators can pay handsomely. UDE has made some efforts in this field. They are, however, insufficient in relation to the challenges.

## 4. DYNAMIC CHANGE: KEEPING REGULATIONS UP-TO-DATE

The OECD *Report on Regulatory Reform* recommends that governments review regulations systematically to ensure that they continue to meet their intended objectives efficiently and effectively. For many decades, the Mexican legal system accumulated regulations and formalities without any effort to review their compatibility or their adequacy in changing social and economic environments. In the past few years, however, substantial progress has been made to review and improve or eliminate this stock of regulatory requirements. Five initiatives are discussed below.

*Review of existing formalities.* Formalities, and in particular licences and permits, are seen as a major problem and a major contribution to the cost of doing business. In some cases, they have functioned as entry barriers, particularly for SMEs. According to a World Bank estimate, without considering transaction and opportunity costs, opening a business could take up to a year and a half, while the costs of complying with all the formalities governing business operations in some cases account for about 3% of a large firm's operating expenses.[56] Additionally, the previous existence of an unspecified number of formalities – sometimes regulatory agencies did not know how many formalities they were responsible for – created a state of uncertainty and opportunities for corruption. Hence, reforming formalities became a high priority in the regulatory reform programme. The ADAE sets out a precise review procedure to "eliminate or simplify unnecessarily burdensome information requirements". At the end of this review and any reforms, a list of the official "deregulated" formalities for each ministry is published in the *Diario Official*. At publication, the formalities listed are included in the Federal Registry of Business

Formalities. Through this process, the Registry should be comprehensive – that is, the Federal Registry must include the full set of enforceable formalities – and should provide legal security to businesses.

The review programme had four stages. First, an inventory was drawn up, through a detailed reporting requirement in which all ministries needed to answer a range of precise questions for each one of its formalities. This systematic analysis enhanced regulatory communication, as most of the ministries did not know the exact number of their formalities. It was also a deregulation mechanism, as ministries "cleaning up their house" voluntarily eliminated outdated and illegal formalities, rather than reporting them. In December of 1996, the inventory was published on the CDE web page.

Second, once a ministry's formalities were identified, the UDE began reviewing the formalities for each ministry in a sequential order (see Box 10).

The process has not been completed, but the mechanism has been launched through the whole of the administration. To date, ten out of twelve federal ministries subject to review have completed the first step of the formality reviews, that is, each minister has presented to the CDE and committed specific reforms to the formalities they are in charge of (see last column of Table 5). According to the latest report, the review process has resulted in official commitments to eliminate around 50% of the mandatory formalities already reviewed.[57] In addition, ministries have agreed to simplify and improve 97% of the remaining formalities. Although the programme seems to be taking the right steps to improve the administrative

---

### Box 10.   Reviewing a formality in Mexico

1.  A ministry's inventory of formalities and related documentation is handed to a special advisory group composed of business persons and other interested parties. A deadline is established for receiving individual proposals.

2.  In parallel, a UDE desk officer and team examines each formality in detail and prepares proposals based on the regulatory reform criteria established in the ADAE. The review is based on the following checklist:
    - Can the formality be eliminated?
    - Can an alternative be found, for instance changing a permit into a notification or a set of general rules to be verified *ex post*?
    - Can the authority's response time be reduced and an automatic approval system established?
    - Can individual information requirements (including annex documents) that constitute the formality be eliminated?
    - Can other elements of the formality been improved?

3.  A document presenting the final proposals for each formality is presented to the regulatory agency and after a negotiation process generally lasting between three and nine months and meetings of the executive commission (in which the private sector participates actively), the package is presented to the CDE by the corresponding minister for approval.

4.  The regulatory agency, with the help of the UDE, implements the approved proposals. This stage is a delicate and resource intensive process due in part to the Mexican civil law system. At least three distinct legal instruments must be prepared depending on the elements to be reformed. Formalities may be established in a law, in a presidential regulation (reglamento), in a ministerial instruction, or in a combination of these. The simplest, and hence more rapid, reforms modify a ministerial instruction. Changes to laws and presidential rulings require the involvement of the CJEF. Finally if a law is reformed, Congress must be involved. A "deregulation package" is negotiated and passed. Complete implementation of a ministry approved proposal that includes legislative changes can take up to two years.

5.  After publication of a detailed description of reviewed formalities in the Federal Official Gazette, the UDE registers them in the Federal Registry of Business Formalities.

6.  The Comptroller General verifies the administrative implementation of the reforms through a set of performance indicators developed by the Modernisation of the Public Administration Programme.

environment for business by increasing transparency and simplifying federal formalities, the overall regulatory burden reductions and estimated potential cost-savings are not yet studied nor documented.

The process for the review of formalities is well designed, incorporating a significant level of involvement from affected parties and a strong role for the regulatory reform body, which is able to take an "independent" view. At the same time, dialogue and negotiation with the administering Ministry provides a means of ensuring implementation of the reform as well as a check on feasibility. However, the progress of the reform has been slower than originally expected. In the three and a half years since the programme started, 63% of the stock of business formalities has been reviewed and 28% of the agreed changes are not yet implemented in law and subordinated regulations (see Figure 1).

Two main problems have slowed the reaping of benefits by consumers and businesses. First, although by the end of the summer of 1999 the UDE will have finalised the review of the whole set of formalities (with the review of the 1 027 formalities of the Ministry of Finance and of the 67 formalities of the telecommunications sector), the implementation of agreed changes would still be a few months away. Indeed, an essential element to produce results is the needed enactment in laws and subordinated regulations of the changes agreed by ministries and agencies at the CDE. Although 64 legal instruments directly related to the implementation of the regulatory reform programme have been adopted since 1995 (17 laws, 19 *reglamentos* and presidential decrees, and 28 ministerial decrees), Figure 1 shows that, in the last year, the gap between reviewing and implementing changes has grown. This situation is attributable to complex factors. One reason refers to the structure of Mexico's legal system where a reform needs to start at the level of a law before being consolidated in a subordinate regulation. As discussed in Section 1 the emergence of a cohabitation government has meant that more time is needed to prepare and enact legal reforms through Congress. Another reason is that a large number of formalities from the Ministry of Communications and Transportation and from the Ministry of Finance (two-thirds of the total) were the last to be reviewed. Nevertheless, because the typical lag time between review and legal implementation of formalities approximately eight to ten months, most of the legal and regulatory implementation phase should be finalised by the end of 1999 or early 2000.

Table 5. **Progress in the review for existing formalities (June 1999)**

| Ministries | Number of formalities before the review process | Percentage of formalities eliminated upon full implementation of reform commitments made to the OCDE | Degree of legal implementation of reform commitments | Percentage of remaining formalities simplified and improved[1] |
|---|---|---|---|---|
| Trade and Industry | 227 | 37% | 100% | 85% |
| Foreign Affairs | 24 | 8% | 100% | 76% |
| Health | 115 | 42% | 89% | 98% |
| Labour | 72 | 47% | 99% | 92% |
| Tourism | 67 | 27% | 99% | 92% |
| Environment | 155 | 13% | 42% | 99% |
| Education | 146 | 71% | 81% | 100% |
| Agriculture | 48 | 13% | 90% | 100% |
| Energy | 179 | 18% | 90% | 99% |
| Communications and Transport[2] | 736 | 67% | 20% | 100% |
| Interior | 77 | 0% | 0% | 100% |
| Finance | 1 027 | Review not yet completed | | |
| Communications and Transport[3] | 67 | | | |
| Total | 2 940 | 47% | | |

1. For the definition of a mandatory formality, see Note 59. The percentage applies only to the number of mandatory formalities reviewed.
2. Without the Postal Service and the telecommunication sectors.
3. Only the telecommunication sector.

Figure 1. **Progress made in improving business formalities**

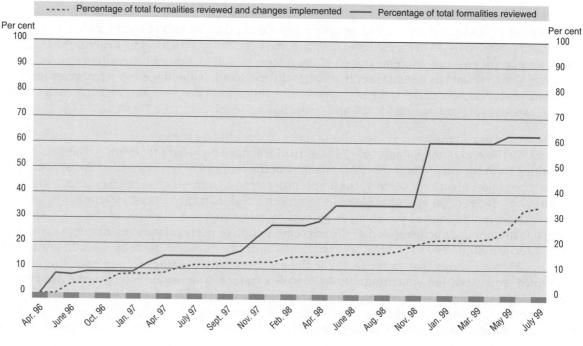

Source: UDE June 1999.

A second point is that the review process has to date included only those formalities with an impact on business. Considerable benefits may flow to citizens from implementing a similar process for formalities impacting on their daily lives. Adopting such a programme could also help broaden understanding of, and support for, the broader reform process.

*Improvement of the concession system.* Where an activity is defined as a public service, there are legal constraints on the form of regulatory instrument that the Mexican government can use. The Constitution provides that such services may be provided by the private sector under a concession. The concession creates legal rights and duties that are different than those in a licence or a permit. A concession, unlike a permit or license, entails federal jurisdiction over labour, fiscal and other regulatory matters. Thus, when federal road transportation shifted to a permit system in 1989, regulatory powers devolved to the states and municipalities. Design of concessions also has economic consequences. If a concession period is too short, incentives to invest are reduced, and temptations for abuse increase. The concession title also has accounting and fiscal effects, resulting from the fact that the firm does not own the assets. And concession titles can also raise administrative problems, as loosely defined concessions may permit excessive discretion and legal uncertainty. This, however, has not significantly deterred private sector entry.

In the last few years, Mexico tried to limit the use of this *ex ante* regulatory instrument and improve the concessions that still are needed. In some cases, the status and definition of public service for a given activity was reformed to allow the creation of licences and permits or other instruments needed to regulate private property rights. In other cases, where the public service concept was maintained, the concession system has been revamped with longer terms, nearly automatic renewability, precise performance requirements, or dispute resolution mechanisms. These new forms of concession more closely emulate permitting or licensing systems. Indeed, in some cases they are more transparent and efficient. The improvements have dramatically reduced regulators' discretion. The mining concession and the related auction procedures are good examples.

*Ad hoc review of existing regulations.* Mexico has not established an institutionalised process to systematically review existing regulations as it has done with business formalities. Rather, the UDE has taken an *ad hoc* approach. The review of federal business formalities has led to a *de facto* review of many existing regulations. Since formalities are imbedded in an array of laws and regulations, the reviews have inevitably considered broader aspects of the regulations. This occurred particularly in the case of the reviews of the ministries of environment, health and labour where formalities and regulations were comprehensively reformed as part of a comprehensive package.

*Sectoral work groups.* In 1998, to accelerate reforms in important sectors of the economy, the UDE/CDE established advisory working groups to consider regulation in four economic sectors: textiles, tourism, mining and construction. These groups worked with a similar approach to those concentrating on a single ministry. However, due to lack of resources this group approach has been abandoned.

*Elimination of out dated regulations.* As part of its enacting decree in 1992, the Federal Metrology and Standards Law required that all minor rules related to standards on health, safety, environmental risks or consumer information covered by the Law should be replaced by a NOM. The law also mandated a 15 months transition period, after which the remaining rules would become void. No study has been done on this measure but anecdotes indicate that this radical "housekeeping" exercise resulted in a considerable deregulation.

In December 1997, the UDE and the CJEF, after an exhaustive analysis, published in the Federal Official Gazette a decree abolishing 181 laws and regulations considered obsolete.

*Sunset approach for reviewing* NOMs. Looking forward Mexico has initiated the use of sunsetting measures. One of the 1997 amendments to the Federal Metrology and Standards Law was the mandatory review of all technical standards (NOMs) every five years. Every regulatory agency must study the effectiveness of each of its NOMs before the end of every five-year period since its inception, and present the results of the analysis to the corresponding consultative committee. If the study shows the NOM to be deficient, the regulatory agency must initiate procedures within the committee to eliminate of modify it. If the quinquennial review is not performed, the NOM in question is no longer enforceable. Additionally the law now also stipulates that all NOMs must be reviewed within their first 12 months of operation to determine whether they are operating as anticipated.

*Support SMEs and other initiatives to improve the regulatory environment.* Together with the initiative to install one-stop shops (*Ventanillas Unicas de Gestion*) in most of Mexico's cities (see Section 3.1.6), virtually all federal ministries have created, individually or together with other agencies, specialised offices to provide information or help to process formalities. In addition, many one-stop shops created by business and industrial associations and state and municipal governments allow businesses to process most of their formalities. The National Industrial Association (CANACINTRA), for example, has created 8 such one-stop shops, the National Restaurant Association (CANIRAC) 2, the Mexico City National Chamber of Commerce (CANACO) 7, the National Architects Association 2, state governments over 90 and municipal governments over 20. In Mexico City there are now over 30 different offices to which business people can go to for information on local regulatory requirements or to directly present applications for business licences and permits.

## 5. CONCLUSIONS AND POLICY OPTIONS

### 5.1. General assessment of current strengths and weaknesses

Regulatory reform in Mexico is part of an historic process of social, political and economic change, and while it is a key contributor to these broader changes, it is, in turn, constrained and shaped by them. The future prospects of regulatory reform are therefore inextricably linked with the evolution of these wider reforms.

Mexico has moved further and more quickly in bringing its regulatory system up to international standards than has most OECD countries. The only countries that compare in terms of the magnitude of the policy response are eastern European countries involved in the transition to market democracies. This review has shown, however, that the distance yet to travel is large, and warns that future progress depends on the support of new actors and interests in the multi-party and federal system. Given that the regulatory reform programmes are relatively recent and have moved so quickly, gaps in concept, design, and implementation have inevitably opened and remain to be resolved. This is recognised in Mexico. What is needed now is a moderate rebalancing of the programme toward a broader vision of social welfare to help build a wider constituency, combined with a multi-year period of consolidation, sustained implementation, and refinement of the legal and policy reforms already on the table. This will permit legal and policy reforms to trickle down through the administration so that citizens and businesses see concrete benefits.

The Mexican experience offers lessons that should be considered by other Member countries. Regulatory reform has received clear and sustained support at the highest level of the federal government – a factor that has been of key importance in empowering the bodies within the administration charged with co-ordinating, monitoring and promoting reform. These administrative bodies have been given clear, well formulated roles and high quality staff and have been active in pursuing reform. Other key strengths include a well-formulated set of RIA requirements including, unusually, consideration of the feasibility of implementation.

The process for developing technical standards is a well designed reform, embracing both procedural and technical safeguards, and is of interest in the development of best practices in this important area. Development of on-line searchable databases of regulatory formalities is well advanced and will put Mexico at the forefront in the use of this important tool for better communication on regulatory standards. Progress has been made to review and streamline administrative formalities and reduce paperwork barriers to entrepreneurialism. Integration of federal, state and local government regulatory reforms is also an area in which Mexico is in the front rank. Virtually all states have now agreed to implement reform programmes based on consistent principles, and have made progress in encouraging commitments from municipal governments to do likewise. Consequently, the overall level of reform activity seems to have been successfully "leveraged" by the federal reform strategy. Transmission of reform to the sub-national levels of government should help broaden its base and deepen its roots.

Five important challenges should be faced to deepen the transformation or the regulatory environment and to improve prospects for further reform.

– The most pressing concern is the implementation gap. Mexican officials have expressed concern that problems with the quality of human resources and public management continue to hamper the effective implementation of reforms. This is compounded by compliance and enforcement issues, including judicial weaknesses, in ensuring that regulatory reforms are translated into real benefits to society. This issue has importance for a range of issues beyond regulatory management and reform *per se*. Over the longer-term, a cultural change among regulators is needed. Development of a more transparent, results-oriented, and accountable means of operating is slowly emerging, but is very fragile and not well supported by the broader legal and administrative environment.

– Transparency has improved significantly at both policy and implementation levels through a series of mechanisms to release more information, clarify regulatory requirements, and standardise the use of administrative discretion. Yet, Mexico still falls far short of international good practices, particularly in the use of public consultation. Procedural requirements exist in some areas, such as standards, but there is no comprehensive, standardised consultation requirement for regulations. Mexican citizens still have no general right to comment on regulatory decisions affecting their lives.

– Regulatory reform should be more clearly harmonised with other structural reform policies, in particular with competition advocacy and administrative reform policies.

– The central locus of reform which has always been situated in the Ministry of Commerce and Industry may gain in power, effectiveness and efficiency if moved to a higher and more central management position.

– The *need to rebalance the reform programme* between deregulation and good regulation, particularly sectoral governance and consumer protection, is urgent in Mexico, as it is in Japan. Notwithstanding the extensive support from the business community, a fundamental issue to sustaining regulatory reform will be to broaden its constituency to consumer and citizens and, in parallel, to increase involvement of the Congress, which is expanding its role in policy development in Mexico. This will require that the move, already launched, toward regulatory quality rather than deregulation as the guiding principle for reform should be more explicit and its implications clarified to a wider range of social interests.

## 5.2. Policy options for consideration

The policy options below suggest concrete actions that should be considered to address the five challenges identified above. The strategies recommended are in accord with basic good practices in other countries. Some of the recommendations can be carried out quickly, while others would take some years to complete.

- *Establish consistent government-wide standards for regulatory quality by closing gaps, eliminating exemptions in the current policy framework and expanding the review programme beyond "business" regulations to all significant regulations.*

Good regulatory practices already established for significant portions of Mexican regulatory activity should be expanded government-wide. Broad exemptions to ADAE, the Administrative Procedure Law, and the technical standards law, combined with the non-mandatory nature of some policies, has resulted in a fragmented policy regime for the use of regulatory powers. The focus on business regulations can distort the establishment of an efficient, consumer-oriented regulatory framework and reduce the general public support for the programme. These gaps undermine the use of regulatory impact analysis, independent review, codification, and public consultation. The Administrative Procedure Law, which sets down the powers that may be exercised by administrative agencies, principles governing those powers, and legal remedies to those aggrieved by administrative action,[58] would be an important vehicle to improve and strengthen the regulatory process – from "cradle to grave", and any exemptions should be very narrowly drawn.

- *Further improve transparency by extending legal requirements for notice and comment procedures, already required for technical standards, to all ministries and agencies during the development and revision of regulation. Procedures for openness should be standardised for all advisory bodies.*

Adoption of a general consultation requirement covering all substantive new laws and lower-level rules would promote both the technical values of policy effectiveness and the democratic values of openness and accountability of government. Notice and comment processes are based on clear rights to access and response, are systematic and non-discretionary and are open to the general public as well as organised interest groups. Advisory groups may continue to be needed to establish dialogue with experts and interest groups, and standard procedures for their use are necessary to ensure that they do not undermine the transparency of the regulatory system. The system could also be strengthened by requiring that all regulatory projects be published together with the regulatory impact analysis (see below).

- *Improve the efficiency, independence and accountability of the new regulatory agencies by strengthening their systems of governance, policy coherence, working methods, and relations with the competition authority. A first step should be the launching of a comprehensive, high-level and independent review of the performance of the new*

171

*regulatory agencies, followed by appropriate revisions to their missions, authorities, and work methods in laws and other regulations.*

The rapid increase of Mexican autonomous and semi-autonomous regulatory agencies is changing the legal and administrative environment where businesses operate. This is even more consequential when new utility and network industries are privatised, opening new markets that were reserved to the State to competition, and when new regulatory frameworks for state monopolies are devised. However, this institution-building has been done without a consistent framework for efficiency, accountability, and transparency. Performance has not been assessed in most cases, and questions remain about, for example, the relationships between sectoral regulatory agencies, linkages with the competition authority, and accordance with procedures of the judiciary. It may be useful to evaluate the feasibility in Mexico of a multi-sectoral regulatory institution to share resources, facilitate learning across industries, reduce the risk of industry or political capture, and deal with blurring industry boundaries.

An independent expert group should review the institutional architecture for market-oriented regulation in order to determine if a new harmonised framework would improve efficiency and competition in the regulated areas of the economy. Recent experiences in the United Kingdom, where a *Green Paper* was recently prepared,[59] and the in-depth work done by the inter-ministerial commission of Chile could be models.

- *Promote quality regulation by transferring the CDE/UDE to a location at the centre of government with cross-cutting management and co-ordination authorities, such as the president's office, and by strengthening its attention to consumer protection and citizen welfare.*

The Ministry of Trade and Industry has carried regulatory reform very far indeed, reflecting its strong position in economic policy and commitment to competitive markets. The next step in the reform process is integration of regulatory quality concepts and processes into the core policy-making machinery of government. Experiences in some OECD countries suggest that placing central regulatory management in the centre of government linked to the offices of the president, prime minister, or budget enhances the authority and oversight needed to steer the process and obtain results. This is particularly likely in the Mexican setting, where administrative hierarchy has high value. Another important concern is to improve co-ordination with other entities in charge of structural reform policies, as well as with those closely related to budget and public human resource policies. A new setting could also be the occasion to widen the reform strategy and involve more actively Congress and non-businesses interests.

Moving from a line ministry to the centre of government has important implications for the content and scope of the programme. The UDE should consider broadening its responsibilities, reducing exemptions, and pursuing a government-wide approach to regulatory quality. In particular, a wider view of how good regulation and deregulation together can maximise social welfare would be necessary to maintain the legitimacy and effectiveness of the UDE at a higher management level. The role of consumer protection measures within comprehensive reform strategies should be more prominent in the programme. Many countries have neglected to install consumer protection regimes that work well in new market conditions. In some countries, abuses against consumers have caused backlashes against reform itself. This failure stems from the mistaken notion that market liberalisation means less of all kinds of regulation. On the contrary, in some areas it may mean more. Balancing business interests with consumer interests will increase the credibility of a new unit, and broaden its appeal. For instance, the UK's Deregulation Unit, moved in 1996 from the Trade and Industry Ministry to the Cabinet Office and changed in 1997 its name to the Better Regulation Unit.

- *Strengthen disciplines on regulatory quality in the ministries and agencies by refining tools for regulatory impact analysis, lawdrafting, and use of alternatives to regulation, and training public servants in how to use these tools for regulatory quality.*

Since its creation the UDE has been instrumental in designing and implementing new tools to improve tools for regulatory quality, such as those contained in the Federal Metrology and Standards Law, the Federal Competition Law, and RIA requirements. However, a tool needs not only to be well designed but used, that is, incorporated into daily administrative practices. Implementation should be backed up by adequate resources and incentives for compliance. Action would be useful in four areas:

i) *Require that RIAs be systematically published during the notice and comment process for each regulation.* RIA can be a powerful tool, especially if integrated into notice and comment procedures that can generate better information about the consequences of regulation. RIA can also help increase transparency and accountability across the administration. It can help the Mexican government effectively manage increasingly complex regulatory policies, in a way similar to the management of budget policy. In the short run, the UDE could use its discretionary powers to supplement the list of proposals with addition of the RIA.

ii) *Train public sector employees in how to conduct regulatory impact analysis.* If the RIA programme is to deliver its potential benefits, two steps should be taken. First, the development of skills in regulatory agencies must be improved. Currently, skill levels are low, and the level of quantification and data analysis remains poor. Second, adoption of a "notice and comment" requirement open to the broadest possible range of interests provides an excellent opportunity to collect better information and to provide quality assurance on RIAs. RIA should be fully integrated with notice and comment procedures.

iii) *Promote the adoption of alternatives to traditional regulation by developing guidance and training.* Regulatory and non-regulatory alternatives to traditional "command and control" regulation can increase policy effectiveness and lower cost. Regulators must be motivated through results-oriented management to consider the use of alternatives and to design appropriate ones for particular policy problems. This requires strong encouragement from the centre of government, supported by training, guidelines and expert assistance where necessary. Where rigid laws and legal culture inhibit use of more effective alternatives, broader legal reforms to allow more innovation and experimentation may be necessary.

iv) *Improve regulatory clarity and simplicity through better lawdrafting.* An important problem with regulatory quality in Mexico is the complexity in the structure of the regulatory regime and in the comprehensibility of regulatory text. The principle of plain language drafting should be adopted, and quality controls on technical law drafting should be put into place in each ministry. Such controls could be supplemented by measures to improve the skills of lawdrafting staff and to standardise approaches through guidelines and training.

• *Speed up effective reform by adopting a systematic and comprehensive approach to the review of existing laws and regulations.*

More attention should be placed on systematic review and upgrading of regulation through, for example, a rolling review process based on a prioritisation of policy areas, as is already beginning by the UDE. Structuring of an effective review process will be key to its results, and may require strengthening the capacities of the UDE and co-ordination with the competition authority. The Australian competition principles review, which includes both federal and state governments, provides an interesting model. Such reviews should be based on benefit-cost principles, that is, on maximising social welfare. In key sectors, the reinvention principle should guide the reviews. The effectiveness and speed of more comprehensive sectoral plans based on all policy measures needed for results, including regulations but also other forms of intervention such as subsidies, procurement policies, and tax policies has been demonstrated in other countries. The "reinvention" of sectoral regimes – based in part on international benchmarks – allows reformers to consider policy linkages and related measures needed to make reform effective, to package related reforms into a coherent programme, and to reassure market entrants that reform is credible and predictable. Adopting reform steps in law, as opposed to leaving the timing or steps to the ministries, will further strengthen the accountability, credibility, and sustainability of reform.

• *Review laws and regulations to improve concession processes.*

In the past, regulation of the private sector in the Mexican network and natural resources industries though concessions has sometimes been costly, complex, opaque and overly discretionary. The design

*173*

of concessions has improved markedly in recent years in some sectors. A more precise delimitation of which activities are considered public services has transformed many concessions into permits and licences or replaced them with other regulatory alternatives. This line of work should be continued and systematised for remaining concessions so as to reduce use of this instrument to a small core of public services and improve constitutionally required concessions to reduce any unnecessary discretion in their management.

- *Further encourage regulatory reform by co-ordinating with the states and helping them to develop management capacities for quality regulation.*

While initiatives to date in this area are pioneering, the process is far from complete and evidence exists that state level regulation may be frustrating reforms made at federal level. Progress in decentralising and deconcentrating regulatory powers to bring them closer to citizens and business may also create potential concerns for a coherent and efficient national regulatory system in the future The adoption of state based programmes of reform based on consistent principles should form the basis for more formal co-operation measures, including consideration of establishing for a for resolving issues arising from regulatory conflicts. An additional and complementary strategy should continue to be developed to help the states encourage municipalities to launch regulatory reform programmes. Continued leadership from the centre to encourage experimentation will be needed to promote efforts.

A particular concern refers to improving regulatory frameworks for private participation in states' and municipalities' utilities and public services. One possible model to be further investigated is the one used by the *Fondo para la Vivienda* (FOVI) to provide concrete incentives to implement reform proposals.

# NOTES

1. OECD (1997), *Issues and Developments in Public Management*, Paris, pp. 209-225.

2. "Notes: Liberlismo contra Democracia: Recent Judicial Reform in Mexico", *Harvard Law Review*, 1995, Vol. 108:1919, pp. 1919-1936.

3. Sempe, Carlos (1997), *Tecnica Legislativa y Desregulacion*, Editorial Porrua, pp. 193-201.

4. Taylor, Michael (1997), "Why No Rule of Law, in Mexico? Explaining the Weakness of Mexico's Judicial Branch", *New Mexico Law Review*, Vol. 27, winter, p. 143. It should also be noted that citizens are allowed to carry out any activity that is not prohibited by law. Authorities, on the other hand, may only regulate activities or impose specific obligations if instructed to do so by a specific law or *reglamento*. No other type of subordinate regulations (except NOMs) may impose obligations or requirements on citizens.

5. See OECD (1999), OECD *Reviews of Regulatory Reform – Regulatory Reform in the United States*, Chapter 2, Paris.

6. López Ayllón, Sergio (1995), "Notes on Mexican Legal Culture" in *Social and Legal Studies*, Sage, Vol. 4, p. 481.

7. López Ayllón, Sergio (1997), *Las transformaciones del sistema jurídica y los significados sociales del derecho. La encrucijada entre tradición y modernidad*, México, UNAM, p. 470. See also, Elizondo, Carlos (1993), "The Concept of Property of the 1917 Mexican Constitution", Working Paper 10, Division de Estudios Politicos, Centro de Investigación y Docencia Economica, p. 15.

8. López Ayllón, S. (1997), p. 202 and p. 221.

9. World Bank (1990), *Mexico Industrial Policy and Regulation*, pp. 23-28.

10. According to López Ayllón, S. (1995), NAFTA also introduced some elements that are characteristic of a common law system into Mexico, in particular the concept of law according to which norms may be applied to their most minimal detail and the external enforcement scrutiny exists, for instance, concerning the possibility of the Mexican State being subject to international procedure of dispute.

11. For the first two periods see Levy, Santiago (1993), *Trade Liberalization and Economic Deregulation in Mexico in Public Administration in Mexico Today*, Fondo de Cultura Economica y Secretaria de la Contraloria General de la Federacion, p. 121. For the last period see UDE (1998), direct communication from the UDE, July.

12. OECD (1997), *Issues and Developments in Public Management. Survey 1996-1997*, Paris, pp. 209-213. On previous achievements see Vazquez Cano, Luis Ignacio (1993), *Administrative Simplification in Public Administration in Mexico Today*, Fondo de Cultura Economica y Secretaria de la Contraloria General de la Federacion, pp. 204-206.

13. OECD (1997), *The OECD Report on Regulatory Reform: Synthesis*, Paris, p. 37.

14. OECD (1995), *Recommendation of the Council of the OECD on Improving the Quality of Government Regulation*, Paris.

15. Acuerdo para la Desregulacion de la Actividad noviembre de 1995, Empresarial (ADAE), Diario Oficial de la Federacion, 23 November 1995.

16. Business formalities are procedures related to the authorisation and/or certification of business activities that involve the exchange of information between businesses and regulatory agencies, or rules that require businesses to conserve information for eventual review by regulatory authorities.

17. Acuerdo para la Desregulacion de la Actividad Empresarial (ADAE), p. 2.

18. The Comptroller General sent a letter to the deputy ministers responsible for regulatory reform to comply fully with their obligations relating to new regulatory proposals and regulatory impact statements.

19. OECD/PUMA (1998), Mexico's Responses to the Review Questionnaire on Competition Policy, p. 22.

20. Noyola, Pedro and Enrique Espinosa (1997), "Policy Competition and Foreign Direct Investment: The Case of Mexico", SAI Laws & Economics Paper, May, pp. 38-43.

21. Noyola, Pedro and Enrique Espinosa (1997), pp. 41-43.

22. See Box on the contracting out of a municipal water system by a northern Mexican municipality in World Bank (1997) *The Private Sector in Infrastructure: Strategy, Regulation and Risk*, p. 11.

23. Morales Doria, Juan (1998), "The Role of Regulatory Reform/Deregulation. The Private Sector as Main Participant in the Deregulation Process", presentation to the APEC Regulatory Reform Symposium, August.

24. Consejo Coordinador Empresarial (CCE) (1999), *Estudio Comparative de la Calidad del Marco Regultorio en los Estados de la República Mexicana*.

25. It is worth to note that the NAFTA negotiations were not only external but also domestic. According to government data, more than 2 500 meetings were organised with the business, social and academic sector before and during the negotiations (Lopez Ayllon, S. (1995), p. 490).

26. Lopez Ayllon, S. (1995), p. 482.

27. Exemption from sanitary controls does not imply exemption from health or workplace safety standards.

28. ECODAM (1998), Programa "Usuario Simulado". Carpeta Ejecutiva. Coordinacion General de Estudios Especiales. June.

29. Ozorio de Almeida, Anna Luiza, Leandro F Alves, Scott E.M. Graham (1995), "Poverty, Deregulation and Employment in the Informal Sector of Mexico", Education and Social Policy Department, The World Bank, March, p. 18.

30. OECD (1997), *Economic Survey*, Paris, p. 72-73.

31. Ozorio de Almeida, A.L., Leandro F.A., Scott E.M.G. (1995).

32. The evaluation of this phenomenom is complex, in particular because of the definition of open unemployment in Mexico. However, from the end of 1990 to the end of 1994 (the time of the peso devaluation), all unemployment measures increased, while employment measures did not increase. For instance, in 1994 employment in non-maquiladora industries decreased 3.1 (see Figure 16 of the OECD (1997), *Economic Survey: Mexico*, Paris, p. 74, and OECD (1999), *Economic Survey: Mexico*, Paris, p. 30). Since 1996 this situation has markedly changed: nearly 3 million formal sector jobs were created, almost half in exporting companies and maquiladoras.

33. For instance, unemployment rates increased from 1991 to 1995. About the impact of rationalisation and the informal sector see Ozorio de Almeida, A.L., Leandro F.A., Scott E.M.G. (1995), pp. 14-15.

34. Tokman, Victor (1992), *Beyond Regulation. The Informal Economy in Latin America*, Lynne rienner Publishers, Boulder, London, p. 9.

35. Some studies have shown that the relationship between the size of the unofficial economy and the quality of the Rule of Law is strong and consistent and "countries with more corruption have higher shares of the unofficial economy." See Johnson Simon, Daniel Kaufmann, Pablo Zoido-Lobaton (1998), "Regulatory Discretion and the Unofficial Economy", *Goverment in Transition*, Vol. 88, No. 2, p. 391.

36. Ozorio de Almeida, A.L., F.A.Leandro, E.M.G Scott (1995), p. 26.

37. Ozorio de Almeida, A.L., F.A. Leandro, E.M.G Scott (1995), p. 83.

38. In Fix Fierro, Hector (1998), "Poder Judicial" in Gonzáles, Ma. del Refugio y Sergio López Ayllón, eds. *Transiciones y diseños institucionales*, México, UNAM, (in press), p. 32.

39. The institution and term come from the colonial tradition where and individual could ask for "proteccion"(*amparo*) and shelter from abuses of power from the King. See also Fix Zamudio, Hector, (1965), "Sintesis del derecho de amparo" in *Instituto de Derecho Comparado, Panorma del Derecho Mexicano*, Mexico, UNAM, Vol. 0, pp. 113-156. See also Lopez-Ayllon, S. (1995), p. 485.

40. However, *amparos* are not class actions – only the plaintiff is granted relief. Industry-wide or class-action suits for generalised regulatory correction do not exist in Mexico.

41. Plan Nacionl de Desarrollo, 1995-2000, Mexico, p. 20.

42. "Notes: Liberlismo contra Democracia: Recent Judicial Reform in Mexico", *Harvard Law Review*, 1995, Vol. 108:1919, pp. 1919-1936.

43. Tribunal Superior de Justicia del Distrito Federal (1997), "Justicios presentados en materia mercantil y civil, juzgados de Primera instancia del D.F. 1989-1997".

44. OECD (1998), *Environmental Performance Reviews: Mexico*, Paris, pp. 135-151 and Procuraduria Federal del Medio Ambiente (1998), Press Communication, Mexico, April.

45. OECD (1997), *Regulatory Impact Analysis: Best Practices in OECD Countries*, Paris.

46. Broder, E., John F. Morall III (1997), "Collecting Data and Using Data for Regulatory Decision-making" in *Regulatory Impact Analysis: Best Practices in OECD Countries*, Paris.

47. OECD (1997), *The OECD Report on Regulatory Reform: Synthesis*, Paris.

48. Lopez Ayllon, S. (1997), pp. 239-242.

49. For instance, the CRE has independence to grant concessions and permits in Natural Gas but COFETEL does not have such freedom an thus access decisions are subordinated to the Ministry of Communications and Transport. in Tovar Landa, Ramiro (1997), "Policy reform in networks infrastructure. The Case of Mexico", *Telecommunications Policy*, Vol. 21, No. 8, p. 731.

50. A series of financial reform proposals are been discussed in Congress since Spring 1998 aimed to give to the CNBV a higher degree of independence from the Finance Ministry, and even from the Executive.

51. See discussion in Tovar Landa, R. (1997), p. 731.

52. Noyola, Pedro, Enrique Espinosa (1997), p. 31.

53. Tovar Landa, Ramiro (1997), p. 731 and OECD/ DAFFE (1998), Note by Mexico. Mini-Roundtable on Relationship between Regulators and Competition Authorities, (DAFFE/CLP/WD(98)20), Paris, p. 6.

54. Ruster, Jeff (1997), "A Retrospective on the Mexican Toll Road Program (1989-94)", *Public Policy For the Private Sector*, World Bank, Note No. 125, p. 4.

55. Gil-Diaz, Francisco (1998), "The Origin of Mexico's 1994 Financial Crisis", *The Cato Journal*, Vol. 17, No. 3.

56. World Bank (1990), *Mexico Industrial Policy and Regulation*, pp. 23-28.

57. Business formalities are divided into two categories: voluntary and mandatory. Mandatory formalities include formalities that must be complied with by all businesses (certain tax requirement, official business registrations) and those that are obligatory for businesses in specific sectors or activities (regulations pertaining to transportation of dangerous substances, for example). Most mandatory business formalities are licenses, permits or authorisations. Voluntary formalities are usually related to a service or promotional programme provided by the government. The latter include duty draw-back schemes, rules of origin formalities or requests for the provision of electricity. A total of 2 940 federal business formalities have been reported to the UDE and the CDE, of which 2 147 (or 73%) were mandatory.

58. Schwartz, Bernard (1984), *Administrative Law*, quoted in Guasch, J. Luis and Pablo T. Spiller (1997), *Managing the Regulatory Process: Design, Concepts, Issues and the Latin America and Caribbean Story*, World Bank, New Direction for Development series.

59. DTI (1998), A *Fair Deal for Consumers. Modernising the Framework for Utility Regulation*.

# BACKGROUND REPORT
# ON THE ROLE OF COMPETITION POLICY
# IN REGULATORY REFORM*

\* This report was principally prepared by **Michael Wise** in the Directorate for Financial and Fiscal Affairs of the OECD. It has benefited from extensive comments provided by colleagues throughout the OECD Secretariat, by the Government of Mexico, and by Member countries as part of the peer review process. This report was peer reviewed in June 1998 in the OECD's Competition Law and Policy Committee.

# TABLE OF CONTENTS

OECD 1999

## Executive Summary

## Background Report on the Role of Competition Policy in Regulatory Reform

Competition policy should be integrated into the general policy framework for regulation. Competition policy is central to regulatory reform, because (as Chapter 2 shows) its principles and analysis provide a benchmark for assessing the quality of economic and social regulations, as well as motivate the application of the laws that protect competition. Mexico has adopted a modern competition policy as part of a larger, deliberate effort to open itself to the world economy. Though much has been done, competition policy's role in the process is still being established. The competition law, incorporating up-to-date economic analysis intended to promote efficiency, is new. The tradition of state control and protection is much older. Until recently, major sectors of the economy were either in state hands or subject to price controls, so the economy is still getting accustomed to new competitive realities. In the government, arguments for the protection and promotion of competition confront traditional arguments for the protection of incumbent national firms. In the private sector, larger businesses resist the introduction of significant domestic competition. Many newer firms that owe their existence to the liberalising process support competition enforcement, but in the larger public, interest and support are less clear.

As regulatory reform stimulates structural change, vigorous enforcement of competition policy is needed to prevent private market abuses from reversing the benefits of reform. A complement to competition enforcement is competition advocacy, the promotion of competitive, market principles in policy and regulatory processes. Mexico's competition laws and enforcement structures are sufficient to prevent or correct collusion and unfair practices. The conception of competition policy contained in the competition law is thoroughly modern and entirely consistent with pro-competitive reform. Indeed, it was drafted with that purpose in mind. The competition agency has tried to assert competition principles in newly deregulated and privatised industries. In this process, it faces strong opposition. Some decisions, particularly at the early stages, seemed to anticipate opposition by tolerating anti-competitive conditions, in some cases rationalising those actions as appropriate to a newly expanded North American or global market. But competition policy decisions, including some in connection with regulatory proceedings, have nonetheless curtailed the plans and operations of some nationally prominent firms. Competition problems arising from regulatory and privatisation actions still call for high priority attention, in enforcement and advocacy. For dealing with market power, the division of responsibility between the competition policy agency and other bodies, although conceptually plausible, seems to be difficult to implement well. To make competition policy effective in these matters, it may be necessary to give the competition agency even stronger tools to ensure that its identification of competition problems in regulated industries leads to effective measures to solve those problems.

## I. THE CONCEPTS OF COMPETITION POLICY IN MEXICO: FOUNDATIONS AND CONTEXT

Mexico's competition policy is part of a larger reform effort, initiated in the mid-1980s, to move away from protection and central control and instead develop a market-based economy. The major elements of this effort were ending price controls, liberalising trade and investment, privatising state enterprises, reforming regulation, and adopting a modern competition policy. Thus, the motivation underlying Mexico's competition policy is to cement a general market-liberalising reform program.

Competition policy objectives are set out explicitly in the competition law: "to protect the competitive process and free market participation by preventing and eliminating monopolies, monopolistic practices and other restraints of the efficient functioning of markets for goods and services.[1]" The relationship between competition policy and regulatory policy is recognised in the structure of the laws that now regulate sectors, such as telecommunications and transportation, that were one characterised by state-owned monopoly. In several of those laws, regulation of prices or other conduct is only authorised if there is substantial market power in the industry. Whether there is market power is determined by the competition agency, under the principles of the general competition law.

Efficiency is the primary, and perhaps the sole, criterion for applying the competition law. Other commonly encountered competition policy concerns are subsumed in the efficiency-based analysis. For example, there are no doctrines or interpretations about fairness or fair competition, nor about protecting the interests of small enterprises or limiting industrial concentration. The explicit bases for competition policies and laws in many OECD countries have tended to emphasise efficiency in recent years, so in this respect, and in others, Mexico's relatively new law takes advantage of the evolution of competition policy and theory elsewhere. Although the law is part of a program to develop a more market-oriented economy, the law takes no explicit note of the goal of promoting economic growth. Of course, it is implicitly understood that growth should follow from greater competition and efficiency.

In principle, other laws that affect competition policy, such as those governing former state enterprises, must be applied consistently with the competition law. Regulatory policy complements the competition law to address the market power of a former monopolist in deregulated sectors. Price regulation can be applied to prevent exploitative abuse of dominance, while the competition law prevents and corrects exclusionary abuses of a dominant position. In practice, though, other ministries involved in the regulatory process may advance development-related goals that may not be consistent with promoting competition conceived as efficiency. In several sectors, notably transport and energy, public policy seems to include the goal of creating or protecting a large, nationally based firm. In the division of responsibility over market power between the competition authority and the regulator, it is the regulator that most often has the final say in designing the rule, and thus it is the regulator's conception of policy balance that governs as a practical matter. That conception is not always consistent with efficiency-based competition.

Competition policy, in the sense of promoting and protecting free competition rather than controlling prices and investment, is a new phenomenon in Mexico. The Constitution has prohibited monopoly since 1917[2] (indeed, since the mid-1800s), but the constitutional prohibition was only a statement of political aspiration, not a basis for government policy. Instead, by the 1970s, much of the Mexican economy was under price or entry control or in the hands of state-owned monopoly, in an environment of import protection and strong state supervision. The goal of competition policy was to eliminate the evils of private monopoly, and this goal was accomplished by price control and state ownership. The result was nonetheless monopoly, albeit publicly sanctioned. The effective policy about competition was to suppress it, not protect or promote it. By the mid-1980s, as a number of factors led to financial and economic crisis, it became clear that the old economic policies, including the policy about competition, could no longer support growth. The government changed economic direction, to replace control with market competition.

Two fundamental steps, both rooted in competition policy principles, led the reform effort. The government ended most domestic price controls and reduced constraints on new entry. And the government moved on several fronts to open the economy to trade and investment. Mexico eliminated most compulsory import licenses, abolished official import prices, reduced the maximum tariff by 80% (and cut the average tariff in half), adhered to the GATT, and entered the North American Free Trade Agreement (NAFTA). From 1984 to 1995, imports quadrupled (as did exports). Import liberalisation stimulated domestic competition in tradable goods sectors.

Another avenue to greater competition was privatisation of state enterprises, to reduce the temptation for protectionist intervention and increase the potential for market-based discipline. The largest single effort was the 1991 sale of the telephone monopoly for US$6 billion. Eighteen commercial banks were privatised in 1991 and 1992, for a total of US$13 billion. Formerly public firms in steel, sugar, airlines, TV broadcasting, satellite services, and railroads are now privately owned. Licenses and concessions for activities that were formerly performed by the state, such as natural gas storage, transportation and distribution, and seaport facilities, have been auctioned to the private sector.

Deregulation and regulatory reform accompanied privatisation. The sequencing was not always what might have been hoped for. Telecommunications illustrates the problems. There, a general regulatory structure was not in place until after the privatisation (although concession titles contain provisions that address some of the problems of monopoly), and inadequate consideration seems to have been given to the post-privatisation industry structure. In addition to longer-term objectives such as modernising the network and expanding coverage, a major short-run privatisation goal was evidently to maximise revenue by selling market power. Reform should prevent former state-owned monopolies from turning into private monopolies, as well as remove constraints on competition and eliminate unnecessary egulations.

The final step was the introduction of a general competition law. In 1993, the basic legal framework for reform was completed when Mexico adopted the Federal Law of Economic Competition (LFCE),[3]

---

Box 1.    **Competition policy's roles in regulatory reform**

In addition to the threshold, general issue, whether regulatory policy is consistent with the conception and purpose of competition policy, there are four particular ways in which competition policy and regulatory problems interact:

- Regulation can **contradict** competition policy. Regulations may have encouraged, or even required, conduct or conditions that would otherwise be in violation of the competition law. For example, regulations may have permitted price co-ordination, prevented advertising or other avenues of competition, or required territorial market division. Other examples include laws banning sales below costs, which purport to promote competition but are often interpreted in anticompetitive ways, and the very broad category of regulations that restrict competition more than is necessary to achieve the regulatory goals. When such regulations are changed or removed, firms affected must change their habits and expectations.

- Regulation can **replace** competition policy. Especially where monopoly has appeared inevitable, regulation may try to control market power directly, by setting prices and controlling entry and access. Changes in technology and other institutions may lead to reconsideration of the basic premise in support of regulation, that competition policy and institutions would be inadequate to the task of preventing monopoly and the exercise of market power.

- Regulation can **reproduce** competition policy. Rules and regulators may have tried to prevent co-ordination or abuse in an industry, just as competition policy does. For example, regulations may set standards of fair competition or tendering rules to ensure competitive bidding. Different regulators may apply different standards, though, and changes in regulatory institutions may reveal that seemingly duplicate policies may have led to different practical outcomes.

- Regulation can **use** competition policy methods. Instruments to achieve regulatory objectives can be designed to take advantage of market incentives and competitive dynamics. Co-ordination may be necessary, to ensure that these instruments work as intended in the context of competition law requirements.

and the Federal Competition Commission (CFC) was created to enforce it. Liberalising trade was a critical step toward competition, but could not by itself be enough. Removing official trade barriers could not assure competition if those were simply replaced by private barriers. Dominant domestic firms, or export or import cartels, might hinder competition by collusion or by imposing exclusivity on domestic distributors and retailers. And import liberalisation could not ensure competition in non-traded sectors. Moreover, as a party to NAFTA, Mexico committed to adopting measures to proscribe anti-competitive business conduct.[4] The competition law was being prepared during the same period that Mexico was negotiating NAFTA, although the law was adopted before NAFTA came into force.

The competition law adopts many of the most advanced ideas and practices from around the world. The experts in the ministry of trade and industry who prepared the law consulted with colleagues from academia and competition agencies in other countries (and from the OECD). The law balances efficient and strong treatment of the most harmful competitive constraints with economically sensitive analysis of others, and it applies an integrated treatment of market power in all relevant situations. The law's elegant logical organisation and clear conceptualisation reveal its origin as a product of technical expertise, more than political creativity and compromise.

The level of support for the new direction of competition policy in the wider public or business communities is uncertain, although it is evidently growing now that the institutions have been in place long enough for people to become familiar with them. A number of factors, including the CFC's economics-based approach, its observance of careful, and sometimes time-consuming, procedures, and the delays from frequent judicial challenges, as well as the impression that some of its decisions have accommodated non-competition interests, have led to a public perception that the agency is not strong. Uncertainty about the extent of support for competition policy could be especially troublesome in the changing Mexican political situation. The government's present lack of majority in the legislature may considerably narrow its margin of manœuvre. There are indications of support for competition policy among legislators, although some of that support is interested in using competition policy to achieve purposes that would not be consistent with the CFC's economics-based approach. Neither the CFC nor others in the government have done much yet to educate the general public about the benefits of a modern competition policy. The lack of a clear public message and broader support could make competition policy less effective, just as Mexico's reforms are entering the stage in which general, horizontal principles like competition law, rather than sectoral regulatory decisions or trade policies, will be more important tools for ensuring that the promised benefits of reform are achieved.

## 2. THE SUBSTANTIVE TOOLKIT: CONTENT OF THE COMPETITION LAW

The general competition law shares its substantive foundation with a program of reform based on market principles. The absence of a competition law had probably encouraged the business and government behaviours and policies that made reform necessary. Now, legislation for sectoral privatisation and deregulation is taking advantage of its new competition policy institutions' capacity for making economically-based judgements about the definition of markets and the assessment of market power or effective competition. The competition law is self-contained and generally coherent. Its conceptual framework could make the law the touchstone for measuring the adequacy and success of other reforms.

The principles of Mexico's competition policy appear in three documents. The Constitution, Article 28, bans monopolies and monopolistic practices; however, the ban on monopolies is subject to significant sectoral exceptions. The Federal Law of Economic Competition (LFCE) implements the Constitutional provision by preventing and penalising anti-competitive conduct and mergers. The law does not provide for correcting monopoly as such, despite the Constitutional authority; rather, the law addresses particular practices by which monopoly might be attained or strengthened. And Regulations to implement the LFCE, which were published in March 1998, develop specific aspects of the law. In addition, provisions of other regulatory laws refer to the CFC and its powers.

The LFCE classifies practices as either absolute or relative. Absolute monopolistic practices are prohibited *per se* and are legally void *ab initio*. Parties to these practices cannot defend them by claiming

---

### Box 2. The competition policy toolkit

General competition laws usually address the problems of monopoly power in three formal settings: relationships and agreements among otherwise independent firms, actions by a single firm, and structural combinations of independent firms. The first category, **agreements**, is often subdivided for analytic purposes into two groups: "horizontal" agreements among firms that do the same things, and "vertical" agreements among firms at different stages of production or distribution. The second category is termed "**monopolisation**" in some laws, and "**abuse of dominant position**" in others; the legal systems that use different labels have developed somewhat different approaches to the problem of single-firm economic power. The third category, often called "**mergers**" or "**concentrations**", usually includes other kinds of structural combination, such as share or asset acquisitions, joint ventures, cross-share-holdings and interlocking directorates.

**Agreements** may permit the group of firms acting together to achieve some of the attributes of monopoly, of raising prices, limiting output, and preventing entry or innovation. The most troublesome **horizontal** agreements are those that prevent rivalry about the fundamental dynamics of market competition, price, and output. Most contemporary competition laws treat naked agreements to fix prices, limit output, rig bids, or divide markets very harshly. To enforce such agreements, competitors may also agree on tactics to prevent new competition or to discipline firms that do not go along; thus, the laws also try to prevent and punish boycotts. Horizontal co-operation on other issues, such as product standards, research, and quality, may also affect competition, but whether the effect is positive or negative can depend on market conditions. Thus, most laws deal with these other kinds of agreement by assessing a larger range of possible benefits and harms, or by trying to design more detailed rules to identify and exempt beneficial conduct.

**Vertical agreements** try to control aspects of distribution. The reasons for concern are the same – that the agreements might lead to increased prices, lower quantity (or poorer quality), or prevention of entry and innovation. Because the competitive effects of vertical agreements can be more complex than those of horizontal agreements, the legal treatment of different kinds of vertical agreements varies even more than for horizontal agreements. One basic type of agreement is resale price maintenance: vertical agreements can control minimum, or maximum, prices. In some settings, the result can be to curb market abuses by distributors. In others, though, it can be to duplicate or enforce a horizontal cartel. Agreements granting exclusive dealing rights or territories can encourage greater effort to sell the supplier's product, or they can protect distributors from competition or prevent entry by other suppliers. Depending on the circumstances, agreements about product combinations, such as requiring distributors to carry full lines or tying different products together, can either facilitate or discourage introduction of new products. Franchising often involves a complex of vertical agreements with potential competitive significance: a franchise agreement may contain provisions about competition within geographic territories, about exclusive dealing for supplies, and about rights to intellectual property such as trademarks.

**Abuse of dominance** or **monopolisation** are categories that are concerned principally with the conduct and circumstances of individual firms. A true monopoly, which faces no competition or threat of competition, will charge higher prices and produce less or lower quality output; it may also be less likely to introduce more efficient methods or innovative products. Laws against monopolisation are typically aimed at exclusionary tactics by which firms might try to obtain or protect monopoly positions. Laws against abuse of dominance address the same issues, and may also try to address the actual exercise of market power. For example under some abuse of dominance systems, charging unreasonably high prices can be a violation of the law.

**Merger control** tries to prevent the creation, through acquisitions or other structural combinations, of undertakings that will have the incentive and ability to exercise market power. In some cases, the test of legality is derived from the laws about dominance or restraints; in others, there is a separate test phrased in terms of likely effect on competition generally. The analytic process applied typically calls for characterising the products that compete, the firms that might offer competition, and the relative shares and strategic importance of those firms with respect to the product markets. An important factor is the likelihood of new entry and the existence of effective barriers to new entry. Most systems apply some form of market share test, either to guide further investigation or as a presumption about legality. Mergers in unusually concentrated markets, or that create firms with unusually high market shares, are thought more likely to affect competition. And most systems specify procedures for pre-notification to enforcement authorities in advance of larger, more important transactions, and special processes for expedited investigation, so problems can be identified and resolved before the restructuring is actually undertaken.

---

that they are efficient; rather, their inefficiency is presumed conclusively. Violators are subject to administrative sanctions under the LFCE. In addition, the CFC may report associated criminal conduct to the public prosecutor. Relative practices may be found illegal only if the agents have substantial power in a defined relevant market. The sanctions for relative practices are limited to civil remedies under the LFCE, and parties may offer efficiency defences.

## 2.1. Horizontal agreements: rules to prevent anti-competition co-ordination, including that fostered by regulation

The absolute monopolistic practices that are subject to *per se* prohibition include four kinds of hard-core horizontal agreements among competing agents: price fixing, output restriction, market division, and bid rigging. The statute indicates some particular kinds of conduct along with the general categories. For example, the price fixing clause prohibits information exchanges with the purpose or effect of fixing or manipulating price; the output restriction clause prohibits commitments relating to frequency or volume; the market division clause covers both potential and actual markets; and the bid rigging clause covers agreements about participation as well as about bid levels. The listing of relative monopolistic practices includes only one specific kind of horizontal agreement, collusive boycotts, but it also includes a catch-all provision,[5] which would subject other kinds of horizontal arrangements to economically-based case-by-case treatment.

The absolute prohibition of these hard-core horizontal agreements cements one of the important reforms, the elimination of publicly sanctioned, but privately arranged, price control. Until the mid-1980s, prices for most goods and services were fixed by law, and the ostensibly regulated price level was often the result of an agreement among the members of the industry. Industries were, and are, organised into "business chambers" subject to the supervision of the Ministry of Trade and Industrial Promotion (SECOFI). As in other countries with corporatist traditions, semi-official industry trade bodies have been a common source of competition policy concerns. The laws providing for these business chambers were recently revised to limit their powers of exclusion, by making membership voluntary rather than compulsory, and to discourage their temptation to collusion. The old structure provided a convenient forum for reaching and enforcing agreements about regulated prices. Nearly all prices are now decontrolled, although SECOFI retains authority over the few that are not.

Much of the CFC's enforcement work, especially at first, has been directed at rooting out the old habits that this system of business chambers and price controls had supported. The CFC has fined a number of industry associations that fixed their members' prices.[6] In March 1995, the CFC fined the National Road Transport Chamber for horizontal price fixing. The chamber had distributed a reference price guide for negotiations between users and motor carriers. Despite the formal deregulation of this industry between 1989 and 1993, the guide specifically established the aim of setting minimum prices. The March 1998 LFCE Regulation announces that a price fixing violation will be presumed where a trade association communicates an instruction or recommendation and competitors set prices that are identical or, in the case of tradable goods or services, that are higher than world market prices (adjusted for trading costs).

Use of *per se* prohibitions balances the policy criterion of strict economic efficiency with an administrative criterion of enforcement efficiency. There may be some instances where *per se* rules condemn practices that have no anti-competitive effect in the particular circumstances. If many sellers face a single buyer and the price is inefficiently low because of the buyer's market power, permitting the sellers to act together might in theory improve efficiency, for example. To preserve simple rules, though, the law does not permit sellers to do this. Any problem of buyer market power has to be addressed directly, and not by permitting sellers to collude. Agreements between competitors with a small total market share are unlikely to harm competition, but these too are nonetheless subject to the law. Theory suggests that price fixing agreements between firms with small market shares would be uncommon, because those firms lack the market power that would make those agreements effective. But experience shows that small firms nonetheless collude enthusiastically, perhaps showing that in small markets they may indeed have at least short-term market power when they act together. In addition, small firms may

187

not know what the law prohibits or may lack good legal advice. And small firms may be tempted to act together in response to new economic conditions and uncertainties. In any event, the CFC has brought exemplary enforcement actions against small firms. This runs some risk of alienating potential allies in small business. On the other hand, collusion among small businesses may also have a directly observable effect on another important constituency, consumers. Smaller firms may co-ordinate some activities without violating the law by joining together in "integrating companies." This is a program, managed also by SECOFI, to assist small and medium sized firms to take advantage of scale economies and purchasing efficiencies. The CFC has determined that price standardisation by such integrating companies would not necessarily violate the law.[7]

The ban on horizontal agreements has been applied to agreements that were evidently sanctioned by local government, although not imposed by regulation. For example, an agreement among local tortilla producers allocated areas of the market in order to prevent entry of new competitors who provided home delivery services. The CFC penalised the firms involved and issued a recommendation to the state government to prevent the municipal authorities from supporting this type of action in the future.[8] And the law has been applied to agreements concerning sales to state-owned monopolies, despite the constitution-based exemption for these monopolies themselves. Five sellers of barium oxide to Pemex, the state oil monopoly, agreed to fix sales terms and conditions in order to neutralise Pemex's bidding process. All five suppliers were fined.[9]

The *per se* prohibitions have been applied in reforming sectors, notably transport, to good effect. So far, the law's no-compromise approach has not led to legislation providing for less-competitive exemptions or other arrangements, at least at the national level. Although a *per se* rule can be a temptation to run up a large number of relatively trivial cases against small firms that cannot defend themselves, not all small firm cases are trivial, and there is much to be said for clarity in the law. On balance, the law about horizontal agreements is excellent.

## 2.2. Vertical agreements: rules to prevent anti-competitive arrangements in supply and distribution, including those fostered by regulation

All kinds of vertical agreements are treated as relative monopolistic practices. The LFCE specifically identifies market division, resale price maintenance, tied sales, and exclusive dealing. The March 1998 LFCE Regulations also specify exclusive dealing in exchange for special discounts. Other types of vertical agreements may be reached under the catch-all provision. Relative monopolistic practices are illegal only if they demonstrably harm competition in the particular case; that is, the practices must unduly displace other agents from the market, substantially limit their access, or establish exclusive advantages in favour of certain persons. And the responsible party must have substantial market power in the relevant market. Parties may offer a defence on the grounds of efficiency, for which the burden of proof lies upon the presumed responsible party.[10] Unlike in most other OECD countries, there is no *per se* prohibition against resale price maintenance.

Treating all vertical agreements as relative practices, subject to case-by-case analysis, reflects the law's thoroughgoing economic basis. The main criterion is substantial market power, so vertical agreements are allowed if the producers or distributors involved face sufficient horizontal competition. The same result has been reached in practice in many other jurisdictions even under laws that do not draw such an explicit distinction. One benefit the CFC sees in this rule, which presumes efficiency and requires a market-power showing before finding a violation, over a rule that presumes violation but then permits exemptions based on efficiency, is that it imposes less of a regulatory burden, both on parties and on the agency involved. To be sure, "prohibitive" rules such as those of the EU give the administrator more power to intervene, but they also increase the enforcement workload and lead to complex, difficult regulatory distinctions.

Enforcement concerning vertical agreements seems to have had little to do with regulatory or privatisation situations or issues. The CFC finds no indication that anti-competitive agreements in supply or distribution have been required or encouraged by existing or previous regulations. In any event, the

LFCE fully applies to regulated sectors and even to conduct of legally protected monopolists that falls outside the scope of their protection. One of the CFC's early decisions required Pemex to change its practices about dealing with distributors in order to improve retail-level competition. And some actions have been taken under the LFCE to ensure that the pro-competitive intentions of market opening have not been defeated by private exclusive dealing or market division agreements.

The approach to relative practices thoroughly embodies the CFC's economic approach. Mexico's treatment of vertical price controls is an interesting contrast to the practices of other Member countries, which usually apply something akin to a *per se* prohibition.

## 2.3. Abuse of dominance: rules to prevent or remedy market power, especially arising from reform-related restructuring

Monopoly is prohibited, both by the LFCE and by the Constitution, but there is no separate section of the law about monopolisation or abuse of dominance. Rather, single-firm practices that may be defined as abuse of dominance or monopolisation in other countries are treated as relative monopolistic practices under Mexico's law. Some of these practices are specified in Article 10 of the law and Article 7 of the LFCE Regulations: refusal to deal, boycott, predatory pricing, price and other forms of discrimination, cross-subsidisation, and raising rivals' costs. Other practices could be reached by the catch-all provision, if done by firms with market power and if there were an adverse effect on competition. The Regulations clarify the criteria applied for defining the relevant market and for determining the existence of market power. The same legal predicate for LFCE liability, of showing market power, is applied in other, sectoral regulatory programs, thus providing a critical link between competition policy and regulatory policy.

The LFCE does not address abusive (high) pricing.[11] Violation is defined in terms of exclusionary practices at the expense of competitors, and not in terms of exploitative practices at the expense of consumers. The idea behind this approach is that if a firm exploits its market power by charging supra-competitive prices to consumers, that conduct will normally invite new competitors to enter, and it is thus self-correcting. Only if the dominant firm tries to maintain or enhance its dominance by engaging in a monopolistic practice – that is, excluding competitors – will the CFC step in.

Restructuring a monopolised network industry is not within the law's powers, because the Constitutional prohibition of monopoly as such is not implemented in the LFCE. Sector-specific laws and privatisation programs deal with this issue. Some of the early privatisations, notably in telecommunications, paid too little attention to the need for restructuring, with the result that the newly private industry was born as an inadequately regulated monopoly. More recently, though, CFC advice has been sought in these processes, which are discussed further below. Problems of network access, where the concern is discrimination or cross-subsidisation that harms competition in complementary markets, might in principle be reachable under the LFCE. But the usual approach has been for the sectoral legislation or regulation to set out rules governing access, rather than to apply the LFCE's general principles and procedures.

Similarly, because monopolistic pricing is something the LFCE does not remedy, other agencies apply sector-specific regulations to control abusive pricing by dominant firms. A necessary precondition for this price regulation is the existence of market power. Laws about railroads, airlines, natural gas and telecommunications include this market power standard. The CFC is responsible for assessing and identifying market power in those sectors. If the CFC finds there is market power, that finding becomes the basis for price controls imposed by the sectoral regulator.

The LFCE has been applied to other practices involving dominant firms in protected, privatised, or deregulated industries. In 1995, for example, the CFC took action against price discrimination by a subsidiary of Pemex, even though Pemex still has a constitutionally-based monopoly over crude petroleum and certain basic petrochemicals. This protection no longer extends to many intermediate petrochemicals, though. Pemex illegally discriminated between two types of users of ethylene oxide, an intermediate product for which Pemex is still the only producer. And the CFC challenged one of the major domestic airlines, Aeroméxico, for vertical division of markets and refusal to deal with travel agencies that sold other airlines' tickets.

Some abuses are also subject to sector-specific regulations. For example, the 1995 Federal Telecommunications Law contains *per se* prohibitions of cross-subsidisation and discriminatory treatment. This approach is not quite the same as under the LFCE, where such practices would be analysed case-by-case to determine their actual net effect. To be sure, it may be that the sectoral agency is considering policy objectives and values other than competition policy, something which the CFC itself would not do in similar circumstances. The continuing controversies over access to telecommunications markets suggest that standards which sectoral regulators apply are not always those of an economically-based competition policy.

Although the LFCE does not address exploitation of market power, it has been applied to address predatory pricing. The LFCE Regulations define predation as sustained pricing below average total cost or occasional pricing below variable cost. Although this pricing tactic is treated as an exclusionary device, the legal standard does not include a judgement about the likelihood of post-success recoupment of losses suffered to force a competitor out. The CFC has spent considerable time and resources on a predatory pricing case. After two rounds of proceedings over several years, the CFC found that Warner Lambert dominated the chewing gum market, with a share between 65% and 73%, that it had power to control price, that its prices were persistently below average total cost, and that the victim's losses were caused by Warner Lambert's conduct. The CFC imposed a fine and injunction; the matter is now on appeal. The standard in the Regulations was developed in deciding this case.

Treating dominance solely in the context of particular practices incorporates a lesson from the experience of others, that using legal tools to restructure monopoly can be costly and difficult, perhaps futile. It may represent a judgement that, despite the economic costs of monopoly, the costs of breaking it up and of forgoing some of its possible productive efficiencies are likely to be greater. Unfortunately, that means the law has few tools for dealing with structurally dominant firms that were inherited from before. The CFC can take action if they do something exclusionary, but it may not be easy to make those cases, because fear of commercial retaliation may inhibit customers and would-be competitors from complaining.

The lack of a means for dealing with monopolistic structure except in the context of privatisation means the law must tolerate conditions contrary to its purpose of eliminating monopolies. Of course, the cost of the remedy might be so high that toleration actually is, in some sense, efficient. But if no structural remedy is adopted, it is necessary to ensure that highly concentrated industries face real competition through other means. The principal source would be international trade. Yet some highly concentrated industries are protected by anti-dumping duties or other constraints against significant imports. A feasible, and perhaps even more effective, alternative to breaking up companies would be preventing or undoing anti-competitive trade arrangements, including both private agreements limiting competitive entry and official acts with the same effect.

### 2.4. Mergers: rules to prevent competition problems arising from corporate restructuring, including responses to regulatory change

Mergers whose objective or effect is to reduce, distort or hinder competition are prohibited. The CFC considers factors such as whether the merging parties would obtain the power to fix prices unilaterally or to substantially restrict competitors' access to the market, and whether actual or potential competitors likely would inhibit such power. The LFCE Regulations now provide for an explicit efficiency defence, assigning the burden of proof to the merging parties. The firms' financial conditions and prospects may also be taken into account in the evaluation of harm to competition, although there is no explicit "failing firm" defence. The Regulations also clarify the criteria applied for defining the relevant market and for determining the existence of market power.

Merger activity has increased in Mexico recently, as it has around the world. In its first (partial) year of operation, the CFC concluded 34 merger reviews; in the second year, that number nearly tripled to 89, and it has grown steadily until in 1997 it reached 218 and represented 46% of all cases. Few mergers have been challenged. In 1997, the CFC objected to only two, and imposed conditions on three others. A significant proportion of CFC cases – 32% in 1997 – has involved reviews of participants in privatisations and public auctions for licenses and concessions. These cases require an analysis similar to that of mergers.

Most mergers are occurring in industries that are restructuring or consolidating either because of trade liberalisation and deregulation or because of financial crisis. Commercial banking, for example, has undergone substantial restructuring. First, privatisation encouraged new entry, domestic and foreign, but then the peso crisis of the mid-1990s required many mergers and acquisitions. The CFC has not blocked any mergers in the banking sector. The relevant product market has typically been found to be the whole range of banking and credit services provided by commercial banking institutions, and the geographic market has been found to be national, on the grounds that there are no legal impediments to branching throughout the country and the major banks have national coverage. These conclusions have led the CFC to find smaller structural changes and less risk of anti-competitive effect. A 1993 merger (after privatisation, but before the major financial crisis struck) between two privatised, second-tier banks was one of the first mergers that the CFC reviewed. The CFC has reviewed several post-crisis acquisitions by foreign banks, which have increased their market share from 1.4% in 1994 to 15.6% in 1996. Because the acquirers brought needed financial strength and competition against the traditionally dominant position of the Big Three national banks, these transactions did not raise the commonly asserted trade-off between the protection of competition and the protection of stability.

Substantive criteria for merger analysis appear in a regulation issued in July 1998.[12] The regulation sets out structural criteria, which are applied in the context of general principles for defining markets and identifying barriers to entry in Part III of the March 1998 LFCE Regulations. The July 1998 regulation is one response to a concern, expressed by some in the business community, that the CFC's standards for deciding about mergers were not transparent or comprehensible. One structural criterion is based on the Herfindahl index (HHI), that is, the sum of the squared market shares of all the firms in the market. The regulation sets out a "safe harbour" for combinations that raise the HHI by less than 75 points, or that result in an HHI below 2 000. In addition, the regulation applies criteria based on an index of dominance. This is similar to, and derived from, the HHI: it is the sum of the squares of each firm's share of the HHI. Two additional safe-harbour rules follow: a transaction is considered unlikely to affect competition adversely if it does not increase the index of dominance, or if that index's resulting value is less than 2 500. These concentration-based indicators are not determinative. The CFC will also examine other factors that are relevant to determining whether letting the firms merge would lead to substantial market power, that is, to the power to control prices or substantially restrict competitors' access to the market.

Premerger notification obligations are indexed to the minimum general wage (fixed at 30.20 pesos in 1997). One basic threshold is 12 million times that reference. Notification is required if a transaction exceeds that level, or if it results in holding more than 35% of the shares or assets of a firm with sales or assets over that level. Notification is also required if the parties' assets or annual sales total more than 48 million times the index and the transaction involves an additional accumulation of assets or shares over 4.8 million times the index. Mergers outside Mexico must in principle be notified to the CFC if they produce effects within the country; however, the LFCE Regulations exempt from notification mergers between foreign firms that do not imply additional control over a firm located in Mexico. All notified transactions are subject to inquiry, which is subject to strict deadlines. So far, the CFC has generally been able to resolve cases in less than 100 days; the average is about 35 days.[13] Sanctions for failure to notify may include a fine, up to 100 000 times the index. The CFC may contest a merger that does not need to be notified, but only if it does so within a year after the transaction.

At least as important as the merger review process, at least so far, has been the closely-related responsibility to review privatisation proposals and procedures. Procedures for reviewing participants in privatisations and auctions for licenses and concessions differ from those for mergers, and indeed may vary with particular proposals or programs. There are no thresholds and deadlines may depend on specific auction rules. The CFC performs these functions pursuant to an administrative directive of the

Inter-Ministerial Divestiture Committee and powers granted by a number of particular statutes and regulations. These typically require that potential participants not be blocked by the CFC. In general, in its analysis the CFC applies criteria that are highly similar to those of merger reviews. Of the 154 reviews concluded in 1997, the CFC objected to two and imposed conditions on another. The CFC prohibited two firms from bidding for rural grain storage facilities. One of these firms, a maritime transport company, had already obtained one of the three regions of the privatised national railroad system. The acquisition of the storage facilities would give it too much strategic control over the transport and storage of national and imported grain.

Remedies for mergers with anti-competitive aspects are either corrective or preventive. Few mergers have been blocked. A combination of two sugar refineries was rejected because corrective remedies would probably be unsuccessful, and the CFC opposed a merger of two packaged meat companies whose combined share of national supermarket sales for some products would have been nearly 60% (and which would have controlled the national refrigerated distribution network). Preventive remedies consist of obligations such as to notify about future mergers, antidumping complaints, or applications for exclusive permits. Remedies like these were imposed on transactions involving sugar refineries, petrochemical firms and natural gas distributors. Contractual remedies may require the elimination of exclusivity clauses or the commitment to facilitate competitors' entry, prevent discrimination, or guarantee the commercial independence of the companies involved in the merger. Measures of this kind were used in mergers in the textile and metal industries and in radio and TV broadcasting, among others. Finally, structural remedies require the divestiture of assets. Such remedies were imposed in the Kimberly Clark-Crisoba merger.[14]

Several notable merger-related decisions have involved privatised and deregulated industries. CFC investigation and informal communication of concerns evidently halted a proposed reconfiguration in the telecommunications and television industries. The proposed transaction would have given Telmex, the historic national telephone monopoly, control over a major group of cable TV firms, while the broadcast company, Televisa, would maintain control over a number of applicants for UHF and MMDS concessions. The CFC and others were concerned about the evolution of subscription TV and basic local telephone markets, particularly in the Mexico City metropolitan area. The measures that the CFC indicated would have been necessary to eliminate the threats to competition could have substantially altered the parties' plans, and they decided to withdraw before the investigation was concluded.

In airlines, a complex and difficult structural matter has been underway for several years. Airline deregulation had already begun to lead to new entry, increased services, and greater price competition, when financial reverses stalled the process. CFC has countenanced the combination of the two major domestic air carriers, Aeroméxico and Mexicana, into a holding company, whose acronym is CINTRA. Before the competition law was adopted, Aeroméxico had acquired control over Mexicana, with the authorisation of the Ministry of Communications and Transport (SCT). A condition of that authorisation was that the combination would be subject to the new competition law when it became effective. The airlines' deteriorating economic and financial situation led to their being taken over by creditor banks. CINTRA was incorporated at the banks' initiative, to be a holding company charged with improving the airlines' financial situation. Since then, shifts in bank capitalisation and ownership have led to the government holding a controlling interest in CINTRA.

The holding company arrangement is clearly unattractive from a competition policy perspective. It may have been thought inevitable, both because of support from the banks and the other ministry and because limitations on foreign investment in this sector meant there were few if any realistic alternative purchasers, so that blocking the combination would not have improved the situation. In any event, the CFC's acceptance of the holding company was subject to conditions that were intended to maintain competition between the two airlines: separate accounts, independent management, and performance monitoring and periodic reporting on market conditions by a consultant appointed by the CFC. Such conditions are difficult to apply effectively and are obviously a second-best substitute for clear structural separation. If the CFC finds there is no competition, then the SCT may set fares, and if the CFC finds unlawful practices, the parties must suspend them or take corrective action. The CFC may order that the combination be dissolved if there is substantial damage to competition.[15] Despite these safeguards, there are doubts about the vigour of the airlines' continued competition. Board memberships at first were identical; CFC intervention reduced that some, but did not eliminate board overlaps completely, and managerial relationships too have not been kept distinct. The CFC has been investigating whether fare levels show the exercise of market power in some city-pair markets, calling for remedial action. This situation is a major test of the effectiveness of Mexico's competition policy and institutions.

The law about structural combinations is generally complete and modern, but in one respect more clarity might be useful. A party's financial weakness may count in the assessment of likely competitive effects, but beyond that there are no principles describing how it is to count, and what presumptions, if any, are applied. This leaves a great deal of room for non-transparent discretion. Some transactions, in banking and the CINTRA combination in particular, have probably been motivated by concerns about disposing of assets in virtual bankruptcy. The CFC's reported decisions note that motivation and the concern that failure would diminish competition, but the reports are conclusory. The factual basis underlying that reasoning should be made clearer.

## 2.5. Competitor protection: relationship to rules of "unfair competition"

The law treats unfair competition in a way that is consistent with its economic motivation. The law's provisions about relative monopolistic practices address actions that harm competitors, rather than those that affect consumers directly. Thus, they have the appearance of measures aimed at unfair competitive practices. But the underlying purpose of the law is efficiency, and the CFC specifically rejects the idea that it should be based on fairness. As a consequence, some practices that are often considered "unfair competition" are not addressed. Sales below cost is now included in the LFCE Regulations' list of relative monopolistic practices, but it is evaluated under predatory pricing standards and subject to a market power test.

The CFC has received complaints about alleged abuse of economic dependence. The LFCE's market power standard means it deals with such complaints about vertical contract relationships if horizontal competition is impaired.

## 2.6. Consumer protection: consistency with competition law and policy

Despite the mutual support they might offer each other, in the Mexican legal system the competition and consumer protection laws are enforced separately by two different agencies. The Federal Consumer Protection Law is enforced by the Federal Prosecutor for Consumers. This office is located in the same ministry, SECOFI, where the CFC is assigned for administrative purposes. The consumer law's stated objectives are to promote and protect consumer rights and to procure equity and legal security in relationships between suppliers and consumers. That office also enforces the remaining price controls and the rules about weights and measures. The CFC finds there are relatively few overlaps between that conception of consumer policy and the issues that arise under competition policy, and consequently there is little communication between the two agencies.

On one occasion, the CFC was asked for an opinion on a proposed regulation of comparative advertising. The CFC responded based on the likely effects on competition, and advised that comparative advertising is unlikely to adversely affect the competitive process, although problems might arise related to intellectual property rights or to the quality of information given to consumers. Thus, the CFC recommended that any consumer regulation about this issue not be concerned about relations between competitors, but rather should concentrate on relations between suppliers and consumers. The Prosecutor for Consumers evidently followed this advice, since it did not proceed with the proposed change in this regulation.

The CFC has had no program to explain the benefits of competition and competition law enforcement to consumers, although a division devoted to public outreach has just been established. It would have to undertake such an effort on its own, for there is no significant national consumer organisation to work with. In light of the potential complementarity of their purposes and the relationship of the responsible agencies to the same ministry, the lack of more formal co-ordination between consumer and competition policies in SECOFI is surprising. Contacts now appear limited to exchanging information about cases that might affect each others' jurisdiction. The SECOFI consumer office issues a consumer-oriented magazine that might be a vehicle for telling consumers about how they benefit from preventing anti-competitive conduct.

## 3. INSTITUTIONAL TOOLS: ENFORCEMENT IN SUPPORT OF REGULATORY REFORM

Reform of economic regulation could fail if vigorous action is not taken to prevent abuses in developing markets. The CFC has an adequate set of substantive tools; the next question to examine is whether they are effectively employed.

### 3.1. Competition policy institutions

The CFC, which has sole responsibility to apply the LFCE, is a separate entity attached to SECOFI. The CFC decisions are made by majority vote of the plenum of five commissioners. The CFC president chairs the plenum meetings, co-ordinates the CFC's work, issues its annual report, represents the CFC publicly, and can appoint and remove personnel. The Executive Secretary, appointed by the CFC president, is responsible for operational and administrative co-ordination, and for legally certifying undertakings such as plenary sessions. The CFC's work is done by general directorates for legal affairs, economic studies, concentrations, investigations, privatisation, regional operations, international issues, administration, and public information. The CFC's principal formal ties to other regulatory authorities are through its participation in inter-ministerial committees, generally as an observer, where it advises about design of regulations and privatisation strategies. Competition policy issues related to regulation are also considered by the Economic Deregulation Unit in SECOFI, described in Chapter 2. The EDU participated in drafting the LFCE, and continues to participate in review of regulations and proposals, including those of the CFC.

Decisional independence is protected by the terms of the commissioners' tenure. The CFC's president and the other four commissioners are appointed by the president of Mexico for staggered ten year terms, and are removable only for cause. The CFC commissioners are thus insulated from the usual practice of virtually complete personnel turnover after presidential elections every six years. In contrast to some sectoral agencies, the basis for the CFC's independence is in the law, not a lower-level normative act, and the commissioners are appointed by the president, not by ministers. They are still exposed to political pressure and other persuasion, but their tenure protects them somewhat from consequences of decisions that conflict with other ministries' designs. Officials at the highest levels have tried to lobby CFC commissioners. The CFC's official position in response is that it has to act on its own. Although connected administratively to SECOFI, the CFC is technically and operationally autonomous and thus is not responsible to the Minister for its decisions. This formal independence is important. The finance ministry and the Congress are responsible for the CFC's budget and so maintain a means of indirect control over policy.

Some have criticised the CFC for lack of transparency in its decision criteria. So far, the principal means of explaining its decisions has been its annual report, which includes summaries of the most illustrative cases. The CFC has now begun publishing its decisions and reasoning in a periodical gazette; in addition, summaries will also be published in the Official Journal of the Federation. The complete texts of the law, the regulations and annual reports, and summaries of decisions since July 1997 are available at the CFC's Internet website.[16] The CFC has also begun to announce when it is undertaking investigations, naming the industry but not the likely target. This practice has had the desired effect of attracting evidence, as well as the less desirable effect of alerting targets and encouraging them to take pre-emptive legal action.

The CFC participates in several inter-ministerial groups that are concerned with issues that affect competition policy, such as privatisation. It is not usually a voting member of those groups, though. It participates principally in order to assist in analysing competition issues and to prepare for quick issuance of opinions. Without a vote, the CFC may be perceived as a less important factor in these groups' deliberations. Of course, the CFC exercises significant power in the ensuing processes, by determining whether firms can participate. The CFC's relations with other regulators have sometimes been difficult. Not only is the CFC's jurisdiction under the LFCE very broad, but also several sector-specific laws give the CFC authority over important issues in other ministries' or agencies' jurisdiction. The LFCE and sector-specific laws may lead to different results. Some competition-related sectoral rules are more stringent than the generally applied competition policy, for example. And in some sectors, notably telecommunications, there have been disagreements about the design of competition-related regulations and remedies.

## 3.2. Competition law enforcement

The LFCE is a prohibition-based law, implemented through *ex post* law-enforcement, rather than an administered one based on reviewing applications for permission or exemption. The high level of economic content may makes its application appear discretionary, though. The CFC may begin a law enforcement or other matter either in response to a complaint or on its own initiative.[17] Increasingly, the CFC is treating complaint-based matters as *ex officio* ones. The CFC's information-gathering powers are the same regardless of the matter's origin or object. Remedial powers are substantial. The CFC may impose fines or order the suspension or correction of the forbidden practice. This includes the power to dismantle illegal mergers.

The LFCE and the CFC's Regulations set out a procedure which gives parties a chance to make a formal response to the case and order against them. Further appeals to the courts can take two forms. A party who claims that a legally protected interest has been infringed by CFC action may resort to the *amparo* action before a Federal District Court, to challenge the legality or constitutionality of the CFC's decisions.[18] Parties have often availed themselves of this constitutionally-granted process right, and the result has been to delay CFC proceedings. Not only do parties challenge final CFC decisions, but they

---

Box 3.   Enforcement powers

**Does the agency have the power to take investigative action on its own initiative?** The CFC, like most Member country agencies (19), has power to issue prohibitory orders on its own initiative. In one-quarter of the countries, even such "cease and desist" orders can only be issued by a court or separate decision-maker. About half of Member country agencies, including Mexico's, can impose financial penalties directly. Mexico's CFC also has the power to issue mandatory orders, such as divestiture.

**Does the agency publish its decisions and the reasons for them?** Virtually all Member country enforcement agencies publish their decisions and reasoning in some form. Where agencies do not do so themselves, effective decisions are made by courts that do. The CFC has now begun to publish summaries of its actions regularly, without waiting to collect them in an annual report.

**Are the agency's decisions subject to substantive review and correction by a court?** All Member country competition agencies must defend their actions in court if necessary.

**Can private parties also bring their own suits about competition issues?** Some kind of privately initiated suit about competition issues is possible in nearly all jurisdictions. In a majority of countries, agencies explain the reasons why they do not take action in a particular case, and a party who is disappointed by the competition agency's inaction can challenge the agency in court. In Mexico, the right of private suit is limited to a follow-on proceeding to collect damages.

also take the CFC to court to dispute preliminary and intermediate actions. Once the *amparo* is initiated, the judge can enjoin the administrative proceeding pending the judicial decision. Until its comprehensive regulation appeared in March 1998 explaining how the law was being interpreted and applied, many *amparo* suits complained (generally unsuccessfully) that the LFCE was unconstitutionally vague. In addition to the *amparo* challenge, it is possible to challenge fines by appeal to an administrative court, the Federal Tax Appeal Tribunal.[19] The CFC believes its success rate in both *amparo* suits and administrative appeals has generally been good, at least on important substantive issues.

Clear deadlines and time targets control CFC proceedings. Some deadlines are in the LFCE, and others are set by the Regulations. For ordinary law enforcement matters, the CFC has committed to reaching a final decision within about 90 to 150 days after receiving a complaint. Merger matters are to be concluded within 90 days, although that time can be extended in exceptional cases. If a party petitions for reconsideration (within 30 days after a CFC decision), the CFC will act on that petition within 60 days. Some observers have criticised the CFC for deciding slowly, but often the reason has been either delays due to *amparo* appeals or punctilious observation of necessary procedures to reduce the risk of losing such appeals.

### 3.3. Other enforcement methods

The CFC and its processes control application of the LFCE. There is no other source of substantive law about competition policy issues, either at the state or federal level. Rights of private action are limited to a claim for damages, after the CFC has found a violation. This avenue has not yet been used. When it is, the court is likely to ask the CFC its views about the appropriate amount of damages. Proceedings before the CFC may be started by the CFC itself, acting on its own initiative, or in response to complaint from a private party. Complaints about absolute monopolistic practices can be filed by any person. Complaints about relative monopolistic practices and mergers should be filed by the affected party. Provided that the complaint meets the conditions for standing set out in the LFCE and the Regulations, the CFC must deal with the case; it does not have the discretion to reject it without reaching some decision. A disappointed complainant may have some recourse to the courts to correct an alleged error, through the *amparo* process.

### 3.4. International trade issues in competition policy and enforcement

Mexican competition policy is one element of a program that began with major steps toward market openness. Thus, is it unsurprising that the CFC and the decisions under the LFCE attend to this substantive dimension, in defining relevant geographic markets and determining the existence of market power. Analysis of market conditions in Mexico must take into account increased competition from abroad since import liberalisation began in the mid-1980s. And actual or potential new entry made possible by less restrictive foreign investment rules can make a difference in assessing market power. Still, in many cases the CFC defines markets as national, because of market and demand characteristics. But it does take into account the effect that imports and foreign investment may have on the market power of firms operating in Mexico.

Three types of practices related to international markets affect domestic competition, and thus are of concern for the CFC. First, import liberalisation in Mexico may be impaired by private barriers to trade raised by domestic firms with market power. Those firms could hinder the entry of foreign goods, for instance, by pre-empting access to essential distribution channels. The CFC can take action when the responsible parties are established in Mexico. For example, in 1995 the CFC fined two producers of domestic appliances, with a combined Mexican market share over 80%, for colluding to grant discounts to retailers who promised not to sell appliances produced outside the NAFTA area. Second, anti-competitive practices abroad may have adverse, cross-border effects on competition in a Mexican market. The most common case is a foreign export cartel that is permitted in the country of origin. Third, mergers abroad may also affect competition in Mexico, for example, because one or more of the merging parties have subsidiaries or important sales in Mexico. In these last two cases, the CFC's possible responses are limited, for although it has legal power to address the substantive issues, it is not empowered to investigate or impose (and collect) fines on firms located abroad. Of course, the CFC's power to act in Mexico can encourage parties to co-operate with its processes, even where that cannot be compelled. For addressing these kinds of issues effectively, co-operation with the competition authorities of the country where the practice takes place seems essential.

Competition policy also is concerned about the analysis of allegedly unfair practices in international trade. Mexico implemented an antidumping and countervailing duty mechanism after it adhered to the GATT in 1986. This subject is now governed by the 1993 Foreign Trade Law and its Regulations, which are applied by another part of SECOFI, the Unfair Trade Practices Unit (UPCI). The CFC is concerned that enforcement of unfair trade laws against imports may in practice distort competition in domestic markets. Antidumping duties imposed by the UPCI have protected national producers with a dominant position in the domestic market. In other cases the duties simply delay an effective market clearing process by protecting inefficient domestic firms. This problem is not limited to Mexico, of course. Other countries' competition authorities have found that alleged dumping practices are not inconsistent with healthy competition, typically because the exporter lacks power to monopolise a market in the country of import. The CFC follows the antidumping and countervailing duty decisions through participation in the inter-ministerial Foreign Trade Commission, which must approve UPCI resolutions. The CFC cannot block the UPCI's resolutions, because it has no veto power, but on several occasions it has ventilated its concerns about the effects of antidumping and countervailing duties on domestic competition.

Procedures for responding to complaints about anti-competitive behaviour under the LFCE make no distinction between foreign or national firms. Hence, both have the same right to file complaints. Of course, asserting jurisdiction over practices abroad is often difficult. Mexico has no formal co-operation agreements with other countries about competition policy. The CFC follows the general co-operation principles established in NAFTA and in other trade agreements, as well as co-operation principles promoted within the framework of international organisations, particularly the OECD. It has used these channels to notify, or receive notification, about possible problems on a few occasions. The CFC believes it has ample, informal communication on technical issues, with agencies in other countries, especially those of the NAFTA partners.

---

Box 4.   **International co-operation agreements**

Eight Member countries have entered one or more formal agreements to co-operate in competition enforcement matters: Australia, Canada, Czech Republic, Hungary, Korea, New Zealand, Poland, and the US. And the EC has done so as well.

---

### 3.5. Agency resources, actions, and implied priorities

Commitment to effective enforcement, as measured by resources employed, has been reasonably stable. In terms of personnel, CFC staffing has held steady for several years, at about 165 employees. In terms of budget, though, the picture is different: it fell about 30% (in real terms) between 1994 and 1997. This drop reflects budget and economic troubles that have hit Mexico since the 1995 financial crisis. For 1998, the budget for personnel has been increased significantly, despite a budget total that is about the same as in 1996. The budget stringency may be impeding work, to some extent, as the total budget per employee for 1997 was only about half what it was in 1994.

Among the five commissioners, there are three economists and two lawyers. In the CFC as a whole, there are about 30 economists, 30 lawyers, and 50 officials with other professional backgrounds. About

20 staff are occupied with regulatory issues: opinions about new regulations, trade policy, and other government programs. Investigation and prosecution of anti-competitive actions takes about another 35 staff from the directorates of Investigations and Legal Affairs. And about 25 staff from the Concentrations and Privatisation directorates are involved in merger and privatisation reviews. Directorates often collaborate and support each other. A high priority, in terms of staff time, has been given to regulatory and related issues.

Many complaints were submitted during the first year of the CFC's operation, probably due to the expectations generated by the enactment of the law. The high rate at which those early complaints were dismissed – 90% – is probably explained by the complainants' lack of knowledge and experience. That rate has declined, as complainants have been receiving better advice about what the law can and cannot do. Some cases dismissed for procedural shortcomings were nonetheless pursued *ex officio*. During the first years, actions against anti-competitive conduct relied largely on *ex officio* investigations, and concentrated on three aspects: recently deregulated sectors afflicted with anti-competitive inertia, economic activities shielded by administrative barriers to entry, and concentrated markets characterised by exchange of information between competitors.[20] Activity picked up markedly in the next years, for several reasons. The business community became increasingly aware of the law and CFC's functions. Many more mergers and acquisitions were filed. And the CFC became involved in decisions about privatisation of state companies, issuance of public permits and concessions, and granting rights concerning ports, telecommunications and natural gas distribution.[21]

The latest case data shows the CFC's emphasis on *ex officio* proceedings and the high proportion of matters that conclude with no finding of violation. In 1997, the CFC handled 60 proceedings against conduct-based problems. Of these, most (35) were *ex officio* investigations, and 25 were private complaints. Of the 52 cases that were concluded, one-quarter (13) resulted in penalties or recommendations. The rest were either withdrawn or summarily dismissed, or no violation was found. In 1997, the CFC also

Table 1. **CFC enforcement activity**

| | Horizontal agreements | Vertical agreements | Mergers* | Interstate trade barriers |
|---|---|---|---|---|
| **1997**: investigations or matters opened | 8 | 45 | 351 | 7 |
| Sanctions or orders sought | 7 | 2 | 8 | 3** |
| Orders or pecuniary sanctions imposed | 6 | 1 | 17 | – |
| Total pecuniary sanctions imposed (pesos) | 911 156 | 2 209 675 | 1 492 312 | – |
| **1996**: investigations or matters opened | 9 | 17 | 236 | 3 |
| Sanctions or orders sought | 4 | 2 | 11 | 4** |
| Orders or pecuniary sanctions imposed | 4 | 2 | 10 | – |
| Total pecuniary sanctions imposed (pesos) | 38 053 | 39 946 | 360 005 | – |
| **1995**: investigations or matters opened | 14 | 19 | 149 | 1 |
| Sanctions or orders sought | 3 | 5 | 13 | 0** |
| Orders or pecuniary sanctions imposed | 3 | 0 | 4 | – |
| Total pecuniary sanctions imposed (pesos) | 276 682 | 27 450 | 354 000 | – |
| **1994**: investigations or matters opened | 3*** | | 94 | |
| Sanctions or orders sought | 5*** | | 2 | |
| Orders or pecuniary sanctions imposed | 2*** | | 2 | |
| Total pecuniary sanctions imposed (pesos) | 139 705*** | | 1 556 726 | |
| **1993**: investigations or matters opened | 32*** | | 63 | |
| Sanctions or orders sought | 0*** | | 2 | |
| Orders or pecuniary sanctions imposed | 0*** | | 1 | |
| Total pecuniary sanctions imposed (pesos) | 0*** | | 512 000 | |

\*    Includes privatisations, licenses, and permits.
\*\*   Recommendations to the corresponding authorities.
\*\*\*  Horizontal and vertical combined.
*Source*:   CFC.

examined 212 mergers and acquisitions, most of them the result of pre-merger notifications (22 were *ex officio* investigations, and one originated as a complaint). The CFC concluded 219 merger cases, approving 192, requiring conditions for 20, and blocking two (five were dismissed or withdrawn by the parties).[22]

Although the CFC has not adopted explicit enforcement priorities, it has paid special attention to official barriers to interstate trade imposed by state governments. In recent years, the CFC has taken action against barriers imposed by several state governments on interstate trade in flowers, eggs and fresh meat, among others. And in recently deregulated sectors, the CFC has taken actions against price fixing in transport and against consolidation in telecommunications.

## 4. THE LIMITS OF COMPETITION POLICY FOR REGULATORY REFORM

### 4.1. Economy-wide exemptions or special treatments

There are few exceptions from the LFCE. Some of the activities excluded are like those excluded in most countries: legally constituted labour associations, copyright and patent holders, and export trade associations (of small producers). Another important set of exemptions applies to the "strategic sectors" identified in Article 28 of the Mexican Constitution, which are not considered monopolies although the LFCE does apply if they engage in monopolistic practices.

Technically, authorisation by a federal or state government official does not excuse private conduct that violates the LFCE. Practically, the CFC recommends that other authorities not encourage or issue rules or orders that put parties in that position. The CFC rejects the claimed excuse as a matter of principle, but it may lead to a reduction in the penalty. The party who has to pay for the LFCE violation might complain against the other agency for giving bad advice or instructions. No court has faced and decided this issue, though.

Public enterprises are not exempt as such. The state, its agencies, and its companies as economic agents are subject to the LFCE. State-owned enterprises involved in the strategic areas established in the Constitution are subject to the law with respect to monopolistic practices that are not specifically within the strategic sectors. Pemex has been subject to several actions for practices outside the sector where it enjoys constitutional protection. Government entities whose conduct restricts competition may get an admonition, rather than an order or a fine, where they are not participating in conduct as economic agents and the CFC thus does not have jurisdiction over them. For example, an action against a collusive boycott in notarisation services concluded with economic sanctions against the private parties involved and a recommendation to the public official whose action formed the basis for the boycott effort.[23]

---

### Box 5. Scope of competition policy

**Is there an exemption from liability under the general competition law for conduct that is required or authorised by other government authority?** Unlike the majority of Member countries (15 out of the 27 reporting), Mexico's law does not recognise an exemption from the general competition law for conduct required by other regulation or government authority.

**Does the general competition law apply to public enterprises?** Mexico, like every Member country except Portugal and the US, applies its general competition law to public enterprises.

**Is there an exemption, in law or enforcement policy, for small and medium sized enterprises?** Four Member countries reported some kind of exemption or difference in treatment for small and medium sized enterprises: Belgium, France, Germany, and Japan.

---

One important area of enforcement against public bodies is aimed at state government action that restricts trade between the states. The LFCE[24] implements the Constitution's prohibition against such action by holding that "acts performed by state authorities with direct or indirect objectives to prevent the entry or exit of goods or services from state territories, of domestic or foreign origin, shall have no legal force or effect." In theory, then, after the CFC makes such a ruling, private parties could ignore the local officials' acts with impunity. Restrictions on interstate trade are nevertheless pervasive. Many of them pre-date the LFCE and the effective enforcement of the constitutional ban. The CFC lacks the power to punish a local government or to issue a mandatory order constraining its conduct. Thus, the CFC's usual action about a government entity's restraint is a recommendation; if the local government does not take action itself to remove it, that is followed by a declaration that the restraint is legally void.

Small and medium sized firms receive no special treatment under the LFCE, other than what would follow from economic principle. There is no *de minimis* rule, and hard-core horizontal agreements are prohibited *per se*, regardless of the size of the firm. But there is a degree of implicit protection in the rule-of-reason approach taken for all other conduct (although substantial market power depends on firm's size relative to its market, not its absolute size).

## 4.2. Sector-specific exclusions, rules and exemptions

The LFCE applies to all areas of economic activity, including those areas subject to specific, sectoral economic regulations. The strategic sectors reserved to the state under Article 28 of the Constitution are excluded from the law's prohibition of monopoly, but entities engaged in the exempted strategic sectors might be found to violate the law's strictures against monopolistic practices. The strategic areas now include coinage and paper money, postal service, telegraph and radiotelegraphy, petroleum and other hydrocarbons, basic petrochemicals, radioactive minerals, nuclear energy, and electricity. Recently, satellite communications and railroads were taken off the list (by constitutional amendment), in order to open up those sectors to competition And electricity sector has been partially opened up to private participation, despite its status as strategic area. Under certain circumstances, private parties may now generate electricity for their own use or for sale to the state-owned electricity monopoly.

For several regulated sectors, independent regulatory agencies have been established: telecommunications (the Federal Telecommunications Commission, or COFETEL, which is in the Ministry of Communications and Transport), electricity and natural gas (the Energy Regulatory Commission, CRE; its role in electricity is limited because that sector is still largely state-owned), insurance (the National Insurance Commission) and pension funds (the National Pension Fund System Commission). Some other sectors, such as transport and pharmaceuticals, are directly regulated by federal ministries. The financial sector is regulated by the Ministry of Finance, the National Banking and Securities Commission, and the Mexican central bank. None of these government entities have authority to apply the LFCE, nor are these sectors exempt from it.

Since 1995 several sectoral laws and regulations have included provisions to promote competition, which are applied by reference to the CFC. In addition, the CFC must appraise the prevailing conditions of competition prior to the introduction or elimination of official prices by the regulatory authorities. (The government has some power to establish price ceilings without regard to firm or industry market power. The Federal Executive determines which products are eligible, based on the statutory criteria (that they are necessary to the national economy or essential for basic needs), and SECOFI sets the ceilings after negotiation with interested parties. In the mid-80's, about 70% of all products were subject to some form of price controls, but as of 1996 that was reduced to only two products, tortillas (which were subsidised by the government) and medicines.

## 5. COMPETITION ADVOCACY FOR REGULATORY REFORM

The LFCE empowers the CFC to comment on the effects that existing laws, regulations, agreements and administrative acts may have on competition, on the effects of contemplated changes to federal programs and policies, and, upon request by the Federal Executive, on the effects on competition of new laws and regulations proposed to Congress. And the CFC has played a central role in the processes of privatisation and of awarding concessions and licenses, both in the design of the necessary law and regulations and in implementing them.

The CFC participates in inter-ministerial committees in order to inject competition policy into regulatory decisions. The CFC's role has been principally to prevent administrative measures that could produce anti-competitive effects. The committees include the Inter-ministerial Privatisation Commission, the Inter-ministerial Public Spending and Financing Commission, the Consulting Committee for the Opening of Local Telephone Services, the National Standards Commission for, and the Foreign Trade Commission. The CFC thus participates in competition-related policy making about privatisation, licensing, standards, regulation, and foreign trade.

The CFC is directly concerned with competition aspects of sector-specific regulation and in the allocation of licenses and permits, including reviewing applicants for these assets. Partly as a result of its competition advocacy, the CFC has been given this role explicitly, under the Seaport Law, the Law on Roads, Bridges and Road Transport, the Navigation Law, the Railroad Services Law, the Federal Telecommunications Law, the Civil Aviation Law and the Airport Law, and the regulations on natural gas and on pension funds.[25] The CFC has two functions under these rules. First, the CFC can determine which economic agents may participate in auctions for public enterprises, concessions, licenses and permits. Second, the CFC may determine whether effective competition exists, or whether one of the agents has substantial market power, as a condition for a sectoral regulator to impose regulation such as price caps. In that connection, the CFC may also determine that competition has been restored, because of changes in market conditions, so the regulation should be terminated.

**Telecommunications deregulation.** Liberalisation of telecommunications began in 1991 when the telephone monopoly, Telmex, was privatised. Competition though wireless telephone services began in 1993. As part of the privatisation process, Telmex retained its monopoly in long distance telephony until the end of 1996. After the privatisation, and before the end of that period of Telmex exclusivity, the Ministry of Communications and Transport designed the telecommunications regulatory framework. In that process, the CFC urged that the number of competitors in long distance and local not be limited (that is, that all qualified applicants should obtain a license), and that new competitors (which would be principally those in long distance and in wireless telephony) should obtain unrestricted and non-discriminatory access to the local network, still controlled by Telmex. The CFC also contributed to other competition-related aspects of the telecommunication legislation, such as those dealing with terms for public network concessions, access to value-added services, open-architecture networks, interconnection agreements, and exclusive contracts.

**Incumbent market power.** The sector regulator, COFETEL, can regulate the tariffs and services of dominant firms in order to facilitate entry and enhance competition. But that power depends on the CFC, for it is up to the CFC to determine whether a carrier is dominant. The CFC has now made such a formal determination. During the second half of 1997 the CFC carried out an *ex officio* investigation, which concluded in December 1997 that Telmex does indeed have substantial market power in five relevant markets: local telephony, interconnection services, national long distance, international long distance and the resale of long distance. The market power in local telephony, national long distance services, and international long distance services is directed at final consumers, while the market power for access or interconnection services and transport services most directly affects other carriers. Telmex owns virtually all of the local public networks and provides local and interconnection services. Entry has occurred in long distance services, but the entrants' infrastructure is still modest compared to Telmex's network. Thus, long distance companies rely on Telmex's capacity for their access to final consumers and to provide long distance services in some routes. Telmex's vertical integration and its ability to fix prices without other competitors being able to offset such power, as well as the existence of important entry barriers, were taken into account in determining its dominant position. This decision, which the CFC reaffirmed in February 1998 and submitted to COFETEL, is likely to be appealed by Telmex. The

201

only issues on appeal will be procedural or constitutional, though, as the CFC determination of market power is conclusive. The next step is for COFETEL to design and implement appropriate regulations.

**Local telephony rules.** COFETEL's local telephony rules incorporate some of the CFC's recommendations to promote competition in local telephone services, but COFETEL rejected others. One that was included is the definition of local telephone service areas. The number of local service areas, which are based on switching groups, will be gradually reduced from 1 500 to 485 over a five-year period. The intention is to reduce the investment requirements for new carriers and so reduce barriers to entry while promoting scale economies in the use of capacity. A contentious issue is the settlement paid to local operators for terminating an international call. The rules about this were intended to be non-discriminatory among different local service firms, but there has been considerable dispute about how these rules affect other parties. Local providers are also required to register at least five unbundled interconnection components, subject to separate rates and billing. Services are to be provided at non-discriminatory rates, making no distinction among service suppliers performing similar operations, including its subsidiaries or affiliates. Non-discrimination is to be enforced by the relatively weak means of requiring an integrated firm to keep separate accounts for its own operations, though. The rules introduce the principle of "calling party pays" in mobile service. In countries where this charging system has been implemented, mobile telephony has developed much faster than in Mexico, where the receiver paid for the call. But CFC concerns about the need for a clearer separation in the rules between mobile and fixed telephony were ignored. A difficulty in addressing the separation issue is that controls over fixed telephony are contained in the Telmex concession agreement.[26]

**Satellites.** The CFC has been involved in the design of the framework for the privatisation of the satellite system. The communications satellite system was sold off in 1997. There was a discussion of whether to sell the whole satellite system (consisting of three geostationary satellites and one additional orbit slot currently not occupied) in one package or to split it up in two packages. Selling it as a unit might create a dominant position at the expense of users, but also might yield a system that could take advantage of economies of scale and scope. It would also likely fetch a higher price. In the end, the CFC did not object to the privatisation of all satellite assets in one package because it considered that the eventual winning bidder would still face sufficient competition from services provided by foreign satellite systems, which have become possible due to agreements reached with the US and other countries. In addition, there may be competition from optic fibre and microwave technologies, and eventually from low-orbit satellites. The CFC also did not object to any of the participants in the privatisation process, finding that, because of these other sources of competition, acquisition by any of them would not threaten to create market power.

The CFC promoted the incorporation of competition criteria into the privatisation framework. Here again, one important element was conditioning the Minister's power to impose special regulatory obligations on a CFC finding of market power. In addition, the CFC argued for rules against discrimination or cross-subsidisation. To prevent satellite users from accumulating satellite capacity in order to impede the entry of new competitors, a party that acquires the right to satellite capacity must use it within 180 days or lose that right to another claimant. The CFC is also involved in determining who may obtain a license to bring in signals from foreign satellite systems.

**Spectrum auctions.** Radio spectrum frequency licenses are issued through an auction process. Interested parties must get CFC authorisation in order to participate in the auction process. In the design of auction programs, the CFC has made efforts to include measures to rationalise frequency allocation, facilitate the entry of interested parties, and prevent anti-competitive practices. Thus, it has supported the establishment of simultaneous ascending auctions, the imposition of spectrum caps, the establishment of clauses to discourage collusion between competitors, and the application of the "use it or lose it" principle. Different conditions or requirements have resulted, depending on the particular market conditions and prospects for each band auctioned.

One 1997 auction was aimed at building a capacity supply market for microwave point to point and point to multi-point systems. Restrictions ensured the presence of at least five operators in every geographical market, with each acquiring no more than 20% of the spectrum auctioned. The CFC did not oppose any particular bidder's participation, because the structural conditions were deemed sufficient to protect competition. By contrast, the CFC imposed some conditions on another 1997 auction for frequencies used by fixed and mobile wireless and PCS services, because these wireless access services can affect competition in local telephone markets. The CFC and COFETEL agreed to limit the accumulation of frequencies and licences. In addition, the CFC imposed conditions on Telmex's participation, because it had already determined that Telmex has market power in the markets for local telephony and interconnection. Telmex would be subject to an audit in order to review the conditions of competition in the market, and more importantly, Telmex would have to wait 24 months before starting its commercial operations (except for rural telephony services) in order to ease the entrance of new competitors. A principal reason for nonetheless permitting Telmex to participate at all, despite the risks to competitive conditions, was that Telmex alone still has a "universal service" obligation in rural areas, which might be best served by these newer technologies rather than traditional ones. Participation could also permit Telmex to continue upgrading its technology.

Some conditions were imposed to ensure competition in mobile radio-paging services, where 24 parties expressed interest in the 27 regional concessions and nine national ones. One party would be limited to the equivalent of four of the national concessions (through some combination of national and regional licenses). In any region, no single party could have more than four concessions (regional, national, or a combination). And no one could get more than two concessions of the three concessions offered in each region. The limits applied to groups of companies connected common shareholders and other corporate links. Because the telephone network is an input into paging services, competition depended on establishing non-discriminatory access to this network. Thus, the CFC subjected the participation of a Telmex subsidiary to an agreement for interconnection fees between Telmex and the paging service companies. The other bidders were all approved, with the exception of a firm that already held four national concessions.

A few limits were imposed on an auction of frequencies for pay TV and radio in 46 regional markets, to ensure continued competition from alternatives. There were already 190 companies with cable networks, and licenses for microwave (MMDS) systems had been granted throughout the country. Other pay TV services are available too, such as direct satellite broadcast, but the extent of competition among them is limited, to the extent that they are aimed at populations with different income levels. Cable and MMDS operators were only allowed to apply for licenses in geographic areas that were not covered by their previous licenses. This CFC decision had the effect of permitting a major firm, Cablevisión, to bid for spectrum in the rest of the country. Cablevisión already had an important presence in the pay TV market, but mainly in the Federal District, where no licenses were auctioned.

Few issues arose in the auctions for mobile aeronautical radio communications and point-to-point microwave links. The auction rules excluded parties who already held a concession or permit to provide these services, in order to ensure a minimum number of competitors. Otherwise, the CFC determined not to reject any particular bidder. But the CFC did suggest that, because increased demand and technological change could affect future values, the frequencies be granted to administrators who would then market them among final users.

**Railways.** Privatisation is now underway. Licenses to build and operate railways have been granted through a two-part competitive bidding process, involving technical qualification as well as money. Licenses are only granted to Mexican companies, in which foreign investment may not exceed 49% of equity. The CFC participated in the process of drafting the law and regulations, and several features of the privatisation program respond to CFC recommendations. In particular, the CFC urged that railroad concessions in different regions should be granted to different companies. Competition with road transport would be promoted by eliminating the possibility of cross subsidies between railroad regions and by stimulating the efficiency of the network. Competition within the rail network would also be encouraged by a structure that permitted regional comparisons of costs and prices. The CFC has issued opinions about the bidders for five railways: Coahuila-Durango, Nacozari, Pacífico-Norte (FPN), Noreste (FNE), and Tijuana-Tecate. The CFC and the Ministry, SCT, agreed on rules placing some limits on cross-ownership. Ferrocarril del Noreste (FNE) was limited to 5% ownership in FPN, and FPN was limited to 5% of the companies licensed for the main south-east route. In some situations, notably the Coahuila-Durango route, an obligation to grant tracking and haulage rights was imposed in order to avoid market power abuses.

The CFC was also involved in the process of developing the basic Railroad Service Regulations, which define trackage and haulage rights and establish procedures for applying for those rights and for setting the applicable terms, conditions and fees. They also set out procedures for setting rates when, in the CFC's opinion, conditions of competition do not exist. These can be initiated at the request of the affected user or at the initiative of either the Ministry or the CFC. Rates are to be set equal to those that would be charged by an efficient carrier, using a method previously submitted to the CFC. The regulations also set out means for granting third parties concessions to provide a specific transportation service when the original concessionaire ceases to do so.

**Ports.** The CFC is involved when port administrations are privatised or operating license rights are auctioned. The rules prevent combining directly or indirectly two or more terminals that provide the same kind of service in the same relevant geographic market. And the CFC must approve particular bidders here, as in similar auction proceedings.

**Air transport.** Starting in 1995, the CFC participated in the discussion and preparation of the drafts for the airports and civil aviation laws, in conjunction with SCT. The provisions in the Airports Law related to competition include transparent criteria for concessions and permits for managing, operating, and building airports, allocation of concessions through public auctions, regulation of mergers and acquisitions, obligation to provide services without discrimination and to make available open access to suppliers of auxiliary services, and guidelines for regulating rates and prices when, in the CFC's opinion, conditions of competition do not exist. The actual process of privatising the airports began in 1998. There are similar powers concerning airline fares; if the CFC determines that there is market power in a relevant market, typically a city-pair or associated airport markets, then the Ministry may regulate the fares. The civil aviation law is still being applied in ways that prevent potentially efficient new entry, though. The Ministry includes a test of likely profitability in permit and route decisions, ostensibly to protect safety.

**Natural gas distribution.** The CFC must approve participation in auctioning exclusive distribution permits for natural gas. As elsewhere, the CFC applies a merger-like analysis. The CFC determines the participants' market shares and whether there is market power or restraints on competition. So far, the CFC has not opposed or placed conditions on participation in these auctions. It decided to bar one bidder in Mexico City, but changed that decision on reconsideration.

The CFC also contributed to the 1995 regulations that laid the groundwork for introducing private market competition. The process is complicated by the fact that the incumbent in much of the country is Pemex, which retains a constitutional monopoly on natural gas production and also still owns much of the pipeline network. The regulations call for removal of restrictions on natural gas imports, in order to promote the functioning of market forces at the primary sales level. Transportation, storage, distribution, and marketing activities are to be unbundled and provided independently, without the sale of one service depending on the acquisition of another. Vertical integration of transport and distribution within a single region is permitted only if it leads to greater efficiency. Because it was thought critical to promote investment in infrastructure, concessions would be exclusive, at least for a period of time, and competition would be for the market, not within it. Exclusive distribution permits would be awarded on the basis of the best service and lowest prices. And the concessionaires' market power is limited by giving resellers free access to the concession area and by granting permits for self-supply. Participation in auctions for exclusive distribution permits is subject to the approval of the CFC. Price and rate regulations may be removed when, in the CFC's opinion, conditions of competition exist.

## 6. CONCLUSIONS AND POLICY OPTIONS FOR REFORM

### 6.1. General assessment of current strengths and weaknesses

The Mexican government recognised the imperative need to move the basis of its economy away from protection and privilege and undertook a long-run plan to do so. From ending price control through liberalising trade and investment and privatising state-owned enterprises to adopting a modern competition law, the plan is founded on free market competition.

The analytic quality of the competition law is a significant strength. The law is consistent and coherent, based on economic analysis and the goal of economic efficiency. It affords a solid foundation for applying competition policy both in law enforcement and in other policy issues. This modern analytic approach is continued in the recent LFCE Regulations. All are models of well-balanced economic sophistication. Some details might be touched up. The predatory pricing test seems loose and likely to find violations too often; a corrective could be adopting a clear "recoupment" requirement. And in merger review, more transparency in the treatment of the competitive effect of poor financial health would be welcome.

The CFC has spent a commendable proportion of its effort on advocacy and dealing with competition policy problems outside of traditional law enforcement. Here, the regulatory structures sensibly assign critical tasks to the CFC, to make analytically consistent judgements about presence of market power. The same standards are applied by the same expert body whether the issues is merger or other competition law enforcement, or licensing, privatisation or natural monopoly regulation. This consistency integrates competition policy into regulatory policy.

Expert craftsmanship is a clear strength. But that strength implies a weakness as well. The competition law, like the rest of the reform program, is the product of experts in the government. The competition law and policy lack a clear base of support in the public at large. Although legislators are reportedly interested in the CFC's work, and the CFC receives an increasing number of complaints now that the public and smaller businesses are more aware of its existence, the constituency for competition policy is not well identified. Moreover, there has little visible effort to develop a public constituency, through media relations, systematic relationship with consumer protection institutions (which are admittedly rudimentary), or otherwise. Perhaps the strongest constituency supporting competition policy is new entrants, which appreciate how liberalisation has made their businesses possible. But even for them, support may fade unless the CFC is clearly seen as an important instrument in market-opening, barrier-lowering action. Major, established businesses, which have not shaken habits learned under the old system, would prefer market arrangements to be managed so they would not be taking any investment risk, and are not above making direct appeals at the highest levels of government in a effort to preserve their privileges.

Uncertainty about how far to commit to real competitive reform is demonstrated in some of the divisions of labour. Giving the CFC the important task of identifying market power is analytically sound. Having another body, such as COFETEL for telecommunications, decide what will be done about that problem shows that someone else has the ultimate voice about that competition policy issue. Additional evidence of mixed priorities about competition policy is the fact that the market-opening and privatisation processes have left a few highly concentrated industries in place from the pre-reform era, without providing for means to break them up or even exposing them to effective import competition.

Uncertainty about the degree of support may be one reason for what looks like temporising in some early CFC decisions, and it may also underlie the persistent assessment by others in the government and the private sector that the organisation is "weak." The perception of weakness may be unavoidable for an organisation founded on policy and ideas, particularly ideas as complex and ambiguous as those of industrial organisation economic theory, in a society that values personal power, contacts, and influence. But one result of following analytic principles is that interested parties could portray some CFC decisions to look like compromise positions that avoided confronting powerful economic players. In privatisation proceedings, the national liner shipping firm was permitted to buy one of the major rail concessions, the major cable firm was allowed to participate in related spectrum auctions, and Telmex was allowed to bid in the wireless phone auction, albeit with mild conditions. Some claim the CFC has bowed to financial industry interests, in permitting CINTRA to continue to exist and in taking few actions concerning competition in financial services markets. In each of these controversial cases, the CFC defends its decisions by pointing out the strength of the conditions it imposed or the lack of a demonstrable anticompetitive effect in the circumstances.

And on the other hand, the CFC has taken some visible and vigorous actions against major economic interests. Its ruling about Telmex's market power, its actions against abuses by Pemex, and its findings about CINTRA's market power would counter the image of weakness – provided other regulators follow up with action consistent with those rulings. Is it a measure of the CFC's increasing independence and strength, rather than weakness and irrelevance, that the CFC was not involved in negotiations to settle the controversies about entry and pricing in telecommunications? Perhaps it was strength, for the CFC warned the negotiating parties, public and private, that an agreement about price levels could attract law enforcement attention. Often, CFC decisions are only a first step, and other parts of the government must take the effective actions, which the CFC cannot require or control. If other government bodies ignore or evade CFC findings, that fact will demonstrate the value Mexico actually places on competition policy as a tool for reform. For competition policy and enforcement to cement reform, other agencies must learn to accept its results, rather than resist them on behalf of industry clients.

### 6.2. The dynamic view: the pace and direction of change

The CFC may be tempted to get away from the politically charged problems of regulatory policy and focus more on law enforcement. Whether that is a sound strategy depends on the reasons and the results. It could establish the CFC's credibility, if it produces a number of tangible, credible successes. But if it looks like a retreat from controversy, the shift could confirm, rather than correct, the impression of weakness. Some of that impression stems from public misunderstandings of what is involved in litigating competition issues. Already, because well-financed parties often take the CFC to court, the CFC feels it must move carefully, follow clear procedures, and avoid the appearance of result-driven decision-making. That care is thought by some, probably unfairly, to be a sign of ineffectiveness. More enforcement may help overcome this misunderstanding in the long run, by educating the businesses and the public about the complexities of competition policy, and along the way working out novel procedural methods and substantive doctrines in the courts so that enforcement will become increasingly efficient.

The notion of an independent decision-making agency is a new phenomenon in Mexico. Whether any of the "independent" agencies can really act independently of the government is yet to be established. The CFC has been bolder than COFETEL. The most independent regulators, such as the energy commission and CFC itself, seem to have a better understanding of competition policy values than ministries such as SCT or agencies with close ties to a ministry such as COFETEL. The CFC's comparative boldness may be explained by the stronger legal basis for its independence of action. Its decision about market power in airlines tends to contradict the policy that the transport ministry would like to pursue, of consolidating the two national airlines into one. And its decision that Telmex has market power requires the communications ministry to take regulatory actions which will be inconsistent with its contention that the Mexican telecommunications industry is already competitive. It would be valuable to review the experiences of these new institutions, to evaluate how their structures impact their effectiveness and to assess whether a single, multi-sector regulator might better implement competition-based policies and resist industry capture (see Chapter 2, Government Capacity to Produce High Quality Regulation, for further discussion of these issues).

### 6.3. Potential benefits and costs of further regulatory reform

The primary performance objective of competition policy in Mexico is efficiency. In telecommunications and some other sectors subject to economic regulation, protection, or inherited and persistent market power, Mexico still endures inefficiencies. As the regulated and protected sectors are opened to competition, it can be expected that prices and the quality of products and services will move toward competitive levels.

It can also be expected that producing these public benefits will entail some private costs, as competition erodes the security of those who benefit from market power. Thus shareholders and labour interests in these sectors are likely to resist change, in order to avoid those losses to themselves. Efforts to avoid costs to these parties will impose costs on the economy and the consumer, as the competitive benefits of lower prices and greater choice are deferred.

## 6.4. Policy options for consideration

- *Maintain emphasis on regulatory issues and regulated and privatising sectors, with analysis, publicity, and enforcement, as long as competition is still impaired by controls on entry and by other kinds of official favouritism.*

Focus should be maintained on the sectors where regulation and privatisation are still important issues, despite the difficulty and the political and resource cost, until better outcomes are achieved in the major sectors affected. Analysis and advice should be accompanied by law enforcement in these sectors, too. The CFC can take advantage of the law's comprehensive reach, for few industries, even regulated ones, are technically exempt. This emphasis would have the additional, desirable effect of focusing attention on higher-impact matters concerning collusion and exclusion. If more enforcement is desirable for institutional reasons, it would be better to target the largest economic forces, the largest consumer and market harms, and the most important anti-competitive situations. These are likely to coincide with the subjects of privatisation and deregulation, that is, the same sectors that are now receiving the CFC's regulatory-policy attention.

In trade matters, too, the CFC should play an important role. Some of the remaining competition policy issues in Mexico are the product of still-incomplete opening of its markets. Liberalisation has not yet improved the competitive structure of several major industries. If the law is not amended to add a power to cure monopoly through divestiture, then it should give the CFC more power in the trade law process to prevent achieving or protecting anti-competitive outcomes. At a minimum, the CFC could, through advocacy, ensure that the competitive implications of trade issues are well publicised.

- *Make the CFC part of the Economic Deregulation Council (CDE), to ensure that competition policy issues are regularly considered at the highest levels in regulatory reform efforts.*

The CFC is not regularly involved in the CDE's review process. Although it is consulted on an *ad hoc* basis, the lack of formal, regular ties and responsibilities inevitably diminishes the significance of competition policy issues in this important process. Bringing the CFC into the CDE could lead to a more stable process for resolving disputes among competing policy interests. If promoting market-based approaches is an important goal, then that importance should be represented by high-level participation in this body. Continuing participation will also help ward off regulations that are more anti-competitive than necessary to accomplish their purposes, thus economising on enforcement efforts in the long run.

- *Provide for effective power to ensure that regulations to remedy market power actually achieve that aim, by requiring CFC approval for those regulations or a right of intervention and appeal concerning regulatory decisions that implement its market power findings.*

In form, the method for incorporating competition principles into the regulatory system appears sensible. The CFC applies its general expertise about assessing market competition to determine whether there is a market power problem that needs a solution, and if there is, then a regulatory body that is expert about the particular sector designs and implements that solution. The practice, however, demonstrates that the formal arrangement has weaknesses. In some sectors, capture appears to be a significant problem. Regulators protect "national champions" in communications and transport, and the constitution protects them in energy and petroleum. Competition policy confronts development concerns in telecommunications. In energy, it must compromise with national history. And in many sectors, it is in conflict with financial interests. Regulators who share industry interests in preserving established institutions are unlikely to apply competition policy effectively.

207

The division of authority in regulated markets needs to be reconsidered. The CFC's finding of market power is merely precatory and insignificant if the relevant ministry's regulation does not actually solve the problem, or if its solution creates new problems and complicates the CFC's ability to deal with them. The CFC should have an oversight role. One option would be to require CFC approval of the proposed regulation before it could become effective. A less intrusive option would be for the CFC to accompany its market power findings with clear, performance-based standards and necessary controls that regulations must include. And the CFC could be more effective if it had the clear power to intervene in actions that apply those regulations, to ensure that the other agency is following through correctly and effectively.

Alternative institutions or additional remedies might be considered to deal with monopoly problems. For deciding about access pricing in network industries that remain regulated, and overcome sectoral regulators' traditional tendency to protect the incumbent, one possibility is a new broad-based agency that would deal with these common questions of "utility" regulation across sectors. That would free the CFC of any duty to compute prices but maintain contact with the CFC for making determinations about competitive conditions and effects. Such a multi-sectoral agency would centralise expertise, promote consistency, and reduce the risk of capture by a particular interested sector. And it is worth considering whether to add provisions to the LFCE to deal more directly with the problem of monopoly as a structural matter. To be sure, relief is difficult to achieve at acceptable costs. But it could be useful to have the tools available, kept in reserve for occasional use in exceptional, but important, cases in which it is difficult to establish clearly illegal monopolising conduct (perhaps because victims are reluctant to come forward), yet structural market power is unacceptably persistent.

- *Broaden the base of support, through greater media exposure and co-ordination with consumer protection activities.*

The CFC should publicise its actions to a wider audience than the business press. To accomplish the goal of wider public understanding of the benefits of competition, it will be necessary that enforcement actions result in consumer benefits that can be clearly and convincingly communicated. And it should develop a structure of co-ordination with consumer protection activities, which could also help build a broader base of understanding and support. It would be consistent with the economic foundation of Mexico's competition policy for the CFC to take on responsibilities for some "consumer protection" issues that are also often treated as matters of unfair competition doctrine, like deceptive advertising, which have direct effects both on consumers and on the health of market competition.

- *Broaden the available enforcement resources by expanding the right of private action.*

As a supplement to the CFC's resources, and a potential corroboration or corrective for its policy positions and decisions, the right to take private action should be expanded. Making all decisions under the LFCE completely dependent on the CFC ensures consistency, but risks leaving problems unaddressed because of resource limitations. Private lawsuits about access and pricing in the context of network monopolies could assist the CFC in overcoming sectoral regulators' resistance to introducing competition. Expanding private actions will require addressing other institutional problems, though. The federal district courts that are most competent to hear these cases do not usually handle private disputes. These would more likely go to the state courts that also hear other kinds of commercial cases. In the state courts, analytical capacities and decisional independence are more variable.

- *Enter international co-operation agreements to improve enforcement efficiency in transnational matters.*

The CFC should enter international co-operation agreements to regularise its relationships with other enforcement bodies and improve its capacity to deal with global problems. Mexico's opening to foreign trade and investment will inevitably produce many enforcement matters with significant international dimensions, and not just with its NAFTA neighbours. Clear prior arrangements for co-operation with other enforcement authorities will improve enforcement efficiency and effectiveness.

## 6.5. Managing regulatory reform

The CFC needs to be strengthened in stature, and perhaps in resources. It is not clear how to do the latter, when budgets are tight across the government. Other budget-strapped governments, such as Japan's, have found ways to increase funding for competition matters despite cutbacks elsewhere. The CFC may have been short-changed compared to other agencies with narrower jurisdictions. COFETEL has a budget four times larger than the CFC's, and CRE's budget is twice as large. Yet the CFC took on additional responsibilities about regulatory issues despite the decrease in its budget. The Ministry of Finance has authorised a substantial increase in the CFC's 1998 budget as well as an important expansion of its administrative structure. Still, it is not clear that the CFC is being stretched to do the job with the resources it has. The CFC may need to identify particular, compelling enforcement problems it cannot resolve with its current staff and budget, to support the call for greater resources.

As reform proceeds and competition spreads across the economy, problems due to remaining pockets of market power will become even more obvious. Economic distortions will result from trying to sustain monopolies in economically competitive industries. Mexico will have to consider carefully the benefits and costs of the remaining state monopolies.

# NOTES

1. Article 2, Federal Law of Economic Competition (LFCE).

2. Constitution, Article 28.

3. The Competition Law was published in the Official Journal of the Federation on 24 December 1992, and came into force on 22 June 1993.

4. North American Free Trade Agreement, Article 1501(1).

5. LFCE, Article 10 (vii).

6. These cases are described in the annual reports of the CFC for 1993-94 (p. 34, laundries and dry cleaners), 1994-95 (p. 56, purified water producers, and p. 58, road transport), 1995-96 (p. 64, maritime and airport cargo deconsolidation services, and p. 68, customs brokerage services) and 1997 (p. 64, road transport).

7. OECD Competition Law and Policy Committee (1997), Aide-Memoire of In-Depth Examination of Competition Policy in Mexico.

8. Comision Federal de la Competencia (1998), Annual Report [to OECD Competition Law and Policy Committee] on Competition Policy Developments in Mexico (1997).

9. Comision Federal de la Competencia (1997), In-Depth Examination of Competition Policy in Mexico (1995-96), submitted to OECD Competition Law and Policy Committee, 21 January 1997.

10. This was added in the 1998 Regulations.

11. OECD Competition Law and Policy Committee (1997), Aide-Memoire of In-Depth Examination of Competition Policy in Mexico.

12. Diario oficial, 24 July 1998, p. 20.

13. OECD Competition Law and Policy Committee (1997), Aide-Memoire of In-Depth Examination of Competition Policy in Mexico.

14. OECD Competition Law and Policy Committee (1997), Aide-Memoire of In-Depth Examination of Competition Policy in Mexico.

15. Comision Federal de la Competencia (1997), In-Depth Examination of Competition Policy in Mexico (1995-96), submitted to OECD Competition Law and Policy Committee, 21 January 1997.

16. At www.cfc.gob.mx.

17. Article 24(I), LFCE; Article 50, Regulations of the LFCE.

18. See Richard D. Baker (1991), Judicial Review in Mexico: A Study of the Amparo Suit.

19. OECD Competition Law and Policy Committee (1997), Aide-Memoire of In-Depth Examination of Competition Policy in Mexico.

20. OECD Competition Law and Policy Committee (1997), Aide-Memoire of In-Depth Examination of Competition Policy in Mexico, Paris.

21. Comision Federal de la Competencia (1997), In-Depth Examination of Competition Policy in Mexico (1995-96), submitted to OECD Competition Law and Policy Committee, 21 January 1997, Paris.

22. Comision Federal de la Competencia (1998), Annual Report [to OECD Competition Law and Policy Committee] on Competition Policy Developments in Mexico (1997). The data in the table come from the questionnaire response, and do not correspond precisely to the data in the annual report.

23. Comision Federal de la Competencia (1998), Annual Report [to OECD Competition Law and Policy Committee] on Competition Policy Developments in Mexico (1997).

24. Article 14.

25. For an overview see Etienne, Fernando Heftye, "Promoción y protección de la competencia en legislaciones sectoriales y tratados internacionales", in Comision Federal de la Competencia *Report* for the second semester of 1996.

26. The CFC has nonetheless been able to take account of distinctions between fixed and mobile telephony in determining relevant markets. In its decision about Telmex's dominance, the CFC separated local basic telephony from cellular service. Even though they both provide local communications, they differ in price, quality, and mobility. Telmex's market power in basic local service justifies asymmetric regulation under the telecommunications law, and that would in turn emphasise regulatory differences between it and wireless service.

# BACKGROUND REPORT
# ON ENHANCING MARKET OPENNESS
# THROUGH REGULATORY REFORM*

\* This report was principally prepared by **Denis Audet**, of the Trade Directorate. It has benefited from extensive comments provided by colleagues throughout the OECD Secretariat, by the Government of Mexico, and by Member countries as part of the peer review process. This report was peer reviewed in September 1998 in the Working Party of the OECD's Trade Committee.

# TABLE OF CONTENTS

## Executive Summary

### Background Report on Enhancing Market Openness through Regulatory Reform

Does the national regulatory system allow foreign enterprises to take full advantage of competitive global markets? Reducing regulatory barriers to trade and investment enables countries in an expanding global economy to benefit more fully from comparative advantage and innovation. This means that more market openness increases the benefits that consumers can draw from regulatory reform. Maintaining an open world trading system requires regulatory styles and content that promote global competition and economic integration, avoid trade disputes and improve trust and mutual confidence across borders.

Regulatory reforms were instrumental in the significant transition that Mexico has undergone in the last decade and a half moving away from an inward-oriented economy based on import-substitution policies towards a market-based open economy integrated into the world economy. Mexico's accession to the GATT in 1986 and negotiation of NAFTA in the early 90s have had profound and lasting influence on Mexican policy and regulatory formulation processes. Mexico's multilateral and regional commitments have effectively worked as policy anchors during the financial crisis of early 1995. Far from backtracking, an extended deregulation programme was launched in the aftermath of the crisis to improve and quicken Mexico's regulatory reform programme.

Extensive and transparent public consultations in the revision of all existing Federal regulations and the preparation of new regulations are carried out under the extended deregulation programme. The Internet is used for disseminating the whole range of Federal formalities and regulations and for soliciting comments on proposed new regulations. Mexico is also using modern electronic transmission systems for Customs procedures and government procurement, thereby improving the transparency of these procedures and facilitating transactions for foreign participants. The enhanced transparency in the elaboration process of Federal regulations acts as an important check and balance feature in this regulatory formulation process.

Ministries and Regulatory Agencies are now required to prepare "regulatory impact assessments" (RIAs) for new regulations having potential impact on business activity. With respect to the elaboration of official technical standards, the combined features of the openness of consultation process, the publication of draft standards and the public availability of respective RIAs altogether act to minimise potential incidences of regulatory capture by domestic groups.

While Mexico has made significant investment in setting up a comprehensive framework for carrying out regulatory reforms at the Federal level, this study identifies a number of policy options for pursuing reform from the perspective of market openness:

- *Continue to foster good regulatory practices already instituted in areas such as transparency; and make public through the Internet the RIAs prepared for proposed regulations.*

- *Take measures to ensure uniformity in the preparation of RIAs and in the implementation of regulatory requirements by all Federal and Regulatory Agencies.*

- *Complement the current sets of guiding principles for the preparation of regulatory impact assessment with the additional principle of "avoidance of unnecessary trade restrictiveness".*

- *Heighten awareness of and encourage respect for the OECD efficient regulation principles in state and local regulatory activities affecting international trade and investment.*

- *Intensify efforts to use existing international standards and to participate more actively in the development of internationally-harmonised standards as the basis of domestic regulations.*

- *Seek to ensure that bilateral or regional approaches to regulatory co-operation are designed and implemented in ways which will encourage broader multilateral application.*

## 1. MARKET OPENNESS AND REGULATION: THE POLICY ENVIRONMENT IN MEXICO

Mexico has undergone a significant transition in the last decade and a half moving away from an inward-oriented economy based on import-substitution policies towards a market-based open economy integrated into the world economy. The accession of Mexico to the GATT in 1986 consolidated key commitments in terms of transparency, non-discrimination and trade liberalisation. Other market-based reforms were also adopted as necessary complementary policies. Barriers to foreign investment were lifted, except in a few sectors reserved to the State, and a comprehensive programme of privatisation was implemented covering banks, airlines, steel, telephone services and ports.

An initial regulatory reform programme was launched in 1989 and orchestrated by the Economic Deregulation Unit (EDU), based in the Ministry for Trade and Industry "Secretaria de Comercio y Fomento Industrial" (SECOFI). The programme consisted of rationalising certain economy-wide regulatory requirements, including technical standards and general administrative procedures, in targeting economic sectors in which the benefits of deregulation would be greatest including tourism, railways, air transport, ports, land transport, petrochemicals, electricity, telecommunications, satellites, customs administration, foreign exchange, water supply, financial institutions, mining and fishing.

Efforts were concentrated on removing rent-generating restrictions and on eliminating bureaucratic red tape at the Federal level. An antitrust law was prepared to set the stage for improved domestic competitive conditions and resulted in the creation of the Federal Competition Commission in 1993. All these policy and regulatory reforms were considered necessary to create new and equitable market opportunities in order to accelerate the modernisation of the Mexican production capacity and to stimulate the growth of its economy.

The negotiation of the North American Free Trade Agreement (NAFTA) has had a profound influence on the Mexican policy formulation given the scope and pace of the policy reform involved. Under NAFTA, almost all trade in goods, including agricultural products, and services is subject to complete liberalisation over fixed time periods. A comprehensive set of domestic policies having trade-related dimensions was subject to specific disciplines and exchanged on a reciprocity basis in such areas as the transparency of domestic regulations, technical standards and certification procedures, investment, government procurement, intellectual property rights, customs procedures and a binding dispute settlement procedure.

With the experience gained in NAFTA, Mexico negotiated several other free trade agreements with Central and South American countries and is actively participating in multi-country trade initiatives in the context of the Asia-Pacific Economic Co-operation (APEC) and the Free Trade Area of the Americas (FTAA). Mexico's simple average tariff remained stable at about 13% between 1993 and 1997 but the weighted average tariff fell from 7.8% to 2.7% during the same period when the calculation is done on the basis of applied tariff rates which incorporate the effects of regional and unilateral tariff reductions.[1] Mexico has also extended, on a non-discriminatory basis, to all WTO Members the benefits of its free trade agreements in such areas as investment, customs procedures and intellectual property. Mexico wishes to continue to negotiate WTO-compatible regional free trade agreements with its trading partners and is interested in pursuing trade liberalisation at the multilateral level through a new round of comprehensive negotiations within the WTO.

With the financial crisis of early 1995, Mexico was confronted with difficult policy decisions, in many respect its WTO and NAFTA commitments have effectively worked as policy anchors. Far from backtracking, an extended deregulation programme was launched in the aftermath of the crisis to improve and quicken Mexico's regulatory reform programme. The privatisation programme was accelerated and the Mexican investment regime was further liberalised, opening up to foreign ownership sectors previously reserved to the State, such as railways, satellite communications, natural gas storage and distribution. A reform of the pension system was launched based on individual capitalisation accounts managed by the private sector in order to stimulate domestic saving, thereby reducing external exposure.

_217_

Recent economic indicators for 1997 and early 1998 show that Mexico has staged an impressive recovery from its crisis with Gross Domestic Product (GDP) growing at a rate of 7% in 1997 and at above 5% during the first half of 1998. One indicator of the strength of the Mexican economy is revealed by the recorded inflows of foreign direct investment in fixed assets amounting to US$12.5 billion in 1997 (see Table 1).

Table 1. **Flows of foreign direct investment into Mexico**
US billion

| | 1990 | 1991 | 1992 | 1993 | 1994 | 1995 | 1996 | 1997 |
|---|---|---|---|---|---|---|---|---|
| Total FDI | 6.0 | 17.5 | 22.4 | 33.3 | 19.2 | −0.2 | 22.6 | 17.5 |
| Direct FDI | 2.6 | 4.8 | 4.4 | 4.4 | 11.0 | 9.5 | 9.2 | 12.5 |
| Portfolio FDI | 3.4 | 12.8 | 18.0 | 28.9 | 8.2 | −9.7 | 13.4 | 5.0 |

Source: Banco de Mexico, Statistics on foreign direct investment include temporary imports of fixed assets by in-bond industries as of 1995.

Mexico's foreign trade sector played a key role in leading the recovery starting in 1995. Between 1994 and 1997, total exports in US dollars jumped by 95.5%. The trade balance moved from a deficit of $18.6 billion in 1994 to a surplus of $6.1 billion in 1996 (see Tables 2 and 3). In 1997, the trade balance was in a slight surplus position of $1.6 billion, as strong domestic demand increased total imports by 30.7%.

While NAFTA's imports and exports respectively accounted for 83.8% and 86.3% of total imports and exports in 1996, it is interesting to note that about two thirds of the incremental imports in 1997 originated from non-NAFTA regions. This suggests that the Mexican economy is not exclusively NAFTA-oriented and partly reflects multilateral trade opening measures.

Mexico is currently hard hit by the impact of the Asian crisis and the ripple effects spreading throughout the world. Despite substantial depreciation of the peso, Mexican products have lost competitiveness relative to the much more depreciated Asian currencies, with the textiles, clothing and electronic equipment sectors being particularly vulnerable. With slower world growth rate now expected for 1998 and 1999, Mexican growth rate will most likely slow down during the second half of 1998 thus putting additional pressure on the fragile fiscal balance. With oil-related income accounting for about 36% of the total governmental income in 1997, the steep drop in world crude oil prices is having a real dampening effect on the Mexican economy. Continuing deregulation efforts in the near future are thus likely to be made against a less favourable world environment than in 1996 and 1997.

Table 2. **Mexican imports by regions**
US billion

| | 1990 | 1991 | 1992 | 1993 | 1994 | 1995 | 1996 | 1997 |
|---|---|---|---|---|---|---|---|---|
| Total imports | 31 058 | 38 124 | 61 923 | 65 271 | 79 335 | 72 453 | 89 466 | 116 932 |
| NAFTA | 21 458 | 26 804 | 46 532 | 46 876 | 56 433 | 55 347 | 74 958 | 84 151 |
| EU 15 | 5 075 | 5 875 | 7 252 | 7 795 | 9 055 | 6 731 | 6 873 | 9 903 |
| Other Americas | 1 264 | 1 656 | 2 316 | 2 483 | 2 912 | 1 626 | 2 020 | 2 709 |
| Rest of world | 3 262 | 3 788 | 5 823 | 8 117 | 10 935 | 8 748 | 5 615 | 20 169 |
| Total exports | 26 854 | 26 655 | 45 945 | 51 698 | 60 644 | 79 278 | 95 657 | 118 609 |
| NAFTA | 18 981 | 19 194 | 38 111 | 48 022 | 52 753 | 67 271 | 82 527 | 96 690 |
| EU 15 | 3 411 | 3 291 | 3 414 | 1 248 | 2 809 | 3 666 | 3 500 | 4 019 |
| Other Americas | 1 877 | 2 035 | 2 683 | 1 481 | 3 195 | 5 047 | 5 721 | 6 055 |
| Rest of world | 2 585 | 2 135 | 1 737 | 947 | 1 887 | 3 293 | 3 909 | 11 845 |

Source: OECD *Annual Foreign Trade Statistics*, Harmonised System Revision 1 (1998) for the 1990-1996 Data; and OECD Series A monthly data for 1997. Figures for 1990 and 1991 exclude in-bond trade.

Table 3. **Mexican composition of trade**

US billion

|  | 1990 | 1991 | 1992 | 1993 | 1994 | 1995 | 1996 |
|---|---|---|---|---|---|---|---|
| Total imports | 31 058 | 38 124 | 61 923 | 65 271 | 79 335 | 72 453 | 89 466 |
| Manufactures | 18 713 | 23 877 | 40 948 | 44 004 | 53 975 | 49 876 | 61 294 |
| Semi-manufacturing | 6 727 | 8 554 | 13 449 | 14 145 | 17 000 | 16 217 | 19 175 |
| Agriculture | 4 493 | 4 351 | 5 795 | 5 552 | 6 892 | 4 854 | 7 115 |
| Oil products | 1 126 | 1 342 | 1 731 | 1 570 | 1 468 | 1 506 | 1 882 |
| Total exports | 26 854 | 26 655 | 45 945 | 51 698 | 60 644 | 79 278 | 95 657 |
| Manufactures | 8 923 | 10 290 | 28 029 | 33 489 | 41 329 | 53 241 | 65 886 |
| Semi-manufacturing | 4 829 | 4 905 | 6 465 | 7 035 | 7 691 | 11 589 | 12 111 |
| Agriculture | 3 145 | 3 486 | 3 332 | 3 894 | 4 408 | 6 245 | 6 262 |
| Oil products | 9 957 | 7 974 | 8 119 | 7 281 | 7 216 | 8 202 | 11 399 |

*Source:* OECD *Annual Foreign Trade Statistics*, Harmonised System Revision 1 (1998). Figures for 1990 and 1991 exclude in-bond trade.

With the Presidential election scheduled for the year 2000, a new National Development Plan will have to be proposed. This will provide the opportunity to reaffirm the importance of pursuing the deregulation programme at the Federal level and to ensure its application at the state and local levels. As improvement of the Mexican social network will certainly rank among the high priority items in the next Plan, the implementation of the six efficient regulation principles, discussed below, will be useful for underpinning a sound regulatory framework.

## 2. THE POLICY FRAMEWORK FOR MARKET OPENNESS: THE SIX "EFFICIENT REGULATION" PRINCIPLES

An important step in ensuring that regulations do not unnecessarily reduce market openness is to build the "efficient regulation" principles into the domestic regulatory process for social and economic regulations, as well as for administrative practices. "Market openness" here refers to the ability of foreign suppliers to compete in a national market without encountering discriminatory, excessively burdensome or restrictive conditions. These principles, which have been described in the 1997 OECD *Report on Regulatory Reform* and developed further in the Trade Committee, are:

– Transparency and openness of decision making.

– Non-discrimination.

– Avoidance of unnecessary trade restrictiveness.

– Use of internationally harmonised measures.

– Recognition of equivalence of other countries' regulatory measures.

– Application of competition principles.

They have been identified by trade policy makers as key to market-oriented and trade and investment-friendly regulation. They reflect the basic principles underpinning the multilateral trading system, concerning which many countries have undertaken certain obligations in the WTO and other contexts. The intention in the OECD country reviews of regulatory reform is not to judge the extent to which any country may have undertaken and lived up to international commitments relating directly or indirectly to these principles, but rather to assess whether and how domestic instruments, procedures and practices give effect to the principles and successfully contribute to market openness. Similarly, the OECD country reviews are not concerned with an assessment of trade policies and practices in Member countries.

In sum, this report considers whether and how Mexican regulatory procedures and content affect the quality of market access and presence in Mexico. An important reverse scenario – whether and how inward trade and investment affect the fulfilment of legitimate policy objectives reflected in social regulation – is beyond the scope of the present discussion. This latter issue has been extensively debated within and beyond the OECD from a range of policy perspectives. To date, however, OECD deliberations have found no evidence to suggest that trade and investment *per se* impact negatively on the pursuit and attainment of domestic policy goals through regulation or other means.[2]

## 2.1. Transparency, openness of decision making and appeal procedures

To ensure international market openness, foreign firms and individuals seeking access to a market (or expanding activities in a given market) must have adequate information on new or revised regulations so that they can base their decisions on an accurate assessment of potential costs, risks, and market opportunities. Regulations need to be transparent to foreign traders and investors. Regulatory transparency at both domestic and international levels can be achieved through a variety of means, including systematic publication of proposed rules prior to entry into force, use of electronic means to share information (such as the Internet), well-timed opportunities for public comment, and rigorous mechanisms for ensuring that such comments are given due consideration prior to the adoption of a final regulation.[3]

Market participants wishing to voice concerns about the application of existing regulations should have appropriate access to appeal procedures. Mexico implemented a comprehensive deregulation programme in recent years which was reinforced in 1995. This sub-section discusses the above transparency and transparency-related considerations in Mexico and how they are met. Also covered in this sub-section are a brief synthesis of significant reforms applied in Mexican procurement and Customs procedures, as making procedures more transparent was one of the major objectives of these reforms.

### 2.1.1. Mexico's overall regulatory setting

This assessment needs to begin with a brief overview of the overall deregulation infrastructure that set up in order to better evaluate whether transparency and transparency-related considerations are taken into account. An extended deregulation programme to improve and accelerate Mexico's regulatory reform programme referred to as the *Acuerdo para la Desregulación de la Actividad Empresarial* (ADAE) was launched in 1995. Under the ADAE, the Economic Deregulation Council (the Council) was established and composed of high level business, labour, academic, agricultural and several Cabinet Ministers. The creation of this Council provided the already formed Economic Deregulation Unit (EDU), located within SECOFI, additional political leverage in promoting reform within the Federal public administration.

The task of the EDU is to promote and co-ordinate Mexico's regulatory reform programme in conjunction with the Council and with the Deputy-Ministers in charge of regulatory improvement in each Ministry. The strategy for reform is based on four pillars: the review and reform of all existing Federal business formalities (stock); the review and reform of all new administrative or legislative proposals (flow); the proposal of economy-wide legislative reforms to improve Mexico's regulatory framework; and providing support to regulatory reform programmes at the state and local levels.

Improved transparency was one of the most immediate results emerging from this programme as virtually all Federal business formalities were identified and published on the Council's Internet site (http://www.cde.gob.mx) by December of 1996. Since February 1998, a compendium of all current laws and other major legal regulatory is continually updated on the Council's Internet site. As a result, foreign participants have an open access to a comprehensive set of Mexican laws, regulations and business formalities at their computer tips through the Internet.

Another transparency-related feature of the Mexican regulatory regime is the preparation of the "National Development Plan". The Plan sets the economic, political and social objectives of the government actions and it is published at the beginning of each 6 year presidential term. From the Plan, a series of different programmes are developed for different sectoral policies, including regulatory activities. These programmes are drawn up in consultation with interested parties and set out the major activities that individual Ministers will undertake during their terms. A yearly progress report must be submitted by the President to Congress. The National Development Plan as well as all other sectoral programmes can be downloaded from the Internet or obtained from the corresponding Ministries. Upon prior registration, it is also possible to access the Internet version of the Mexican Official Diary (http://cde.gob.mx/prontuario/frpron1.htm).

### 2.1.2. *Federal administrative procedure law*

Transparency considerations are intimately related to the administrative procedures put into place for the elaboration and adoption of domestic regulations. It is therefore essential to review some of the key steps involved in order to assess the transparency-friendliness of these procedures.

Mexico's Federal Administrative Procedure Law (FAP Law) sets out the general guidelines for the government's interaction with the public in all administrative procedures. All regulations must be published in the Official Diary before they can be enforced and must comply with the criteria the Law sets relative to: the publication of rules; the validity of administrative actions; the responsibilities of regulatory authorities; the rights of the general public; the way documents and responses may be submitted; the maximum response times by authorities; and the manner in which inspections and verifications are carried out.

---

### Box 1. **Regulatory Impact Assessment**

The FAP Law requires that all draft regulations with a potential impact on business activity be submitted to the EDU along with a regulatory impact assessment (RIA). In order to help regulatory Agencies prepare RIAs and to disseminate the regulatory criteria specified by the ADAE, the EDU prepared a RIA elaboration manual which specifies instructions for completing the six sections of a RIA:

- *Purpose of the regulation.* Agencies must list all behaviour to be regulated and the reasons for which government intervention is deemed necessary. Providing explanations and evidence of the existence of problems that the proposed regulation purports to solve is essential. Agencies must justify government intervention. There are no standardised criteria or threshold tests used to evaluate these justifications. This section of the RIA must also include an explanation of the legal basis for the regulation. A description of all related regulations, including any international obligations, as well as the reasons for which they have been unsatisfactory must be provided.

- *Alternatives considered and proposed solution.* Regulators are asked to think of all possible regulatory and non-regulatory options available to deal with the problems at hand, including the option of doing nothing. The alternatives must be described and the reasons for rejecting them clearly stated. International standards must always be taken into consideration and preferentially applied in order to promote harmonisation of technical regulations.

- *Implementation and enforcement.* Implementation and enforcement schemes must be described in detail (sanctions, verification mechanisms, etc.). It is particularly important for the regulatory agency to explain where it expects to obtain the resources needed to apply them effectively.

- *Public consultation.* Ministries are required to list all parties consulted, including names and telephone numbers, and their respective opinions.

- *Identification of business formalities.* All formalities created, modified or maintained by the proposed regulation must be listed and described.

- *Anticipated benefits and costs.* RIAs must include a structured description of the potential costs and benefits of the proposed regulation. The level of quantification and detail of the costs and benefits section is expected to be proportional to the importance of the project. Only regulations of major impact need to extensively quantify benefits and costs. Only incremental costs and benefits must be taken into account and all data sources must be duly noted. The different types of costs and benefits must be identified and discussed (effects on capital costs, operation costs, salary costs, consulting/legal costs, conformity assessment costs, health environment or other social costs, administrative costs, etc.), and their distributive implications made explicit.

---

The FAP Law does not specifically set any public consultation procedures but recognises the need for them. It leaves the issue of public consultation to be decided in sector specific laws, while stating that if a specific law establishes that proposals must be published for public comment, the period of time allowed should be of at least 60 days, unless otherwise specified.

The Council and the EDU also play an important role in promoting public consultation and transparency by making public all proposed regulations they review. For every meeting of the Council's executive commission, the list of proposed regulations is made available in the Council's Internet site. Although the EDU's statutory powers allow it to review proposed regulations and to make public its opinion, it remains that it cannot oppose the implementation of poor regulations.

The preparation of RIAs requires time and efforts by bureaucrats and the task could become over time repetitive or prepared in haste unless internal quality control measures are applied. Since RIAs are only performed since the end of 1997, the issues are rather about the quality of the assessment performed and its uniformity of application among Regulatory Agencies. Mexican authorities recognise that the quality of the data is generally poor in the costs and benefits section of RIAs. As a result, Regulatory Agencies are not asked to calculate net benefit for fear of creating additional incentives to distort data.

Concerning uniformity in the preparation of RIAs among Regulatory Agencies, the use of RIAs is still recent, thus time will tell whether some Agencies are well accomplishing the task or are *de facto* escaping or circumventing key areas of the required assessment. Evidence shows that Regulatory Agencies are generally complying with new requirements. Furthermore, a list of all regulatory proposals under review by the EDU and the Council is published and updated weekly on the Internet and RIAs for those projects are available to the public upon request. In coming months, proposed regulations and their respective RIAs will be directly available on the Internet. The ease of access availability would further assist the public, including foreign participants, in better understanding potential implications of proposed regulations.

Mexican authorities are also of the view that the review of new regulations allows the Council and the EDU to make sure that there is no backtracking on the advances that have been made in previous deregulatory processes. It allows for significant pre-emptive regulatory reform. It is much easier to change regulatory measures before they are actually implemented. It is easier for the EDU to promote greater co-operation and regulatory understanding with the use of regulatory impact statements.

From a transparency perspective for foreign participants, the comprehensiveness of the type and range of regulatory information made available through the Internet is notable and probably is among the most comprehensive within OECD countries. The regulatory framework provides for no distinction between nationals and non-nationals wishing to participate in public consultations. Mexican authorities have confirmed that non-nationals are effectively submitting comments on draft regulations and there comments are duly taken into consideration along with other comments.

In one way, the public availability of draft regulations issued at the Federal level and opinions expressed with the list of consulted parties acts as a check and balance feature which help to minimise instances of regulatory capture by specific groups with vested interests. So far, the foreign business community in Mexico has been supportive of the regulatory reform at the Federal level.

### 2.1.3. *Federal Metrology and Standardisation Law*

Another important regulatory area where the transparency of the overall procedures is essential for foreign participants relates to the formulation and adoption of standards and conformity assessment procedures. In the absence of full transparency or open consultation process, the risk exists that domestic groups might be able to capture the process of standards formulation and adversely impact on the competitiveness of imported products. The Mexican Federal Metrology and Standardisation Law (FMS Law) was revised in May 1997 with the view, *inter alia*, to provide for improved transparency-related provisions.

The responsibility for the development of technical regulations and their use rests in nine governmental ministries, including SECOFI through the National Standards Office *"La Dirección General de normas"*

(DGN). Besides the national standardisation bodies, the DNG is the only government agency that is allowed to issue voluntary standards. The DGN is the recognised member body to the International Standardisation Organisation (ISO), the Commission for the CODEX Alimentarius, the International Electronic Commission (IEC) and the Pan American Standards Commission (COPANT). It serves as the Mexican enquiry point under the WTO TBT Agreement, NAFTA, the Group of Three (Mexico, Colombia and Venezuela) and the Free Trade Agreements with Costa Rica, Bolivia and Nicaragua. It also serves as the support secretariat for the National Standardisation Commission which is established to assist and co-ordinate standardisation-related activities that fall under the responsibility of the various Federal Regulatory Agencies and under the responsibility of the established of National Standardisation Bodies.

The FMS Law provides for specific administrative procedures for the drafting and publication of technical regulations and standards. It provides for a unified adoption process for technical regulations or *Normas Oficiales Mexicanas* (NOMs) and voluntary standards or *Normas Mexicanas* (NMXs). Technical regulations shall have the goal of establishing characteristics which products and processes must fulfil as they may pose a risk to the safety of persons or harm the health of human, animals, vegetables, the general environment and work environment or for the purpose of preservation of natural resources. NMXs are of voluntary application and cannot have lower specifications to those established in NOMs. In mid-1998, there were approximately 585 NOMs and 5 500 NMXs. A catalogue of all NOM and a list of NMX standards is available since early 1998 on SECOFI's Internet site (http//:www.secofi.gob.mx/dgn1.html).

The transparency of the formulation process of Mexican standards finds concrete forms through several means, including the preparation of a National Standardisation Programme, the consideration of draft standards by national consultative committees, the publication of draft proposals in the Official Dairy and opportunities provided to the public for comments. All these various components are discussed below.

In recent years, many complaints were expressed by trading partners about the lack of transparency of Mexican standards, the rigidity in the implementation of labelling and marking requirements and the lack of time for traders to keep up with modifications in standard-related requirements. Concerns were particularly expressed on labelling requirements for imported beers and the marking of origin for textiles articles.

As a result of these complaints, Mexican authorities have examined the relevant cases and used the so-called "fast track procedure" of the FMS Law (Article 51) to provide more flexibility for traders in

---

### Box 2.  National Standardisation Programme

FMS Law adopted in July 1992 and revised in May 1997 requires the preparation of an annual publication containing the National Standardisation Programme (the Programme). It is published in the Official Diary and is publicly available through any of the consultative committees in charge of designing and approving technical standards and through SECOFI's Internet site. It contains a list of all technical regulations and standards and technical specifications (*normas de referencia*) to be considered during the coming year by each of the 22 national consultative committees (*comités consultivos nacionales de normalización*), the national technical committee (comités técnicos de normalización nacional), the reference committees (comités de normas de referencia) and the national standardisation bodies.

The Programme must be adopted by the National Standardisation Commission. Each committee must list the name, address and telephone number of its president, who is responsible for disseminating information and organising the activities of the committee. The national consultative committees must include a brief description of the objectives of the technical regulations proposed for their incorporation in the Programme. The time frame for the consideration of each regulatory topic must be indicated within the Programme in order to give all participants and the general public an idea of when the corresponding technical regulation or standard might be issued. Only technical regulations and standards listed in the Programme can be elaborated in that year.

223

meeting labelling requirements for beer imports and marking requirements for imported textiles articles. The fast track provision enables to bypass the normal public consultation process in order to rapidly modify standards that are causing unforeseen harmful consequences. To counterbalance the absence of open public consultation, the revised standards cannot impose new or stricter requirements. In the two above mentioned cases, the use of the fast track procedure resulted in more market openness.

The FMS Law also provides for the adoption of emergency mandatory standards to deal with exceptional and unforeseen circumstances which might result in irreversible situations (Article 48). Emergency standards can be in force for a maximum period of six months which can be extended for another period of six months. In the latter case, a RIA must be prepared and the process is considered by Mexican Authorities to be compatible with relevant provisions of the WTO TBT Agreement.

Overall, technical standards in Mexico reflect a mixture of government and private sponsored standards with the overwhelming majority of approved standards being in the category of voluntary standards sponsored by the private sector – the proportion of voluntary versus official standards is ten to one. This decentralised process of elaboration of standards however requires that they be based on a consensus of the interested sectors, after public consultations, and also based on international standards unless they are determined to be inefficient or inappropriate. The FMS Law provides for no distinction between nationals and non-nationals and foreign participants can participate in any of the 22 national consultative committees or in the work of NSBs. The combined features of the openness of the consultation process, the publication of draft standards and the public availability of RIAs altogether act to minimise potential incidences of regulatory capture by domestic groups.

---

### Box 3. National consultative committees

All technical regulations, NOMs, are mandatory and must be drafted within one of the 22 national consultative committees, each of which represents a different sector of economic activity and NMXs must be drafted by one of the National Standardisation Bodies (NSBs) or SECOFI in those areas not covered by them through technical committees. There are currently six NSBs and 35 technical committees in Mexico.* The 22 consultative committees are presided over by a representative from the lead Regulatory Agency for the sector in question and are comprised of government and private sector representatives. The participation of private sector representatives in individual committees is open to all interested parties, nationals and non-nationals without distinction.

Once a committee has agreed on the characteristics of a new or revised standard, the lead Regulatory Agency publishes the draft proposal of the standard in the Official Diary for public comment. Proposed new or revised NMXs standards are prepared by NSBs or national consultative bodies and they must publish a summary of their draft proposals in the Official Diary.

Prior to the publication of the draft proposal for a technical regulation NOM, the lead Regulatory Agency must submit for discussion to the respective consultation committee a regulatory impact assessment. This statement must contain explanations about: the standards' objectives; the proposed measure; alternatives considered and the reasons for not proposing them; the advantages and disadvantages of the proposed standards; and the technical feasibility available for the verification and certification involved. For proposed standards that may have a broad impact on the economy, the statement must also include a financial assessment of the potential costs and benefits for the proposed standards and for the alternatives considered, as well as a comparison with international standards. All such information is available to the public at the DGN's information centre.

Sixty days later, the consultative committees or NSBs have 45 days to review and analyse comments received. After that period, responses to comments must be published no sooner than 15 days before the publication of NOMs in their final form.

---

\* SECOFI is empowered to issue NMXs in areas not covered or insufficiently covered by NSBs.

### 2.1.4. *Government procurement at the federal level*

The Mexican legal framework on government procurement procedures is based on the principle of transparency. However, the cost of retrieving relevant information through traditional means could be substantial for national small and medium-sized enterprises and enterprises based in foreign countries. Similarly, due to the possibility of time lost in retrieving and in submitting bids, deadlines could be missed and bids disqualified. In this connection, foreign participants have legitimate expectations in terms of the degree of transparency that domestic government procurement procedures should abide with.

In March 1996, Mexico began an innovative process of government procurement through the Internet, known as COMPRANET, with, as the declared objective, improvement in the transparency of overall procedures. Through the use of the Internet, significant efficiency gains can be realised for both government purchasers and suppliers in terms of time and cost saved in retrieving and delivering electronically relevant technical tendering documentation, government laws and regulations. Small, medium-sized and foreign enterprises in remote locations can have the same access to procurement information as large domestic enterprises. Government agencies also gain by improving the competitive process as more bids can be submitted. Government procurement in Mexico is substantial amounting to US$22.4 billion in 1996.

Under NAFTA and other Free Trade Agreements with Bolivia, Costa Rica, Nicaragua, Colombia and Venezuela, goods, services and construction service markets in Mexico are gradually accessible in increased stages over a maximum period of 8 years. National treatment and non-discrimination are guaranteed for American, Canadian, Bolivian, Costa Rican, Nicaraguan, Colombian and Venezuelan suppliers. The coverage of the different agreements is basically the same.

In the future, Mexican authorities want to further develop COMPRANET to make it possible for participating agencies to carry out all necessary follow-up and control of the procurement process through

---

#### Box 4.   COMPRANET: transparency in procurement

In March 1996, the Ministry of Comptroller and Administrative Development (SECODAM) created an Internet site COMPRANET through which it is possible to consult a range of information about open tendering procedures of the Mexican government procurement system (http://www.compranet.gob.mx).

Each year the Ministry of Finance and Public Credit authorises the budget for the "Annual Acquisitions Programme of Goods and Services and Public Works" (PAASOP) for participating Ministries and Federal entities to establish their procurement requirements. SECODAM establishes the necessary standards based on the Law of Acquisitions and Public Works (APW) and oversees government procurement procedures. The annual acquisitions programme (PAASOP) is also available on COMPRANET.

The process of open tendering may be national or international. It is national when only Mexicans can participate and the goods to be procured must have at least 50% of local content. It is international when: it is mandatory under free trade agreements; for procurement financed by loans from international organisations; national offers cannot fulfil requirements; or in the case of price convenience.

Invitations to participate are advertised through a notice published in the Official Diary and in COMPRANET. The notice indicates various technical information, including whether the tendering is national or international and how to obtain tender documentation.*

---

* Tenders must be submitted in writing in two sealed envelopes, one for the technical and the other for the economic tender. The opening of tenders is performed in two phases. In the first phase, the opening of technical envelopes takes place in a public meeting and tenders that do not meet all conditions are rejected. In the second phase for the qualified technical tenders, the opening of economic tenders is done and the one with the lowest bid is awarded the contract. A new tendering procedure takes place when all tenders submitted do not comply with the conditions established. Decisions on contract awards are noticed in public meetings in which all bidders can freely participate. Bid challenges must be notified to SECODAM for actions that contravene the Law of Acquisitions or trade agreements signed by Mexico.

electronic means. With the development of electronic signatures, cryptography and international standards in the electronic data transmission, possibilities will emerge for the submission of bids through COMPRANET.

Mexico has innovated in making Federal procurement procedures much more transparent than before through the use of the Internet. Foreign participants now enjoy more equitable treatment in terms of costs and time as: they can more rapidly identify that tendering opportunities exist in Mexico; they can electronically retrieve relevant technical tendering documentation, laws and regulations; and they are less subject to miss submission deadlines. As a general rule, the APW Law provides that 100% of the total value of acquisitions, leasing, services and public work obtained by entities should be done through public tendering. However, there are exceptions to the general rule which are specified in the APW Law.

### 2.1.5. *Reforms in customs procedures*

In any country, foreign participants can be frustrated by the lack of transparency or uneven applications of Customs regulations and procedures between various ports of entry. The corruption of Customs officials is encouraged when regulations provide them with wide discretionary powers. Similarly, importers can incur significant cost overruns when shipments are held in Customs warehouses as a result of inefficiencies in Customs procedures.

---

Box 5.   **Customs procedures in Mexico**

In Mexico, import transactions must be processed through certified Customs brokers and customs duties are payable in commercial banks to improve the duty collection system and to minimise incidences of frauds and corruption. Customs brokers are responsible, on behalf of their clients, for import declarations and duty assessment.

The principle of 100% physical inspection was dropped for a random system of inspection where about 10% of all shipments are subject to a physical inspection. A second level of inspection is carried out at random by private firms to detect potential malfeasance practices by Customs officials in collusion with brokers. At each stage, the maximum time granted to Customs officials for the inspection is limited to two hours. After this time limit, shipments must be released, unless exceptional circumstances. Post-audit verification of importers' files and transactions can be performed to detect false declarations and frauds.

Mexico has established an Integral Automated Customs System (SAAI) which allows for the electronic exchange of information between the General Customs Administration, Customs offices, Customs brokers, warehouses and authorised banking institutions to collect duties. Under SAAI, entry documents can be validated or refused prior to the actual clearance of goods, thereby providing for more transparency and predictability for traders.

Since May 1997, Mexico, the United States and Canada began experimenting an electronic-based commerce system called "the North American Trade Automation Prototype (NATAP)" for truck carriers. Six cross-border sites are covered for this programme of which four sites are on the Mexican-United States borders (El Paso/Juarez, Laredo/Nuevo Laredo, Otay Mesa/Tijuana, and Nogales/Nogales). The NATAP system is based on the Electronic Data Interchange (EDI) technologies using the EDIFACT standards. The required Trade Software Package (TSP) is freely available in three languages (English, Spanish and French).

In a nut shell, this Internet-based system links traders, Customs brokers, carriers and Customs offices. Encoded stickers attached on the truck's windshield are laser read as trucks approach border facilities and information is transmitted to the Customs official's computer. The information is immediately matched against pre-sent information for the shipment in question and Customs officials have instant access to the whole file. Officials then send a light signal to the drivers: a green light means go, and red means stop for inspection.

Preliminary indications suggest that NATAP has so far been little used. This may be partly due to the lead time required by all participants to get acquainted with the software and for training staff to properly operate the system.

---

As a necessary complementary measure in the Mexican trade liberalisation orientation, several important changes were made in its Customs procedures and administration. Customs procedures are now based on the principles of: transparency and clear appeal provisions; self-determination and self-observance of legal obligations; integral automation of procedures and re-engineering through the use of new technologies; and maximum reduction of discretionary power by Customs officials.

The reform of Mexican Customs procedures represents a total revamp of administrative procedures and attitude. Mexico is now among the leading countries in the implementation of an integrated electronic-based system. These changes have resulted in several efficiency gains for all concerned parties in terms of: the improvement in the transparency of procedures; the maximum clearance time fell from anything up from 24 hours to a few minutes; the number of certified Customs brokers increased from approximately 380 in 1989, 800 in 1993[4] and 995 in 1997;[5] the number of Customs officials in entry ports fell by more than 20% between 1994 and 1997 while the number of import and export operations increased respectively by more than 25% and 62% during the same period; the more transparent system resulted in improved efficiency in duty collection; and the reduction of discretionary power by Customs officials and improved integrity practices.

The simplification and automation of Customs procedures and the investment in infrastructure have reduced significantly the possibilities of an uneven application of Customs procedures between ports of entry. Mexican authorities believe that the task of assuring even application of all Customs practices in their 47 ports of entry is a major challenge in itself due to: the large investment required to link electronically all ports; the diversified nature of operations carried out by Customs officials; and the complexity of co-ordinating training programmes with the frequency of modifications in regulations which Customs officials are called upon to administer.

### 2.1.6. *Mexico's multilateral transparency commitments*

SECOFI oversees the implementation of transparency provisions relating to Mexican obligations contained in the WTO and other trade agreements. This oversight concerns not only obligations regarding transparency but those concerning non-discrimination; national treatment; prohibition of unnecessary obstacles to trade; the use of international standards, recommendations and guidelines; and considerations of equivalency. SECOFI plays a co-ordinating role in encouraging government-wide awareness of and respect for international obligations relating to domestic regulatory matters, such as the WTO/GATT Article III (national treatment on internal taxation and regulation) and regulatory commitments arising from other WTO Agreements, such as the Technical Barriers to Trade (TBT) and the Sanitary and Phytosanitary Measures (SPS). The "Information Centre of the General Directorate of Standards" of SECOFI acts as the inquiry point to respond to requests for information only as foreseen in the TBT and SPS Agreements of the WTO.

Mexican regulation regarding the Foreign Trade Law also establishes a two-level *Comisión de Comercio Exterior* (COCEX) or Commission on Foreign Trade at the Deputy-Minister level and at Director-General level from various Ministries, including External Affairs (SRE); Finances (SHCP); Social Development (SEDESOL); SECOFI; Agriculture and Rural Development (SAGAR); Environment, Natural Resources and Fisheries (SEMARNAP); Health (SSA); the Central Bank; and the Federal Competition Commission. COCEX is headed by SECOFI and its main functions are to provide opinions on all issues concerning trade policy formulation. No changes in Mexican trade and trade-related laws and regulations can be adopted without the proposed regulations being reviewed by this Commission. With its direct involvement in COCEX, SECOFI is able to review draft regulations submitted by other participating Ministries and to verify their conformity with Mexico's international obligations and commitments.

### 2.1.7. *Assessment*

The Mexican Ministry for Trade and Industry, SECOFI, is overseeing a comprehensive deregulation programme which involves extensive and transparent public consultations in the revision of all existing regulations and the preparation of new regulations and legislation. The regulatory framework provides for no distinction between nationals and non-nationals who wish to participate in public consultations. Efforts are also made at the Federal level to support state and municipal levels to initiate regulatory reform programmes.

The extensive use of the Internet to disseminate the whole range of Federal formalities, regulations and laws places Mexico among the most advanced OECD countries for the use modern electronic information exchange. The Internet is not only used to disseminate formalities but more importantly it is used as a medium to solicit comments from all sources on proposed new regulations. In terms of opportunities for public consultation and comment, publication of draft regulatory measures and notification to international organisations, Mexico also ranks among the top OECD performers. The potential publication through the Internet of all RIAs would greatly assist the general public and in particular, foreign participants, to better understand some of the potential implications of proposed regulations prior to their adoption.

The absence of a specific deregulation infrastructure would in itself raises questions about the real impact of deregulation efforts. That is not the case in Mexico. The overall evidence is that Mexico has set up a comprehensive and transparent infrastructure to oversee deregulation efforts required by Federal Ministries and Agencies with specific responsibilities at senior levels for implementation and action. It remains that some of the key features of the deregulation programme are still very recent and there are signs that some Regulatory Agencies are escaping or circumventing some of the requirements (see Section 3, Telecommunications services). Time will tell whether the quality and uniformity in the implementation of regulatory impact assessments are performed as expected.

From the perspective of foreign participants, the degree and quality of the transparency of procedures regarding government procurement and Customs procedures are crucial for ensuring their ability to pursue business opportunities in Mexico. In both fields, Mexico has made significant investment in putting into place electronic-based systems which are improving the transparency of procedures involved which in turn should result in transaction cost-savings for traders and added opportunities in submitting bids in due time for foreign participants. Recurrent complaints about the uneven application of Customs procedures in different ports of entry and difficulties encountered at the municipal levels with government procurement contracts are reminders that Mexican authorities should apply vigilance and that the improvement in the transparency of various regulatory procedures should be actively pursued at the state and municipal levels.

Mexico operates a decentralised process of elaboration of technical standards with the overwhelming proportion of standards being in the category of voluntary standards. Altogether it is found that the combined features of the openness of the consultation process, the publication of draft official standards and the public availability of their RIAs act to minimise potential incidences of regulatory captured by domestic groups.

## 2.2. Measures to ensure non-discrimination

Application of non-discrimination principles aims to provide effective equality of competitive opportunities between like products and services irrespective of country of origin. Thus, the extent to which respect for two core principles of the multilateral trading system – Most-Favoured-Nation (MFN) and National Treatment (NT) – is actively promoted when developing and applying regulations is a helpful gauge of a country's overall efforts to promote trade and investment-friendly regulation.

International treaties subscribed by the President and ratified by the Senate are supreme law in Mexico. They do not require the adoption of domestic legislation for their internal application. However, several domestic laws have been modified to make them fully compatible with international commitments and to facilitate their application. Accordingly, despite the fact that there is no overarching requirements in Mexican law to incorporate MFN and NT principles into domestic regulations, all agencies are obliged to comply with the principles as contained in those international agreements. It falls upon SECOFI to act as an oversight agency to ensure that the implementation of non-discrimination provisions stemming from the WTO and other international trade and trade-related investment agreements are effectively implemented. Within the WTO dispute settlement process, there were no complaints from trading partners alleging infringement of Mexican MFN or NT obligations in the WTO.

Overtly discriminatory regulatory content is fairly exceptional when viewed from an economy-wide context and against the wide WTO and regional trade commitments entered into by Mexico. Existing measures which discriminate against foreign ownership tend to be fairly limited in scope and complete or partial deregulation across many sectors of the economy has already generated attendant pro-competitive effects for international market openness. Few areas however deserve some attention such as: preferential trade agreements; and trade in services. Each of these are reviewed below.

### 2.2.1. Preferential trade agreements

While preferential agreements give more favourable treatment to specified countries and are thus inherent departures from the MFN and NT principles, the extent of a country's participation in preferential agreements is not in itself indicative of a lack of commitment to the principle of non-discrimination. In assessing such commitments, it is relevant to consider the attitudes of participating countries towards non-members in respect of transparency and the potential for discriminatory effects. Third countries need access to information about the content and operation of preferential agreements in order to make informed assessment of any impact on their commercial interests. In addition, substantive approaches to regulatory issues such as standards and conformity assessment can introduce potential for discriminatory treatment of third countries if, for example, standards recognised by partners in a preferential agreement would be difficult to meet by third countries.

Preferential agreements to which Mexico is a party include six free trade agreements[6] and a network of bilateral investment agreements. Mexico is currently negotiating several free trade agreements with various countries including the European Union.[7] It also participates actively in large multi-country initiatives, such as the Asia-Pacific Economic Co-operation (APEC) and the Free Trade Area of the Americas (FTAA). As reflected in the number of free trade agreements signed and under negotiation, Mexico is keen to exchange on a reciprocal basis significant liberalisation commitments, that go beyond those applied in the WTO. Simultaneously, it supports current talks for the launching of a new round of multilateral trade negotiations.

More concretely, Mexico has extended on a non-discriminatory basis to all WTO Members the benefits of its free trade agreements in the areas such as investment, Customs procedures and intellectual property. The Foreign Investment Law was first amended in December 1993 to materialise its commitments under NAFTA and more generally to promote Mexico as a host country for foreign direct investment. Mexico's accession to the OECD in 1994 was instrumental in the extension of NAFTA's investment commitments to non-NAFTA countries. The Law was subsequently amended in 1996 to allow for additional liberalisation measures and to open up to foreign ownership some sectors previously reserved to the State, such as railways, satellite communications, natural gas storage and secondary petrochemical products.[8]

As a result of these investment liberalisation measures, out of 704 activities included in the Mexican Activities and Products Classification; 606 had been opened up to 100% FDI; 37 accepted up to 100% subject to favourable rulings by the National Foreign Investment Commission; 35 allow for minority interests; 16 are reserved to Mexicans; and ten are reserved to the States.[9]

Mexico's trade and investment agreements are managed in a highly transparent manner. Generally, information on actions to be taken by Mexico and requests for comments on proposed actions are published in the Official Diary. In addition, information on preferential agreements is made available by Mexican Ministries and agencies concerned through a variety of means, including press statements, and the Internet (http://www.secofi.gob.mx). Submission of information to relevant WTO bodies in accordance with WTO obligations establishes another avenue for information, and both of the FTAs to which Mexico is a party encourage and require transparency through public notice. Overall there are few complaints formulated by trading partners concerning Mexico's participation in free trade agreements.[10]

229

Overall, available evidence points to well-orchestrated and good faith efforts in Mexico to share information about its trade and investment agreements as widely as possible. Mexico's attitude demonstrates a desire to extend on a non-discriminatory basis some of the key liberalisation measures achieved under regional agreements, *i.e.* investment.

### 2.2.2. *Trade in services*

Mexico participated in and signed the WTO General Agreement in Trade in Services (GATS) and more recently the Financial Services Agreement concluded in December 1997. Mexico's commitments are annexed to its Schedule to the GATS and they grandfather certain deviations from the non-discrimination and national treatment principles. For example, foreign financial institutions must obtain authorisation from the Ministry of Finance and Public Credit (SHCP), financial institutions must remain under effective control of Mexican shareholders and there are thresholds limiting foreign investors' holdings. These levels were, however, raised from the 1995 commitment of 30% to 40% for insurance companies, multiple-banking institutions and securities firms (49% for limited-purpose financial institutions, foreign exchange houses, investment companies, etc.). In addition, foreign investment by governments and official agencies is not permitted.[11]

Under the GATS, specific market access and national treatment commitments are made according to four modes of supply for each services sector concerned (cross-border supply, consumption abroad, commercial presence, and presence of natural persons). Mexico's services schedules show that it undertook sector-specific commitments in a large number of sectors. For two modes of supply (consumption abroad and cross-border supply), there are no market access or national treatment limitations for almost all sectors, except financial sectors. In terms of commercial presence, limitations generally relate to conditions for foreign participation in activities reserved for Mexican nationals and land ownership on the coastline and along the frontiers. Concerning the presence of natural persons, several commitments are made for intra-corporate transferees.[12] Under NAFTA, limited exceptions are permitted to the universal application of the agreed principles of MFN, national treatment and local presence. Given the architectural differences in which commitments are structured under NAFTA and the GATS, it would be too long to draw a list of these differences and outside the purview of this review. It is however fair to say that, at this point in time, Mexico's services commitments are broader in NAFTA than in the GATS.

### 2.3. Measures to avoid unnecessary trade restrictiveness

To attain a particular regulatory objective, policy makers should seek regulations that are not more trade restrictive than necessary to fulfil a legitimate objective, taking account of the risks non-fulfilment would create. Examples of this approach would be to use performance-based, rather than design standards as the basis of a technical regulation, or to consider taxes or tradable permits in lieu of regulations to achieve the same legitimate policy goal. At the procedural level, effective adherence to this principle entails consideration of the extent to which specific provisions require or encourage regulators to avoid unnecessary trade restrictiveness and the rationale for any exceptions, how the impact of new regulations on international trade and investment is assessed, the extent to which trade policy bodies as well as foreign traders and investors are consulted in the regulatory process, and means for ensuring access by foreign parties to dispute settlement.

In Mexico, the principal tool for measuring the effects of new federal regulations is the regulatory impact assessment (RIA) (see Section 2.1.4). While Mexico has put into place a whole structure for organising regulatory reform within a coherent framework, including the requirement for regulatory impact statement for all new regulations, the principle of avoidance of unnecessary trade restrictiveness is not specifically mentioned among the guiding principles for the reform. It may be argued that this principle is informally taken into consideration when due account is made that alternative regulations may accomplish the same objectives at a lower cost and that the proposed regulations must minimise the negative impact they have on business. As well, nothing bar SECOFI from suggesting or promoting alternative regulations that are least trade restrictive. However since the principle of avoidance of unnecessary trade restrictiveness is not included with the retained guiding principles when regulatory impact assessments are carried out, there is no guarantee that it would be effectively taken into consideration.

Mexico still requires import licences for products covered under some 184 tariff lines. In many cases the licences are a mere formality which can now be obtained through computer links.[13] For the imports of used motor vehicles and used computer equipment, licences are simply not granted except for the imports of used computers by non-profit schools. The regulatory instrument applied in these cases results in a total import prohibition which is the most trade restrictive regulatory instrument. The purpose of this review is not to question the policy legitimacy of the decisions to protect Mexican automotive and computer industries. However, these cases illustrate the need to complement the current guiding principles for regulatory reform with an additional principle of the "avoidance of unnecessary trade restrictiveness" which would be systematically checked along with the other principles when regulatory impact assessments are carried out.

## 2.4. Measures to encourage use of internationally-harmonised measures

Compliance with different standards and regulations for like-products often presents firms wishing to engage in international trade with significant and sometimes prohibitive costs. Thus, when appropriate and feasible, reliance on internationally-harmonised measures as the basis of domestic regulations can readily facilitate expanded trade flows. National efforts to encourage the adoption of regulations based on harmonised measures, procedures for monitoring progress in the development and adoption of international standards, and incentives for regulatory authorities to seek out and apply appropriate international standards are thus important indicators of a country's commitment to efficient regulation.

For WTO Members, a broad requirement to use international standards as the basis of domestic regulations stems only from adherence to multilaterally-agreed trade rules. However, departures from this basic obligation are permitted. Article 2.4 of the WTO TBT Agreement requires Members to use relevant international standards (or relevant parts of them) as a basis for their technical regulations "except when they would be an ineffective or inappropriate means for the fulfilment of legitimate objectives pursued". A parallel orientation in Article 3 of the Agreement on the Application of Sanitary and Phytosanitary Measures (SPS Agreement) requires Members to base their sanitary or phytosanitary measures on international standards, guidelines, or recommendations, where they exist, although Members may introduce or maintain measures based on more stringent standards under certain narrowly-defined conditions.

As noted above in Section 2.1.3, the FMS Law calls upon the lead Regulatory Agencies and the National Standardisation Bodies (NSBs) to base technical standards on international standards, except when they are considered to be inefficient or inadequate to achieve the desired objectives. When elaborating NOMs, relevant agencies must justify on scientific bases the reasons for not using or deviating from international standards. Mexican Authorities consider that approximately 65% of the NOMs are partially or totally in accordance with international standards.

Although the burden of the proof falls on Regulatory Agencies and NSBs to make such a demonstration for each proposed standard, there is the risk of expediency consideration and comparison. This risk is however minimised as regard official standards, NOMs, as such considerations are taken into account during the preparation of associated RIAs. Furthermore, since RIAs are publicly available during the consultation process of proposed standards, attempts to ignore or improperly disqualifying international standards could be found with embarrassing consequences for the lead Regulatory Agencies in question.

As regard voluntary standards, it is a moot point whether NSBs are making genuine efforts to base their proposed voluntary standards on international standards. On the one hand, NSBs are no required to prepare RIAs along with their proposed standards, thus there is probably less transparency of factors considered. On the other hand, NSBs are privately-sponsored organisations which should have a priori no objections to adopt available international standards when these are cost efficient and less burdensome. NSBs are also required by the FMS Law to have the capacity to participate in international standardisation activities and to have adopted the WTO TBT Code of Good Practice for the Preparation, Adoption and Application of Standards. These requirements should help them to stay abreast with relevant international developments and best practices applied abroad.

It remains that for all Mexican Regulatory Agencies and NSBs, the adoption of international standards requires considerable human and material resources to get acquainted with them and to implement necessary operational testing and training involved. The task of translating in Spanish language highly technical terms for complex systems can represent significant costs and act as deterrent for the adoption of international standards. Overall evidence however suggests that the Mexican elaboration process of technical standards is favourably disposed towards the adoption of international standards.

### 2.5. Recognition of equivalence of other countries' regulatory measures

The pursuit of internationally-harmonised measures may not always be possible, necessary or even desirable. In such cases, efforts should be made in order to ensure that cross-country disparities in regulatory measures and duplicative conformity assessment systems do not act as barriers to trade. Recognising the equivalence of trading partners' regulatory measures or the results of conformity assessment performed in other countries are two promising avenues for achieving this result. In practice, both avenues are being pursued by Mexico in various ways. Recognising certification given to foreign products by foreign laboratories is one example. Such recognition can be accorded unilaterally, but also through the mechanism of a Mutual Recognition Agreement (MRA) between trading partners.

WTO obligations provide the chief context for the recognition of equivalence of other countries' regulatory measures and conformity assessment results. Both Agreements expressly encourage WTO Members to recognise other countries' technical regulations, SPS measures and results of conformity assessment procedures as equivalent, though in all cases Members retain ultimate discretion in deciding whether a satisfactory basis exists for doing so.[14] SECOFI has overall responsibility for monitoring Mexican compliance with these and other obligations under its trade agreements, in co-operation and co-ordination with relevant Agencies, and for responding to complaints received from foreign governments concerning perceived violations of such obligations.

Conformity assessment procedures are varied and they consist of testing, sampling, calibration, certifying and verifying products against prevailing approved technical standards. These procedures can be performed by several Government Agencies in Mexico and by private conformity assessment bodies. In order to carry out conformity assessment functions, private bodies need to be accredited by SECOFI and also need approval of the relevant Government Agencies to obtain the right to certify the Agencies' standards.

The main criteria followed in the accreditation process are that: the interested conformity assessment body indicates which standards it wants to assess and certify; it demonstrates its technical, material and human capacity; and it offers quality assurance of the good performance for the mentioned activities. The accreditation functions are actually carried out by SECOFI, although it is foreseen that a private entity (EMA) will carry out those activities in the near future after the authorisation process is obtained. SECOFI is responsible for the accreditation of private accreditation entities.

It is the responsibility of SECOFI to conclude agreements with international or foreign institutions for the mutual recognition of conformity assessment results carried out by accredited bodies in Mexico. Mexican accredited bodies can also negotiate mutual recognition agreements with foreign institutions or bodies but they need SECOFI's approval. The establishment of credible grounds for determinations of equivalence is resource-intensive, time-consuming and sometime politically sensitive process.

While there are no foreign-owned conformity assessment bodies currently operating in Mexico, there are no restrictions preventing foreign bodies from obtaining accreditation and the criteria are the same for all applicants. Under NAFTA, Mexico negotiated a four-year grace period, which ended in January 1998, in the obligation to accredit conformity assessment bodies in the territory of the other parties in not less favourable conditions that the ones given to those bodies in its own territory. This grace period gave time to Mexican conformity assessment bodies to upgrade their technical and competitive capacity. Since January Canadian and American conformity bodies can seek their accreditation for certifying relevant Mexican standards. Mexico has negotiated so far two agreements with the USA for the mutual recognition of the test results for tires and telecommunications equipment. Mexico is negotiating with Canada an agreement on telecommunications equipment.

Possible approaches to recognition of results of conformity assessment procedures are also under consideration in APEC. Current discussions are addressing potential arrangements in such areas as electrical safety, electronic equipment and telecommunications equipment. If and when agreed, such arrangements would be open to participation by individual APEC economies. Recognition of standards and conformity assessment issues are similarly on the agenda of other incipient regional economic integration agreements in which Mexico is involved, notably the FTAA. Mexico is participating in these discussions and it is assessing the usefulness of mutual recognition agreements and application in new areas.

Since January 1998, corresponding to the end of the NAFTA grace period for accrediting conformity assessment bodies in the other parties, Mexico is definitely moving in the right direction on the issue of the recognition of equivalence of other countries' regulations and conformity assessment procedures.

## 2.6. Application of competition principles from an international perspective

The benefits of market access may be reduced by regulatory action condoning anti-competitive conduct or by failure to correct anti-competitive private actions that have the same effect. It is therefore important that regulatory institutions make it possible for both domestic and foreign firms affected by anti-competitive practices to present their positions effectively. The existence of procedures for hearing and deciding complaints about regulatory or private actions that impair market access and effective competition by foreign firms, the nature of the institutions that hear such complaints, and adherence to deadlines (if they exist) are thus key issues from an international market openness perspective.

If private conduct affects the competition process impairing access to a particular market by foreign firms, the affected firms may file a complaint before the Federal Competition Commission (FCC). The FCC is an independent administrative agency responsible for the enforcement of the 1993 Federal Law of Economic Competition (LCFE) and its associated regulations. The FCC has no discretionary power to reject a case provided that the complaint fulfils the requirements set out in the LCFE.

The 1995-1996 case involving a complaint by a Mexican subsidiary of a multinational corporation, Singer Mexicana Manufacturera Electronica and Sim against two Mexican firms is illustrative of how market access issues are addressed by the FCC. In that case, the Mexican producers had entered into contracts with domestic retailers, granting a rebate if the retailers would not sell appliances produced outside the NAFTA area. The FCC found that these contracts were anti-competitive and ordered the firms involved to remove these clauses from their contracts. It further warned them that failure to comply would lead in the imposition of fines as provided in the LCFE.

In contrast, the FCC has rather limited powers to address competition problems that might arise from regulatory actions that impair market access for foreign firms. Under the LCFE, and certain other sector-specific regulations, the FCC has a limited competition law advocacy role to other governmental institutions. Although these opinions are not legally binding, they are often taken into account by other regulators in Mexico. Prominent examples of successful advocacy are provided by the Railroad Service Law and Federal Telecommunications Law which incorporate competition provisions that emphasise market access opportunities for both domestic and foreign service providers.

A particular setting for concern is the exertion or extension of market power by a regulated or protected monopolist into another market. The substantive problem, sometimes called "regulatory abuse," is not addressed by laws about monopolisation, or by regulatory laws applied to particular markets. Foreign firms and trade could be implicated in two ways. First, an incumbent domestic regulated monopolist might gain an unfair advantage over foreign products or firms in an unregulated domestic market. Or, an incumbent foreign regulated monopolist might use the resources afforded by its

233

protection at home to gain an unfair advantage in another country. As explained above, beyond advocacy, the FCC has limited formal role to provide appropriate relief to remedy the problems created when regulatory decisions impair competition in other markets.

However, one ex-officio investigation carried out in the first year of operation for the FCC, involving PEMEX (Petroleos Mexicanos), the oil producing state monopoly, concerning gasoline stations shows the potential power of the FCC advocacy role in acting against regulatory abuse. The FCC charged PEMEX with unduly blocking entry to new competing gas stations by protecting the geographic territory of existing stations and erecting substantive barriers to entry. PEMEX imposed a "franchising" system, which required gas stations to obtain pre-clearance from PEMEX to sell anything that was not a PEMEX product (even food, soft drinks and other goods or services), and to pay a fee to PEMEX for such clearance. Some commentators have suggested that some foreign firms are particularly interested in investing in new service stations as a result of this decision, thus demonstrating the international dimension of this case.

The outcome of the FCC action was the signing of a consent agreement by PEMEX to remove all requirements to open up new gas stations, except ecological and safety standards; and to eliminate the "franchising" restrictive scheme. This action, in a period of six months, had already yielded great success. There are now over 400 new gas station contracts with PEMEX, more than PEMEX had authorised in the previous three years, showing greatly boosted investment. These CFC-induced structural remedies show the great benefits that may be obtained by enforcing basic competition concepts and by restraining new regulated monopolies from distorting markets not covered by their legal activity. This case also shows the importance of removing the *de facto* authority that public monopolies have exercised through the years, abusing their overwhelming market power.

## 3. ASSESSING RESULTS IN SELECTED SECTORS

This Section examines the implications for international market openness arising from Mexican regulations currently in place for three sectors: telecommunications equipment; telecommunications services; and automobiles and components. For each sector, an attempt has been made to draw out the effects of sector-specific regulations on international trade and investment and the extent to which the six efficient regulation principles are explicitly or implicitly applied. Telecommunications services are reviewed in greater detail in Chapter 6.

Particular attention is paid to product standards and conformity assessment procedures, where relevant. Other issues addressed here include efforts to adopt internationally-harmonised product standards, use of voluntary product standards by regulatory authorities, and openness and flexibility of conformity assessment systems. In many respects, multilateral disciplines, notably the WTO TBT Agreement, provide a sound basis for reducing trade tensions by encouraging respect for fundamental principles of efficient regulation such as transparency, non-discrimination, and avoidance of unnecessary trade restrictiveness.

### 3.1. Telecommunications services

The Mexican market for telecommunications services is one of the largest and fastest growing in Latin America. Despite uneven geographical service and relatively low telephone line density *vis-à-vis* the rest of the world (9.5 mainlines per 100 inhabitants in 1997, compared to 66 in the United States), the sector has registered dramatic growth in recent years and become a significant revenue earner for the Mexican economy. Public telecommunications revenue as a percentage of Mexican GDP grew from 0.56% in 1985 to 1.90% in 1997. Much of this growth has been precipitated by the opening of the market to long-distance (national and international) competition. International Telecommunication Union (ITU) estimates predict continued strong growth in the sector, presenting important opportunities for new entry into the market. Some foreign competitors have moved quickly to capitalise on these new market conditions, while structuring their investments in a manner consistent with relevant Mexican foreign ownership restrictions.[15]

The current regulatory setting for the provision of telecommunications services (see Chapter 6) is the result of major policy changes introduced from 1990 onwards. In 1990, the Mexican government privatised the state-controlled monopoly *Teléfonos de Mexico*, granting it exclusive rights to domestic and international long-distance service until 1996. Article 28 of the Mexican Constitution was amended in March 1995 to eliminate the State monopoly for the establishment and operation of satellite systems. The enactment of the *Federal Telecommunications Law* (FTL) on 9 June 1995 introduced opportunities for competition and new entry into the market. At the multilateral level, Mexico made specific liberalisation commitments in the GATS negotiations on basic telecommunications covering services such as voice telephony, facsimile services, paging services, and cellular telephone services.[16]

Regulatory roles and institutions were also reorganised as part of telecommunications reform. The Ministry of Communications and Transport (*Secretaria de Comunicaciones y Transportes*, or SCT) acted as the sole regulatory authority for the industry until Telmex's formal legal monopoly came to an end in August 1996. The creation at that time of the *Comisión Federal de Telecomunicaciones* (COFETEL) placed day-to-day regulatory responsibilities such as tariffing, interconnection rates, frequency allocation, and establishment of license fees into the hands of an independent body with technical and operational autonomy. SCT continues to play a role by virtue of its remaining authority for the grant and revocation of concessions[17] and operating permits. SCT and COFETEL consult with interested parties when drafting regulations for the sector. The relationship between SCT and COFETEL is discussed in more detail in Chapter 6.

The administrative procedure followed by SCT for the grant of a concession to install, operate, or exploit a public telecommunications network is set out in Chapter III of the FTL.[18] Applications by prospective service providers must contain, at a minimum: name and address of the applicant; a description of the services to be provided; the technical specifications of the project; investment plans, coverage and quality of service; a business plan; and documentation establishing financial, technical, legal and administrative capacity of the applicant. Additional criteria apply in respect of applicants seeking to use the radioelectric spectrum.

Rulemaking procedures for the sector are subject to the Federal Administrative Procedure Law (FAP Law) and guidelines on government interaction with the public (see discussion in Section 2.1.2). Thus, all draft regulations must be published in the Official Diary before they can be enforced. Mechanisms for public consultation, however, are left to sector specific laws. COFETEL is also required by the FAP Law to submit all draft regulations with a potential impact on business activity along with a regulatory impact assessment (RIA) to SECOFI's Economic Deregulation Unit.

Both COFETEL and the SCT have web sites contributing to transparency in the sector. Nonetheless, some trading partners have expressed concerns about transparency in this sector, citing difficulties in identifying regulatory content and in understanding newly-issued rules as well as uncertainty about procedural avenues to be followed when pursuing complaints about existing regulations.

Regulatory content for the sector has broadly reflected the pro-competitive concepts underlying recent domestic reforms. The termination of Telmex's legal monopoly in August 1996 and opening of the long distance market to competition in January 1997 (when Telmex was forced to interconnect) were important watersheds. A degree of competition was introduced with the speedy grant of licenses to new concession holders.

However, throughout 1998, foreign carriers became increasingly vocal about alleged regulatory barriers to effective market access and presence in Mexico. These concerns culminated in the United States with calls for the launch of a WTO dispute settlement procedure against Mexico in respect of various regulatory issues, notably international settlement rates, foreign ownership restrictions and satellite infrastructure.[19]

Specific aspects of interconnection rate structures have also come under scrutiny. Domestic interconnection rates charged by Telmex to terminate inbound international calls have emerged as a trade

235

concern, with foreign carriers claiming that Telmex's rates are much higher than those charged in other liberalised markets. Foreign competitors have also objected to Telmex's imposition of a 58% surcharge on all inbound switched international calls.[20] US carriers claim that this rate structure extracts from them $857 million per year. They argue that the fees are far above cost and that their combined impact, by severely depressing expected profitability, is effectively discriminatory. Affected foreign carriers also consider that imposition of these fees results from a regulatory failure to rein in abusive market power.[21] As of 1 January 1999, the 58% surcharge was replaced by a rate of 26.1 cents of a peso per minute (approximately 2.6 cents of one US$) for the delivery of the long distance traffic (detailed information is available on Cofetel's Internet site www.cft.gob.mx).

Telmex argues in regard to the interconnection issue that its significant loss of market share to foreign competitors since 1997 shows that competition exists in the market and that the fees are justified to compensate the company for the over $13 billion it invested to prepare the country's infrastructure for competition – improvements which foreign competitors now freely exploit.

Modalities for the negotiation of accounting rate agreements (settlement rates) between national and foreign carriers have been another source of conflict. As in many OECD countries, Mexico's accounting rate framework is established by commercial negotiation. However, foreign competitors object to the fact that under current rules, such negotiations can only be conducted by the dominant carrier Telmex, giving it effective authority over the process.

Finally, under existing regulations, only facilities-based carriers may provide international simple resale (ISR) services – procedures which allow carriers to use private lines for the routing of phone calls. While the rationale behind this approach is to encourage network build-out in support of universal service, non-facilities-based carriers argue that the restriction is a violation of Mexico's WTO commitments in the sector. However, Mexico's agreement to allow ISR is contingent on having the necessary regulations in place, which is still not the case.[22]

Foreign ownership in most sub-sectors remains subject to restrictions. Under the Federal Telecommunications Law, foreign investment participation in concessions for basic and long distance telephony may not exceed 49%. An exception is made in the area of cellular telephone services,[23] where up to 100% ownership may be allowed with prior authorisation of the National Foreign Investment Commission. As a result of Constitutional amendments introduced in 1995, foreign investors may now own up to 49% of a Mexican firm operating satellite communications. No foreign investment restrictions apply in respect of value-added services.[24]

Broader legal authority for wider prohibitions or restrictions on foreign participation also exists. The *Ley de Vias Generales de Comunicacion* stipulates that foreign governments and foreign state enterprises or their investments may not invest, directly or indirectly, in Mexican enterprises engaged in communications, transportation or other general means of communication activities as defined in the law. Article 12 of the law establishes that concessions for the construction, establishment or exploitation of "general means of communication" may only be granted to Mexican nationals or enterprises. Mexican enterprises with one or more foreign partners must show that the latter would accept to be treated as Mexican nationals with respect to the concession, effectively waiving any right of protection from their home governments. Other restrictions apply in respect of telecommunications transport networks, including local basic telephone services, long-distance telephone services (national and international), rural telephone services, satellite services, mobile telephony, and paging. Different legal sources underpin the latter group of possible restrictions,[25] introducing the risk of non-transparency.

The overall picture that emerges is largely positive, though some cautionary remarks are warranted. Faced with the dual challenge of expanding service and fostering competition in the sector, Mexico has made impressive progress towards liberalisation while still in early stages of infrastructure development – a rare achievement relative to many non-OECD countries. Key events such as the passage of the FTL and the establishment of an independent telecommunications regulator have set the stage for a trade- and investment-friendly regulatory regime. However, the experiences of some (mainly US) carriers seeking to compete in a liberalising Mexican long-distance market show that certain features of the regulatory framework may be undermining market openness.

Concerns relating to market openness may dissipate in the future. Still, greater efforts seem to be required in respect of transparency and openness of decision-making in terms of: clearer communication of regulatory content and avenues for complaint by adversely affected foreign parties; avoidance of unnecessary trade restrictiveness through more systematic analysis of proposed rules for the sector from a market openness perspective, including perhaps enhanced consultation with the trade policy community; and enhanced application of competition principles from an international perspective. Specific regulatory content, *e.g.* rules on interconnection fees, may also need to be reviewed in terms of their alleged discriminatory effects on foreign competitors.

### 3.2. Telecommunications equipment

Regulatory functions for this sector are performed by COFETEL. Two important roles are development of the incumbent network's technical interconnection standards and establishment of equipment attachment policies allowing customers and service providers to attach pieces of terminal equipment to the incumbent's network. COFETEL plays the lead standardisation role for the sector and is the only entity authorised to recognise test results from domestic or foreign test facilities.[26]

COFETEL standardisation activities, including administrative procedures for the preparation of official and voluntary standards, are subject to the provisions of the FMS Law discussed in Section 2.4 of this Chapter. Over 100 *Normas Oficiales Mexicanas* (NOMs) are in place for telecommunications equipment.

NAFTA provisions aimed at facilitating trade in telecommunications equipment devote considerable attention to standards issues as a core market access concern. Article 1304(1) requires each Party to ensure that its standards-related measures relating to the attachment of terminal or other equipment to public telecommunications transport networks, including measures relating to the use of testing and measuring equipment for conformity assessment procedures, do not introduce unnecessary obstacles to trade, and establishes a basis for the imposition of standards. Also Article 1304(6) requires each Party to adopt as part of its conformity assessment procedures "provisions necessary to accept the test results from laboratories or testing facilities in the territory of another Party for tests performed in accordance with the accepting Party's standards-related measures and procedures".

A NAFTA Telecommunications Standards Sub-committee was established to develop a work programme aimed at "making compatible, to the greatest extent practicable, the standards-related measures of the Parties for authorised equipment". Though the Sub-committee make considerable progress at the outset, concrete achievements have yet to be realised in this area. This, together with the fact that NAFTA's coverage is limited to terminal equipment – not covering wireless – may be contributing to a shift in focus on the part of the US industry to APEC and US-EU MRA processes.

Apparent differences in interpretation of the obligations arising under NAFTA-related provisions have given rise to growing concerns about Mexican market openness in this sector. Implementation in practice of Article 1304(1) provides a ready example. As noted earlier, that Article establishes a basis for the imposition of standards for terminal equipment attachment under certain narrowly-defined conditions, such as the need to "ensure users' safety and access to public telecommunications transport networks or services". This and four other conditions were in essence grafted to NAFTA from Part 68 of the US Federal Communications Commission regulations – regulations designed to ensure a highly competitive equipment market in the aftermath of the AT&T break-up, in part by deterring the imposition of equipment standards except to address certain narrow issues.

In practice, however, Mexico has not shared this interpretation. Instead of espousing a minimalist regulatory approach, NAFTA partners contend that Mexico has sought to fit its over 100 official equipment-related standards under the five "exceptions" rubrics contained in Article 1304(1), raising questions about compliance with the overall thrust of the Article. While NAFTA clearly recognises the right of each Party to take standards-related measures and to establish the level of protection it deems appropriate, trade frictions surrounding the issue seem to point to an open question – whether the underlying objectives of Mexican equipment standards might be met in a less trade restrictive manner. Here, greater efforts towards recognition of equivalence of other countries' standards – perhaps based on the "functional equivalence" model employed by the US telecommunications regulator – may hold the key to reduced trade tensions.

Similar philosophical differences appear to be thwarting efforts to establish common ground for the mutual acceptance of test data under conformity assessment procedures. NAFTA Article 1304(6) required each Party to adopt, as part of its conformity assessment procedures, "provisions necessary to accept the test results from laboratories or testing facilities in the territory of another Party for tests performed in accordance with the accepting Party's standards-related measures and procedures". Mexico's preferred approach to this issue has been to require government accreditation of laboratories, a stance visibly at odds with the more "hands-off" position taken by the United States and Canada. Both of Mexico's NAFTA partners continue to cite lack of progress in this area as a serious trade concern.[27]

NAFTA also lifted the 49% limit on foreign equity in telecommunications equipment manufacturers, with the result that all firms located in NAFTA countries regardless of national origin may obtain 100% ownership in equipment manufacturing firms without government approval. Mexico is not a signatory to the Information Technology Agreement.

In sum, the nature of the Mexican standards system and the particular approach taken by the regulator with respect to official standards and conformity assessment procedures for this sector have contributed to persistent and significant trade tensions with trading partners. Sector-specific NAFTA provisions on standards-related measures have aimed to alleviate these frictions – and might have provided a model for wider multilateral application – but fundamental differences on implementation issues have clouded concrete results in this area to date. Further efforts to recognise the equivalence of other countries' regulatory measures, particularly conformity assessment procedures and greater reliance on internationally-harmonised measures where appropriate, may go some distance to improving market openness.

Mexico might also look to the US example in moving some products to self-declarations of compliance, removing the need for an additional layer of certification procedures. Finally, given the extent of official standards applicable to this sector, a comprehensive re-evaluation of the fundamental objectives underlying regulations currently in place with a view to ensuring that they do not unnecessarily restrict trade seems warranted. Greater reliance on pro-competitive, industry-driven open standard-setting activities involving all interested players, domestic or foreign may however hold greater promise for easing trade frictions in the long term.

### 3.3. Automobiles and components

Concerns about market openness and domestic regulation of automotive industries around the world are not new. Due to the historic dynamism of global economic activity in the sector and traditionally interventionist policies of some governments aimed at protecting domestic automotive industries, trade tensions related to domestic regulatory issues in general and standards and certification procedures in particular have long figured on bilateral and regional trade agendas. This reflects the fact that automobiles remain among the most highly regulated products in the world primarily for reasons relating to safety, energy conservation, and the environment. Divergent national approaches to the achievement of legitimate domestic objectives in these key policy areas are therefore likely to remain a significant source of trade tension as global demand for automobiles continues to rise.

In Mexico, automotive production and trade is highly regulated under the Automotive Decree (*Decreto para el fomento y modernizacion de la industria automotriz*) not so much for the purposes of safety, energy conservation and environment but to speed up its modernisation and competitiveness through highly trade restrictive regulations albeit set to be eliminated at the end of December 2003.

Imports of new motor vehicles into Mexico remains nevertheless prohibited by individuals and are allowed only by manufacturers that comply with the Automobile Decree. Import licences are therefore only granted to manufacturers on the basis of their recorded import and export balance. For used vehicles, there is a *de facto* import prohibition from all countries as import licences are simply not granted. Under NAFTA, licences will be gradually issued from some imports of used vehicles originating from the US and Canada as of 2009 and the licence requirement will be eliminated in 2019. Mexico has also signed several other free trade agreements which each provide for the elimination of tariff at a given point in time.

---

### Box 6. Mexican automotive decree

The Automotive Decree first introduced in December 1989 and amended subsequently provides for a set of measures designed to facilitate the modernisation of the Mexican automotive industry with a view to making it internationally competitive. Mexico essentially grandfathered the main provisions of the Decree for a period terminating at the end of December 2003 under NAFTA. After that, the horizontal NAFTA provisions will govern trade in motor vehicles within North America. In 1998, Mexico's tariff rate on vehicles is 5.5% under NAFTA and the MFN rate is 20%.

The Decree contains specific local content and trade balancing requirements to be applied by each manufacturer. National content requirement is established at 34% between 1994 and 1998 and it will be reduced by one percentage point each following year to 29% in 2003, and eliminated in 2004. Automotive manufacturers are required to achieve trade balancing requirements established as a percentage of the value of direct and indirect imports of auto parts which manufacturers incorporate into their production in Mexico for sale in Mexico. In 1994, the trade balancing requirement was reduced from $2 of exports for every dollar imported to 80 cents. This percentage will be gradually reduced every year to reach a level of 55 cents in 2003 and eliminated in 2004.

---

While the Automobile Decree still maintains significant trade distorting provisions, the overall approach contrasts sharply with the previous programme based on import substitution. Foreign direct investment is now welcome and the local content and trade balancing requirements are gradually relaxed and set to be eliminated in 2004. The Automobile Decree and Mexico's overall trade liberalisation were instrumental in Mexico becoming a large exporting country of motor vehicles with 11% of total world exports of commercial vehicles in 1997, up from 1% in 1990 (see Table 4). In 1997, Mexico's export

Table 4. **Production, export and registration of motor vehicles in Mexico**

|  | 1980 | 1990 | 1994 | 1995 | 1997 |
|---|---|---|---|---|---|
| **Production** |  |  |  |  |  |
| Passenger vehicles | 303 056 | 598 093 | 856 563 | 699 312 | 853 197 |
| Commercial vehicles | 186 950 | 222 465 | 194 000 | 237 888 | 508 833 |
| **Export** |  |  |  |  |  |
| Passenger vehicles | 13 633 | 249 921 | 497 049 | 598 803 | 591 485 |
| Commercial vehicles | 4 612 | 26 016 | 71 443 | 183 873 | 396 707 |
| **Export ratio** |  |  |  |  |  |
| Passenger vehicles | 0.4% | 41.8% | 58.0% | 85.6% | 69.3% |
| Commercial vehicles | 0.2% | 11.7% | 36.8% | 77.3% | 78.0% |
| **Shares of world exports** |  |  |  |  |  |
| Passenger vehicles | 0% | 2% | 4% | 4% | 4% |
| Commercial vehicles | 0% | 1% | 3% | 7% | 11% |
| **Domestic registration** |  |  |  |  |  |
| Passenger vehicles | 286 000 | 353 000 | 413 819 | 114 658 | 303 558 |
| Commercial vehicles | 166 000 | 198 000 | 205 311 | 72 823 | 82 000 |

*Source:* Comité des constructeurs français d'automobiles, 1997 *Analyses et statistiques*, pp. 45-47, Paris, 1998.

ratio calculated as the volume of exports divided by the volume of production was 69% and 78% for passenger and commercial vehicles respectively. Exports were practically non-existent in 1980.

Tangible benefits have been materialised for Mexico with its new approach to regulate the motor vehicle sector. Automotive production accounts for about 11% of manufacturing production and 19% of total exports (including in-bond exports). Eight vehicle assembly firms are now operating, 16 truck and bus manufacturers and over 500 auto parts suppliers. The Mexican authorities further expect, that between 1997 and the year 2000, new investment in the automotive sector will amount to about US$18 billion to take advantage of the opportunity offered by the Mexican environment and market.

The net benefits are however tempered by the high consumer prices paid by Mexican consumers, with a price premium hovering around 25% above comparable vehicles in the United States for both new and used vehicles (unofficial sources). Given the export success of manufacturers established in Mexico and the fact that the trade balancing requirements are not currently exerting any real restraint on import levels on manufacturers, Mexican authorities should assess whether the high price supported by Mexican vehicle consumers could not be reduced.

Technical standards in Mexico are applied for ensuring the safety of motor vehicles and for achieving environmental objectives. As the Mexican automotive industry is highly integrated in North America, Mexican vehicle production is essentially calibrated to meet the safety and environmental standards set in the United States and Canada which generally provide for high technical requirements. There are few official Mexican technical standards (NOMs) but more than 100 voluntary standards (NMXs). Contrary to the United States, Mexico does not allow for the self-certification of technical safety standards by manufacturers. Safety and environmental conformity assessment procedures can be carried out in relevant Mexican accredited conformity assessment bodies.

Since January 1998, Mexico applies Article 908 of NAFTA which provides that each party shall accredit and recognise certification procedures performed by conformity assessment bodies in the territory of another Party. If appropriate agreements are finalised among NAFTA Parties, US and Canadian environmental standards could be certified by accredited Mexican conformity assessment bodies and vice versa. In view of the self-certification of safety standards applicable in the United States, Mexican manufacturers are already self-certifying their vehicles destined for export to the. United States.

NAFTA also provides for the establishment of an Automotive Standards Council to facilitate the attainment of compatibility among national standards-related measures of the parties. Within this

---

Box 7.   **Global technical regulations for wheeled vehicles**

In recent years, support was voiced for strengthening the legal and administrative capacity of the 1958 Agreement of Working Party 29 of the United Nations – Economic Commission for Europe (UN-ECE) as the principal body for common development of technical standards and regulatory requirements for motor vehicles. As a result of multilateral negotiations, a new agreement was reached on 25 June 1998 on Global Technical Regulations for Wheeled Vehicles which shall facilitate the full participation of countries operating either the type-approval or the self-declaration systems of conformity of standards. The UN-ECE Agreement is entitled "Agreement concerning the establishment of global technical regulations for wheeled vehicles, equipment and parts which can be fitted and/or be used on wheeled vehicles".

The Agreement opens up the possibility for establishing "global technical regulations" proposed by its contracting parties and which must be approved by consensus. The USA has already ratified the Agreement and the adhesion of the EU, Canada, Australia and Japan is expected shortly. Mexico is not a member of the UN-ECE Working Party 29 given the absence of requests from manufacturers operating in Mexico which are all foreign-owned multinational firms. Cost involved in the participation in this Working Party is a consideration for Mexican Authorities.

Council, a mutual recognition agreement was achieved among NAFTA parties for tires. Mexico participates actively in the Council

There are no sector-specific processes in Mexico for the elaboration of technical standards for motor vehicles with respect to both safety and environment. Any proposals for official and voluntary standards must be included in the annual National Standardisation Programme. Proposals must be drafted by one of the consultative committees and are subject to the same procedure of public consultations and availability of related regulatory impact assessments. The majority of Mexican standards applied to motor vehicles are in the category of voluntary. With its high export propensity, it is in Mexico's interest to minimise redundancy in standards and conformity assessment procedures and to negotiate mutual recognition agreements with its major trading partners. This process has began with tires under NAFTA and with the end of the grace period granted to Mexico for accrediting conformity assessment bodies of other NAFTA parties, the stage is set for progress in mutual recognition of the certification of standards.

## 4. CONCLUSIONS AND POLICY OPTIONS FOR REFORM

### 4.1. General assessment of current strengths and weaknesses

An analysis of the OECD indicators questionnaire on market openness undertaken carried out in early 1998 as part of the OECD Project on Regulatory Reform found Mexico to be well ahead of the OECD average with respect to three of the efficient regulation principles and to score relatively low with respect to the application of competition principles (see Figure 1 below). A word of caution should be

Figure 1. **Mexico's trade friendly index by principle**

OECD average = 100

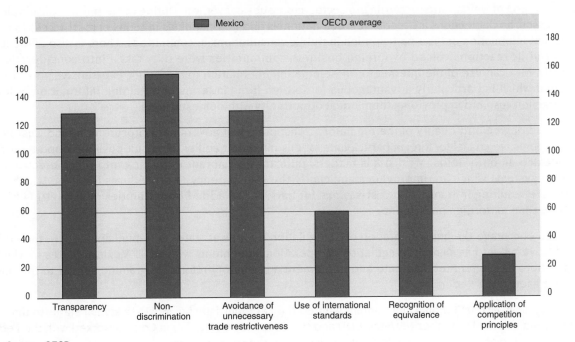

*Source:* OECD.

noted about the results reproduced in this Figure given the large number of answers left blank by Member countries which has complicated the task of country comparison.

The results represented on the Figure are useful as they corroborate, to a certain degree, the results obtained during the country evaluation phase. Overall the Figure suggests uneven results for Mexico in applying the six efficient principles of market openness in comparison with OECD countries, with simultaneously above average OECD results for the first three principles and relative low results with the other three principles. As a result of the country review, however, important nuances most of them on the positive side were found in terms of the overall trade friendliness of Mexican regulatory procedures with the six efficient regulation principles.

While not all of the six efficient regulation principles examined in this review are expressly codified in Mexican administrative and regulatory oversight procedures to the same degree, the weight of available evidence suggests that they are given ample expression in practice. This is most clearly the case for transparency and openness of decision-making and measures to ensure non-discrimination. The formulation of domestic regulation and technical standards is performed on the basis of extensive public consultations and transparent processes. Together these features act as a check and balance which reduce opportunities for regulatory capture by vested interest groups. Concurrently, there are few WTO complaints from trading partners with respect to any of its multilateral obligations and, when they happen, Mexico has shown good faith in seeking to find mutual acceptable solutions.

The overall deregulation programme is structured on a comprehensive and high level organisation encompassing all Mexican Ministries and Agencies. At the top, the Economic Deregulation Council composed of high level representatives from all segments of activities is providing a high political profile to the programme. At the operational level, each Ministry is required to assign a Deputy Minister in charge of regulatory improvements in their Ministry. The overall management of the deregulation programme is co-ordinated by the Economic Deregulation Unit (EDU) of SECOFI for co-ordinating major reforms. This structural arrangement seems particularly adapted to overcome enshrined resistance to change and inertia in Ministries which have developed over the years a closed attitude to opinion coming from outside of their own sphere of influence, particularly when these opinions touch upon essential operations under their purview.

The process of deregulation and review of proposed regulations is subject to public consultation, the duration of which varies according to sector and issues concerned. During these public consultation processes, no distinctions are made between nationals and non-nationals in terms of their access to the relevant information or their participation in public consultations or committees. There is also evidence that public reactions voiced by foreign business communities were duly taken into consideration. Finally, Mexican use of the Internet for disseminating information to the public is extensive and widespread which is particularly advantageous for foreign firms in terms of obtaining information at low transaction cost and in providing them equal opportunity with domestic firms.

The degree and quality of the regulatory transparency of government procurement and Customs procedures are crucial for foreign participants for ensuring their ability to pursue business opportunities in Mexico. In both fields, Mexico has made significant investment in putting into place electronic-based systems which are improving significantly the transparency of procedures involved which, in turn, are resulting in transaction cost-savings for traders and added opportunities in submitting bids in due time for foreign participants.

To encourage the implementation of deregulation reforms at states and municipal levels, the Federal Government has signed deregulation co-operation agreements with all 31 Mexican States in which each state has committed to create and implement a regulatory reform programme similar to the one undertaken at the Federal level.

Although a constitutional amendment granted the Federal District of Mexico a similar status to that of the 31 States as of December 1997, the EDU and the Economic Deregulation Council worked with the Federal District to advance the regulatory reform agenda in the country's largest urban centre. The significant advances are mentioned in the background report on Government Capacity to Assure High Quality Regulation. It is further expected that the current and future administrations will continue along this path.

In accordance with WTO obligations, the Federal Government must take "reasonable measures" to ensure compliance by regional and local governments with international obligations.[28] The ongoing deregulation programme in Mexico seems to recognise the importance of these considerations. Public Seminars are also organised by SECOFI in order to reach a wide and diversified audience with the view to explain the objectives and means put into place under the deregulation programme.

While the third principle dealing with the avoidance of unnecessary trade restrictiveness is not formally included in the guiding principles adopted by Mexico under its deregulation programme, overall evidence suggests that related considerations are informally taken into consideration – and more so than in other OECD countries according to the Figure. However, there are a number of cases where Mexican import licence requirements are resulting in *de facto* import prohibitions, i.e. for used motor vehicles and used computer equipment. The actual uses of highly trade restrictive instruments suggest that the current set of guiding principles for the regulatory reform is incomplete and that an additional principle of "avoidance of unnecessary trade restrictiveness" should be adopted along with the other principles guiding the preparation of regulatory impact statements.

Mexican market openness might be further enhanced by making additional efforts with respect to the recognition of equivalence of other countries' regulations and conformity assessment systems, and reliance on internationally-harmonised standards as the basis of domestic regulations. The Mexican elaboration process of technical standards requires an explicit comparison with comparable international standards and an assessment of the degree of correspondence with them. Overall evidence suggests that Mexico is favourably disposed towards the adoption of international standards but the resource intensity implied for their evaluation acts as a real deterrent factor in view of ongoing fiscal restraint imperatives.

Limited progress has been achieved so far concerning the recognition of conformity assessment procedures performed in other countries. However, since January 1998 Mexico's grace period under NAFTA is over and the stage is now set to work towards reduction in duplicative certification procedures among NAFTA parties. It is however crucial for Mexico to ensure a wider geographical relationships in respect of mutual recognition agreements of conformity assessment procedures. Efforts will therefore be required in this direction. Ongoing negotiations for additional free trade agreements and other multi-country discussion under APEC and the FTAA offer opportunity to concretise positive developments in this field.

Moves towards regulatory harmonisation or mutual recognition of standards or conformity assessment procedures are promising steps, though the substantial commitments of time and resources required for such initiatives are exercising real constraint on the ability of Mexico to negotiate and conclude necessary international agreements. With the proposal to privatise the accreditation functions of conformity assessment bodies, a task currently performed exclusively by SECOFI, the latter will probably be able to free some resources and to reallocate them toward the more important task of negotiating MRAs for the recognition of other countries' regulatory measures and conformity assessment procedures.

Mexican competition law provides for equivalent treatment to foreign and domestic firms as a matter of procedure and substance. With respect to dealing with regulatory abuse which may give rise to market access issues, the competition law also appears to adequately address these concerns. In practice, however, the Mexican approach is weighted on the informal advocacy role of the FCC with less emphasis on the formal investigatory and remedial authority by the FCC. As the Mexican competition law is still relatively recent, this should be watched over time to see whether, or to what extent, this relative informality curtails its effectiveness as a means of dealing with market access problems arising from regulatory abuse.

## 4.2. The dynamic view: the pace and direction of change

Globalisation has dramatically altered the world paradigm for the conduct of international trade and investment, creating new competitive pressures in Mexico and elsewhere. At the same time, the progressive dismantling or lowering of traditional barriers to trade and increased relevance of "behind the border" measures to effective market access and presence has exposed national regulatory regimes to a degree of unprecedented international scrutiny by trade and investment partners, with the result that regulation is no longer, if ever it was, a purely "domestic" affair. Trade and investment policy communities have generally kept pace with these twin phenomena. Concrete steps to increase awareness of and effective adherence to the efficient regulation principles and deepen international co-operation on regulatory issues are encouraging trends in this context.

The economic transition staged in Mexico in the last decade and a half, which is extraordinary by any standards, clearly attests to the understanding by Mexican Authorities of the changing world economic paradigm. In particular, the significant privatisation programme implemented in Mexico in conjunction with the removal of previous restrictions on foreign direct investment and control over many Mexican industries, that used to be deemed as strategic, has already yielded significant opportunities for foreign traders and investors.

Increased reliance on inputs from domestic and foreign business communities is now fully recognised and structured for the pursuit of the deregulation programme and in the elaboration of technical standards. A business-driven approach to market-opening regulatory reform has already yielded concrete results and it should be maintained. As prior experience has shown, continued multilateral liberalisation of trade and investment should bolster future regulatory reform efforts.

### 4.3. Potential benefits and costs of further regulatory reform

The need for all governments to address market failures through sound regulatory action is an undisputed sovereign prerogative. Nonetheless, ill-conceived, excessively restrictive or burdensome regulation exacts a heavy price on commercial activity, domestic or foreign, and places a disproportionately heavy burden on small-and medium-sized enterprises. Foreign firms established in the Mexican market face the same regulatory burden as domestic firms.

Trade and investment friendly regulation need not undermine the promotion and achievement of legitimate Mexican policy objectives. High-quality regulation can be trade-neutral or market-opening, coupling consumer gains from enhanced market openness with more efficient realisation of domestic objectives in key areas such as the environment, health and safety. But it is doubtful that this can be achieved in the absence of purposeful, government-wide adherence to the principles of efficient regulation.

Market-opening regulation promises to promote the flow of goods, services, investment and technology between Mexico and trading partners. Expanded trade and investment flows generate important consumer benefits in terms of greater choice and lower prices, they raise the standards of performance of domestic firms through the impetus of greater competition and boost GDP. The transformation of the Mexican economic policies was instrumental in making Mexico one of the world's largest recipient of FDI among emerging economies, after China, during the 1990s (see Table 5). In 1997, Mexico received

Table 5. **Selected recipient countries of foreign direct investment**

|  | 1990 | 1991 | 1992 | 1993 | 1994 | 1995 | 1996 |
|---|---|---|---|---|---|---|---|
| World net inflows (billion US$) | 197.5 | 152.3 | 166.9 | 213.2 | 233.5 | 331.9 | 330.2 |
| % of world net inflows |  |  |  |  |  |  |  |
| China | 1.77 | 2.87 | 6.68 | 12.91 | 14.47 | 10.80 | 12.17 |
| **Mexico** | **1.33** | **3.13** | **2.63** | **2.06** | **4.70** | **2.87** | **2.31** |
| Brazil | 0.50 | 0.72 | 1.23 | 0.61 | 1.32 | 1.46 | 2.99 |
| Malaysia | 1.18 | 2.62 | 3.11 | 2.35 | 1.86 | 1.24 | 1.36 |
| Poland | 0.05 | 0.19 | 0.41 | 0.80 | 0.80 | 1.10 | 1.36 |
| India | 0.08 | 0.05 | 0.17 | 0.26 | 0.42 | 0.65 | 0.78 |

*Source:* World Development Indicators, 1998, The World Bank.

its highest level of inflows of foreign direct investment in fixed assets of the 1990s, reaching US$12.5 billion as already noted in Table 1.

With about two thirds of exports accounted for by manufactured goods, the Mexican export performance reflects the improved competitiveness of Mexican firms in international markets which itself is partly a reflection of the overall trade and investment liberalisation and domestic deregulation approaches pursued in recent years. The growing importance of trade is reflected in the number of exporting firms in Mexico which has increased from 25 609 to 43 023 firms between 1993 and 1997 for a 68% increase (see Table 6).

Reforms in customs procedures have already resulted in tangible benefits in terms of a drastic fall in the maximum clearance time and labour productivity gains for Customs Officials and overall improvement in terms of integrity. Current integrated Internet-based applications linking the majority of interested parties in trade transactions raise the prospects of additional savings in terms of quicker responding time among parties in completing forms or retrieving them for their correction or modifications and the potential elimination of all paper forms. Mexico is already among the leading countries in the implementation of an integrated electronic-based system and ongoing improvement programmes suggest that it will maintain this leadership in the foreseeable future.

Another regulatory area where Mexico seems to be among the leading countries in innovative applications of the Internet is for government procurement tendering and bidding procedures. Future developments by SECODAM of its COMPRANET Internet-based system offer the possibility of additional efficiency gains in terms of time and cost saved in retrieving and delivering electronically tendering and for submitting bidding.

Table 6. **Number of exporting firms in Mexico by sectors**

| Description | 1993 | 1997* |
|---|---|---|
| Fruit and vegetables | 2 176 | 2 836 |
| Flour, seeds, seasoning | 564 | 649 |
| Various products of animal/vegetable origin, food preparation | 789 | 1 288 |
| Various drinks | 172 | 313 |
| Minerals | 262 | 323 |
| Chemical products and others | 2 946 | 4 744 |
| Leather and leather products | 528 | 963 |
| Wood and wooden products | 881 | 1 711 |
| Textiles | 1 661 | 3 762 |
| Footwear | 532 | 1 183 |
| Mineral manufacturing and ceramic products | 1 149 | 2 144 |
| Glass and glass products | 538 | 1 007 |
| Steel | 1 680 | 2 856 |
| Metal and metal products | 1 621 | 2 682 |
| Capital equipment | 3 072 | 4 587 |
| Machines and electric material | 1 879 | 2 651 |
| Automobile equipment and accessories | 847 | 1 601 |
| Precision instruments | 1 401 | 2 054 |
| Furniture, light articles and pre-fabricated construction materials | 1 116 | 2 822 |
| Toys and sports articles | 356 | 630 |
| Electronics | 1 439 | 2 217 |
| **Total** | **25 609** | **43 023** |

* Data up to end-November 1997.
*Source*: SECOFI.

## 4.4. Policy options for consideration

*Continue to foster good regulatory practices already instituted in areas such as transparency; and make public through the Internet the regulatory impact assessments (RIAs) prepared for proposed regulations.* While Mexico is well advanced in disseminating Federal formalities, regulations and draft regulations through the Internet, the public availability of RIAs for all proposed regulations would further assist the public, including foreign participants, in understanding potential implications of those regulations. It would also act as an additional check and balance feature to minimise potential risk of regulatory capture.

*Take measures to ensure uniformity in the preparation of RIAs and in the implementation of regulatory requirements by all Federal and Regulatory Agencies.* The requirement to prepare a regulatory impact assessment for proposed regulations having a potential impact on business activities is still very recent and there is the need to ensure that this regulatory requirement is uniformly implemented by all Federal Ministries and Regulatory Agencies.

*Complement the current sets of guiding principles for the preparation of regulatory impact assessment with the additional principle of "avoidance of unnecessary trade restrictiveness".* This would allow to systematically check proposed regulations and legislation against a more comprehensive set of principles when regulatory impact statements are carried out.

*Heighten awareness of and encourage respect for the OECD efficient regulation principles in state and local regulatory activities affecting international trade and investment.* Given the important responsibilities of states and cities, the potential exists for conflicting regulations that would frustrate the free circulation of goods and services within the Mexican territory and deregulation reforms sponsored at the Federal level. With improved transparency in the preparation and adoption of Federal regulations and procedures, the absence or lack of transparency in the preparation and adoption of regulations and procedures at the state and municipal levels will also become more visible.

*Intensify efforts to use existing international standards and to participate more actively in the development of internationally-harmonised standards as the basis of domestic regulations.* Reliance on internationally-harmonised measures as the basis of domestic regulations can facilitate the expansion of domestic production capacity and support the export-orientation of Mexican firms.

*Seek to ensure that bilateral or regional approaches to regulatory co-operation are designed and implemented in ways which will encourage broader multilateral application.* Mutual recognition of regulations or conformity assessment procedures and other approaches to intergovernmental regulatory co-operation offer promising avenues for the lowering of regulatory barriers to trade and investment. Efforts carried out under regional agreements should actively be pursued in a broader perspective of international organisations with multilateral applications.

### 4.5. Managing regulatory reform

Mexico's accession to the GATT in 1986 and the negotiation of NAFTA in particular have had profound impact on domestic policy and regulatory formulation processes in Mexico. These trade and investment agreements have acted as catalysts for domestic regulatory reforms and provided strong policy anchors which have contributed to minimise the adverse effects of the crisis in 1995 and helped to stage an impressive recovery. These agreements were instrumental in locking in policy commitments to regulatory reform regarding both generic and sector-specific themes and provided transparent benchmarks by which to gauge progress towards reform objectives. Steady pursuit of additional international commitments in the context of the WTO and comprehensive regional free trade agreements can further strengthen the ongoing process of regulatory reform.

At the same time, time-lag between fast-changing competitive conditions and government-negotiated outcomes can be significant, pointing to the need to supplement these activities with domestically-driven efforts to achieve and maintain optimal market openness. In some cases, identifying and addressing recurrent patterns of trade friction through more focused, systematic application of the efficient regulation principles may dramatically reduce the scope for trade conflicts in the first instance. This alone should generate important gains to government in terms of encouraging optimal allocation of time and resources to pursue given policy objectives, be it at the multilateral, regional or bilateral level. When regulatory styles and content succeed in averting trade disputes altogether, net gains accrue to both Mexican consumers and global economic welfare.

# NOTES

1. See the submission of the Mexican Government in the context of the 1997 WTO Trade Policy Review. Mexico indicated that it had unilaterally eliminated tariffs on an MFN basis on 1 200 products, thus increasing the number of duty-free products from 414 in 1993 to 1 658 in 1997. This tariff elimination primarily concerned inputs and machinery used in agricultural, chemical, electrical, electronic, textiles and publishing sectors.

2. See in particular OECD "Open Markets Matter. The benefits of Trade and Investment Liberalisation", Paris, 1998, OECD "The environmental effects of Trade", Paris, 1994, and the 1995 Report on Trade and Environment to the OECD Council at Ministerial level.

3. See related discussion in Chapter 2 (Regulatory Quality and Public Sector Reform), The OECD Report on Regulatory Reform, Vol. II: Thematic Studies (OECD, 1997).

4. See OECD 1996, Trade Liberalisation Policies in Mexico, Paris, p. 48.

5. *Source*: Confederación de Asociaciones de Agentes Aduanales de la República Mexicana (CAAAREM).

6. NAFTA and the five other Free Trade Agreements, respectively with: Colombia and Venezuela (G-3); Costa Rica; Bolivia; Nicaragua; and Chile. Mexico also grants unilateral preferences to a number of developing countries under the Generalised System of Preferences.

7. Mexico is currently negotiating free trade agreements with: El Salvador, Guatemala, Honduras, Panama, Jamaica, Equator, Peru, Trinidad and Tobago, MERCOSUR and Israel.

8. Concerning secondary petrochemical products, the amendment of the Foreign Investment Law identified the secondary petrochemicals which can be produced privately and clarified the principles for private and foreign investment in the sector. Except for eight listed petrochemical products, all oil derivatives can be privately produced. For existing plants which are to be regrouped into saleable units, private investment is allowed up to 49% of the capital, the Mexican government keeping a majority share holding. For investment in new plants, private and foreign ownership is permitted up to 100% and the approval process for start-ups has been shortened. *Source*: OECD *Economic Surveys* 1998 *Mexico*, p. 77.

9. See the submission of the Mexican Government in the context of the 1997 WTO Trade Policy Review, p. 198.

10. The European Union requested WTO consultations in which it claims that Mexico applies Cost-Insurance-Freight (CIF) value as the basis of customs valuation for imports originating in non-NAFTA countries, while it applies Free-On-Board (FOB) value for imports originating in NAFTA countries. The EU alleges that Mexican procedures are inconsistent with WTO obligations regarding regional trading arrangements. Consultations are following their courses.

11. See Mexico's services schedules in GATS/SC/56/Suppl. 3, 26 February 1998.

12. See WTO 1997, Trade Policy Review, Mexico, pp. 128-129.

13. In 1997, import licenses were required for 184 tariff lines, *e.g.* crude oil and basic petrochemicals, certain pharmaceuticals, arms and explosives, motor vehicles, drugs, and numerous used goods such as clothing, machinery and computer equipment. Even under NAFTA, Mexico was able to retain the import license requirement for new motor vehicles (for a period of 5 years for 10 items and 10 years for 20 items) as well as used motor vehicles (for 25 years for 30 tariff lines). An additional 90 tariff lines in used goods require permits for 10 years. Finally, 17 tariff lines remain prohibited on the 1997 Mexican tariff schedule. *Source*: World Trade Organisation, Trade Policy Review Mexico 1997, p. 52.

14. See TBT Articles 2.7 and 6.1 and SPS Article 4.

15. One example was the creation in 1994 of AVANTEL, a venture between MCI Communications Corporation and Grupo Financiero Banamex-Accival (Banacci) to offer long distance and other telecommunications services in Mexico. MCI owns 45% of the company.

16. On cross-border supply, Mexico agreed "to place no limitations, except on market access, that would require international traffic to be routed through the facilities of an enterprise with a concession granted by the Ministry of Communications and Transport." See Mexico Trade Policy Review, WT/TPR/S/29 p. 143.

17. Concessions (authorisations by SCT to use certain parts of the radioelectric spectrum) are required for the construction of public telecommunications networks; the establishment of private networks using that portion of the spectrum designated as "determined use"; the launching of satellites, and the use of satellite frequency bands; the use of foreign satellite frequencies for national service; and experimental operations. Concessions are renewable and normally granted for a period of twenty years. See "Regulatory Structure" by InfoMex Market Research on the Internet.

18. Ley Federal De Telecomunicaciones, Chapter III, Section III, Articles 24 and 25.

19. By 1998, MCI Communications, partner in AVANTEL, was vigorously objecting to what it deemed to be discriminatory elements of Mexico's regulatory regime, notably "the interconnection fees" (covering settlement rates, termination rates, or call-completion charges) paid by long-distance companies to Telmex for routing incoming international calls through its network to the final customer and rules allowing Telmex to charge long-distance competitors 58% of revenue earned on every incoming international call. Because Mexico receives 2.6 times as many international calls as it places, revenue from incoming calls is huge: estimated at about $850 million in fees in 1996. MCI threatened to cancel $900 million in planned additional investment in Mexico unless the rules were changed and requested USTR to challenge the fee structure in the WTO. Similarly, AT&T, partner in Alestra, formally requested USTR to initiate WTO dispute proceedings on Mexico's telecommunications policies in September 1998. See, for example, "AT&T Calls on USTR To Act Against Mexico On Telecom Policies" in Inside US Trade, 18 September 1998.

20. Telmex's stated justification for the surcharge is to fund infrastructure buildout and universal service.

21. AT&T, for example, has charged that "Telmex is able to extract [these] enormous payments because the Mexican regulatory system, unlike the regulatory systems in most European countries, gives Telmex effective bottleneck control over the termination of US international switched services in Telmex's home country." See "AT&T Moves to Stop Telmex-Sprint Venture" in The Industry Standard: The Newsmagazine of the Internet Economy, 13 August 1998.

22. In the continued absence of such regulations, Telmex has maintained that these services remain unlawful in Mexico. See "AT&T Calls on USTR to Act Against Mexico on Telecom Policies", op. cit.

23. A US firm, IUSACEL, introduced cellular telephony services in Mexico in 1989. In 1990, a subsidiary company of Telmex named Telcel joined the market. Together, these two companies serve the entire area of Mexico City as well as some states. The rest of the country is served by eight concessionaire companies operating in nine different regions. No further concessions are planned in this sector in which foreign investment participation of up to 100% of property is permitted (prior authorisation from the CNIE is required after foreign participation exceeds 49%).

24. See WTO, "Trade Policy Review of Mexico", WT/TPR/S/29.

25. Constitucion Politica de los Estados Unidos Mexicanos; Ley de Vias Generales de Comunicacion; Ley de a Inversion Extranjera; Reglamento de Telecomunicaciones

26. See WTO, "Trade Policy Review of Mexico", WT/TPR/S/29.

27. See "Canada's International Market Access Priorities – 1998" at http://www.dfait-maeci.gc.ca.

28. GATT jurisprudence sheds light on how this obligation has generally been interpreted. A 1992 GATT panel report on US measures affecting alcoholic and malt beverages examined the application of Article XXIV in relation to various measures of US state and local governments relating to imported beer, wine and cider. The panel ruled, inter alia, that some state measures were discriminatory and that the United States had not demonstrated to the panel that conditions for the application of Article XXIV:12 had been met. See DS23/R, adopted on 19 June 1992, in Basic Instruments and Selected Documents, 39S/206.

# BACKGROUND REPORT
# ON REGULATORY REFORM
# IN THE TELECOMMUNICATIONS INDUSTRY[*]

---

* This report was principally prepared by **Darryl Biggar** and **Patrick Hughes**, Administrator of the Directorate for Financial, Fiscal, and Enterprise Affairs, with the participation of **Bernard J. Phillips**, Division Head, of the OECD's Division for Competition Law and Policy, and **Dimitri Ypsilanti** and **Patrick Xavier** of the Directorate on Science, Technology, and Industry. It has benefited from extensive comments provided by colleagues throughout the OECD Secretariat, by the Government of Mexico, and by Member countries as part of the peer review process. This report was peer reviewed in March 1999 by the OECD's Working Party on Telecommunication and Information Services Policies and by the Competition Law and Policy Committee.

# TABLE OF CONTENTS

## Tables

## Figures

# 1. THE TELECOMMUNICATIONS SECTOR IN MEXICO

## 1.1. The national context for telecommunications policies

In the past ten years, the regulatory regime in the Mexican telecommunications sector has undergone significant reform as part of a broad-based effort designed to move away from protection and central control toward a market-based economy. This reform has transformed the telecommunications sector from a state-owned monopoly industry with relatively weak performance, to a sector increasingly reliant on competition to deliver benefits to users and consumers. To date the reform has led to significant growth in competition in long-distance telecommunications services and has laid a foundation for competition in local services.

The telecommunications sector in Mexico, with around US$7.6 billion in revenue is the 12th largest in the OECD, ranking slightly behind the Netherlands (US$7.9 billion) and slightly ahead of Sweden (US$6.9 billion).[1] Telmex, the incumbent telecommunications operator in Mexico, is the 20th largest telephone carrier in the world (10th largest outside the US), roughly comparable in size to KPN in the Netherlands, and a bit larger than Bell Canada and Telia of Sweden.[2] Telmex is one of the largest companies in Mexico, representing 25-30% of the Mexican stock market's capitalisation.

In 1990, many performance indicators for the telecommunications sector in Mexico showed significant room for improvement: telephone penetration in 1990 was about 6.4 lines per 100 persons, the density of public payphones was 0.5 per thousand inhabitants, the percentage of network digitalisation was 29%, and the waiting time for new line installation was two years.[3] Over the subsequent eight years, substantial progress was made. By 1997, the density of public payphones was 2.7 per thousand inhabitants,[4] the waiting time period for a new line was 27 days (substantially less in Mexico City), and 96.7% of the Mexican network was digitalised.[5]

This progress was made in spite of several adverse macroeconomic factors, including lower-than-average GDP per capita,[6] high population growth, a skewed income distribution and, most importantly, a substantial macroeconomic shock in 1995.

In part as a result of these adverse factors, Mexico's penetration of telecommunications access lines per capita remains very low. In 1997, there were only 9.8 access lines per 100 inhabitants in Mexico,[7] almost half the next-lowest of 19.4 in Poland, and well below the OECD average of 48.9 lines per 100 inhabitants.[8] Furthermore, prices for telecommunications services in Mexico remain relatively high. According to the OECD basket methodology, prices for telecommunications services in Mexico are among the highest in the OECD.[9]

In the past few years many key steps have been taken to establish a regulatory regime in Mexico setting out the framework for competition in the telecommunications industry. Virtually all telecommunications markets are now open to competition and in some markets competition has developed rapidly. In the long distance market new entrants gained market share more quickly than in many other OECD countries. In the medium term, with certain adjustments to the existing regulatory regime, the challenges Mexico faces, such as low penetration, present significant opportunities for the growth of rival networks, and the further development of network competition, to the ultimate benefit of Mexican users and consumers.

## 1.2. General features of the regulatory regime, telecommunications market and market participants

### 1.2.1. Brief history

Prior to 1990, telecommunications were provided by a monopoly incumbent, Teléfonos de México ("Telmex") which was nationalised in 1972.[10] Throughout the 1970's and 1980's, the government maintained a controlling interest, but partial private ownership remained and Telmex shares were quoted and traded on the Mexican stock exchange. During this period, the quality of service provided by Telmex was very poor and penetration rates were low.

In 1988, the Mexican government embarked on a major investment to expand and modernise the network in preparation for privatisation, and later, the opening of competition. Important events in the history of regulatory reform are outlined in Box 1.

In 1990, Telmex was partially privatised. The government sold a controlling interest to a consortium led by a Mexican conglomerate, Group Carso, and including Southwestern Bell and France Telecom as foreign partners.[11] As part of the privatisation, Telmex was granted a new concession containing many important provisions that established the foundation of a new regulatory regime for telecommunications in Mexico. The concession was granted for 50 years, from the date of the original concession, 10 March 1976. The new concession expires in 2026.

The concession includes provisions relating to universal service, price controls, quality of service, competition safeguards, and rules regarding accounting separation. The concession maintained a monopoly for Telmex in long distance and international telephony until August 1996, to allow Telmex time to achieve network expansion targets and to "rebalance" its rate structure – i.e., reduce long distance rates and increase local rates in a revenue neutral fashion.

The concession was not exclusive in regard to other services. Entry into wireless, paging, trunking, VSAT networks, customer premises equipment and value added services was permitted. Entry into local service was also permitted, but no concessions were granted.

Quality of service requirements for the first four years of the concession were set out in an annex to the concession itself. The concession specifies that quality of service targets for subsequent periods of four years are to be set through negotiation between the Ministry and Telmex. At the end of 1994 and concurrent with the peso crisis, the government and Telmex agreed on a set of less onerous performance targets.

At the same time, Telmex delayed planned rate rebalancing in line with government policies in response to the crisis.[12] During this period network expansion dropped off sharply to a level that was insufficient even to keep up with population growth.

Competition in wireless telephone services began in the early 1990s when duopoly cellular concessions were granted for nine regional markets throughout the country. In each of the nine regions, two concessions were issued, one reserved to the wireline incumbent while the second was issued to a competitor. Telmex's entry into cellular was accomplished through a subsidiary, Telcel. This market structure is parallel to what was introduced in cellular communications in Canada and the US.

Before the end of the long-distance monopoly period, the Mexican government implemented an entirely new telecommunications law, the Federal Telecommunications Law (the "FTL").[13] The FTL completed the foundation for the introduction of competition that was first sketched out in the Telmex concession. The FTL also foresaw the establishment of a new regulatory authority. Key features of this law and the Telmex concession are described in the appendix.

Throughout 1995 and 1996 concessions were granted to a number of new entrants for fixed domestic and international long-distance services. In late 1995, Telmex and the new long distance carriers initiated private negotiations to establish interconnection rates. As no agreement could be reached, and as stipulated in the Telmex concession, the regulatory authority stepped in. In a resolution of April 1996, the SCT set the interconnection tariffs to be applied for origination and termination of long-distance charges during 1997 and 1998.

This resolution was challenged on 4 October 1996, in a formal action filed by all new long distance entrants. After an initial industry hearing hosted by the authorities in December, Cofetel delayed the resolution of the disagreement for more than a year. A court injunction ultimately ordered the authorities to answer the carriers' petition. This resulted in Cofetel issuing a resolution on 11 March 1998, backing the SCT's previous interconnection resolutions of July 1994 and April 1996. Under these circumstances, on

> ### Box 1. Important events in the regulatory reform of the telecommunications sector
>
> - In August 1990, the *Secretaria de Communicacions y Transports* (SCT) agreed to a new concession for Telmex, providing Telmex with a monopoly in domestic and international long distance until 1996.
> - In October 1990, a new regulatory framework (*Reglamento de Telecommunicaciones*) was adopted which spelled out SCT's responsibilities and provided for the grant of new concessions in all areas except those reserved for the government.
> - In 1993 the Foreign Investment Law enhanced foreign investment participation in the telecommunication sector. Foreign investment of up to 49% ownership of capital stock of operators of a fixed network was permitted. Higher levels of foreign investment were permitted in cellular carriers, provided a favourable resolution from the National Commission of Foreign Investment was obtained.
> - On 1 July 1994, SCT published a resolution on how interconnection agreements between long distance carriers and the incumbent were to be established. The same resolution established a calendar for the opening of equal access competition, beginning with 60 cities in 1997, and spreading to the whole country by 2000. The resolution also established that interconnection would be cost-oriented and in line with international norms and benchmarks.
> - In March of 1995, the Mexican Constitution was modified to allow foreign private investment in satellite communications.
> - On 7 June 1995, the Federal Telecommunications Law (FTL) was enacted, substituting in large part the old "*Ley de Vías Generales de Comunicación*" which had applied since 1940.
> - On 26 October 1995 and 5 January 1996, SCT published the rules under which concessions would be granted to long-distance (interstate) operators and local networks, respectively. During late 1995 and 1996, concessions were granted to new entrants into fixed domestic and international long-distance services.
> - On 26 April 1996, following the failure of the carriers to reach agreement (filed with SCT in March 1996), the SCT issued a resolution determining the interconnection charges for long-distance service to be applied during 1997 and 1998, and establishing that the charges for "special projects" needed to provide interconnection would be determined by an expert hired by all long distance carriers.
> - On 21 June 1996, the Long Distance Service Rules were published together with the new national numbering and signaling plans.
> - On 9 August 1996, a sector specific regulator, the Federal Telecommunication Agency ("Cofetel") was set up by Presidential Decree. Late November the same year the first auction for paging services took place.
> - On 11 December 1996, Cofetel published rules governing the provision of international long-distance services, setting out the proportional return system. On 16 December 1996, the regulation governing resellers of pay phones was implemented.
> - On 1 January 1997, competition began in those long distance services that required interconnection.
> - During 1997, Cofetel auctioned spectrum for the purposes of providing microwave point to point and point to multi-point links (10, 14, and 23 GHz), for fixed or mobile wireless access, local wireless telephony and pay TV and Audio services (MMDS).
> - In August 1997, Cofetel published the regulation governing communication via satellite (*reglamento de comunicaciones vía satélite*). In the same month Satmex was privatised.
> - On 23 October 1997, Cofetel published the Local Service Rules.
> - In December 1997, the competition authority concluded that Telmex had "substantial market power" and in March 1998 it confirmed its resolution.
> - During 1998, Cofetel auctioned spectrum for the purposes of providing land mobile radiocommunications systems, point-to-point links (37-38 GHz) and narrowband personal communication services.
> - In December 1998, Cofetel published a resolution setting out the interconnection charges to apply for 1999 and 2000. Interconnection charges were lowered, and a system of calling-party pays introduced for mobile. In addition Cofetel published rules for accounting separation, reductions to the number of local service areas and a program to expand national numbers from 8 to 10 digits, according to the basic numbering plan.

2 April 1998, Avantel filed an *amparo* against the 11 March 1998 Resolution. The District Court granted Avantel a suspension of the relevant payments until the merits of the *amparo* are resolved.

In August 1996, competition was permitted in non-switched national and international long-distance services. In the same month, a new sector-specific regulator – *the Comisión Federal de Telecomunicaciones* ("Cofetel") was created by delegation of the powers of the SCT, through presidential decree. In December 1996, Cofetel established a "proportional return" system for international traffic under which all international carriers would receive a share of the in-bound traffic in relation to their share of outbound international traffic.

Competition in the Mexican long distance market began on 1 January 1997, when six new carriers started to operate.[14] Competitive entry into domestic and international long distance quickly put downward pressure on rates and erosion in the incumbent's market share. By the end of 1997 the new entrants had gained 18.8% of the domestic long distance market and 31.6% of the international market. This represents a rapid erosion of the incumbent's market share relative to the experience in other OECD countries.[15]

Throughout 1997 and 1998, customers in the 100 largest cities opening to competition were polled to determine their preferred long-distance carrier. This process, known as "pre-subscription" defined for each customer his or her default long-distance carrier.[16] Non-voting customers remained, by default, with Telmex. By the end of 1998, 6.7 million users had either actively chosen their carrier or defaulted to Telmex. This represents 80% of the 8.2 million lines that are open to competition. (Approximately 83% of the installed lines in the country are open to long-distance competition.)

As in many other countries, the introduction of competition has been associated with high-profile disputes and litigation as both the incumbent and the entrants seek to clearly establish their legal rights and to use all political and legal mechanisms at their disposal to influence regulatory decisions in their favour. These disputes have often given rise to legal injunctions. In Mexico, any act of authority deemed to violate the constitutional rights of a plaintiff can be suspended by means of an *amparo* (injunction) until the underlying merits of the case are resolved in court. A*mparos* are not class actions – only the plaintiff is granted relief. Industry-wide or class action suits, with their promise of generalised regulatory correction, do not exist in Mexico.

As an example, the 1990 Telmex concession set out a requirement that interconnecting operators would be required to pay the costs incurred by Telmex necessary to establish and maintain interconnection. In the April 1996 ruling (at the same time as determining the interconnection charges that would apply), SCT set out a procedure under which the costs of investment projects needed to provide interconnection services (the so-called "special projects") would be scrutinised by an international expert to determine their validity. Bellcore was hired for that purpose and decided that the amount due was US$422 million dollars. Cofetel issued the respective resolution on 28 May 1997, including the formula for distribution of this payment amongst all the long-distance carriers including LADA (Telmex's long-distance arm), based on their relative usage of the projects. Alestra, Avantel, and Miditel appealed these charges. Currently, none of the competing long-distance carriers are paying for these special projects pending the resolution of this issue.

At the time of the introduction of competition, Telmex still had not completely rebalanced its prices, in part due to the delay in the rate of rebalancing during the 1995 crisis. Therefore, in the first two years following the introduction of competition (from January 1996 until the first quarter of 1998) local service prices increased rapidly in real terms until they reached the individual price-caps originally scheduled for 1996. At the same time, and in accordance with the overall price-cap on Telmex's operations, Telmex substantially lowered domestic and international long-distance prices. Revenues from local service have risen rapidly as a portion of total revenues, from about 40% in 1996 to about 60% in 1998, while long distance revenues (domestic and international) have fallen from about 57% in 1996 to about 34% in 1999.

During the second half of 1997, the competition authority (the "CFC") carried out an *ex officio* investigation, which concluded in December 1997[17] that Telmex has substantial market power in five markets: local telephony, interconnection services, national long distance, international long distance, and the resale of long distance. The CFC resolution was confirmed in March 1998, following a Telmex petition for reconsideration. Cofetel is authorised by the FTL to impose specific obligations on concessionaires that are deemed by the CFC to have substantial market power. Cofetel has publicly declared that the new obligations will include provisions for avoiding predatory pricing in competitive markets and to restrict supra-competitive pricing in less competitive markets as well as additional conditions on quality and information. Telmex has filed an injunction against the decision of the CFC, which is currently "on hold" pending the decision by Cofetel as to the nature of the new regulations. In March 1999, some competitive carriers formally asked to be included in the process of forming these new regulations on the grounds that dominant carrier restrictions have an effect on the whole market. However, Cofetel believes that because the FTL does not mention such participation, to do so would open the decisions to legal challenge.

Progress in opening the market for local service to competition has been somewhat slower than in the case of the long-distance market. The SCT published procedures for applying for new concessions for local networks in January 1996. The local service rules were published in October 1997. In late 1997 and early 1998, Cofetel auctioned a substantial amount of spectrum suitable for the provision of PCS and wireless local loop applications. The winning bidders at these auctions received concessions to provide fixed or mobile local services.

Competition in the local telephony market is expected to begin in 1999. To date, four firms have been granted a concession for fixed-wire local service. A further eight firms have acquired spectrum through the PCS and WLL auctions, and six have received local-service concessions (the remaining two have not yet paid the amount they bid for the spectrum). One firm, Pegaso, launched commercial operations in February 1999 with a nation-wide mobile PCS network. (Commercial operations of Pegaso have so far been limited to the Tijuana area. Its operations in Monterrey and Mexico City are due to begin in mid to late 1999). Another two firms, Axtel and MaxCom, began commercial operations in April 1999 using wireless technology. Altogether the new local operators have committed to 9.5 million new lines, which offers the promise of doubling the number of telecommunications lines in Mexico.

### 1.2.2. Market participants

As mentioned, the dominant incumbent telecommunications operator is *Teléfonos De México, S.A. de C.V.* ("Telmex"). In 1997 Telmex received around US$7.6 billion in revenue, had 55 000 employees and maintained around 9.2 million access lines.

Telmex is the second largest company in Mexico, the largest company listed on the Mexican Stock Exchange, and is the largest non-government employer in the country. Telmex's subsidiary Telcel, is also the largest mobile carrier, with total revenue of about US$521 million in 1997. Other subsidiaries of Telmex provide long-distance and other services.[18] Telmex also owns 49% of a cable TV provider.[19]

Telmex has achieved an operating income of between 14.5% and 19.4% of total assets (in real terms) over the 1993 to 1997 period.[20] Telmex weathered the macroeconomic crisis fairly well, in part because its revenues from in-bound international traffic were not directly affected, and in fact, appreciated in relative value given the decline in the value of the Mexican peso on international markets. For the last several years, Telmex has been engaged in a share buy-back program which has returned more than US$1.5 billion to the shareholders per year. Telmex has announced plans to purchase around US$2 billion of shares during 1999. Despite being the 12th largest telephone company in the world (by revenue), Telmex's stock market capitalisation place it second in the world, next only to BT.

Telmex currently has the largest market share in local, domestic and international long distance and mobile markets in Mexico. (Telmex provides around 100% of all local telephony, 80% of domestic and international long-distance telephony, and 60% of mobile telephony). Telmex completed construction of a 30 000 km fibre optic network (*e.g.* trunks between exchanges) in 1995, which replaced a less reliable and lower capacity microwave network. An intercontinental submarine segment known as "Columbus II" supports the new long distance network. Through an international alliance signed in 1995, Telmex co-operates with Sprint (a major US long distance carrier) to provide seamless international services between Mexico and the US since 1996 (including for example voice, video and data) and, through a joint venture company, long distance services in the US since August 1998.[21] Through the Sprint alliance, Telmex also has access to "Global One" and provides 800 services.

As of March 1999, 17 firms held concessions to operate in long-distance domestic and international markets. The first major new entrant in the long distance market was Avantel, established by MCI and Banamex. It has built a 5 365 km high capacity fibre optic network based on MCI's technology and Concert services with three main switching centres. The second major entrant was Alestra, established by AT&T and the Mexican group Alfa (Bancomer-VISA joined as a second Mexican partner). It has built a 4 596 km high capacity fibre optic network employing AT&T technology including three 5ESS digital switches in Mexico City, Guadalajara, and Monterrey.

Of the 15 long-distance concessionaires (not counting the incumbent carrier Telmex with its main regional subsidiary Telnor), eight have commenced operation: Avantel, Alestra, Iusatel, Marcatel, Miditel, Protel, Bestel and RSL ComNet. The seven remaining carriers, who are currently in the process of building infrastructure are: Maxcom, Intelcom, LadiMex, Presto Telecomunicaciones, Axtel, Telereunión and Unión Telefónica Nacional.

Concessions have been granted to six companies that will start competition in local markets (Maxcom, Megacable, Resetel, Unitel, Axtel and Avantel servicios locales). These companies have promised to invest more than US$1.2 billion in investment over the next five years. In 1998 licenses to operate PCS and wireless local loop were granted in nine concession areas. Three firms (Maxcom, Extensa and Axtel) were granted concessions and have ambitious five year plans relying on a combination of wireline and wireless technologies. Maxcom's five-year plan calls for 500 000 new lines covering 25% of the population. 40% of the lines will involve wireless technology. Extensa's five-year plan involves coaxial and wireless technology, covers 40 cities, and involves 1 900 miles of fiber-optic cable. Axtel's five-year plan involves 2 million lines, using mostly wireless technology for 210 cities.[22] Overall, the new local players have committed to building 9.5 million new lines over the next 5 years.

In mobile, the largest operator is Telcel, a subsidiary of Telmex that provides a nation-wide mobile service. Telcel's market share is about 60%, similar to the market share of the largest mobile carrier in most OECD countries.[23] The largest competing mobile operator is Iusacell, majority-owned by Bell Atlantic. Iusacell has cellular operations in four of the nine regions in Mexico (covering about 70% of the population). Iusacell also holds a long-distance concession and facilities. The number of cellular subscribers in Mexico was 1 million in October 1996 reached about 2.3 million by May 1998 and (projected) 3.3 million by the end of 1998 – though penetration rates remain low compared to other OECD countries.[24]

Satellite providers are an additional source of potential competition in telecommunication service markets. In 1990, a decentralized state-owned organization named *Telecomunicaciones de México* (known as Telecomm) was created to provide telegraphy, packet switching, microwave, and satellite services. It is also a signatory to Intelsat and Inmarsat services. In 1995, the Constitution was modified to allow private investment in satellite communications. Later, during 1996 and the first half of 1997, Telecomm was divested from its satellite services, to create the company *Satélites Mexicanos* S.A. ("Satmex") which was privatized on August 1997 through a public tender. The assets of this company are three modern geostationary satellites using the Ku and C bands to provide services in Latin America and selected cities of the US. The L band transponders provide mobile services within the Mexican territory.[25]

In December 1997, a concession was granted to GE Capital Spacenet Communications Services de México. This concession allows the company to install, operate and exploit a public telecommunications network to offer services of transmission and reception of signal, writing, image, voice, sound, or any other form of information for private networks. Cofetel has given a favourable opinion to granting companies like Iridium, Globalstar and Orbcomm a concession to exploit the rights of emission and reception of signals from frequency bands associated with their respective satellite systems. The approval of the SCT is still pending.

Public payphones have been open to competition since a *reglamento* governing payphones was issued on 16 December 1996. To date 29 permits have been granted to commercialise the service and Cofetel is processing 18 additional applications. According to the business plans of the permit holders, investment in this service for the next five years will be close to 400 million pesos (US$40 million) with the installation of 150 000 pay phones, additional to those installed by Telmex. The most ambitious of new pay phone operator, a firm called "World Centre of Video Conferences" intends to install 25 000 and US$60 million worth of pay phones in 200 cities over three years. Another firm, Aditel, intends to install 300 telephones in subway cars and stations in Mexico City

Competition has existed in trunking and paging services since 1991. In trunking services there are 48 concessionaires, 12 provide local services and 26 regional service covering 215 cities and the main highways. In paging there are 107 concessionaires, 62 provide local services, 30 regional services and 15 national service. They provide service in 86 cities. As Table 1 shows, the penetration of paging has increased significantly since competition began.[26]

Table 1.   **Growth in trunking and paging services**

|  | 1991 | 1992 | 1993 | 1994 | 1995 | 1996 | 1997* | 1998** |
|---|---|---|---|---|---|---|---|---|
| Trunking (thousands of users) | 3 | 15 | 30 | 54 | 64 | 79 | 111 | 135 |
| Paging (thousands of users) | 53 | 88 | 129 | 167 | 207 | 273 | 445 | 544 |

\*   Preliminary.
\*\*  Estimated.
*Source:*   Cofetel.

Competition has existed in value-added services since 1990. Since 1995, 280 *Constancias de Registro* for value added services have been granted. The services considered by Cofetel to be value-added services are: audiotext, electronic data interchange, videotext, teletext, access to internet, remote data processing, electronic data mail and facsimile, voice mail, and remote access to databases.

## 2.   REGULATORY STRUCTURES AND THEIR REFORM[27]

### 2.1. Regulatory institutions and processes

Reform of sectoral regulatory structures were an important part of the initiative to introduce market forces into the telecommunications industry. Prior to reform, telecommunications regulation was the responsibility of the *Secretaria de Communicaciones y Transportes* ("SCT") – a ministry that has a broad mandate encompassing not only telecommunications but also highways, railways, aviation, ports, the postal service, and the national merchant marine. Within SCT was the *Subsecretaria de Comunicaciones* under which telecommunications was regulated. For the first five years of the Telmex concession, SCT was the sole regulator.

On 9 August 1996, the *Comisión Federal de Telecomunicaciones* ("Cofetel") was created through a Presidential Decree published in the *Official Gazette*. The then SCT Under-secretary was appointed to be its chair. Cofetel is autonomous from but not independent of the SCT. Cofetel derives its powers through delegation of the powers of the SCT, as set out in the Presidential Decree. Cofetel's budget is determined separately from the budget for the SCT.

Table 2. **A synopsis of telecommunications regulation in Mexico**

| Category | Regulatory restrictions | Notes |
|---|---|---|
| **Entry regulations** | | |
| Facilities-based carrier | Entry on the basis of a concession. The FTL requires that certain conditions and obligations be imposed on concessionaires. Concessions specify network coverage and investment obligations. | No limit on the number of concessions, permissions or registrations. |
| Reseller | Entry on the basis of a permit. | To date no requests for permits for pure resale have been granted. Cofetel says that requests for permits will be granted once the respective regulation is in place. |
| Value-added service provider | Entry on the basis of registration. | |
| Line-of-business restrictions | Telmex cannot exploit, directly or indirectly, any concession for television services to the public in the country. Separate application and approval is required whenever a business plan is changed. | |
| Foreign ownership restrictions | No concessionaire can be majority foreign owned, except in the case of cellular telephone services. | Limited rights shares do not count in calculating foreign ownership proportions. |
| **Price controls** | | |
| Telmex | A system of price caps on total average revenue, allowing flexibility on the individual prices. The price-cap rises with inflation less a productivity factor. All prices must at least cover incremental cost. Price of residential local service should not be above its incremental cost. | |
| Other operators | Prices must be registered. | All carriers' prices are publicly available on the Internet. |
| **Interconnection controls** | | |
| Telmex | The obligation to interconnect is set out in the Telmex concession and the FTL. Prices are set by Cofetel within 60 days in the event of failure to reach agreement between the parties. All parties must allow desegregated access to services, capacity, and functions of their networks based on non-discriminatory rates and must respect reciprocity of rates and conditions for concessionaires providing each other similar services, capacities, or functions. | Cofetel believes that in the absence of alternative mechanisms to support residential service and given limitation to further increases in local rates, interconnection charges should contribute to a deficit on Telmex's local residential service. |
| Spectrum allocation | Concessions for the use of spectrum are auctioned. | |
| Numbering policy | Rules for carrier pre-selection for long-distance and international service were established in 1996. Policies for local number portability are not yet established. | Call-by-call selection of long-distance carrier is not possible in Mexico. |
| Universal service | There are limited coverage obligations set out in the Telmex concession. New concessionaires must meet minimum network build-out obligations to obtain a concession. | Cofetel has the intention to establish a "universal service"-type fund to cover the deficit on residential local service. |
| International Issues | Competition for termination of in-bound international calls is not allowed, given Mexico's use of a proportional-return and uniform-settlement-rate system. The right to negotiate the common terms and conditions for international settlements with a foreign carrier is given to the domestic carrier with the highest market share in each route for the previous six months (which, in the past, has been Telmex). | The termination charge for inbound international traffic is well above cost and the ratio of incoming to outgoing traffic is around 2.5 to 1, so international traffic is an important source of revenue. |

*Source:* OECD.

Cofetel has four commissioners, including its president, who are appointed by the President of the Republic from a list provided by SCT. Commissioners do not have a fixed term of appointment. They remain in office until they resign or are replaced. Commissioners can be appointed and dismissed by the President of the Republic, on the advice of SCT. The three commissioners other than the president assume specialist responsibilities in, respectively: legal matters; economic planning and analysis; and engineering and technology. Matters are decided through majority vote, with the president having a tie-breaking vote. These arrangements concentrate significant power with the chair, who prevails in a decision unless all three commissioners vote in a contrary manner. In practice, Cofetel indicates that all decisions have been taken unanimously.

In matters related to the issuing, enforcement and revocation of concessions, Cofetel cannot act on its own. Cofetel merely issues an opinion to SCT who takes a decision whether or not to act. In all other areas (in the resolving of disputes, the authorisation of prices and the issuing of rules and regulations), Cofetel acts independently of SCT. SCT cannot issue, enforce or revoke concessions without an opinion from Cofetel.[28]

Cofetel currently employs around 300 staff. Under Mexican law, government employees cannot take up employment in the sector with which they have been directly involved for one year from the date of resigning from the public sector.

Serious concerns have been raised in Mexico regarding the actions and independence of Cofetel. Some new entrants and Telmex have alleged that Cofetel has been selective and discretionary in its implementation and enforcement of the existing regulatory regime and that Cofetel's decisions have lacked transparency.

The establishment of Cofetel as a regulatory agency distinct from the SCT was an important step towards developing an independent and transparent regulatory framework in Mexico. However, the independence of Cofetel, and the transparency and accountability of its decisions, do not go as far as is desirable. Regulatory independence from day to day political pressures is essential to build confidence of all market participants that government intervention in the telecommunications market will be transparent. Further, independence from the regulated companies, is needed to ensure transparent, fair, and reasonably predictable decisions. Arrangements differ in each country, but the essential features include complete independence from the regulated companies, a legal mandate that provides for separation of the regulators and the regulatory body from political control (e.g., by removing the power over appointments to the regulatory body from political control), a degree of organisational autonomy, well-defined obligations for transparency (e.g., publishing decisions) and for accountability (e.g., appealable decisions, public scrutiny of expenditures). The combination of transparencies – of objectives, powers, processes, decisions, and information – enables the public to evaluate how the regulator is fulfilling its role as a neutral arbiter of market competition and enforcer of regulation.

Cofetel derives much of its power from its ability to recommend the approval or denial of concessions, or to recommend the imposition of conditions on concessions. In addition, although Cofetel has developed and disseminated formal regulations on two occasions, Cofetel develops and disseminates its policies primarily through administrative rules and official resolutions of disputes. Cofetel has implemented the decisions set out in the rules through the mechanism of conditions on concessions. Unlike formal regulations (reglamentos), administrative rules are not subject to the requirement to be reviewed by the president's legal counsel (Consejería Jurídica del Ejecutivo Federal) and are not signed by the president.

Since 1995, the government has established a horizontal programme to register all formalities imposed on businesses and to review all new regulations under a programme called ADAE (Acuerdo para la Desregulación de la Actividad Empresarial). In 1997, a reform of the administrative procedure law reinforced this regulatory oversight capacity and established the requirement for a regulatory impact analysis regarding all new rules and regulations. However, Cofetel and SCT are still in the early stages of compliance with this regulatory control policy (see Section 2.2.9 below). Cofetel has said that it will combine the assorted rulings and case by case decisions into a single uniform body of regulation (Reglamento de Telecomunicaciones). It is important that SCT and Cofetel comply rigorously with the regulatory oversight control for such regulation as well as future other regulations.

Since its creation, Cofetel has had to establish its own processes and procedures for operation. Like many new agencies, this process has involved learning from experience. On more than one occasion Cofetel has been challenged in the courts. In part, this litigation reflects a change in attitudes in

Mexico to the role of government in industry. Informal, around the table negotiations are being replaced by formal, arms-length regulatory procedures. In part, this litigation reflects the strategic use of the legal system by the major players. In Mexico, government actions against individual interests can be blocked by means of the legal mechanism of *amparo* – a form of injunction which stays the government action pending the adjudication of the underlying argument. This adjudication can take years to resolve. All of the major firms in the telecommunications industry have made use of this tool, including the incumbent.[29] To win an *amparo* a plaintiff must make a convincing case to the court that an authority has acted in violation either of the constitution or of the nation's written body of law and regulation. The new entrants have won interim injunctions against the special projects charges and the interconnection regime established by Cofetel, pending the resolution of these disputes in the courts.

Although Cofetel has widely consulted with the industry on an informal basis, Cofetel has not, to date, implemented a formal public process of consultation before taking important decisions. Before the second semester of 1998, Cofetel did not publish the reasoning behind its decisions, contributing to a general lack of transparency in the decision-making process, and enhancing the scope for legal challenge. The adoption of processes involving a public, transparent and accountable procedure of notifying for comment, publicly accepting or rejecting other positions based on reasonable standards and the regulatory framework, and issuing final resolutions based on such procedures, would result in a more credible, less contentious and more efficient regulatory process.

Cofetel indicates that it intends to adopt a formal public consultation process during 1999.[30] This process will involve formal timelines, distinct steps, the keeping of detailed records and the publication of the reasons for all decisions. It is hoped that the introduction of such a process will enhance transparency and limit the probability of legal challenge of Cofetel's decisions. Cofetel should move quickly to implement policies to enhance the transparency of its decision-making, such as those stated in the SCT 1999 Work Program.

A regulatory institution such as Cofetel would be powerless without a mechanism for enforcing the regulatory regime, including its own decisions. The FTL sets out the maximum sanctions that may be applied in the case of violations of the provisions of this law. The fines to be imposed range from 2 000-20 000 "minimum wages" for minor violations (such as failure to register rates); 4 000-40 000 "minimum wages" for medium violations (such as non-compliance with obligations and concessions set forth in concessions) and 10 000-100 000 "minimum wages" for serious violations (such as providing telecommunications services without a concession). Since the current minimum wage is around US$3, the largest possible penalty on a carrier is US$300 000, for the most serious violations. This amount is small relative to the revenue of US$7.6 billion of Telmex, the largest carrier. The largest penalty that Telmex could receive under the FTL is less than 0.004% of its revenue. These monetary penalties are unlikely to be a sufficient deterrent.

Cofetel (through the SCT) has the power to revoke a concession (either immediately, in the case of certain serious violations, or only after three violations in the case of minor violations). However, the revocation of a concession is a draconian measure that would disrupt telecommunications services for millions of users and have a serious adverse impact on investors and is therefore unlikely to ever be used for a large company such as Telmex. For other companies, revocation is such a severe penalty that even the threat of a minor sanction is met with legal action. It is unlikely that the other concessionaires will ever accept a sanction without first exhausting every possible legal recourse. In either case the enforcement of concession violations is difficult.[31]

In addition to Cofetel, the Mexican competition authority, the *Comisión Federal de Competencia* (CFC) plays an important role in the telecommunications sector. The CFC has played an active role in screening applicants in the process of spectrum auctions. In addition, the FTL provides an explicit role for the CFC in determining when a telecommunications firm is dominant. As explained further below, Mexico's general competition law fully applies in this sector. Thus, in principle, anti-competitive actions such as horizontal arrangements between firms, abuse of dominance and predatory pricing can be controlled through the prohibitions set out in the competition law. The CFC's responsibilities include responding to formal complaints of anti-competitive behaviour by an economic agent found to have substantial market power in the relevant market. Telmex has been the object of such complaints for abuses such as cross-subsidies, charging for dialling to 800 numbers from public telephones, resale of both switched and un-switched interurban transport capacity to new entrants, and abuses of the local data base, among others.

As in other countries, the competition authority and the telecommunications regulator play complementary (but sometimes overlapping) roles. Although Cofetel is given specific powers with respect to resolving certain disputes and insuring compliance with all aspects of concessions (including those requirements in the Telmex concession forbidding anti-competitive actions), Cofetel's primary role is in establishing the regulatory framework. On the other hand, the role of the CFC is primarily to respond to complaints regarding anti-competitive behaviour as well as investigate on its own initiative when it has reason to believe monopoly abuse may be occurring. The new entrants, frustrated with what they see as Cofetel's inability or unwillingness to resolve complaints of anti-competitive actions in an effective and timely fashion, are increasingly turning to the CFC for resolution of such matters.

Furthermore, as mentioned earlier, Cofetel cannot act on its own – the final power to issue, enforce and revoke concessions rests with the SCT and not with Cofetel. For example, as noted earlier, although Cofetel has recommended the approval of concessions for Iridium, Globalstar and Orbcomm, to date, the SCT has not issued the concessions.

## 2.2. Regulations and related policy instruments in the telecommunications sector

### 2.2.1. *Regulation of entry and service provision*

The requirements for entry into markets for telecommunications services in Mexico are set out in the FTL. The FTL requires that all facilities-based providers of telecommunications services obtain a concession before offering service. Non-facilities-based telecommunications service providers must obtain a permit, while value-added service providers need only be registered. The concession system is the mechanism by which services deemed to be "public services" by the Mexican constitution may be opened to private entry. Concessions are transferable, but only after three years from the date of the issue.

As mentioned in the previous section, the issuance of concessions and permits is carried out by the SCT, on the advice of Cofetel. The FTL stipulates the information that an application for a concession must contain. An application must include: a statement of investment and coverage commitments; a business plan; and evidence of legal, technical, financial and administrative capacity. If the concession is granted, the FTL requires that a concession must specify at least: the different services to be rendered by the concessionaire; the rights and obligations of the concessionaire; and the commitments of geographical coverage of the network. Cofetel must issue its opinion on a concession within 120 days from the date of application. In practice, some concessions have taken more than a year to grant. Cofetel states that these delays arise when applications have been filed with incomplete information.

The FTL obligates Cofetel to scrutinise the business plan and legal, administrative, financial and technical capacity of each potential entrant. In addition, the FTL requires Cofetel to set out in the concession that the services the concessionaire can offer and the obligations and coverage requirements of the new concessionaire. One consequence is that concessionaires are, in practice, subject to a form of line-of-business restriction. For example, a cellular provider who (after receiving its initial concession) wishes to enter the long-distance market must re-apply to Cofetel for an extension to its concession.

The FTL does not specifically limit what conditions can be set out in a concession. In the absence of body of regulation (such as the proposed *reglamento* that is mentioned in the previous section) Cofetel uses its ability to impose conditions on concessionaires as a mechanism for regulating the industry. In practice, this occurs through a process of negotiation over the business plans of individual companies, with Cofetel/SCT delaying or withholding the concession if the business plan of the intended entrant is not in line with Cofetel/SCT's intentions.

263

The intention of the FTL is that, as a mechanism for network expansion, new concessionaires will be required to undertake obligations to build out new infrastructure. Before accepting applications for concessions, Cofetel has adopted the practice of specifying (for certain services) the minimal coverage commitments and obligations that new concessionaires will have to undertake. For example, long-distance operators are required to commit to link at least three cities in three different states of Mexico with their own transmission facilities. An operator planning to offer only long-distance service between two cities with its own facilities, or between several cities in the same state, would not be granted a long-distance concession.

New concessionaires, even in the absence of any obligation, would normally choose to build some new infrastructure. The focus of this provision is therefore on obligations on new entrants to construct more infrastructure than they would otherwise choose. A requirement or obligation to build out more infrastructure than an entrant would normally choose is a form of "tax" on entry. The objective seems to be to promote faster network build-out at the risk of foregoing higher levels of competition, lower prices, efficiency and innovation. This policy trade-off is most clearly seen in the decision to grant a monopoly to Telmex for six years in exchange for (amongst other things) network build-out obligations.

To date a number of concessions have been granted in many different segments of the market, including 15 concessions in long-distance and a further 10 in local service (not counting the incumbent). A certain level of competition is therefore developing under the current policies. Nevertheless, in the longer term, the policy approach of regulating entry to promote infrastructure development can be questioned:

First, competition itself provides powerful incentives to enhance network penetration. By diminishing competition in the market place, it is possible that the mechanism is reducing the overall level of new investment relative to the situation in which there are no restrictions on entry. There need be no policy trade-off between network build-out and competition. Competition itself provides strong incentives for new investment. Second, as a tax on entry, this tax is relatively non-transparent. It is difficult to observe the price that consumers are paying in the form of reduced competition. Third, the network investment obligations set out in the concession (which must be specified many months or years in advance) may restrict the ability of the new entrants to respond to new technological, demand and market developments in the industry as they arise.

Fourth, and more important, the discretion of Cofetel to impose conditions on entry may itself become a problem. All existing concessionaires have a strong incentive to induce Cofetel to raise the requirements for new entry over time. Cofetel has already been criticised by the incumbent firms for granting "too many" concessions. Existing concessionaires might also argue for a relaxation of their concession obligations, while insisting upon maintaining the same obligations on new entrants. Indeed, concession obligations have recently been relaxed for existing cable TV concessionaires in response to pressure from the concessionaires themselves. Cofetel states that, overall, the conditions on concessions for both existing and new entrants have been gradually relaxed.

Finally, one of the conditions that Cofetel seeks to impose is a requirement to abide by the rules established by Cofetel itself.[32] This amounts to a waiver of the legal right to challenge those rules. The ability to challenge legal rulings is an important tool for ensuring that rulings are efficient, appropriate and do not exceed the scope of the powers of the regulator. By insisting on waiving the right to challenge those rules, Cofetel can enhance its powers, possibly at the expense of new entrants, and possibly raising barriers to entry.

Given Mexico's constitutional requirement that the private provision of "public" services such as telecommunications be regulated through concessions, the FTL was an important step forward in liberalising entry into the telecommunications industry. The further steps suggested here would extend the liberalisation provided for by the FTL to further promote competition and ensure that new barriers are not raised to entry in telecommunications.

### 2.2.2. Resale

Cofetel has not yet established a procedure for granting permits to carriers proposing to offer simple resale of domestic and international long distance services. Cofetel argues that this is a consequence of a wider policy to encourage facilities-based carriers in preference to resellers, at the initial stages of reform.[33] In addition, international simple resale is not allowed because it is incompatible with the proportional returns and uniform settlement rate system for international traffic (see Section 2.8).

Section 54 of the FTL requires that pure resellers "shall be subject, without exception, to the respective regulatory provisions". At this time, such provisions only exist for the resale of pay-phones.

In the long-run resale competition is not as effective at lowering prices and delivering benefits to consumers as facilities-based competition. Nevertheless, pure resale may be a legitimate entry strategy for an entrant who wishes to establish a market presence prior to investing in sunk facilities of its own. In addition, a prohibition on resale entry may actually reduce the incentives for infrastructure investment. Preventing the entry of resellers eliminates one class of customer of network operators, thereby potentially limiting the value of the network.

In practice, the prohibition on domestic resale may neither promote network expansion nor act as a restriction on entry because concessionaires are allowed to resell to other concessionaires. Since the requirements for becoming a concessionaire are not unduly onerous, concessionaires can follow a largely resale-based or facilities-based strategy as they wish. Indeed, the concessionaire Bestel appears to be following a policy of constructing facilities with the primary purpose of reselling the network to other concessionaires.

Cofetel's 1999 work programme considers the initiation of a consultation process with the industry in order to set the regulatory provisions needed for pure resale, in line with Mexico's WTO commitments.

### 2.2.3. Line of business restrictions

At present, the only line of business restraint in the Mexican telecommunications regulatory regime is set out in the Telmex concession. The concession states that "Telmex cannot exploit, directly or indirectly, any concession for television services to the public in the country".

As a result of convergence, it is increasingly likely that, in future, voice telephony, Internet services, and cable television services will be provided off the same infrastructure. Line of business restraints that prevented, say, voice telephony and cable television services from being offered over the same infrastructure may, in the long run, hinder the process of convergence.

### 2.3. Regulation of interconnection

Both the 1995 FTL and the 1990 Telmex concession contain provisions under which interconnection is to be made available to a public switched telephone network. The FTL specifies that where one firm seeks interconnection to another, the parties are first to negotiate. In the event of the failure of the negotiation, after 60 days either party can appeal to Cofetel to rule on any outstanding issues, including the level of interconnection charges. Cofetel is required to make a decision within 60 days.

The FTL states that concessionaires must "allow desegregated access to services, capacity and functions of their networks based on non-discriminatory rates". Furthermore, reciprocity must be respected in the interconnection among "concessionaires providing each other similar services, capacity or functions". Volume discounts are explicitly prohibited.

There have been allegations that the process of resolving interconnection disputes has taken far longer than the statutory 60 days. For example, Megacable, after 60 days of unsuccessful negotiation with Telmex, appealed to Cofetel to resolve its interconnection dispute on 5 June 1998. Sixty days later Cofetel asked for further information (on the basis that Megacable's request did not specify exactly what terms and conditions Cofetel was to specify). Cofetel did not issue its final resolution until eight months after the formal start to negotiations, despite the fact that the FTL clearly contemplates this process to take no longer than four months.

Resolving interconnection disputes is never easy. Given the amounts at stake these disputes are intensely controversial. Nevertheless, delays in the resolution of interconnection disputes unambiguously favour the incumbent and slow the development of competition.

### 2.3.1. Interconnection of local networks with other fixed networks

In 1996, after negotiations between the new long-distance companies and Telmex failed, Cofetel stepped in to determine interconnection rates. At the time, Telmex had not completed its rebalancing of local and long-distance rates as permitted under the concession. Telmex claimed that, as long as the structure of prices remained unbalanced, it was entitled to receive a contribution in interconnection charges towards the deficit it incurred on its residential local service. SCT upheld this view. In its April 1996 interconnection resolution, the SCT imposed a relatively high interconnection charge equivalent to 5.3 US cents per minute (at each end of a long-distance call, not including the additional revenue from billing the customer directly for the local call component) to be applied during 1997 and 1998.[34] This charge included a basic rate equivalent to 2.5 US cents (0.19 peso, indexed to inflation) and a surcharge on the termination of incoming international calls equal to 58% of the settlement rate, which increased the estimated average interconnection rate by 2.8 US cents. The total contribution from these two rates was calculated so as to cover an alleged deficit on Telmex's residential local service while rates were being rebalanced. The SCT resolution also established that in 1999 the total interconnection charge would not be more than 3.1 US cents, similar to the average interconnection rate prevailing in the US at the time.[35]

During 1996, 1997, and 1998 Telmex engaged in rapid rebalancing of its local and long-distance prices, increasing local rates in real terms to the levels originally scheduled under its concession. This rebalancing substantially reduced the deficit on the residential local service. Correspondingly, in December 1998, Cofetel substantially reduced the interconnection charges. The 58% surcharge for each minute of international traffic terminated by Telmex was allowed to lapse. The effect of this measure was to cut the interconnection charge by more than half, to an equivalent of 2.6 US cents. This new rate will apply throughout 1999 and 2000.[36]

It is important to note that interconnection charges are not the only source of revenue for Telmex for covering the costs of originating and terminating long-distance and mobile calls. In addition to billing the long-distance or mobile operator for interconnection services, Telmex also directly charges the local customer the price of a local call. Local calls in Mexico are charged a flat rate per call of about 12.07 US cents. In addition, residential customers receive the first 100 calls per month for free. Around 45% of residential callers do not exceed this limit. If it is assumed that an average call length of 3.5 minutes, the average revenue per minute per end is around 1.7 US cent. If it is assumed that 40-60% of all local calls are charged, the additional revenue per minute per end received by Telmex for providing local service, over and above the interconnection charges, is in the region 0.7-1.0 US cent. (In other countries, local telephony providers also sometimes benefit from sources of revenue beyond interconnection charges in the maintenance of the local network, such as the "subscriber line charge" in the US. In the case of the US, this additional revenue is equivalent to an additional 1-1.5 US cent per end minute on interconnection charges).

The absolute level of interconnection charges in Mexico are high by international standards (see Figure 1).[37] Cofetel notes that for the purposes of the comparisons below, the basic rate of 2.6 cents should be adjusted to reflect the charge for uncompleted calls. If this were included the tariff would be approximately 2.76 cents. In addition, Avantel asserts that interconnection port charges should also be added, yielding (by Avantel's estimates) around 2.84 cents. This compares with rates less than 1.5 US cents per minute per end for Bell Atlantic and less than 1 US cent per minute per end for BT.

Cofetel recognises that the 2.6 US cents interconnection rate is above the cost of providing the service, because it includes a contribution to cover what it believes is a deficit on the provision of residential telephone service. The contribution is necessary, Cofetel believes, to prevent an additional sharp increase in the residential service rates.

In December 1998, Cofetel issued a resolution on the interconnection of Telmex with other fixed local and mobile networks. In that decision Cofetel held that the interconnection rate should be the same for the termination of calls in Telmex's network for calls originating in fixed local and mobile networks, as the service provided by Telmex is the same in each case. Moreover, the new fixed local carriers (wired or wireless) will be paid 2.6 US cents per minute for terminating calls in their networks when their networks provide (or are committed to provide) significant coverage of the local service area, including a relevant percentage of the residential users in the local area. In contrast, local fixed networks with a limited coverage of the local service area (like fibre rings) that are not intending to provide services to a significant percentage of residential users, will be paid only 1 US cent per minute (the underlying cost).[38]

Furthermore, the December 1998 resolutions set out specific provisions relating to the interconnection of Telmex with other local networks that cover residential areas. In this case Cofetel considered that the reciprocal application of an interconnection rate well above cost represents a threat to the financial viability of the new entrant since it is likely that, at the beginning of its operations, traffic will be unbalanced against the new network. Therefore, Cofetel mandated the application of "bill and keep" agreements for a reasonable range of unbalance. On these grounds, Telmex and Axtel agreed that they will pay each other only the minutes exceeding a ratio of outgoing minutes to total interconnection minutes of 70%, during the first two years. This means that Axtel can send up to seven minutes of traffic to Telmex for every three minutes it receives from Telmex without payment.

As in all countries, issues surrounding interconnection have been in Mexico an intense source of controversy. Cofetel states that its broad intention is to abide by their WTO undertakings to have "cost-oriented" interconnection charges. They acknowledge that the costs of providing call origination and

Figure 1. **International comparison of interconnection charges**

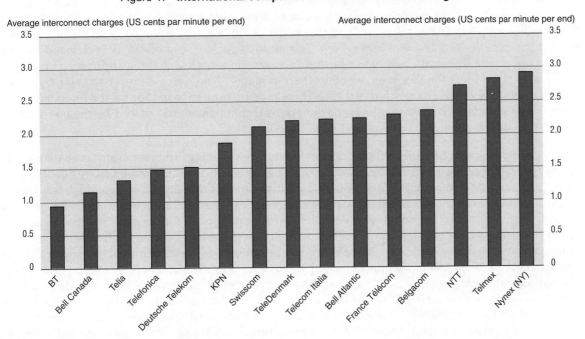

Average interconnect charges (US cents par minute per end)

*Source:* OVUM Quaterly Update, April 1999, Cofetel.

termination services (including a contribution to joint and common costs) is around 1-1.2 cent. However, they argue that a higher charge for origination and termination in Telmex's network is necessary to cover the losses incurred by Telmex on its residential local service. Estimating the number of access minutes in 1999 to be around 25 billion, the excess of 1.6 cent per access minute over cost yields Telmex a contribution from interconnection charges of around US$400 million. To this should be added the contribution that Telmex receives by directly billing customers for a local call each time a long-distance call is made. This amount of about 0.86 cent per end minute, yields an additional US$215 million. In other words, Telmex is receiving around US$615 million each year in contribution to the non-traffic-sensitive costs of providing local service. In 1997 this represented around 20% of the revenues of Telmex's local service. (However, the total revenue flows to Telmex's local service were taken into account when the three independent experts considered the level of the "initial value" and the X factor in the price cap, thus in principle, interconnection charges above cost should be translated into lower retail prices for local services). Cofetel has initiated consultations with the industry in order to create a fund to support the provision of residential services in non-profitable areas (where consumers do not have the ability to pay cost-based residential rates) that will allow the elimination of any implicit contribution in the interconnection rate.

Box 2 sets out some basic principles for setting access prices. As the box emphasises, it is not possible to set access or interconnection prices efficiently without taking into consideration all the other local service charges – and, in particular, the monthly rental and local calling charges for business and residential customers. The full set of charges should satisfy two conditions. First, the price-cost margin for each service should be inversely related to the elasticity of the service and second, the overall level of charges should be sufficient to allow an efficient operator to just recover his or her costs of providing the local service. These two principles will be used as a basis to examine and critique the local service charges in Mexico.

In regard to the elasticity of services, traditionally telecommunications operators maintained low monthly rental charges, by increasing the contribution from long-distance services. Mexico has been rebalancing, and thereby lowering interconnection charges. There are some signs that, at least in the case of residential customers, this rebalancing has proceeded as far as it is possible to go. Cofetel point out that during 1997 and 1998 nearly half a million users disconnected each year and an increasing percentage (currently 45%) of residential users have been limiting their calling to the free calls included in the monthly rent. Telmex has acknowledged that in the last months of 1998 and the first months of 1999 Mexico has experienced negative line growth. Technically speaking, the elasticity of demand for residential telephone lines with respect to further increases in monthly charges appears to be high. It remains an open question, however, whether there remains further scope for rebalancing by raising business monthly rental charges further. Thus there may be further scope for basing interconnection charges on the number of business lines (or the equivalent in bandwidth) served by the new entrants (rather than on the number of interconnecting minutes).

In general, it might be expected that demand for business calling is more inelastic than demand for residential calling. It makes sense therefore for business calls to be charged more than residential calls. In its December 1998 decision, Cofetel implemented this form of discrimination in a rough way by distinguishing interconnection charges with significant coverage of the local area (which would include residential customers) and networks with very limited coverage of the local service area (that serve primarily business customers). Networks which primarily serve business customers (such as the network of Megacable) must pay the higher rate of 2.6 cents per minute to terminate local (business) calls on Telmex's network (and other residential networks), while other networks can terminate calls on Megacable's network for just 1 cent per minute. This approach has two problems. First, the distinction made by Cofetel is on a network-by-network basis rather than a subscriber-by-subscriber basis. This forces Cofetel to make arbitrary and intensely controversial decisions as to what constitutes a network with limited coverage of the local service area. Because of the higher charges, a network which is designated a "limited coverage" network could not expect to compete effectively for residential customers. The second problem with this approach is that, because not all calls originate or terminate on the other network, some calls avoid paying the surcharge. This could be avoided by basing the interconnection charges on the *total* number of local business minutes provided by the entrant (rather than the number of *interconnecting* business minutes).

To date, Cofetel has provided no public information justifying the levels of Telmex's local charges. As Box 2 notes, Telmex's local service should only receive enough revenue to cover the costs of an efficient operator today. Because of technological developments and increasing incentives for efficiency, these costs do not necessarily correspond to the historic costs incurred by Telmex as revealed in Telmex' accounts.

---

Box 2.   **Access deficits and the theory of access charges**

"Local telephone service" is a group of services comprising the provision of local calls and the provision of the local (originating or terminating) component at either end of a long-distance or mobile call. The provision of local telephone service exhibits substantial economies of scale and scope. This means that if each service (local calls and originating/terminating of long-distance/mobile calls) was charged at marginal cost, the provider would not be able to recover its full costs, including fixed costs and common costs. In most countries, some or all of the fixed and common costs are recovered through a two-part tariff – customers (both residential and business) are charged a monthly rental fee in addition to a usage fee. If the monthly rental fee can be set high enough (with little or no effect on telephone penetration), the usage fees can be set low, close to marginal cost. Economic theory says that this would be the efficient outcome.

In practice however, it may not be possible to raise the monthly rental fee to this level, especially in a poorer country, such as Mexico. The higher the monthly rental fee, the more likely are customers to drop off the network. In this case the optimal price for local services would involve trading off the economic losses from higher monthly charges against the economic losses from higher usage fees (local call charges and interconnection charges). Economic theory says that the price-cost margin should be higher on the less elastic services. In general, monthly rental will be more inelastic than usage. Therefore monthly rental charges (especially on businesses) should be raised as high as possible before raising usage (especially long-distance call origination/termination) charges.

It is important, of course, that all competitors contribute on a competitively neutral basis to covering the fixed and common costs of the local service. Raising only the incumbent's monthly rental charges for businesses to cover a local service deficit will invite "cream skimming" competition in this section of the market and will prevent the incumbent from sustaining the necessary cross-subsidies. Although, in principle, it might be possible to structure the interconnection fees as a charge per business line of the competitor, it is more common in practice to recover such revenues in a competitively neutral manner through the use of a fund.

In general, an efficient set of prices for local telephony services satisfy two conditions: First, the margin between prices and marginal cost for each of the services should reflect the elasticity of the service and second, the overall level of prices should just allow the provider to recover the total costs. Laffont and Tirole* suggest that these conditions could be met with a simple price cap incorporating both final prices and interconnection prices. One of the difficulties in practice is determining the appropriate level of total costs. The books of the incumbent can, at best, reflect historic costs. The right measure of costs is the forward-looking cost of an efficient replacement technology.

With all the charges set optimally, there would be no deficit on local telephone service only if the elasticity of monthly rental was such that the monthly rental could be raised high enough to cover all the fixed and common costs of local service, without any significant effects on telephone penetration. In the more likely case in Mexico, it will be necessary to cover at least some of the costs through usage charges. In this circumstance there would still be a "deficit" on local telephony service even once all the charges are set optimally. On the other hand, if the revenues from interconnection and/or a universal service fund are taken into account, the local telephony service should always fully cover its costs.

---

\*   See Laffont, J.-J. and Tirole, J., "Creating Competition Through Interconnection: Theory and Practice", 10 *Journal of Regulatory Economics*, 227-256, (1996).

The revenue to cover fixed and common costs need not all derive from charges related to interconnection. Another approach is to raise this revenue via some form of fund to which all competitors contribute, such as the fund described in Section 2.2.6. This fund could be (and should be) structured in a way as to "tax" most heavily the most inelastic telecommunications services (such as business line rental). Cofetel has expressed its intention to develop such a fund. Indeed, Cofetel has repeatedly stated that the interconnection rate will be lowered when a fund is created to finance network expansion.

There are two further comments which can be made in regard to the interconnection policy in Mexico. Under the current policy, Mexico has followed international precedent in charging for interconnection on a per minute basis. However, economic theory suggests that interconnection charges should be structured according to the underlying costs. Whenever the structure of prices is unrelated to costs, the pattern of consumption is distorted and there may arise opportunities for anti-competitive behaviour. As an example, although the underlying costs of terminating calls may be in the vicinity of 1 cent per minute on average, there are likely to be important differences in the cost of terminating calls at peak and off-peak times. At off-peak times, once a call is established, the cost of maintaining the call is very small indeed (and possibly indistinguishable from zero). A flat per-minute charge for interconnection is therefore likely to under-compensate at peak times and over-compensate at off-peak times. This is likely to distort consumption. More importantly, a positive off-peak interconnection fee may allow the incumbent to act anti-competitively. Since the cost of maintaining a call at off-peak is close to zero, the incumbent can offer a simple flat fee-per call. An entrant paying for interconnection on a per-minute basis may not be able to match this price as it knows that it will lose money on all calls which are maintained beyond a certain length of time. This problem arises with respect to local calls, which are charged a flat fee in Mexico, whatever the length of the call. If the entrant is charged on a per-minute basis, the entrant has an inefficient incentive to seek customers whose calls are shorter than the average and to offer reduced rates for short calls.

It is more efficient to have interconnection charges closely match the underlying cost structure. This involves adequately discriminating between call set-up and call maintenance charges and between peak and off-peak, etc. In particular, if the underlying cost structure more closely matches the flat fee-per-call than a per-minute charge, the interconnection charges should reflect this with a flat fee per call.

In a high-inflation country such as Mexico (inflation was around 18% in 1998), fixing the interconnection charge in nominal terms would imply that real prices for interconnection services would be rapidly declining. It is more appropriate, therefore, to incorporate an adjustment for inflation. Presently, Telmex's interconnection prices are allowed to increase monthly to reflect changes in the consumer price index. There is a real question, however, whether it is appropriate for interconnection prices to fully adjust to reflect inflation. If interconnection charges are cost based and if costs are declining, it is more appropriate for interconnection charges to decline to reflect those costs. It makes sense, therefore, for the interconnection charges in Mexico to decline, in real terms, in line with the productivity adjustment factor (current 4.5% *p.a.*) in Telmex's price cap.

### 2.3.2. Interconnection of local and mobile networks

The December 1998 resolutions also made some important changes to the interconnection tariffs for the interconnection of mobile and local networks. First, for calls originating in mobile networks and terminating in a fixed local network, the interconnection charge was reduced, consistent with the above decisions, from around 3.1 cents per minute to 2.6 cents.

On the other hand, for calls originating in a fixed local network and terminating in a mobile network, the new resolutions introduce the concept of an asymmetric interconnection rate that recognises the higher termination cost on mobile networks. The resolution sets this interconnection rate equivalent to 18 US cents, (and establishes that it will be revised in six months based on additional information of the actual costs of providing the service). Since local carriers are allowed to pass this higher rate to its users, plus billing and collection costs, this means the introduction of the system of calling-party-pays ("CPP").

Under the previous regime, the fixed user paid the local call charge plus a supplement of 1.6 cent per minute. The fixed network did not pass this supplement on to the mobile company. The entire termination costs were charged to the mobile recipient of the call. Under the new regime, if the mobile user opts for called party pays, the charges are essentially the same, except the 1.6 cent surcharge is eliminated. If the mobile user opts for calling party pays, the fixed caller pays local call charges plus a surcharge of 25 cents per minute for calling a mobile number; the fixed network pays the mobile network 19 cents (inflation adjusted) for termination in the mobile network.

The authorities have praised CPP as a key instrument to promote competition based on reciprocal cost based interconnection charges and to expand cellular penetration. CPP allows mobile users to better control their telecommunications charges and reduces the incentive to leave the phone switched off. However, the rule set CPP as an optional service, while the existing Mobile Party Pays remained the default system. Users opting for CPP had to ask for the service, include a 044 prefix to their old number and inform their callers of the change. Following the introduction of the service on 1 May 1999, Cofetel accepted a petition of the cellular carriers to adopt CPP as the default system.

The tariff set for CPP service is 25 US cents per minute (in addition to the normal cost of a local call). This includes a payment of 19 US cents to the mobile carrier, and a charge of 6 US cents per minute covering billings and collections. Since Telmex must already bill its own customers, the incremental cost of billing on behalf of mobile companies is likely to be negligible. This charge for billing and collection appears unnecessarily high. Cofetel accepted the price based on Telmex assumptions of higher costs for uncollectables and for attending to customers' complaints on their bills, but the price will be revised in November based on new information on actual costs.

### 2.3.3. *Technical aspects of interconnection*

"Equal access" or pre-subscription was a component of the regime from the start of competition in 1 January 1997. Starting in 1997, on a city-by-city basis assignment of subscribers to long-distance carriers as the "default" or "1+" carrier was accomplished through balloting – *i.e.* Telmex subscriber was sent a ballot 60 days before competition was opened in a particular city which allowed it to choose among long distance carriers. At the end of 1998, such ballots had been carried out in 100 cities, accounting for 80% of the population of Mexico.

In another component of the December 1998 resolutions, Cofetel made adjustments to the number of local calling areas, and expanded the stock of numbers available. The number of local service areas, which are based on switching groups, will be gradually reduced from 1 406 to 406 over a three-year period. This will increase the size of the smaller local calling areas. The intention is to provide all carriers common and well defined geographic areas, in order to allow them to plan their networks efficiently, reducing the investment requirements and so barriers to entry while promoting economies of scale in the use of capacity.

Overall, in a few years Cofetel has made important steps to develop interconnection policies in a highly contentious environment. Interconnection charges have reduced rapidly to a level that is at the upper end of a range of world prices. The policies set out here would build on these steps to ensure that in the future interconnection charges in Mexico are established in a transparent manner, using transparent, broadly acceptable cost information and pursuing broadly accepted telecommunications objectives.

## 2.4. Regulation of prices

### 2.4.1. *Regulation of Telmex's prices*

The Telmex concession sets out a system of control of the prices of Telmex. The most important component of this is a price cap, which operates over a basket of basic controlled services including local and long-distance. In addition, for the period from 1990-1996 further individual controls operated on the individual local service prices that were intended to limit the rate of rebalancing between local and long-distance prices.

The concession permits Telmex to set its rates subject to an aggregate ceiling on the price of a "basket" of services – essentially volume weighted prices of basic telephone services. Basic telephone services, as defined under the concession, include installation charges, basic monthly rent, measured local service, domestic long distance service, and international long distance service. In effect, the cap takes the form of a constraint on the average revenue received by Telmex for basic retail telecommunications services.

For the years 1990-1996, the overall price cap increased regularly to take into account inflation in the previous period, permitting Telmex to increase its nominal rates to offset inflation (as measured by the "Mexican National Consumer Price Index"). From 1 January 1997, onwards through 1998, the price cap was adjusted by 0.74% per quarter less than the rate of inflation, leading to a real price decline of approximately 3% per year.

The specific formula for the revenue cap on prices is set out in Section 6.3 of the 1990 Telmex concession. It specifies that prices can adjust quarterly such that the product of the price, times by one-period (i.e. three-months) lagged volumes for each component of the basic basket, summed over all products, remained constant in real terms from 1990 to 1996 and, during 1997, fall by 0.74% per quarter (equivalent to 3% per annum). What this means is that if one price falls significantly in a given period (e.g., national long distance), there is increased scope to raise other prices in the basket (e.g., local measured service rates, although residential rates cannot be higher than incremental cost).[39]

Beginning 1 January 1999, and every four years thereafter, the level of the adjustment factor is e set by Cofetel after administrative hearings with the articulated purpose of "allowing Telmex to maintain an internal rate of return equal to the companies' weighted average cost of capital". The procedure is as follows: Telmex has to submit a study on the incremental costs of providing controlled services, as well as a tariff proposal. Based on the long run incremental cost methodology, the initial level of the basket and the value of the X factor are set in order to produce a net profit such that the internal rate of return of the controlled services will be equal to the weighted average cost of capital (WACC). If no agreement on the initial increase or the X factor can be reached between Cofetel and Telmex, then three experts' opinions will be requested. One of the experts is to be chosen by Cofetel, the second by Telmex and the third one should be chosen by mutual consent. As no agreement occurred for the 1998 renegotiation, three experts were chosen and their verdict submitted to Cofetel in February 1999. For 1999-2002 the X factor was set at 4.5% per year. On 9 March 1999 Cofetel announced a nominal price increase for Telmex of 14% in long distance and 4% in local service (with further local service price increases of 4% on 1 July 1999 and on 1 October 1999 depending on the inflation rate registered from April to June).

In addition to the price controls set out above, the Telmex concession also specifies that the price of residential local service must never be above its incremental cost.

The global cap under which Telmex currently operates heightens the likelihood of anti-competitive behaviour. When the cap covers prices in both competitive and non-competitive markets, there may be an enhanced incentive for the incumbent to engage in anti-competitive cross-subsidisation.

*[A cap on the average price in the two markets] can distort competition by making the incumbent excessively aggressive in the competitive market. As the incumbent reduces prices to win custom in the competitive market [a revenue cap] enables it to charge a higher price to customers in the captive market. This has the effect of reducing the incumbent's costs of serving the competitive market. It is quite possible that pricing below marginal cost, which is often regarded as predatory pricing, could be induced by average revenue regulation. As a result, competition from rivals may be thwarted even if they are more efficient than the incumbent. [...] In sum, the way that the pricing structure is regulated can have an important influence upon the nature of competition faced by a multi-product incumbent. In particular, regulating average revenue in a way that allows the incumbent complete freedom over price structure may have serious anti-competitive consequences.[40]*

The Telmex concession explicitly forbids pricing below incremental costs, but there is room for a strategy where most of the burden of common costs is recovered in the local business service (local residential rates have their own ceiling equal to incremental costs), while reducing prices closer to incremental costs in the long distance service.

Indeed, following the introduction of competition in the long-distance market there have been sharp allegations of anti-competitive behaviour and cross-subsidisation, since the prices of long distance services have declined sharply while local rates have increased. However, Cofetel claims that the only reason for the increase in individual local rates since 1997 is to allow Telmex to reach the price caps originally scheduled for 1996, but delayed due to the peso crisis.[41]

As noted earlier, in December 1997, CFC found that Telmex was dominant in five markets. As a consequence of this ruling, Cofetel has authority to impose additional price regulation on Telmex. Cofetel indicates in its 1999 work programme that it intends to implement a system of separate caps for Telmex's local and long-distance prices.

### 2.4.2. Regulation of other retail prices

The FTL states that all concessionaires shall "freely determine the rates for telecommunications services, in terms that will allow the rendering of such services within satisfying conditions of quality, competitiveness, safety and permanence". The FTL requires that all concessionaires register their prices with Cofetel before they are used.

According to Cofetel's procedures, concessionaires must apply to Cofetel to register new prices 15 days before the new prices come into effect. Cofetel must make a decision on whether or not to grant registration within 10 days. The FTL specifies that all prices must be available for inspection on a public register. Cofetel facilitates such inspection by posting all registered prices on the Internet. Cofetel registers most tariffs within the 10-day period. Delays of tariff registration have, however, been as long as a month.[42]

Aspects of this system give rise to competition concerns. First, the system facilitates collusion among competing firms. Sustained profitable collusion requires the detection of "cheating" on the agreed prices. If firms are required to publicly disclose all their prices, the detection of such cheating is much easier. Under the current system, firms have advance notification of their competitors price changes even before those price changes take effect. Firms cannot discount without it becoming public knowledge even before the discounts apply. Although it is common practice in other industries to publish official price lists, an important source of competition is in the size of discounts off official prices. In the telecommunications industry in Mexico all such discounting is completely transparent. Long-distance prices have fallen significantly in Mexico, but with a relatively small number of large players, collusion remains a long-term threat in this industry.[43]

Second, the process diminishes incentives for innovation in pricing and marketing schemes. Since a new pricing plan must be publicly disclosed to a firm's rivals before the new plan can be implemented, the rivals have several days head start on the introduction of a similar competing plan themselves (although the rivals also have to enter the same process).

Third, although the FTL states that, in general, concessionaires shall freely determine their tariffs, Cofetel has a degree of discretion in interpreting when tariffs are sufficient to ensure "quality, competitiveness, safety and permanence". This discretion might potentially become a tool exercised in the interests of the industry. As an example, in 1998, in the presence of an intense price war in the long-distance market, the major players came to Cofetel to assist them to prevent further price declines through denying registration to new, lower prices. This request was carefully considered by Cofetel, but was not taken up.

Economic theory suggests that regulation of prices, terms and conditions is only warranted for a firm in a dominant position. A well-known economist, Roger Noll, in a comment on the telecommunications sector in Mexico notes "[...] regulation of prices, profits and investment decisions by entrants is unnecessary, for entrants must beat the regulated offerings of the dominant carrier in order to gain a foothold in the market. And, establishing detailed conditions for entry is also unnecessary, since the presence of alternative providers that are seamlessly interconnected protects consumers against loss arising from a firm that is under-financed or incompetently managed. Thus there is simply no need to engage in detailed licensing processes for competitors...[44]"

In summary, the price registration system set out in the FTL may threaten the development of competition under certain circumstances. The system of disclosure of all prices greatly facilitates the possibility of collusion amongst the major players. Second, the requirement of registration before using prices limits the opportunities and incentives for introducing new pricing innovations. Third, given the importance of pricing decisions to the industry, the power to refuse registration may become a focal point for industry lobbying to promote price increases or prevent price declines.

In addition to exercising its regulatory authority over prices charged by non-dominant firms, Cofetel also controls the contractual terms and conditions offered by those firms. Certain concessions contain a provision that forces the concessionaire to obtain prior authorisation from Cofetel for the contract boilerplate it intends to use with its end-user customers.

The price registration provisions of the FTL do not adequately distinguish between dominant and non-dominant firms. Economic regulation should be reserved for dominant firms. In contrast, the price registration, accounting separation and other provisions of the FTL apply to all firms. This imposes unnecessary compliance costs, and as the discussion above illustrates, can in fact threaten competition.

The system of price regulation introduced in the Telmex concession was advanced for its time and a major step towards a system of transparent non-political price setting. The proposals here build on this base with minor improvements to minimise the undesirable side effects of the regulation and oversight of telecommunications prices.

### 2.5. Quality of service

The 1990 Telmex concession specifies concrete targets for certain quality of service indicators and network expansion. If the indicators were not met, Telmex was required to provide a rebate to subscribers. The level of these indicators was initially set at low levels that became increasingly demanding over time. The required targets are negotiated every four years between Telmex and Cofetel.

As Table 3 illustrates, in 1994 at the end of the first four-year period, the quality of service targets were reduced downward significantly, thus allowing quality of service to deteriorate.[45] This occurred at the time of the macroeconomic crisis triggered by the peso devaluation. By 1996, the quality indices had recovered their 1994 levels, although the ICAL index in 1997 remained below the level achieved in 1994.

Given the quantity of variables in the quality indexes and the size of the universe of users they are applied to, it becomes virtually impossible to prove non-compliance with the title's quality indicators. Individual quality parameters are integrated into quality indexes and are not taken into account independently of each other. Compliance with the quality indexes is assessed on the basis of the whole universe of Telmex users (commercial clients together with long distance carriers).

Table 3. **Quality of service indicators under the concession**

| | | 1990 | 1991 | 1992 | 1993 | 1994 | 1995 | 1996 | 1997 |
|---|---|---|---|---|---|---|---|---|---|
| 1. Service continuity Index ("ICON") | Target | 80.20 | 83.42 | 86.19 | 87.07 | 87.95 | 83.86 | 85.60 | 87.46 |
| | Actual | 84.72 | 86.27 | 89.53 | 90.89 | 92.17 | 89.94 | 92.45 | 92.73 |
| 2. Quality Index ("ICAL") | Target | 90.84 | 91.66 | 92.38 | 92.82 | 93.64 | 86.80 | 88.74 | 89.98 |
| | Actual | 89.55 | 92.36 | 93.68 | 95.93 | 97.31 | 95.91 | 96.39 | 97.23 |
| 3. Private Line/Circuit Index ("ICIRC") | Target | n.a. | n.a. | n.a. | 69.62 | 79.86 | 60.00 | 67.60 | 77.15 |
| | Actual | n.a. | n.a. | n.a. | 35.59 | 81.12 | 79.95 | 81.44 | 87.52 |

*Source:* Cofetel.

The concession also contained targets on network expansion and related targets on indices of the availability of service such as waiting time for new lines. Targets for the reduction of waiting time have been achieved much more quickly than required under the concession.[46] Telmex also met the network expansion requirement of 12.2% average annual rate of expansion until 1994. This is discussed further in Section 3.3.

## 2.6. Resource issues

### 2.6.1. Access to spectrum

The FTL requires that concessions for the use of spectrum be granted through a public bidding mechanism. Cofetel fulfils this obligation through public spectrum auctions.

To date, Cofetel has conducted public auctions of spectrum for various services including paging, point to point links, MMDS, Personal Communications Services ("PCS") and wireless local ("WLL") access. The PCS auction brought in revenues of US$802.2 million. For the provision of PCS, Cofetel allocated four frequency bands for each region, two for 30 MHz of bandwidth and two for 10 MHz. Concessions to operate PCS and wireless local loop were granted in nine concession areas which coincided with the original nine geographic regions in which cellular concessions were granted.[47]

The bidding process adopted is a "simultaneous ascending auction", whereby participants submit daily bids via computer. In the wireless services market, the process prohibits cross-subsidisation of concessionaire and competitive services and states that concession holders for public wireless service may not receive subsidies or preferential treatment from other telecommunications concessions. All wireless concession and permit holders must be completely independent of other organisations, and must have their own accounting, administrative, operational, maintenance, development and supervisory staff. In addition, wireless concessionaires are prohibited from using equipment or installations belonging to other telephone concessions, unless they can prove that they are renting at market prices, and that all wireless groups are being offered the same arrangement.

Mexico's approach provides concessionaires flexibility on how to use assigned spectrum. Area, rather than site-by-site, concessions, and desegregation and partitioning rights have expanded options for concessionaires to make the most productive use of the spectrum. Broad flexibility for concessionaires enhances efficient use of the spectrum, and permits concessionaires and the marketplace to develop the products that consumers want. In terms of transparency, fairness and competitive access, the system for spectrum allocation has been successful.

One unfortunate consequence of the use of spectrum auctions is that they provide the government with a financial interest in the artificial creation of spectrum scarcity and consequent reduction in competition. In order to minimise this potential problem, Cofetel publishes each year the annual auction program, assessing the demand for spectrum by potential investors given the available technology and equipment. Cofetel argues that it will follow a policy of auctioning spectrum as long as the marginal value of spectrum is positive.

### 2.6.2. Access to right-of-way and related facilities

Access to rights-of-way is an important requirement for new entrants. Entrants must in many cases negotiate with incumbents in telecommunication markets, other utilities (such as power, water and railroad companies), and local governments to secure access to necessary rights-of-way or facilities. Sometimes access entails the right to install facilities (e.g., to dig to install cable in the case of fixed networks, or to erect towers for mobile communications), and other times may involve access to facilities already in place (such as poles, ducts, and conduits).

In general, the issue of access to rights-of-way and related facilities is a matter appropriately left to private negotiations. In some instances, however, there may be jurisdictional problems in extending

275

initiatives to reduce barriers to entry adopted at the national level to local authorities. In addition, incumbents can sometimes protect their market power by denying access to new entrants.

The FTL specifically includes provisions addressing access to rights of way. Article 45 states that "whenever the technical, safety and operational conditions may allow it, the rights of way of the general communication ways, of the electric transmission and radio-communication towers; the set of posts with electric distribution wires; adjacent land plots to oil and other hydrocarbon ducts; as well as posts and ducts with public telecommunications networks wiring that may be available to a public network concessionaire must be equally available to other concessionaires on a non-discriminatory basis".

The Mexican initiatives to promote local competition do not effectively address the issue of rights-of-way. Specifically, the initiatives do not appear to provide a regime establishing the rules under which new entrants are provided access to the incumbent's ducts, conduits, and other relevant facilities. An absence of such rules could delay local competition by leaving scope for the incumbent to raise the costs of its rivals. The absence of such rules could also delay mobile competition by raising the costs of securing permission to install towers. The experience of other OECD countries indicates that the establishment of rules and arbitration mechanisms can be helpful steps to lower barriers to entry.

### 2.6.3. *Numbering issues*

Number portability refers to the ability of customers to change their location, service provider, or service without being required to change their number. An absence of provisions to allow for number portability acts as a disincentive for customers to switch from the incumbent to a new entrantbecause such switching imposes costs, such as the burden of informing others of their new number. In the administration of their numbering plans, regulators in most OECD countries have been gradually moving forward to achieve number portability.[48] While it is possible to provide number portability through "call forwarding" variants (under which a customer in effect is given two or more numbers), there is general agreement that solutions involving Advanced Intelligent Network is superior (though more costly) since the former puts pressure on the availability of numbers.[49] Longer-term solutions based on Advanced Intelligent Network functions require the establishment of a data-base and signalling systems such as common channel signalling/Signalling System 7 (SS-7). In Mexico, a Committee was created, with the industry and Cofetel, to decide on the specific features of SS-7 to be adopted by all carriers. The conclusions were adopted in the National Basic Signalling Plan.

---

Box 3.    **Changes to Mexico's telephone numbering regime**

By December 1998, Mexico faced the prospect of running out of numbers in major cities. In Mexico City, for example, 8 120 000 of the available 8 180 000 numbers had been assigned – leaving less than 1% available for new subscribers or new carriers. In Tijuana, a little less than 90% of the available numbers had been assigned. Thus, the Local Competition decision adds an extra digit to numbers across the country in stages, beginning with Mexico City in February 1999. The decision also aligns Mexico's international dialling prefixes with international norms. The old and new dialling prefixes are as follows:

| | OLD DIALLING PREFIXES | NEW DIALLING PREFIXES |
|---|---|---|
| To the US and Canada: | 95 + Area code + number | 00 + 1 + Area code + number. |
| To other countries: | 98 + Country code + City code + number. | 00 + Country code + City code + number. |
| Domestic Long-distance: | 91 + City code + number. | 01 + City code + number. |

Mexico does not yet have an agreed plan for number portability, either through a "call forwarding" variant or through a solution involving Advanced Intelligent Network. Mexico is, however, currently in the process of adopting a new dialling plan. Mexico will add an eighth digit to numbers in Mexico City in February 1999 as well as Guadalajara and Monterrey by the year 2000. By increasing the stock of available numbers, Mexico is making the initial steps to facilitate a more comprehensive number portability scheme at a later date.[50] It is important, however, that further concrete steps be taken to introduce number portability, which include geographic mobility as well as mobile numbering mobility. The new dialling plan is outlined in Box 3.

It is not currently possible for telecommunications users in Mexico to select a long-distance carrier on a call-by-call basis. Plans for call-by-call selection of the long-distance carrier were set out in the numbering plan published in June 1996, with the intention of commencing the service in September 1997. Each of the 11 carriers holding long-distance concessions at that time were allocated an "identification code" using the mechanism set out in the numbering plan. However the concessionaires requested Cofetel to delay the process until April 1998 and Cofetel agreed. At the beginning of 1998, concessionaires asked once more to defer the process. Cofetel resolved to establish the basis for the start of the service and on 30 March 1998 Cofetel published the "Resolution by which it establishes the conditions and operational characteristics to start the system of call by call selection of the long distance carrier". This resolution sets out the guidelines under which call-by-call selection will be provided as well as the guidelines for local carriers to comply with their obligation to provide this service. By the start of 1999 call-by-call selection service had not commenced operation.

In the absence of call-by-call selection of carrier, competition between long-distance carriers is focused on becoming a user's default or pre-subscribed carrier. To the extent that there are costs involved in switching from one carrier to another (in the form of delays or paperwork), competition is likely to be less intense than if users can select the long-distance carrier on a call-by-call basis. The switching costs can also be used as a barrier against new entry by firms that did not participate in the original balloting process. This may partly explain why the existing concessionaires have opposed the introduction of this service.[51] The lack of call-by-call selection of the long-distance carrier is a weakness in the Mexican regime.

## 2.7. Universal service obligations

Mexico currently has one of the lowest penetration rates of telephone lines of any country in the OECD. Mexico's teledensity also appears low in comparison with its neighbours in South America, taking into account the GDP per capita (see Figure 6). Accordingly, the promotion of network expansion and "universal service" has been a central policy goal of Mexico.

As stated earlier, the 1990 Telmex concession included requirements for network expansion. Specifically, the Telmex concession states that:

> Between [10 September 1990] and 31 December 1994 Telmex must expand its number of basic telephone service lines in operation excluding public telephone booths, by an average minimum rate of 12% annually except in fortuitous circumstances or force majeure.[52]

As Figure 2 shows, Telmex complied with these requirements in its concession. However, network expansion has lagged in subsequent years. In part this is due to the effects of the macroeconomic crisis, a skewed income distribution, and the rapid rebalancing which has taken place.

In addition, the SCT, together with the governments of the States (Mexico is composed of 31 states and the Federal District) has established a Rural Telephone Program to provide telephone service for towns with between 100 and 499 inhabitants. From the Census of 1990 it was determined that there were 32 230 such towns in Mexico. In 1995 this program was changed to allow new technologies (such as cellular telephones) to participate in the program. Cofetel reports that during the present administration approximately 21 000 localities have been connected.

For the last few years Mexico has relied primarily on the forces of competition to expand the network. To that end, policies have been put in place to enhance competition in local service, including rebalancing of local and long-distance tariffs, auctioning of spectrum suitable for PCS and wireless local loop applications, and the establishment of interconnection rules for local access. With these policies now in place, the outlook for network expansion is better. It is the government's opinion that through the auctioning of the spectrum for the supply of wireless telephone services (together with investments in cable telephony projects), teledensity could be doubled with the installation of 9.5 million new lines in five years.

However, as this report demonstrates, overall telecommunications prices in Mexico, especially for local telecommunications services remain high and penetration low. It is to be hoped that the growth of competition in local service will drive down local service prices. If this can be achieved, this will likely have a major impact on teledensity in Mexico.

Telecommunications networks exhibit a characteristic known as "network externalities", meaning that the value of a connection to the network depends upon the number of people who are also connected. There are ways for individuals to internalise this externality – that is, mechanisms by which firms or consumers can subsidise the cost of telecommunications services for others with whom they want to remain in contact. For example, businesses that value being reached by their customers can offer to pay for the charges themselves through "free call" or 0800 numbers. Some telecommunications firms offer "private 0800 numbers" under which individuals can offer to pay the charges for specific callers to their telephone. Of course, individuals can always make private arrangements to subsidise or reimburse the telephone costs of friends or relatives with whom they desire to remain in contact.

However, it is possible that these private arrangements do not work perfectly. It is therefore possible that setting a structure of prices so that individuals are encouraged onto the network at the margin could enhance total welfare. In rich countries, the elasticity of demand for telephone service with

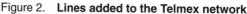

Figure 2. **Lines added to the Telmex network**

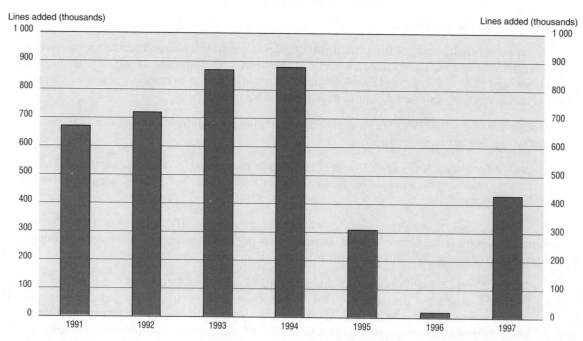

*Source:* Telmex.

respect to prevailing prices is so small as to make such programs largely ineffective. However, the situation in Mexico may be different. In some cases it appears that Telmex has already raised the local service charges to the point where Mexican subscribers are having difficulty remaining on the network. Prices for telecommunications services in Mexico are very high in relation to Mexican incomes.

As discussed earlier in this chapter, it may be that, in Mexico, overall welfare could be improved by setting the structure of telecommunications prices in a manner which encourages subscribers onto the network at the margin. As discussed earlier, in a competitive environment, the structure of the prices of the incumbent cannot be adjusted without inducing competitive entry into the high margin services. In a competitive environment, a readjustment of prices (raising on some prices and lowering of others) can only be achieved through the establishment of a portable, competitively and technologically neutral fund.

Cofetel has expressed the intention to establish such a fund. Some general economic principles to guide the establishment of such are fund can be articulated. First, the funds should be raised in a manner that distorts competition as little as possible. This usually implies that the fund should be financed to the extent possible from general tax revenues.[53] Alternatively, if it is necessary to finance the fund from the telecommunications industry, the funds should be recovered in a broad-based manner (so that the "tax" on any one telecommunications service can be as small as possible). In addition, the "tax" should be higher on services that are relatively less elastic. Fixed or non-traffic sensitive charges on subscriber (especially business) lines are therefore preferred to usage charges on interconnection services.

Second, the funds should be available to all carriers, independent of their technology and in a manner that ensures that the service is provided in the lowest cost manner. This is particularly important as a mechanism to prevent the incumbent inflating the alleged size of the necessary contribution. One approach is to tender the right to provide services in loss-making areas.[54]

As emphasised earlier, such a fund would allow the incumbent to recover the costs of any deficit on local residential service is a manner which distorts all prices (including interconnection charges) as little as possible.

## 2.8. International aspects

International issues in Mexican telecommunications are dominated by the important fact that the vast majority of the international telecommunications traffic of Mexico (88.6%) is with just one other country – the USA. The next largest country is Canada with 1.6%. No other country has a volume of more than 1%.[55]

Historically, in-bound calls from the US have exceeded out-bound calls by a factor of two and a half to one. Termination charges for calls (based on the international accounting rate system) have been decreasing since the beginning of this decade, but are still above the underlying costs, yielding a significant revenue stream for Mexico.

From the early days of the deregulation of telecommunications in the US, the concern was expressed that competition between US long-distance companies would drive termination costs down in the US, while foreign monopolies could maintain termination costs at high levels. This would lead to large imbalances in the "trade" of telecommunications services, with US companies making large payments to foreign monopolies. The proposed solution was to restrict competition between US long-distance carriers in the termination of foreign calls. Under the "proportional return" system companies in the US would agree on a common termination charge and incoming traffic would be shared amongst the local carriers in proportion to the outgoing traffic generated by that carrier. Over time, bilateral and multilateral negotiations would seek to lower the accounting rates closer to cost. This system has also been adopted in other liberalising countries.

At the time of the liberalisation of long-distance competition in Mexico, Mexico was not faced with a foreign monopoly in the US, but was concerned about equality of treatment for US companies in Mexico and Mexican companies in the US. Also, Mexico had a very sizeable telecommunications "trade" imbalance in its favour. In order to preserve the revenue flowing to the Mexican telecommunications industry from this imbalance, Mexico decided establish the proportional return system. As in the US, the competing international operators adopt a single, uniform termination charge. Incoming international traffic is distributed amongst them in a manner proportional to the share of outgoing international traffic. The right to negotiate the uniform termination charge was given to the carrier with the largest share of the traffic (which is likely to be Telmex for the foreseeable future). At the time of writing Telmex and AT&T have agreed that the settlement rates for 1998, the first semester of 1999 and the second half of 1999 and the year 2000 will be 37, 31, and 19 US cents, respectively.

Since the termination charges are maintained well above cost, there are strong incentives on the US carriers to seek to "bypass" the official public network to avoid paying the termination charges.[56] Cofetel has rigorously defended the proportional return system by refusing to grant concessions for international simple resale and by prosecuting informal interconnection of networks near the border with the US.[57]

Estimates of the effect of the proportional return system can be seen by comparing prices. Telmex currently offers to certain major domestic customers the ability to call anywhere in Mexico at an average of 11 cents per minute (including both origination and termination charges). In contrast, the rate for terminating international calls from the US border to a telephone in Mexico is charged at 25 cents (average) in 1999. International long-distance prices have come down as a consequence of competition and a decline in the settlement rates. Cofetel note, based on data from registered prices, calls to the US have dropped between 42.6% and 20.6% between 1996 and 1998.

The proportional return system for international traffic in Mexico is due to be reviewed during 1999. Rule 40 of the rules for international long distance services (published in June 1996) state that: "The proportional return system established in these rules cannot be modified before the third anniversary of its entry into force. Despite that, Cofetel, after reviewing the current conditions of competition and reciprocity for the operation of telecommunication services of Mexico with other countries, the evolution of international references for interconnection tariffs and settlement rates for the traffic of Mexico with its main commercial partners, as well as the growth and development of the telecommunications markets of the country, can determine the convenience to make modifications to the proportional return system established in these rules, before the time stated in the previous paragraph."

Foreign ownership remains subject to restrictions in most areas of the telecommunications sector. Under the Federal Telecommunications Law (Article 12) foreign investment participation in telecommunications concessions may not exceed 49%, except for cellular telephone providers. In the case of cellular operators, higher levels of foreign investment participation may be allowed, subject to the approval of the National Foreign Investment Commission ("*Comisión Nacional de Inversiones Extranjeras*"). No foreign investment restrictions apply in respect of value added services. The 1997 reforms to the Foreign Investment Law introduced additional mechanisms to enhance foreign investment participation. An enterprise with 51% of the voting stock in the hands of Mexican investors and 49% in foreign investment is considered as 100% Mexican when acquiring the 51% of the stock of another company. In addition, limited right shares can be considered as neutral investment and not taken into account for the purposes of foreign investment limitations.

International agreements have played a role in Mexico, as in many other countries. The conclusion of the NAFTA agreement significantly increased the degree to which Mexican telecommunications equipment markets were opened to foreign suppliers from Canada and the US.[58] Importantly, with the successful conclusion in February 1997 of the WTO agreement on basic telecommunications, Mexico took a strong step toward promoting foreign participation in the telecommunications services market. Mexico made significant market-opening commitments in the agreement and joined 64 other WTO Members in subscribing to a Reference Paper on Pro-Competitive Regulatory Principles.[59]

## 2.9. Consumer protection

In Mexico, as in many other countries, consumers may designate a long-distance company as their "default" or "1+" carrier to which long-distance calls are automatically directed. In many OECD countries, some carriers have undertaken to be designated as the "default" carrier without proper subscriber authorisation. This is called "slamming". Because in Mexico there is no possibility to select a long-distance carrier on a call-by-call basis, competition to become a user's default carrier is particularly intense.

In Mexico, slamming complaints are a responsibility of Cofetel, and also a general agency responsible for consumer protection called *Procuraduria Federal de Proteccion al Consumidor* ("Profeco"). All three major carriers, Avantel, Alestra and Telmex have been fined for slamming.[60] In November 1997, Cofetel established the obligation that a third party verifies all changes to pre-subscription.

Telmex has also been fined for delays in providing subscriber information from its database necessary for rivals to switch a subscriber's default carrier in cases where the subscriber has legally authorised the switch from Telmex.[61]

A further issue relates to the way Telmex charges for local measured service. In Mexico subscribers are billed for each call made after a certain minimum. However, Telmex did not list the specific numbers called and thus customers could not verify whether the calls were made. Profeco reports that there have been about 39 000 complaints against Telmex relating to charges for local measured service.[62] To deal with this issue, following Profeco recommendations, Telmex introduced a new billing system to provide customers with detailed information since 1998.[63]

## 2.10. Streamlining regulation and application of competition principles

Since 1989, an explicit national policy on regulatory reform has been in place and has steadily expanded in scope and ambition. An important element of this strategy was the creation in 1989 of an economic deregulation unit called the *Unidad de Desregulacion Economica* (UDE) in the Ministry of Trade and Industry, *Secretaria de Comercio y Fomento Industrial* (Secofi).

By the early 1990s, this economic deregulation programme had broadened to include an effort to review obsolete and inadequate regulations and build the necessary microeconomic conditions to increase efficiency and lower costs in all markets. In November 1995, a comprehensive policy, called the *Acuerdo para la Desregulacion de la Actividad Empresarial* (ADAE), was enacted in a new executive order, and was confirmed a few months later in the National Development Plan. It gave the UDE greater review powers, created an Economic Deregulation Council (CDE) and, most important, established a scrutiny process for new regulatory proposals and existing formalities.

In November 1995, a review process was established for all new regulatory proposals likely to have an impact on business activity. According to the UDE, the rate of compliance with this new process has generally been high. As in other countries, minor rules or politically sensitive regulations may still be implemented without following the appropriate review by the CDE/UDE. However, the strong support of the Comptroller General and political support at the highest level may combine to force the establishment of a new regulatory culture in Mexico (see background report on Government Capacity to Produce High Quality Regulation).

The ADAE comprehensive process permitted broader consultation and review through the CDE of any regulatory proposal likely to have an impact on business activity. However, most of the regulations produced by SCT, and later Cofetel, after the enactment of the FTL were not reviewed by UDE/CDE because rules related to concessions were exempted from the ADAE. In December 1996, a reform of the Administrative Procedure Law established a more powerful review mechanism through the obligation to present a Regulatory Impact Analysis to the UDE/CDE for all proposed regulations including those related to rules governing telecommunication concessions.

As mentioned earlier, Cofetel proposes to combine the assorted rulings and case by case decisions into a single uniform body of regulation.[64] The process of implementing such regulation would involve exposing Cofetel's regulation to close scrutiny by the UDE/CDE. As stated earlier, given the importance of the telecommunications industry to the economy and the resources at stake in many regulatory decisions in telecommunications, it is important that Cofetel's rules and policies be subject to external oversight by an agency charged with responsibility for ensuring high-quality regulation such as the UDE.

### 2.10.1. *Application of competition principles*

Many aspects of the interface between competition law and sector-specific regulation are well designed:

– Competition law applies to the telecommunications sector, and the CFC has the authority to take enforcement actions and provide competition policy advice as in other OECD countries. As indicated elsewhere in this chapter, the CFC has been involved in numerous proceedings in the telecommunications sector, including a few merger proceedings. In July 1995, Telmex acquired the major cable provider in Mexico City (in spite of a prohibition in its concession on the provision directly or indirectly of television services to the public). The decision of CFC not to challenge the transaction is controversial since, in the longer-term, the cable infrastructure could provide an important means of entry into local markets.

– The FTL explicitly provides for a role for the CFC in spectrum auctions. As one example, in authorising Telmex's participation in the auction for fixed-wireless services, the CFC placed certain obligations on Telmex, such as the requirement to submit to an outside auditor to monitor compliance with competition principles and a requirement to wait 24 months before commencing operations.[65]

– Lastly, the FTL explicitly provides a role for the CFC in declaring a carrier dominant for the purposes of imposing additional regulation and, as discussed earlier, the CFC has done so in the case of Telmex.

At one level, there is a significant overlap in the responsibilities of Cofetel and the CFC, particularly in the prevention of abuse of a dominant position (including predatory pricing). Indeed, many of the provisions of the Telmex concession and the FTL relating to interconnection and prevention of cross-subsidisation can be viewed as the sector-specific outworking of the more general principle that a firm in a dominant position should not be allowed to use its dominant position to restrict competition.[66] At another level, the roles of Cofetel and the CFC can be viewed as complementary. The CFC, as an enforcement body, is intended to respond to complaints of aggrieved parties (or its own investigations) in the prosecution of anti-competitive behaviour. On the other hand, the primary role of Cofetel is to set policies, issue concessions and arbitrate on interconnection disputes. Recently, partly as a result of dissatisfaction with Cofetel, the new-entrant carriers have been increasingly turning to the CFC to resolve allegations of anti-competitive behaviour in the sector.

Despite the overlap in their functions, the formal interaction between the competition authority and Cofetel has been limited. For example, Cofetel seeks to prevent predatory pricing, and cross-subsidisation through its control over prices, largely independently of any input from the CFC.

In general, in the design of regulatory laws and institutions, there are good reasons to prefer generic as opposed to industry-specific approaches. Generic approaches are more inclined to be based on broad, well-tested underlying principles and are more likely to be immune to special-interest pleading. This is one reason why it is desirable (and the usual practice) for competition law to apply widely to as many sectors of the economy as possible.

In this light, it is desirable for competition enforcement activities in the telecommunications sector to conform as closely as possible to competition enforcement practices in the wider economy. To this end, Cofetel and the CFC should closely co-ordinate on their approach to enforcement activities. This could be achieved through the establishment of mechanisms for co-operation and statements of common approaches to issues such as market definition and enforcement. As one example, there is clear scope for collaboration on the determination of any specific restrictions to be imposed on Telmex following the CFC's determination of dominance. In making its determination the CFC identified specific competition deficiencies in five markets. It is appropriate therefore, that the CFC assists in the identification of specific remedies to address those deficiencies.[67]

More generally, given the expertise of the CFC in assessing how regulatory constraints affect competition, the input of the CFC into Cofetel's regulatory deliberations would be invaluable. This could be achieved by taking into account the views of the CFC as part of the wider consultation prior to taking important regulatory decisions.

As in any sector, it is important that a dominant firm be prevented from enhancing that dominance through acquisition of control over enterprises or assets which would allow it to strengthen its dominant position. Cable television providers are an important source of potential competition in the market for voice telephony and other telecommunications services. A merger of a dominant telecommunications company with a major cable TV provider would therefore raise competition concerns. In July 1995 Telmex acquired 49% of a major cable TV provider in the Mexico City area. In the medium term competition in telecommunications services in the Mexico City area would be enhanced if Telmex were required to divest this holding.

At present the Mexican regime contains no explicit mechanism for the lifting of regulation as competition develops. Although Telmex has been deemed to be dominant today, it may not be so in the future. The price control and other firm-specific requirements should be lifted, on the advice of the CFC, when Telmex is no longer considered to be dominant.

## 2.11. The dynamic view: convergence in communications markets

As technology develops, increasingly broadcasting and telecommunications are being provided over the same infrastructure by the same firm. This phenomenon is known as convergence. Convergence can create tensions for the regulatory regimes for broadcasting and telecommunications by either holding up the benefits of convergence or, where convergence is allowed, encouraging firms to exploit gaps or differences in the respective regulatory regimes. Convergence can also create tensions regarding regulatory institutions as, in some countries, these two sectors are regulated by separate regulatory institutions.

In Mexico, the regulatory regime for broadcasting and telecommunications largely reflects the underlying technological convergence. In Mexico conventional over-the-air broadcasting (or "Open TV and Audio" as it is known in Mexico) is regulated by the Law of Radio and Television and is the responsibility of the *Dirección General de Sistemas de Radio y Televisión* of the Under-Ministry of Communications in the SCT. However, cable broadcasting (known as "Restricted TV and Audio") is considered a telecommunications service and is regulated by the FTL under the responsibility of Cofetel.

The FTL allows concessionaires of restricted TV to offer other value-added services, such as digital music and Internet, among others.[68] In the coming months Cofetel will publish the Rules for Restricted Television and Audio which seek to provide incentives for fair and non-discriminatory competition, protect copyright rights and promote national production regardless of the technology used. As a consequence of these steps, the interest of customers and companies on restricted audio and TV has increased in the past few years. Restricted (*i.e.*, cable) TV has increased demand for programming and encouraged the development of content targeted at specific segments of the population. As in other countries, cable TV also plays an important role in making broadcast services available where over-the-air reception is poor. Today there are 1.1 million users in Mexico.

As of 1996, there were 246 concessions granted for cable TV, increasing to 284 in 1997 and 394 in 1998. 19 concessions have been granted for TV via microwave (MMDS) services, and six concessions to provide satellite direct-to-home television (DTH) services.

Holders of local and long-distance telecommunications concessions can apply to Cofetel to amend their concession to allow them to provide television services. Telmex's concession expressly prevents Telmex from offering directly, or indirectly, public television services.

283

## 3.  MARKET PERFORMANCE

Regulation is not an end in itself. Rather, the final objective of regulation is the efficient delivery of benefits to users and consumers. This section assesses the performance of the Mexican telecommunications industry in the delivery of those benefits to users and consumers, using a variety of indicators related to price, quality, investment, network penetration and so on.

### 3.1. Price and quantity indicators

Price is, of course, one of the most important indicators of performance. In an efficient market, prices are driven down towards the underlying costs. Reliable cost information is, however, difficult to obtain. Therefore, rather than comparing prices directly with costs, it is more common to compare current prices with two alternative benchmarks – price levels in the past and price levels in other comparable countries.

Consider first the movement in prices over time. Competitive entry into the provision of long-distance and international services has led to pronounced decreases in prices in these markets. Prices have fallen by 50%, in real terms, in two years. This has been brought about by general price reductions as well as the introduction of new discount schemes for calls with particular time and destination characteristics and the extension of off-peak and weekend rates.

As in most countries, discount plans have played an important role in the reduction of the effective price of these services. In January 1998, Avantel offered a 33% discount off all national long distance and international calls, when a customer spends 150 pesos a month or more. In July 1998, Avantel enhanced this discount calling plan by launching a *Friends & Family scheme* under which customers receive preferential prices on calls to a limited list of friends and family members. Customers receive a further 10%

Figure 3.  **Trends in Mexican business and residential local service charges**

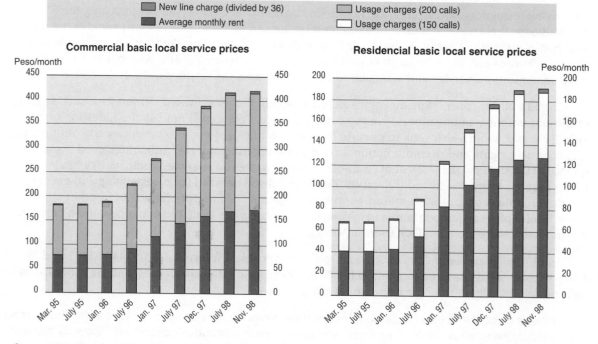

*Source:*  Materials gathered from market participants by OECD.

discount on calls made to other Avantel clients. In the same week Alestra (AT&T) released its AT&T *Destinations Program*, offering low rates on calls made to AT&T customers in the United States.

After being fixed in nominal terms during 1995 (in spite of 59% inflation of that year), local service tariffs subsequently increased faster than inflation. This includes not only increases in the monthly flat rate, but also increases in local measured service charges. Figure 3 illustrates the movement in the nominal price of a basket of local services for residential and business users. The basket includes the cost of installing a new line (at a per month rate, averaged over 3 years), the monthly line rental and the usage cost for a number of calls. For residential customers the number of calls is 150 (for which the first 100 are free) and for business customers, the number is 200 (all of which are charged). As is apparent, the prices for local service have risen rapidly since 1995.

Long-distance volumes have been increasing throughout the 1990s, as Table 4 indicates.

Table 4. **Trends in volumes of lines and calls 1990-1998**

| | 1990 | 1991 | 1992 | 1993 | 1994 | 1995 | 1996 | 1997 | 1998 |
|---|---|---|---|---|---|---|---|---|---|
| Lines in service | 5.35 | 6.02 | 6.76 | 7.82 | 8.493 | 8.801 | 8.826 | 9.254 | 9.927 |
| National long distance calls | 951 | 1 068 | 1 221 | 1 358 | 1 630 | 1 747 | 1 967 | 2 222* | 2 511* |
| International long distance calls | 169 | 210 | 284 | 324 | 461 | 416 | 491 | 555* | 627* |

Note: All figures in millions.
* Estimated by the OECD.
Source: Cofetel, Telmex annual reports.

Price levels in other countries provide a second important source of price benchmarks. For these purposes the OECD collects the prices of a basket of telecommunications for residential and business customers in each of the OECD countries. The basket includes a number of calls distributed at different times of the day, different days of the week and over different distances. The statistics are prepared in US$ using both purchasing power parity (PPP) and current exchange rates. In general, it is considered that the PPP figures provide a more reliable comparison. However, there are reasons to doubt the reliability of PPP figures for those countries experiencing high inflation.[69] For comparison purposes both sets of figures are presented below.

The results of these comparisons with selected OECD countries are displayed in Figure 4. It is apparent that in both cases Mexico's prices are well above the OECD average. In both cases the fixed (*i.e.*, monthly rental) component of the basket is also above the OECD average. These price comparisons do not reflect the nominal price increases announced in March 1999.

## 3.2. Penetration rates

As this chapter has noted, the penetration rate of telephone lines in Mexico remains low in comparison with other OECD counties. As Figure 5 shows, Mexico's performance in terms of penetration rates has lagged behind OECD countries, and Mexico has lost ground since 1990. Indeed, while Mexico is only at about 10 access lines per 100 inhabitants, the next lowest OECD country, Poland, is near 20 lines due to an increase in about 10 lines per 100 inhabitants since 1990.[70]

There is a strong link between GDP per capita and telecommunications penetration. It may be more appropriate, therefore, to compare Mexico with other countries at a similar level of development. Figure 6 compares Mexico's telecommunications penetration with other Latin American countries. Compared with these other countries, Mexico appears closer to the average, although there remains room for improvement.

As indicated elsewhere in this paper it is expected that the new local service concessionaires have committed to build 9.5 million new access lines over the next five years. This will increase Mexico's penetration rate to at least 18-20 access lines per person.

Figure 4. **International comparison of business and residential charges**
**(August 1998)**

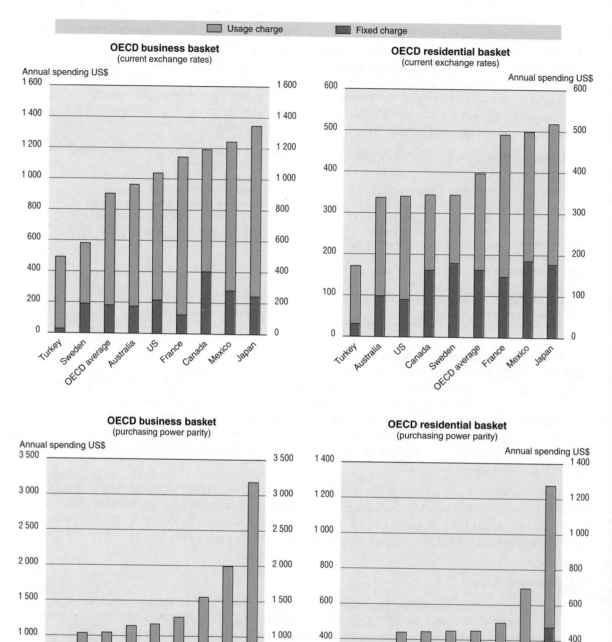

Source: OECD (1999), *Communications Outlook 1999*, Paris.

Figure 5. **International comparison of progress toward network penetration**

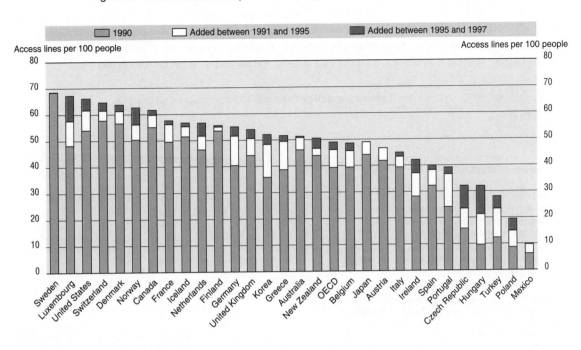

*Source:* OECD (1999), *Communications Outlook 1999*, Paris.

Figure 6. **GDP per capita *vs* penetration rate (selected countries)**

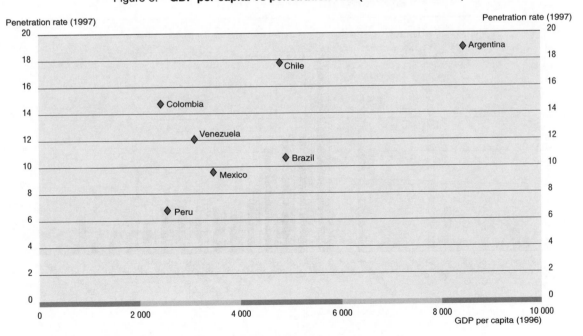

*Source:* ITU, *Basic Indicators: 1997* posted at: <<www.itu.int/ti/industryoverview/index.html>>.

### 3.3. Quality of service

As discussed earlier (Section 2.2.4), Telmex's quality of service has significantly improved since 1990 (with a temporary decline in service quality in 1995-1996), in part due to significant investment in improved telecommunications technology. Table 5 presents the change in key service quality indicators that Telmex is required to meet, according to the terms of its concession.

Table 5.   **Telmex's quality of service 1990 compared with 1998**

| Indicator | 1990 (%) | 1998 (%) |
|---|---|---|
| *Local service*: | | |
| Index of service continuation | 80.2 | 91.4 |
| Percentage of call failure | 10.0 | 2.8 |
| Repair within same day | 45.0 | 80.4 |
| Repair within 3 days | 80.0 | 94.0 |
| Index of quality of service for basic service | 91.2 | 97.8 |
| Obtaining dial tone within four seconds | 97.0 | 99.9 |
| % of calls reaching destination | 92.0 | 98.3 |
| Public payphones out of service as % of total | 13.0 | 1.9 |
| % of calls that are answered by the operator | 90.0 | 92.6 |
| *Long distance service* | | |
| Index for quality of service for long distance | 90.0 | 98.1 |
| % of calls that reach their destination | 90.0 | 99.3 |
| % of calls that are answered by the operator | 90.0 | 95.3 |

*Source*:   Telmex, "El Titulo de Concesion de Telmex y la Apertura a la Competencia en el sector de las telecomunicaciones", 3 November 1998.

Another indicator of quality of service is the number of faults that are recorded. As Figure 7 hows, Mexico ranks fairly well in this indicators.

Figure 7.   **Quality of service faults per 100 lines per annum**

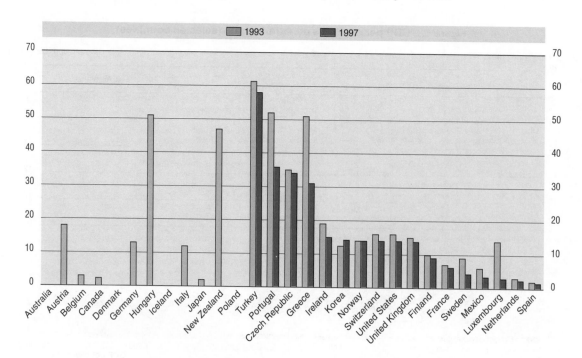

*Source:*   OECD (1997), *Communications Outlook 1999.*

## 3.4. Network investment and modernisation

The degree of network modernisation in terms of digital switching and fibre optic cable provide a measure of non-price aspects of the service provided to subscribers. Digitalised networks allow, for example, faster connections and increased bandwidth (and thus flexibility of uses such as video). An important development in this regard was the replacement of Telmex's microwave long distance network with fibre optic lines. Telmex has installed more than 30 000 km of fibre-optic network

Progress has been made toward network modernisation. From the time Telmex was privatised in 1990 through the end of 1995, the company had invested over US$14 billion, including US$1.3 billion for telephone equipment, US$2.7 billion for transmission equipment, US$3.9 billion for switches and transmission and power equipment, and US$3.7 billion for outside plant. Most progress was made during the 1990 to 1994 period, as shown in Table 6.

Table 6. **Increases in the rate of digitalisation over time**

|  | 1990 | 1991 | 1992 | 1993 | 1994 | 1995 | 1996 | 1997 | 1998 |
|---|---|---|---|---|---|---|---|---|---|
| % Digital: | 29 | 39 | 52 | 65 | 83 | 88 | 90 | 90 | 96.7 |
| Increase in % | n.a. | 10 | 13 | 13 | 18 | 5 | 2 | 0 | 6.7 |

Source: Rates for the period 1990-1996 from COFETEL, Estadisticas de Lenteres Sobre Telecomuniciones "Digitalisation de la Planta Telefonica: 1990-1996," posted at <www.cft.gob.mx/html/5_est/graficas/ Coraf3_pag5.html>. 1998 figures for May 1998.

Public telecommunications investment has fallen off since the investment program undertaken in the late 1980's and the early years of the privatisation. Beginning at about US$16 per capita in the late 1980s and increasing to about US$24 per capita in the early 1990s, the level of investment has fallen in 1997 to about US$10 per capita, well below the OECD average.

## 3.5. Employment

In considering the effects of technological developments, it is also pertinent to recognise the impact on employment levels. Despite considerable "downsizing" by telecommunications carriers in many countries, the number of telecommunication employees in Mexico rose between 1995 and 1996 but fell slightly in 1997. Most of the growth in employment over this period is the result of substantial increases in the radiotelephone (cellular, beepers, paging) industry, which grew at an annual average growth rate of approximately 20%. Since 1990, employment in Telmex has in fact risen by some 12% (see Table 7).

Table 7. **Number of employees in telecommunications service supply**

|  | 1985 | 1990 | 1995 | 1996 | 1997 |
|---|---|---|---|---|---|
| Employees | 37 487 | 50 620 | 50 413 | 57 750 | 56 650 |

Source: OECD, *Communications Outlook* 1999, Paris.

The current and future entry of new operators in the telecommunications industry as a whole will continue to create new jobs in the future.[71] Cofetel estimates that the new wired and wireless local telephony projects will generate 50 000 new direct jobs.[72]

Figure 8.  **Public telecommunications investments as a percentage of revenue**

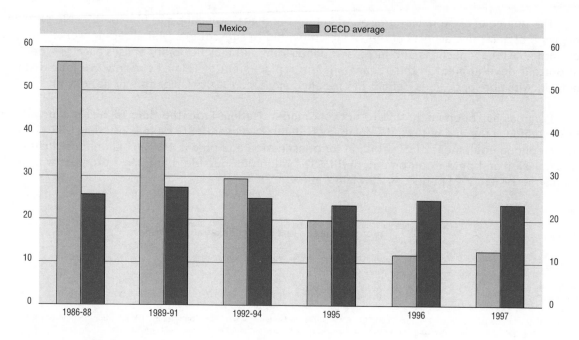

*Source:* OECD (1999), *Communications Outlook 1999*, Paris, Table 4.10, p. 111.

## 4. CONCLUSIONS AND RECOMMENDATIONS

### 4.1. General assessment of current strengths and weaknesses

Overall, Mexico's telecommunications regime has several strengths. Mexico has designed and implemented a sustained long-term process of regulatory reform based on two stages. The first stage, from 1988 to 1994, involved privatisation and a reorganisation of the government's role. The second stage involved the issuing of a completely new law to modernise the regulatory framework and introduce competition in the market for telecommunications services.

The interconnection regime was established before competition started and allowed transitory periods to review interconnection tariffs and adjust them in the light of international references and Mexican market conditions.

In little more than three years Mexico has moved from a statutory monopoly to a situation of active competition in most telecommunications markets. Competition has developed particularly rapidly in long-distance service, and has led to rapid price declines. New entrants in the long-distance markets achieved higher market shares in two years than in most other OECD countries that have liberalised entry. Consumers have benefited from long distance prices that are up to 50% lower in real terms. Competition is expected to start in local service during 1999.

From the Telmex concession in 1990 it is clear that the Mexican regime contemplated and prepared for the development of full competition. The concession itself includes specific competition safeguards that were relatively far-sighted for the time. The 1995 Federal Telecommunications Law is a well-conceived statute that incorporates central elements of effective telecommunications regulation. The FTL promotes market mechanisms for the allocation of scarce spectrum rights and explicitly provides for a role for the federal antitrust authority in assessing market competition. It also sets out a basic framework for interconnection by rivals to the incumbent's public switched telephone network and establishes the basis of the institutional framework necessary for independent regulation of the industry.

Mexico has been aggressive in using market-based mechanisms to allocate spectrum. These mechanisms, together with the active role played by the CFC, have generated a competitive market structure in mobile and wireless communications. This strength is reflected in positive developments in the mobile market. While penetration rates remain low compared to other OECD countries, subscriber growth rates have been strong and the market share of the largest competitor is at about the same level as elsewhere in the OECD. This is an important strength given that wireless (particularly wireless-local-loop) may be more likely to become an alternative to wireline access in countries facing network penetration challenges.[73]

The privatisation of Satmex during 1997 was another major step for regulatory reform, with the issuing of the *reglamento* on satellite communications to establish the basis for competition including the use of foreign satellite signals to provide services in Mexico.

Although there is room for improvement, aspects of the structure of the interface between competition law and sector-specific regulation are well designed. Competition law applies to the telecommunications sector, and thus the CFC has the authority to take enforcement actions and provide competition policy advice as in other OECD countries. As noted in Chapter 3, the quality of the competition law is high. The law is consistent and affords a solid foundation for applying competition policy in law enforcement and in other policy issue

Despite these strengths, there remains considerable room for improvement. The independence of the regulator could be improved, and its methods for coming to decisions can also be improved further to fully meet international best practice standards for transparency, including disclosure of information or arguments supporting major regulatory decisions and consultations with industry players.

---

Box 4.  **Strengths**

- Sustained policy direction in favour of regulatory reform over the last decade.
- The process of policy development and new entry in the transition from monopoly to active competition has been rapid in most telecommunications markets, particularly long distance service.

Substantial improvements have been seen since 1989 in the quality of telecommunications services for businesses and residences.

The Mexican domestic telecommunications market has been attractive for foreign investors, and Mexican consumers have benefited from the capital and new technologies that they have brought into Mexico.

- The fundamental telecommunications law is generally sound, and establishes an institutional basis for independent regulation of the industry.
- The spectrum allocation regime is market-based and well-managed.
- There is an explicit role for competition law.
- The Telmex concession includes competition safeguards and asymmetric regulation that was far-sighted for the time.
- Relatively rapid rebalancing of the price structure in advance of the introduction of competition.
- Rapid downward movement in the interconnection tariffs.
- The establishment of a distinct regulatory agency separate from the government and independent of the major industry players.
- Immediate prospect of sizeable new investment and network expansion.

Cofetel's policies have not been subject to oversight or scrutiny by a third party agency. Given the importance of the telecommunications industry and the amounts at stake in many regulatory decisions, it is important that Cofetel achieve decisions of the highest quality. This can be assured by enforcing the requirements that Cofetel's policies be subject to government-wide regulatory review processes.

Although the FTL is generally a sound statute, it has its flaws. To begin with, the FTL places a great deal of power in the hands of the regulator in its decisions to grant concessions and the conditions placed on those concessions. The FTL also, unnecessarily, requires all concessionaires to register their prices before their use, and to publicise those prices. This facilitates collusion and hinders innovation in pricing schemes. Although the FTL explicitly sets out the sanctions that can be applied, the monetary sanctions are too small (by a factor of about one thousand) to make an impact on a large player and the only alternative is the draconian step of revoking a concession. Enforcement of concessions is unnecessarily difficult.s

The Telmex concession also has its flaws. Although the price-cap system of regulation on Telmex was far-sighted, the inclusion of both competitive and non-competitive prices within the same cap has the effect of enhancing the incentives on Telmex to behave anti-competitively in the competitive sector.

Finally, the existing system of uniform settlement rate and proportional return has prevented prices from decreasing for Mexican and foreign consumers calling to and from Mexico, to the benefit of the telecommunications operators. The Mexican government established this system in 1996 with the flexibility to review it after the third year of entry into force in light *inter alia* of prevailing reciprocity conditions on the US and other foreign markets and domestic market developments.

---

Box 5.   Weaknesses

Institutional arrangements for the regulator do not yet provide adequate independence from the government, which has a direct role (through SCT) in granting and enforcing concessions.

Consultation and transparency in rule-making processes need more development, while the rule-making powers of the regulator are not subject to adequate oversight or review by other agencies.

The concession system gives significant discretionary power over entry to the regulator, and sanctions for violations of concessions are too weak.

Interconnection charges are high relative to international levels and the basis for establishing those charges is not yet sufficiently transparent.

Inclusion of competitive prices in the "basket" of the price-cap regulation system enhances the incentives on the incumbent to act anti-competitively.

- Requirements to register and disclose prices facilitate collusion among competitors and restricts innovation.

- International proportional return arrangements restrict competition and raise prices on international routes.

---

## 4.2. Potential benefits and costs of further regulatory reform

Mexican consumers have received some benefits from regulatory reform. Long distance prices, in particular, have declined rapidly. On the other hand, local service prices have risen, so that average prices (including both local and long distance) remain at high levels. However, further price-reductions in domestic and international long-distance will not be so easily translated directly into increases in local rates. In addition, it is to be hoped that local competition (especially from wireless companies) will eventually contribute to disciplining further the ability of Telmex to raise local rates further.

Further reform of the international proportional return system will yield immediate benefits in the form of lower international charges to and from the US. Lowering of interconnection charges closer to cost will place further downward pressure on long-distance rates.

Further reform will also cement in many of the benefits of competition. The benefits from competition could be eroded if carriers collude or if Cofetel is distracted from promoting competition through industry pressures. Enhancing the role of the competition authority and other government agencies responsible for regulatory reform will ensure that competition continues to thrive and that Cofetel continues to make decisions of the highest quality.

In the longer term, some of the problems that Mexico now experiences appear as opportunities. Although Mexican telecommunications prices are high and teledensity low, provided the regulatory regime can adequately prevent abuse by the dominant carrier, high prices will attract new entry. The low teledensity suggests that there is plenty of room for new entrants to build out networks without fear of duplication of the incumbent's network. Indeed, if Mexico reaches the teledensity that has been achieved in Asian countries in 15 years, there would be room for five telecommunications networks the size of Telmex.[74]

## 4.3. Policy options for consideration

The following recommendations are based on the assessment presented above, and the policy recommendations for regulatory reform set out in the OECD *Report on Regulatory Reform* (OECD, June 1997).

1. **Ensure that regulations and regulatory processes are transparent, non-discriminatory and applied effectively.**

   – *Enhance the independence of Cofetel by: appointing Commissioners for overlapping fixed terms; enhancing their tenure by making removal from office difficult.*

In the long-term, investment in the telecommunications industry requires the assurance that a regulatory framework will be developed, and disputes will be resolved, in an impartial, considered and efficient manner. It is desirable therefore to enhance the credibility and the independence of Cofetel by distancing the Commission even further from the SCT and from the political process in this way.

   – *Delegate the power to issue, enforce and revoke concessions from SCT to Cofetel.*

The value of establishing an independent, transparent regulatory entity is reduced when its powers are limited. The power to issue, enforce and revoke concessions is appropriately exercised by Cofetel.

   – *Establish formal consultation and transparency procedures for Cofetel with the government, the industry and the public to enhance the level of participation and improve the quality of decision making. This consultation process should include an opportunity for agencies such as the CFC to express their views publicly.*

Improved decision-making and consultation processes and publication of the reasons for all decisions would reduce the risk of litigation and would improve the overall quality of Cofetel's decisions. Cofetel has indicated that it intends to implement this policy during 1999. It should make all deliberate haste to do so. In particular, the CFC should have full opportunity to express its views.

   – *Ensure that full use of mandatory quality controls established by the government for the review of its regulatory powers is made in the telecommunications sector.*

The regulatory policies of Cofetel are among the more important regulatory controls in any sector. It is especially important that the powers of Cofetel be subject to the government's regulatory quality controls.

   – *Disclose the total amount of spectrum that could technically be used for a new service prior to auctioning new spectrum.*

Spectrum auctions provide the government with a financial interest in the artificial creation of spectrum scarcity and consequent reduction in competition. In order to offset concerns that more spectrum may be available than is sold, Cofetel should disclose the total amount of spectrum that could be feasibly made available for a particular technology prior to auctioning new spectrum.

*– Implement and enforce asymmetric regulation for the dominant carrier in conformance with Article 63 of the FTL.*

The Telmex concession played an important role in the transition to competition by establishing a fixed timeline for the rebalancing of Telmex's charges and establishing procedures and policies governing interconnection and other competition safeguards. However, this rebalancing is now complete (or almost complete) and the important competition safeguards are more fully set out in the FTL. As has been argued, the price-cap regime in the Telmex concession creates competition problems. Transparency and legal certainty would be enhanced by placing Telmex under the regulation that is appropriate for a dominant firm, applied under Article 63 of the FTL.

2. ***Reform regulations to stimulate competition and eliminate them except where clear evidence demonstrates that they are the best way to serve the broad public interest.***

*– Limit the discretion of Cofetel to grant concessions and to impose conditions on concessions. Issue concessions that do not restrict lines of business. Minimise coverage and commitments required of the concessionaires.*

One of the most important requirements for healthy competition is low barriers to entry. At present Cofetel has the power to impose conditions on concessionaires. Although there is little evidence that the conditions imposed have significantly hindered new entry, this power may itself in the longer term become a potential threat to competition.

*– Reconsider the proportional return system for international traffic with the US and with other countries as competition develops.*

The proportional return system with the US and other countries is a restraint on competition in the international long-distance market which increases prices paid by Mexican consumers.

*– Amend the FTL to eliminate, for carriers which are non-dominant, the requirement for Cofetel to register and publicise prices.*

Competition on prices is one of the most fundamental forms of competition. This competition is threatened by a system in which competitors have advance knowledge of each other's price changes and can observe each other's discounts. This requirement should be eliminated for all except dominant carriers. This would require changes to the FTL.

*– Undertake a number of policies to improve the foundations on which interconnection charges are set, namely: clearly identify the components of interconnection charges which are designed to compensate for the fixed and common costs of local service; allow the process of rebalancing to be completed by allowing Telmex to raise its prices for local service (especially business local service) to eliminate any remaining deficit; and pursue other approaches to the covering a deficit on local service (if one exists) through other mechanisms (such as the fund mechanism below).*

The deficit on Telmex's local service is an important component in Cofetel's argument for above-cost interconnection charges. At a minimum the portion of access charges which is intended to contribute towards this deficit should be separately and clearly identified. Restraining Telmex's rebalancing increases the size of the deficit on Telmex's local service and thereby raises interconnection charges. Ideally, it is more appropriate for the deficit to be funded through a broad-based tax on general revenues or a tax on less elastic telecommunications services, which can be more easily achieved through the use of a formal fund. Finally, under current proposals, Cofetel is forced to make arbitrary, controversial decisions as to when networks qualify for the higher interconnection charges. This could be eliminated by basing charges on whether the originating line serves a residential or business customer.

*– Structure interconnection charges according to the underlying cost – especially, adopt a flat per call charge for interconnection for local calls and reduce real interconnection charges over time according to best practice to ensure that Telmex improves productivity.*

Given that local calls are currently charged on a per minute basis in Mexico, charging interconnection for local calls on a per-minute basis introduces opportunities for distorting and anti-competitive behaviour. Reductions in the costs of providing interconnection services should be passed on to new entrants.

– *Promote network expansion, universal service and economic efficiency objectives by establishing an explicit, portable, competitively and technologically neutral funding mechanism.*

There is some evidence that local service rates in Mexico are approaching consumers' willingness-to-pay. It may therefore be appropriate to subsidise consumers on to the network at the margin, using a mechanism that relies on market forces, is competitively and technologically neutral, and is administered in a transparent fashion.

– *Develop and carry out plans to implement number portability and access to rights of way as soon as possible.*

Plans to introduce number portability and rules to assure access to rights-of-way appear to be at an early stage. An absence of number portability acts as an artificial disincentive for customers to switch from the incumbent to a new entrant because such switching imposes transaction costs, such as the burden of informing others of their new number. Moving forward toward full implementation of a permanent form of number portability would be an important step to assuring that subscribers do not face artificial disincentives to switching between carriers in response to price competition. Similarly, progress on developing an effective regime to assure appropriate access to rights-of-way is also quite important in order to ensure that there are no artificial regulatory barriers to entry into local service markets. This especially applies to the activities of local authorities.

– *Restrict the price cap to only those services in which there is an absence of competition.*

A revenue cap that covers both competitive and non-competitive services enhances the incentives on the incumbent to act anti-competitively in the competitive market. With the present degree of competition in the long-distance market, it is no longer necessary to regulate Telmex's rates. These rates should be removed from the price-cap by relaxing the price regulation set out in the concession or regulating Telmex's prices through some other mechanism, such as Article 63 of the FTL.

– *Dominant local carriers should be prevented from restricting competition by acquiring existing cable television infrastructure.*

Cable television infrastructure is an important source of potential competition in local telephony. In most cases strict enforcement of competition law can prevent a local telephony provider from purchasing a cable television infrastructure (on the basis that it reduces potential competition). In addition, requiring Telmex to divest its existing holdings in cable television should be considered.

## 3. Review, and strengthen where necessary, the scope, effectiveness and enforcement of competition policy.

– *Develop formal co-operation arrangements between Cofetel and CFC for the joint enforcement of competition law prohibitions in the telecommunications sector.*

Given the substantial links between the functions of Cofetel and CFC, it is important for them to develop a consistent approach to preventing anti-competitive behaviour. This could be facilitated through explicit formal co-operation and interaction arrangements.

– *Increase the maximum sanctions set out in the FTL to a level at which the sanctions could have a material impact.*

The current maximum monetary sanctions in the FTL are derisory. The threat to revoke a concession after three violations is a draconian measure that is unlikely to be taken in practice. The monetary sanctions should be enhanced to a level where they could be expected to make a real impact on even the largest concessionaires.

# NOTES

1. OECD, *Communications Outlook* 1999, Table 3.1, figures for 1997.

2. OECD, *Communications Outlook* 1999, Table 1.2.

3. 23.9 months. *Source*: Cofetel.

4. OECD, *Communications Outlook* 1999, Table 8.3.

5. Cofetel. Figure for May 1998.

6. In 1997, Mexico's GDP per capita was US$4 267. Within the OECD, only Poland (US$3 515) and Turkey (US$3 030), are lower.

7. Cofetel estimates this increased to 10.3 lines per 100 inhabitants by the end of 1998 (Cofetel 1999 Work Programme, p. 15).

8. OECD, *Communications Outlook* 1999, Table 4.2.

9. See Section 2.4.

10. Telmex was originally a wholly owned subsidiary of Sweden's Ericsson Group.

11. The government sold all the class AA shares, which embody a minority (20.4%) equity but controlling interest (*i.e.*, 51% of the votes) to Group Carso and the two foreign partners. In turn, 51% of these AA shares are held by the "Mexican Controlling Shareholders" in a trust. Group Carso (now Carso Global Telecom) is the controlling shareholder in this group. Carso Global Telecom is controlled by Carlos Slim. See, Telmex, Form 20-F: Annual Report Pursuant to Section 13 of the Securities Exchange Act of 1934 for fiscal year ending 31 December 1997. For further discussion, see Pankaj Tandon, "Welfare Effects of Privatisation: Some Evidence from Mexico", *Boston University International Law Journal*, Vol. 13, 1995. Employee support was strengthened by selling them a 5% equity position. In 1986, Telmex experienced a work stoppage.

12. The postponement of rate rebalancing initiatives are described by Telmex as "voluntary compliance" with the government's price stabilisation measures of 31 December 1994, which generally froze prices of all public utilities. See Telmex, Form 20-F: Annual Report Pursuant to Section 13 of the Securities Exchange Act of 1934, 1997.

13. Reaction to the FTL when it was enacted in 1995 was generally very positive. For example, the US Federal Communications Commission described the law as "a dramatic new telecommunications law which introduced broad opportunities for competition and new entry". US FCC, "Special Report on Mexico", 26 October 1995. Similarly, Robert Lacy at Avantel (a new entrant) described the FTL as "pro-competitive telecom laws and regulations". See Robert K. Lacy, *Long Distance Competition in Mexico: Regulatory Framework and Enforcement*, 1998.

14. Specifically, these new carriers were Alestra, Avantel, Iusatel, Marcatel, Miditel and Protel.

15. OECD, *Communications Outlook* 1999, Tables 2.1 and 2.2.

16. This process is continuing with an additional 50 cities balloted for pre-subscription in 1999.

17. The decision was, however, not ratified until March 1998.

18. Telnor is a subsidiary of Telmex providing local exchange services in Baja California and Northern Sonora. Telnor's network is small relative to Telmex - *e.g.*, it has less than 5% as many access lines. In August 1995, Telmex purchased Red Uno a leading Mexican company in network services integration and information services. In April 1997, Telmex acquired Kb/Tel Telecommunications, which develops and markets digital wireless communications systems (with applications that include point-of-sale terminals and automatic teller machines). These acquisitions were made by Telmex through a wholly owned subsidiary.

19. In July 1995, Telmex acquired 49% of Cablevision, the largest supplier of cable service in the country which provides cable service in the Mexico City metropolitan area. This purchase which appears to have been authorised despite a prohibition on Telmex operating public television services in Section 1.9 of the Telmex concession, is the subject of a law suit against Telmex by another television concessionaire.

20. Telmex, *Telefonos de Mexico: Annual Report* 1997, p. 1, "Highlights". Operating income and total assets expressed in pesos with purchasing power parity as of 31 December 1997. In a December 1997 report, Morgan Stanley Dean Witter provides a favourable financial assessment, stating: "we to see upside prospects for Telmex shares [...] with a hefty free cash flow, Telmex will probably continue to by back its stock". Morgan Stanley Dean Witter, *Latin America Investment Research*, "Latin America Telecommunications," 3 December 1997.

21. Even though the 214 license to provide long distance international switched resale services was granted to Telmex Sprint Communications ("TSC") on 30 October 1997, the FCC, responding to complaints by AT&T and MCI, delayed the operation of this joint venture until August 1998. Today, TSC is operating under an appeal launched by these two companies.

22. See Gonzalez, Gupta and Deshpande (1998).

23. OECD, *Communications Outlook* 1999, Table 2.2. Based on share of subscribers, 1997.

24. Growth in the number of cellular subscribers from: Cofetel, Estadisticas de Interes sobre Telecomunicaciones, "Usuarios y Lineas telefonicas", which is posted on www.cft.gob.mx. The number of cellular mobile subscribers per 100 persons in Mexico is the lowest in the OECD. See *Communications Outlook* 1999.

25. The L band is still under control of Telecomm as it is used to provide National Security Services, Emergency and Social Services. Telecomm also remains as the signatory to Intelsat and Inmarsat

26. For trunking concessionaires 1997 and 1998 has been a transitional period in the move from analog to digital. During 1998, Cofetel together with the trunking association (AMCOT) has studied the possibility of assigning more spectrum to allow this service to expand from its current infrastructure. If necessary, new auctions will be designed and programmed for these new bands.

27. Figures and charts contained in Sections 2 and 3 include information based on OECD data and methodologies which may differ from those used by Cofetel.

28. This requirement is set out in the Internal Rules of the SCT (*Reglamento Interior de la Secretaría de Comunicaciones y Transportes*), Article 37 bis.

29. Telmex has filed amparos or has pending amparos against the finding of dominance by the CFC, the disclosure of information required to resolve allegations of cross-subsidies in an anti-trust suit by Iusacell in 1995, calling party pays (this amparo was dismissed by a judge in February 1999), the payment of 800 numbers, accounting separation and an anti-trust suit filed against alleged monopoly abuse in the dialling of 800 numbers from public phones.

30. See Cofetel, 1999 Work Programme, p. 20, Paragraph 17.

31. As an indication, the maximum penalty could be increased from 100 thousand to 100 million minimum wages.

32. For example, Cofetel has required the following clause: "The [concessionaire] accepts that in case that the legal provisions and administrative requirements [...] which govern this Concession, are revoked, amended or added, the [concessionaire] shall comply with the new legislation and the new administrative requirements as soon as they go into effect".

33. Cofetel argue that resale is allowed in only 12 countries (Canada, United Kingdom, Sweden, New Zealand, Australia, Netherlands, Norway, Denmark, France, Germany, Switzerland, Japan) all of which have much higher teledensity than Mexico and therefore less need to invest infrastructure.

34. Due to peso appreciation in real terms and the relatively higher growth of incoming international traffic the actual dollar value of the average interconnection rate in 1997 and 1998 was around 6 US cents.

35. In its April 1996 interconnection resolution, the SCT also reaffirmed four key criteria to be used in establishing interconnection rates for 1999-2000. These included, in order *a*) the long-run average incremental cost of interconnection; *b*) the evolution of international benchmarks for interconnection in those countries constituting Mexico's main trading partners, *c*) evolution of international traffic settlement rates between Mexico and those countries, and *d*) the evolution and growth of telecommunications markets in Mexico.

36. However, Cofetel never published the new 1999-2000 rates in the *Diario Oficial de la Federación*.

37. See Cofetel Slide Presentation, "Resoluciones Para Forentar El Desarrolle Y La Sana Competencia," *Mimeo*, 1 December 1998.

38. In defining "significant coverage of the local service area" Cofetel uses the same minimum requirement established in the spectrum auctions for fixed and mobile access: to provide coverage, with the capacity to attend the request for service of any consumer, in an area where at least 40% of the population of the city, municipality or community live.

297

39. Beginning on 1 January 1999, and every four years thereafter, the level of the adjustment factor (which was 0.74 per quarter prior to that date) is set by Cofetel after administrative hearings with the articulated purpose of "allowing Telmex to maintain an internal rate of return equal to the companies' weighted average cost of capital".

40. Armstrong, Mark, Simon Cowan and John Vickers, *Regulatory Reform: Economic Analysis and British Experience*, 1994, p. 131.

41. The Mexican Senate's Committee on Distribution and Administration of Consumer Goods and Services is reported in the press to have stated that: "With Cofetel authorisation Telmex applied disproportionate local telephone tariffs, which permitted it to compete with advantage in the long-distance market". The Committee went on to recommend that the appropriate authorities, together with the Congress, the telephone companies and consumers, begin a public discussion [...] for "reaching a legal framework that is progressively more transparent, fair and just in the telecommunications sector". 20 March 1999, "Senate Committee Issues Formal Determination That Telmex Failed In Its Obligation To Offer Low Tariffs; With Cofetel's Authorisation, The Company Maintains a Local Monopoly and Advantages in Long Distance", El Excelsior, p. 1F.

42. Cofetel notes that where, in rare cases the registration of tariffs has taken longer than the 10 day limit, this has been due to the analysis Cofetel has had to carry out to prevent discriminatory and anti-competitive practices. On these occasions Cofetel has kept in close contact with the concessionaire "so full information is taken into account when registering the tariffs".

43. However, despite the requirement to register tariffs, concerns have been raised that Telmex is surreptitiously discounting by packaging local service discounts with long-distance service.

44. Noll, Roger, (1995), *Telecommunications Competition in Mexico*, mimeo, 18 August 1995.

45. The decline in performance since 1994 is also reflected in OECD cross-country comparisons. In 1994, Mexico's performance indicators ranked fairly well. Mexico ranked 9th on digitalisation rates and 23rd on "answer seizure" rates (*i.e.*, of international calls that are answered on the terminating side) out of 27 countries reporting in 1994. By 1997, Mexico had fallen to 16th on digitalisation and 28th on answer seizure rates out of 29 countries reporting.

46. The concession required the waiting time to drop to six months in 1995, five months in 1996, four months in 1997, three months in 1998, two months in 1999, and one month in 2000. By the end of 1997, the actual waiting time was less than a month, and the backlog of pending applications was 91 400.

47. International Technology Consultants, Latin America & The Caribbean, *Telecom Market Report*, Vol. 7, No. 5, 29 May 1998.

48. The European Commission has been involved in numbering plans for many years (see <www.eto.dk>), and Australia has recently released a new numbering plan (see <www.austel.gov.au/number/index.htm>) Canada and the US are covered by the North American Numbering Plan – number portability in the North American context is discussed at <www.fcc.gov>. Number portability issues in both the UK and North America are discussed in detail in Martin B.H. Weiss and Douglas C. Slicker, "Funding Models for AIN-Based Local Number Portability," *Mimeo*: 1998 TPRC, 8 September 1998.

49. See Martin B.H. Weiss and Douglas C. Slicker, "Funding Models for AIN-Based Local Number Portability", *Mimeo*, 1998 TPRC, 8 September 1998.

50. See Cofetel Slide Presentation, "Resoluciones Para Forentar El Desarrolle Y La Sana Competencia", *Mimeo*, 1 December 1998.

51. There are other reasons why the existing long-distance concessionaires have opposed call-by-call selection. These include high charges by Telmex for performing the necessary billing and collection services, high costs of terminating or originating long-distance calls "off-network" (which involve paying Telmex rates for carrying the call to the nearest network point) and fear of a competitive win-back strategy by Telmex.

52. Telmex Concession, Article 3-2.

53. Collecting funds through general tax revenues is generally less distorting because it is collected from a broader base, so the individual taxes can be lower and thus there is less distortion of relative prices. In practice, few countries (Chile is one exception) fund universal service through general tax revenues.

54. The example of Chile demonstrates the potential benefits of a market-based approach to meeting universal service and network expansion goals. Beginning with a teledensity rate of about four lines per 100 persons in 1988, Chile was able to increase its teledensity to 14 per 100 persons by 1996, and is projected to reach 24 lines per 100 persons by 1999. Over the period 1988 to 1996, the percentage of households with telephones increased dramatically from 14 to over 50%. The universal service plan in Chile incorporated five

main principles: *i)* transparency; *ii)* market neutrality; *iii)* targeted to beneficiaries; *iv)* payments made external from any carrier; and *v)* small and of limited duration.

An innovative feature of the Chilean approach was the auctioning of subsidies to provide telecommunications facilities in unserved areas. While the incumbent carrier won many of the projects, it faced competition from a long-distance rival, Chilesat, which sought to enter these markets through the bidding to build up its long-distance business (in fact, Chilesat bid zero on 16 projects – *i.e.*, no subsidy payment to provide the service – highlighting that services which are alleged to incur a deficit by the incumbent can often be provided without a cross-subsidy). The first bidding round in 1995 involved $2.1 million in direct government funding and gave rise to about US$40 million in private investments, The result was 1 285 rural public telephones at an average cost of US$1 634 per telephone. See World Bank Group, Public Policy for the Private Sector, "Extending Telecommunications Service to Rural Areas – The Chilean Experience", Note No. 105, February, 1997.

55. Telegeography 1998. Based on minutes of international telecommunications traffic. Data based on billing point of traffic. Totals for 1997 include all carriers; route data are for Telmex only.

56. In addition, in a country such as Mexico, with a sizeable imbalance in calls in its favour, the proportional return system has the side-effect that it creates incentives for carriers to fabricate out-going calls in order to increase their share of the lucrative incoming traffic.

57. In a letter to Telmex dated 18 March 1999 opposing proposals by AT&T and MCI to establish arrangements for the termination of international traffic directly with Avantel and Alestra, Cofetel states that "no operator of an international gateway [may] agree to rates other than those approved by Cofetel nor may they carry international traffic outside of the systems of proportional return and uniform rates, as such as violation of the provisions that regulate international long-distance service an would entail the imposition of applicable penalties pursuant to Article 71 of the Act, without prejudice to the revocation of the respective provisional authorisation for the install and operation of international gateways".

58. Prior to 1992, Telmex purchased network switching equipment from the Ericsson and Alcatel groups through long term agreements. In 1992, it signed an agreement with AT&T to provide such equipment, thus providing a second source of supply.

59. With its entry into force on 5 February 1998, the agreement set telecommunications services on the path of progressive liberalisation and pro-competitive regulatory reform in 72 signatory countries, including Mexico and most of the world's major trading nations.

60. The SCT announced that Avantel had switched 6 461 users without their consent, Alestra had switched 3 258 users without their consent, and Telmex had switched 1 103 users without their consent. See *World Telecom Law Report*, "Mexico Sanctions Carriers for 'Slamming' Practices," 9 February 1998, p. 14. Avantel has appealed the decision and is withholding payment of the fine pending the resolution of the issue.

61. Telmex was fined 100 000 times the minimum daily wage for delays in turning over its data base of local subscribers, as well as unauthorised switching of subscribers.

62. "Bueno? Multinationals such as Qualcomm, Bell Atlantic, Bell Canada International and WorldTel Limited will enter Mexico's telecom market," *Business Mexico*, September 1998, p. 24.

63. At present consumers can ask Telmex to provide a list of the calls made during a specified month. However, this service incurs a charge.

64. See Cofetel, 1999 Work Programme, p. 20, Paragraph 16.

65. The CFC's role in spectrum auctions is further set out in Chapter 3.

66. Indeed, in some countries, the national competition law is the primary regulatory instrument in the telecommunications sector.

67. See also the recommendation regarding the role of CFC in remedies implementing its dominance findings in Chapter 3.

68. In 1996, a procedure for obtaining a concession to install, operate and exploit a public telecommunications net was established according to the FTL. This disposition includes the procedure to change from a system status to a public telecommunications network for those concessionaires who were already in the market when the law came into effect. This implies to operate in a band spectrum of at least 450 MHz, and also the obligation to offer interconnection to other networks. A period of four years was established for the companies to do the change. However, in June 1998, the disposition was changed for those who had not opted to do it. They were allowed to present a new calendar, together with technical and financial information that justifies it. This decision has the aim of giving more flexibility to make the conversion, taking into account the real conditions of each place and concession.

69. OECD, *Communications Outlook*, states in Paragraph 215: "Other notable points for these baskets are in relation to Mexico and Turkey where relatively high currency inflation influences the outcome. For Mexico the high price is due to the fact that the latest PPPs always lag actual prices. In most other OECD countries with low inflation rates this does not significantly impact on the price of a basket. In Mexico the pace of inflation means that PPPs and yearly exchange rates are a less useful guide to the prices users pay than current exchange rates. The *Communications Outlook* does not provide an estimate of how much of the observed Mexican PPP basket price is a result of the calculation problem. Given the magnitudes involved, it seems unlikely that the rankings in regard to residential service would be changed significantly, though perhaps Mexico's ranking in regard to the business basket would be improved. Several of the countries at the upper end of the pricing comparison have experienced high inflation in the last year, including: Turkey (76.6%), Mexico (16.7%), Hungary (12.3%), Poland (9.9%) and the Czech Republic (8.2%) in the last 12 months as reported by *The Economist*.

70. OECD data also shows cross-country comparisons of the number of mobile subscribers per 100 inhabitants. It does not appear that, to date, penetration of mobile subscribers has bridged the gap. Thus, relative to other OECD countries, a significant gap remains.

71. "Bueno? Multinationals such as Qualcomm, Bell Atlantic, Bell Canada International and WorldTel Limited will enter Mexico's telecom market" *Business Mexico*, September 1998, p. 24.

72. Cofetel, 1998 *Annual Report*, p. 22.

73. See, for example, International Telecommunication Union ("ITU"), World Telecommunications Development Report 1998: Universal Access.

74. COFETEL, Presentation by Lic. Carlos Casasús López Hermosa (Presidente de la Comisión Federal de Telecomunicaciones), *Telecommunications in Mexico: Evolving Regulatory Framework*, 3 December 1997, Mexico City, Slide No. 63.

# APPENDIX: SUMMARY OF THE REGULATORY PROVISIONS OF THE 1990 TELMEX CONCESSION AND THE 1995 FEDERAL TELECOMMUNICATIONS LAW

## Objectives

- The objectives of the FTL are stated as: "to promote efficient development of telecommunications; to exercise State control over such matters in order to guarantee national sovereignty; to foster open competition among the different telecommunications service providers in order to render services at better prices, diversity and quality for the benefit of the users; and to promote an appropriate social coverage".

## Regulation of entry and exit

- The Telmex concession allowed entry in all markets except for long-distance services. Long-distance services were reserved as a monopoly for Telmex until 10 August 1996. Competition with interconnection to the PSTN was scheduled to start 1 January 1997.

- Under the FTL, a "concession" is required for service providers using frequency or installing, operating or exploiting a public telecommunications network. A "permit" is required for carriers engaged in other non-facilities-based commercial telecommunication operations, and registration is required for value added service providers. Concessionaires must be majority Mexican owned, except in the case of cellular providers.

- The FTL requires that concessions for the use of frequency spectrum be granted through public bidding. A concessionaire who is the sole provider of service in a region cannot withdraw from serving that region.

- The FTL requires that applicants for concessions must specify a business plan, and specific investment and coverage programs and commitments. Concessions granted must set out the different services to be rendered by the concessionaire, the rights and obligations of the concessionaire and the commitments regarding geographic coverage of the concessionaire. Concessions are transferable, on the approval of Cofetel and CFC, after three years have elapsed.

## Interconnection

- According to its concession, Telmex is obliged to negotiate with other operators for the terms and conditions governing interconnection. In the event of failure to reach agreement, the terms and conditions can be set by Cofetel. Interconnecting parties are required to pay Telmex the costs of any procedure necessary to establish and maintain interconnection and Telmex is required to provide a full breakdown of the costs involved. Telmex is obliged to adopt an open architecture design so that other systems can be easily interconnected. Should the long-run incremental cost of interconnection be above the price, Telmex may negotiate an increase in the price.

- According to the FTL, all concessionaires are required to interconnect their networks. Private parties have 60 days to negotiate terms and conditions of interconnection. If this term expires, Cofetel has a further 60 days to establish the relevant terms and conditions that were not agreed by the parties.

- In the interconnection of foreign networks, Cofetel has power under the FTL to establish conditions to which the agreements shall be subject with the purpose of incorporating proportionality (proportional return) conditions.

- The FTL states that tariffs and conditions for interconnection should respect reciprocity for concessionaires providing each other similar services, capacity or functions and must not include volume discounts on tariffs.

## Price Regulation

- The Telmex concession specifies that the rate structure "shall seek to provide an efficient expansion of the public telephone system and provide a basis for healthy competition in the rendering of services". All rates must cover "incremental long-term cost" so that cross-subsidies are eliminated and the necessary incentive exists to expand each service.

- The Telmex concession sets out a specific mechanism for controlling Telmex's prices based upon a price-cap approach. The cap is over the average revenue of a basket including local, long-distance, and international services. The revenue is calculated using the quantities of the previous period. The cap allows adjustments for inflation, less a so-called "X" factor to encourage productivity improvements. For the period 1 January 1991 until 31 December 1996, the X factor was set at zero. From 1 January 1997 until 31 December 1998, the X factor was set at 0.74% per quarter, giving a real price reduction of about 3% per annum. Following 1 January 1999, the X factor as well as the "initial value" of the controlled basket, is set once every four years, based upon a LRIC study submitted by Telmex and approved by an expert. When no agreement is reached between Cofetel and Telmex, the opinion of a set of three experts, chosen by the company and Cofetel, is required. As of 10 March 1999, the X factor is 4.5% for 1999-2002. In addition, for the period 1991-1996 individual price-caps were applied to local services (installation charges, the monthly rental and measured service charge), in order to gradually rebalance rates towards costs.

- The concession states that "the rate structure shall induce Telmex to attain continuous improvement in productivity, in order to allow it to increase profits while gradually lowering rates to users". The "initial value" of the basket and the X factor must allow Telmex to receive an internal rate of return on its regulated services equivalent to the weighted average cost of capital. Telmex's rates for local residential services must not exceed the incremental costs for local service.

- The FTL states that prices are to be set freely by the concessionaires "in terms that will allow the rendering of such services under conditions of quality, competitiveness, safety, and permanence"; prices must not be discriminatory or include cross-subsidies, but if a concessionaire is found to be dominant by the CFC, the Cofetel is authorised to assign specific obligations related to "rates, quality of service and information". Rates must at least cover long-run average incremental cost.

### Universal service and network expansion obligations:

- Between 1990 and 31 December 1994, Telmex was obliged by its concession to expand the number of basic telephone service lines by a minimum of 12% per annum. By 1995 the waiting period for basic telephone service was to be reduced to a maximum of six months. The maximum waiting period was to be reduced by one month in each subsequent year, down to one month in the year 2000.

- By 31 December 1994, Telmex was obliged by its concession to provide telephone service to every town with more than 500 inhabitants and to increase the penetration of public telephone booths from 0.5 per thousand to two per thousand and to five per thousand by 31 December 1998. Every four years Telmex is to arrange with SCT a rural telephone expansion program. Rural telephone rates are not allowed to be higher than the price for basic telephone service.

### Quality of service obligations:

- The Telmex concession sets out a list of performance indicators and sets targets to be achieved for those indicators for each year before 31 December 1994. The indicators include lines with failure, same-day repair, public phones in service, failure reports and so on. From 1 January 1995, Telmex must submit quality of service goals every four years to Cofetel[*] for approval.

### Controls on anti-competitive behaviour:

- The Telmex concession explicitly sets out prohibitions against monopolistic activities, prohibitions against cross subsidies, prohibitions against tied sales and a prohibition against exclusive supplying.

### Other Regulations

- The Telmex concession sets out requirements with regard to accounting separation. While Telmex may distribute the television signals of authorised broadcasters through its network, Telmex is forbidden, either directly or indirectly, from holding a public television concession.

- According to the FTL all concessionaires are required to maintain separate service accounting (accounting separation) and to "allow the portability of any number whenever, at the Secretariat's opinion, this is technically and economically feasible".

- The FTL specifies that all general communications ways (electric transmission towers, radio communication towers, posts and ducts with telecommunications network wiring) that may be made available to one public network concessionaire must be available to all other concessionaires on a non-discriminatory basis. No concessionaire can have exclusive use of such property.

- The FTL specified that no later than 10 August 1996, a new telecommunications regulator was to be established by Presidential decree. The law specifies a timetable for the introduction of competition. Long-distance service not involving interconnection was authorised to start on 10 August 1996. Negotiations for

---

[*] Strictly speaking, the concession refers to SCT, however SCT has delegated most of its powers under the concession to Cofetel.

interconnection were allowed to start on 1 September 1995, and competition in long-distance from 1 January 1997.

– The FTL incorporates (as part of the transitory arrangements) the provisions of the resolution of 1 July 1994 governing the interconnection of competing long-distance networks with Telmex's network. This resolution requires interconnection to be cost-oriented, non-discriminatory, and in line with international benchmarks. It also requires local and long-distance operators to be charged the same prices for interconnection and for interconnection charges to be publicly disclosed.

OECD PUBLICATIONS, 2, rue André-Pascal, 75775 PARIS CEDEX 16
PRINTED IN FRANCE
(42 1999 05 1 P)  ISBN 92-64-17100-2 – No. 50949  1999